Place a program shortcut on the desktop to quickly start a program.

Microsoft Word

Folders can be placed directly on the desktop.

Status Reports

You can easily open a folder with a shortcut.

My Documents

Print documents by dragging them to a printer shortcut. Double-click the icon to check the status of the printer.

Shortcut to HP LaserJet 4-4M

Important documents can be placed directly on the desktop.

Things To Do Today!

11:49 AM

The notification area lets you know what's going on behind the scenes.

D1402004

In-Depth Reference

and Inside Tips from

the Software Experts

RUNNING

Microsoft®

WINDOWS® 95

C R A I G   S T I N S O N

PUBLISHED BY
Microsoft Press
A Division of Microsoft Corporation
One Microsoft Way
Redmond, Washington 98052-6399

Library of Congress Cataloging-in-Publication Data
Stinson, Craig, 1943-
    Running Microsoft Windows 95 / Craig Stinson.
        p.   cm.
    Includes index.
    ISBN 1-55615-674-X
    1. Operating systems (Computers)   2. Microsoft Windows 95.
    I. Title.
    QA76.76.O63.S7555   1995
    005.4'469--dc20   95-24053
                                                  CIP

Printed and bound in the United States of America.

2 3 4 5 6 7 8 9   RMRM   0 9 8 7 6 5

Distributed to the book trade in Canada by Macmillan of Canada, a division of Canada Publishing Corporation.

A CIP catalogue record for this book is available from the British Library.

Microsoft Press books are available through booksellers and distributors worldwide. For further information about
international editions, contact your local Microsoft Corporation office. Or contact Microsoft Press International
directly at fax (206) 936-7329.

Adobe Type Manager and PostScript are trademarks of Adobe Systems, Inc. America Online is a registered
trademark of America Online, Inc. TrueType is a registered trademark of Apple Computer, Inc. Artisoft is a
registered trademark of Artisoft, Inc. Banyan is a registered trademark of Banyan Systems, Inc. dBASE is a
registered trademark and Quattro Pro is a trademark of Borland International, Inc. CompuServe is a registered
trademark and WinCIM is a service mark of CompuServe, Inc. CorelDRAW is a registered trademark of Corel
Systems Corporation. Delphi Internet is a trademark of Delphi Internet Services Corporation. LaserJet is a
registered trademark of Hewlett-Packard Company. Doom is a trademark of ID Software. Intel, Pentium, and
SatisFAXtion are registered trademarks of Intel Corporation. IBM and OS/2 are registered trademarks of International Business Machines Corporation. Helvetica and Times Roman are registered trademarks of Linotype AG and
its subsidiaries. 1-2-3, Ami Pro, Freelance Graphics, and Lotus are registered trademarks of Lotus Development
Corporation. MCI Mail is a registered service mark of MCI Communications Corporation. Micrografx is a
registered trademark of Micrografx, Inc. Microsoft, MS-DOS, Multiplan, PowerPoint, and Windows are registered
trademarks and Natural Keyboard and Windows NT are trademarks of Microsoft Corporation. The Microsoft
Network is operated by Microsoft Corporation on behalf of Microsoft Online Services Partnership. Arial and Times
New Roman are registered trademarks of The Monotype Corporation PLC. NetWare, Novell, and WordPerfect are
registered trademarks of Novell, Inc. PRODIGY is a trademark of Prodigy Services Company. Lap-Link is a
registered trademark of Traveling Software, Inc.

Acquisitions Editor: Lucinda Rowley
Project Editors: Greg Schultz, John Pierce
Manuscript and Technical Editors: Siechert & Wood Professional Documentation

For my son Russell,
window-opener extraordinaire

Chapters at a Glance

Table of Contents

Table of Contents

Table of Contents

Table of Contents

Chapter 20 Connecting with HyperTerminal and Phone Dialer 515

Table of Contents

Table of Contents

Acknowledgments

I am indebted to many people for their contributions to the conception, management, production, and content of this book:

Steve Sagman, Scott Berkun, and John and Jan Weingarten contributed material on The Microsoft Network, Internet Explorer, and the Windows 95 accessory programs.

Lucinda Rowley, Greg Schultz, and John Pierce oversaw the project from their positions as Microsoft Press editors, and did so with admirable grace and humor, despite the many delays and Gantt-chart overhauls. Mary DeJong and JoAnne Woodcock, also of Microsoft Press, provided logistical support, encouragement, and valuable insights.

Craig Gray, of Omnitek Computers, and Esaway Amasha, of International Computer Center, also pitched in at critical moments with logistical help.

The team at Siechert and Wood Professional Documentation—Carl Siechert, Carole Hamilton, Stan DeGulis, and Paula Kausch—combined the traditionally distinct functions of production and technical editing with flair, finesse, and dedication. In addition, Carl logged many hours on the various Windows 95 beta forums, acting as chief intelligence officer for the project. I cannot overstate the value of his collaboration.

Finally, I'd like to thank—once again—my wife and children for their unfailing patience and moral support.

Introduction

Microsoft Windows 95 marks the beginning of a new era in microcomputing. Windows 3.1 and Windows for Workgroups, the last two MS-DOS–based versions of Windows, represent the climax of 1980s sophistication, allowing users to run powerful applications in an easy-to-learn, easy-to-use graphical multitasking environment. Windows 95 improves and extends the capabilities of these systems and provides a new, easier approach to personal computing as well as a number of technical innovations to get the most from today's powerful PCs.

Among the improvements offered by Windows 95 are the following:

- **A completely redesigned user interface**. Starting programs, opening and saving documents, organizing disk resources, connecting to network servers—all these tasks are simpler in Windows 95, thanks to a thoroughly reworked user interface. Highlights of the new UI include the following:

  - ❑ A "Start" menu that provides ready access to your programs, your most recently used documents, Control Panel, your printers, and important system utilities

  - ❑ A simpler way to switch from one program to another

  - ❑ Windows Explorer, a powerful replacement for the File Manager program from earlier versions of Windows (Windows 3.x)

- ❏ A Network Neighborhood icon that lets you browse servers and use network files as simply as you use documents on your own hard disk

- ❏ The ability to create shortcuts for commonly used programs, folders, and documents

- ❏ Property sheets that make it easy to see and change system settings

- ❏ A set of "quick viewers" that let you inspect documents without launching programs

- ❏ A versatile search program to help you locate anything anywhere—on your own computer or on the network

- ❏ A Recycle Bin to help prevent accidental deletions

- ❏ Simpler tools for working with printers and fonts

- ❏ A team of "wizards" that walk you through setup and configuration procedures

- ❏ An improved Help system that includes full-text indexing of help documents

To ease your transition to the new system, Windows 95 includes the Program Manager and File Manager shells that are the centerpieces of earlier versions of Windows, but it's unlikely you'll want to use them for long (if at all).

- ■ **The ability to handle long filenames**. Say good-bye to the filenaming constraints of Windows 3.x and MS-DOS. In Windows 95, filenames can include as many as 255 characters.

- ■ **Built-in networking support**. Unlike most earlier microcomputer operating systems, Windows 95 was designed from the ground up with networking in mind. As a result, facilities for sharing files and devices are completely integrated into the Windows 95 user interface.

- ■ **Plug and Play**. Windows 95 includes built-in support for the Plug and Play initiative, an industry-wide effort to simplify the installation and management of peripheral devices. As a result, Windows 95 provides automatic installation and configuration of devices that meet Plug and Play design criteria, compatibility with legacy devices, and a dynamic environment to support the docking and undocking of mobile components.

- **Support for mobile computing**. In addition to Plug and Play, Windows 95 supports mobile computing with a file-synchronization tool, a utility for transferring files over a direct cable link, and dial-up networking.

- **Better support for multimedia applications**. With its built-in sound, video, and CD capabilities, multimedia applications sizzle. And Windows 95 is the first version of Windows that rivals MS-DOS as a gaming environment.

- **Integrated mail and fax support**. Windows 95 includes Microsoft Fax and a workgroup edition of Microsoft Mail. Microsoft Exchange, your mail and fax inbox, can also serve as an inbox for other mail systems, including Internet mail and the mail component of The Microsoft Network.

The innovations in Windows 95 don't stop at the level of user-interface design or an expanded feature set. The technical advancements made by Windows 95 are just as remarkable. Windows 3.1 and Windows for Workgroups are 16-bit extensions of an 8-bit, single-tasking operating system that, in its very first incarnation, had been aptly nicknamed QDOS—for *quick and dirty* operating system.

The versions of Windows that had been built on the foundation of "QDOS" brought computing to levels of power and convenience that were undreamed of even in the mid-1980s. But they could not adequately support the passage of line-of-business applications from mainframes and minicomputers to desktop networks. This dominant trend of the 1990s demanded 32-bit power and performance, built-in networking support with tools for the centralized management of system configurations, and above all, greater robustness and fault tolerance. To meet these needs, Microsoft developed Windows 95.

Among the technical improvements in Windows 95 are the following:

- **The integration of MS-DOS and Windows**. Windows and MS-DOS are now a single operating system.

- **The use of 32-bit components**. Windows 95 employs 32-bit code wherever possible, for enhanced performance and robustness. It also uses 16-bit code to maintain compatibility with legacy applications and drivers.

- **Preemptive multitasking**. Windows 3.x relies on a "cooperative" system of multitasking, in which applications share processor time by periodically yielding to the next application in line. If an application refuses to yield, the operating system can do nothing about it. Windows 95, in contrast, is a preemptive multitasking environment. The operating system is always in control, applications share resources more efficiently, and an errant program is unlikely to bring the entire system down.

■ **Multithreading**. Windows 95 supports multithreading, allowing appropriately designed applications to multitask their own processes. With a multithreading spreadsheet, for example, you might be able to recalculate one worksheet file while printing a second.

■ **Better support for MS-DOS–based applications**. Windows 95 maintains a smaller "footprint" in conventional memory, allowing it to run many MS-DOS–based programs that are too large to run under Windows 3.x. For programs that are still too big to fit, the system includes an option to run in "MS-DOS mode." In MS-DOS mode, Windows closes all running applications, then removes all of itself except for a small "bootstrap." When you've finished running your MS-DOS–based program, a single keystroke returns you to Windows.

■ **A centralized database of configuration and user-preference information**. The Windows 95 *registry* maintains information about applications and preferences. The Win.ini and System.ini files used by Windows 3.x are supported for the sake of compatibility, but you'll seldom need to concern yourself with those files in Windows 95.

■ **Improved and simplified diagnostic, optimization, and trouble-shooting tools**. Windows 95 makes it easier to optimize your system by including a self-configuring and dynamic disk cache, the ScanDisk utility for checking the logical and physical structure of your disks, the DriveSpace disk-compression system, and an easy-to-use disk "defragger." In addition, to help you troubleshoot resource conflicts, Windows 95 includes Device Manager, a hierarchical list of all devices in your system and the resources assigned to each device.

Get Up and Running Quickly

If you're accustomed to an earlier version of Windows, you might feel a little disoriented on your first day "off the boat" in Windows 95. The following tips will help you master the new environment quickly:

- **Find everything you need on the Start menu**. The Start menu is Windows 95's replacement for Program Manager. You'll find almost every program and document you need on one of its branches. (For details, see "The Start Menu," page 9.)

- **Switch programs with Alt-Tab or click the taskbar**. Alt-Tab works the way it always has, but now you can also switch by clicking a button on the taskbar. And you can make the taskbar "stay on top" or duck out of sight, as you prefer. (For details, see "Switching Between Windows," page 17, and "Personalizing the Taskbar," page 89.)

- **When in doubt, right-click**. Everywhere you go in Windows 95, a right-click provides either a property sheet (allowing you to see and change current settings), a menu of currently relevant commands, or both. Getting in the right-click habit will help you discover everything you can do in this operating system. (For details, see "Object ("Right-Click") Menus," page 26.)

- **Make shortcuts for the programs, documents, and folders you need every day**. Shortcuts save time and trouble by providing direct access to practically anything in your working environment. Shortcuts can be placed on the desktop for easy use. (For details, see "Using Shortcuts to Run Programs and Open Documents," page 71.)

- **Check out Windows Explorer**. If outlines bring up painful memories of high-school English classes, use folder windows to manage your disk resources. But if you *like* outlines, give Windows Explorer a try. This powerful browsing tool lets you take in all your local and networked file resources at a glance. (For details, see Chapter 5, "Managing Folders and Files with Windows Explorer," page 163.)

■ **Drop into your "nethood" to find the file server you need**. The Network Neighborhood icon is your entrée to all servers local and remote. Working with the network files and folders is exactly like working with items on your own hard disk. (For details, see "Using Network Neighborhood to Find Network Files," page 182.)

■ **If you're not sure what's in a document, take a *quick view***. Windows 95 includes "quick viewers" for text documents, spreadsheets, graphics files, and other document types. If you're not sure a particular document is the one you want, right-click it and look for Quick View on the "object" menu that appears. A peek through the quick viewer is faster than opening the file in its parent application. (For details, see "Inspecting Documents and Programs with Quick View," page 67.)

■ **Let the Find command be your skip-tracer**. It's easy to lose things on a large hard disk. It's easy to find them again with the Find command—which you'll find on the Start menu. (For details, see Chapter 7, "Using the Find Command," page 193.)

■ **Tailor the Recycle Bin to your comfort level**. Deleted files in Windows 95 ordinarily go to the Recycle Bin rather than directly into the ether. When the bin is full, the files that have been there longest are finally deleted for good. You can adjust the size of the bin in accordance with your hard-disk size and propensity toward accidental erasures. (For details, see "Restoring Deleted Folders, Files, and Shortcuts," page 150.)

■ **Work in whatever screen resolution you need for the task at hand**. In Windows 3.x, switching from one screen resolution to another might be more trouble than it is worth because you must close your programs and restart the operating system every time you want to switch. In Windows 95, a screen-res switch is as simple as a right-click and a dialog pick. No need to shut or restart anything. (For details, see "Controlling the Amount of Information That Fits On Screen," page 92.)

About This Book

This book has five parts. The first part, encompassing Chapters 1 through 10, provides a detailed guide to the Windows 95 user interface, covering everything you need to know to run programs, manage files and folders, tailor the environment to your personal tastes, access network resources, share folders with other network users, install printers and fonts, and move information between applications and documents.

Part 2, Chapters 11 through 17, offers information about a variety of more advanced topics, including the Windows 95 Control Panel, the system's mobile-computing features, the Backup utility, troubleshooting and performance optimization, and features for users with special accessibility needs. In Part 2, you'll also find details about running MS-DOS–based programs under Windows 95.

Part 3, Chapters 18 through 22, covers several of the accessory programs shipped with Windows 95. Here you'll find chapters on WordPad (the Windows 95 replacement for the Write program included with Windows 3.x), Paint (the updated bitmap editor included with Windows 95), HyperTerminal (the newly refurbished Windows 95 communications utility), Phone Dialer, the multimedia accessories, and (last but surely not least) several of Windows 95's games.

Part 4, Chapters 23 through 26, offers a guide to the major communications tools included with Windows 95 (or with the optional Microsoft Plus! companion package): Microsoft Exchange, Microsoft Fax, The Microsoft Network (MSN), and Internet Explorer.

Part 5 contains an appendix that provides an overview of Microsoft Plus!, an add-on for Windows 95 that provides improved disk compression, clever "themes" that add pizazz to your computing environment, a system agent that runs programs at scheduled times, and other goodies.

Differences Between Windows 95 Versions

This book assumes that you have access to all features included with the CD-ROM version of Windows 95. If you acquired Windows 95 on diskettes, some of the accessory programs and other features described in the book may be unavailable on your computer. For example, the retail diskette version of Windows 95 does not include the games described in Chapter 22. Some of the features and programs described in this book may also be unavailable if Windows 95 was installed on your computer by a network administrator.

Getting Started with Windows

1

Introducing
Windows 95

Whether you're brand new to Windows or a veteran of earlier versions, the screen that appears when you first start Windows 95 is likely to include a few unfamiliar elements. You'll soon feel right at home in Windows 95, but to help you on your way, we'll begin this chapter with a brief survey of the landscape. We'll check out the Start menu, the taskbar, the My Computer and Network Neighborhood icons, the Recycle Bin, and the Windows desktop. Later in the chapter, we'll look at windows themselves (those rectangular frames that we spell with a lowercase *w*), menus, dialog boxes, and the Windows Help system.

If you've used Windows before, you will already be familiar with some of this territory. For example, your experience in working with Windows 3.x menus and dialog boxes will continue to serve you in Windows 95. But we suggest you give the headings, tips, and figures and captions in this chapter at least a quick scan, to be sure that you don't overlook anything new and important.

Whether you're a rookie or a 10-year veteran, welcome to Windows 95!

Starting Windows

You don't need to type a command to get into Windows. Simply turn on your machine and you're there (in a moment or two). If your computer is part of a network, however, you will be invited to type your name and a password when Windows starts. This process is called "logging on." Depending on how your system has been set up, you may be asked to identify yourself, even if your computer is not part of a network.

Also depending on how your system has been set up, once you're past the logon process you may go directly into an application. (Windows 95 provides a means for starting selected programs automatically at the beginning of each session. For information about using "startup" programs, see "Customizing the Start Menu," page 81.) If you find yourself inside an application at startup, you'll want to make your electronic desktop completely visible before following along on this chapter's tour of the Windows 95 landscape. To do that, use your mouse to point to the icon in the upper-right corner of your application's window that looks like this:

Click that icon, along with the similar icons of any other open windows, and your desktop will become completely visible.

Before beginning our tour, let's look for a moment at the logon process.

Logging On for Network Users

Figure 1-1 shows an example of a Windows 95 logon dialog box. (*Dialog boxes* are defined and described later in this chapter. See "Working with Menus and Dialog Boxes," page 25.) If your system requires you to log on, the dialog box you see may look just like this one or slightly different, depending on the type of network you use. But at a minimum it will ask you for your name and password. With most networks, you can enter the password in capital or lowercase letters, or any combination of capital and lowercase. As you type, asterisks appear on the password line to protect your privacy.

FIGURE 1-1.

At startup, you'll be asked to enter your network password.

If you don't want to connect to the network, simply press Esc at the network password dialog box. You'll be able to use all your local disks and printers. When you need a network resource, you can log on by simply connecting to that resource as you normally would. You will then be asked to supply your network password. By not logging on when you don't need network resources, you may be able to improve the performance of your system. Be aware, however, that any local resources you normally share will not be available to your fellow workers while you're disconnected from the network.

If you work on a relatively large network with dedicated servers, you will probably be asked to supply a domain or server name. If you're not sure what to enter in this part of the dialog box, consult your network administrator. Fortunately, at the beginning of each session, Windows 95 fills out both the user name and domain portions of the logon dialog box with the entries that were last used. So, if you're the only one using your computer, you'll seldom have to fill out these lines. All you'll need to do is retype your password to get on to the network.

Logging On for Non-Networked Users

Even if your computer is not part of a network, you may still see a logon dialog box when you start Windows. That's because Windows 95 can create separate "user profiles" for each person who works at a particular computer. A user profile is a collection of information about a user's preferences regarding the appearance of the screen, programs that run automatically on startup, items that appear on the Start menu, and so on. If your system has been set up to allow for user profiles, you will be asked to log on, so that Windows knows which profile to use.

 If your computer is not part of a network and you're the only one who uses it, you don't have to log on to start Windows. If the logon dialog box appears at startup, you can get rid of it. Run Control Panel, choose Passwords, click the User Profiles tab, and select the option button labeled "All users of this PC use the same preferences and desktop settings."

 For information about *user profiles*, see "Taking Advantage of User Profiles," page 87.

What to Do If You Forget Your Password

If you can't remember your password, there's no cause for alarm! Windows won't lock you out of the system. Simply press Esc or click Cancel when you see the logon dialog box. If your computer is normally part of a network, you'll begin your session disconnected from the network. Consult your network administrator to find out what your password is or have a new password established. If your computer is not part of a network but Windows asks for a password so that it can restore your user profile, pressing Esc lets you work with default settings.

See Also: For information about *creating a new password for yourself and reestablishing your preferred settings*, see "Changing Passwords," page 286.

A Quick Tour

Figure 1-2 shows some typical Windows 95 landmarks. At the bottom of the screen is the *taskbar*, your home base for interacting with Windows 95. In the upper left corner are icons labeled My Computer, Network Neighborhood, Recycle Bin, and The Microsoft Network. Additional icons, with little black arrows in the lower left corners, are arrayed in columns in the lower right corner of the screen. These icons with the arrows are called *shortcuts*. The background for these objects—the visual surface on which you work in Windows—is called the *desktop*.

Your own screen may look quite different from the one shown in Figure 1-2. The taskbar may be positioned against a different edge of your desktop. You may have different icons in the upper left corner of your screen, or you may have the same icons with different names. You may have more or fewer shortcuts, and what shortcuts you have are undoubtedly different from the ones in the figure. But chances are your system includes most of the elements shown in Figure 1-2.

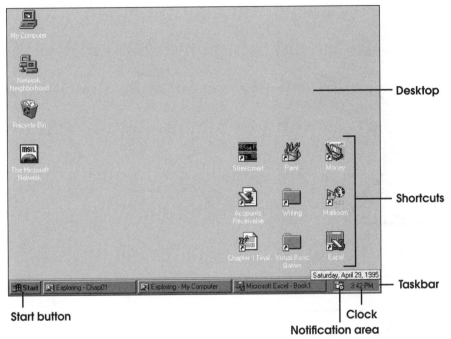

FIGURE 1-2.

A typical Windows 95 desktop includes the taskbar, objects for browsing local and networked computers, and shortcuts for launching documents, folders, and programs.

Desktop

Shortcuts

Taskbar

Start button

Clock

Notification area

The Start Menu

At the left edge of the taskbar (or at the top, if you've moved your taskbar to the left or right edge of the desktop) is a button labeled Start. Clicking here pops up the Start menu, shown in Figure 1-3 on the next page.

The Start menu makes most of your programs, as well as the documents you've most recently used, available with a single mouse click. It's also one of the simplest ways to accomplish several other important tasks, such as personalizing the appearance of your desktop, finding documents and programs on your own or a networked disk, and accessing basic help topics. The Start menu is also a "quit" menu; you'll use its Shut Down command whenever you need to end a Windows session, reboot your computer, or log off to let another person use your computer.

 You can open the Start menu at any time without reaching for your mouse. Simply press Ctrl-Esc.

FIGURE 1-3.

The Start menu provides single-click access to the programs and documents you use most often.

 For more information about *running programs*, see Chapter 2, "Running Programs and Opening Documents," page 55.

For information about *customizing the Start menu*, see "Customizing the Start Menu," page 81.

For more information about *finding documents and programs,* see "Finding Files and Folders," page 195.

For more information about *shutting down*, see "Ending a Windows Session," page 51.

Task Buttons

In the center portion of the taskbar, you will see a button for each program that your system is currently running as well as for each open folder. (For information about folders, see "Working with Folders," page 22.) You can click these buttons to move from one program to another.

If you have a lot of programs or folders open, Windows may truncate some of the text on the task buttons. However, if you rest your mouse for a moment or two on any button whose text is not completely visible, the full text will appear in a pop-up box.

The taskbar with its task buttons replaces the Windows 3.x task list. If you're used to double-clicking the desktop to get the task list, you may be frustrated because that action does nothing in Windows 95. However, you can still get to the task buttons (even if they're hidden or covered by open windows) by pressing Ctrl-Esc.

For information about *other ways to make the task buttons more readable*, see "Personalizing the Taskbar," page 89.

The Clock

In the right corner of the taskbar is a simple clock. You can set this by simply double-clicking it and filling out the ensuing dialog box. If you'd rather not know the time of day, you can banish the clock; for details see "Personalizing the Taskbar," page 89.

The clock also shows you the current date. Simply move the mouse pointer to the clock and leave it for a moment; the date appears in a pop-up box, as shown in Figure 1-2.

If your network is spread across two or more time zones, be sure to let Windows know what time zone your own system lives in. Windows 95 supports a "coordinated universal time format" that provides better tracking of time information for widely dispersed networks. To enter your time zone information, double-click the clock, and then click the Time Zone tab.

For information about *changing the clock's display format*, see "Specifying Regional (International) Settings," page 294.

The Notification Area

In the space just to the left of the clock, Windows occasionally provides information about the status of your system. When a local printer is active, for example, a printer icon appears in this *notification area*. You can double-click the icon to inspect and manage the print queue. If you're running Windows on a laptop computer, icons appear here to let you know whether your computer is currently draining or recharging its battery. If you're running Microsoft Exchange, Windows displays an icon in the notification area when an e-mail message or fax arrives.

My Computer

The My Computer icon lets you browse through all the resources attached to your own system. When you open My Computer, you see a *folder window* similar to the one shown in Figure 1-4. This window includes icons for each of your computer's floppy disk drives, each local hard disk, each local CD-ROM drive, and any network directories that you have connected to your computer. It also shows additional *system folders*, providing access to the Windows Control Panel, your printers, and Dial-Up Networking, a program that lets you dial up network resources via your modem.

FIGURE 1-4.

The My Computer icon opens into a folder window showing all resources attached or mapped to your own computer.

Double-clicking these icons opens additional folder windows. For example, opening the icon labeled "My c drive (C:)" would show you the contents of one of your local hard disks.

See Also: For information about *browsing your own computer,* see "Moving from Folder to Folder," page 119.

For information about *browsing network computers,* see "Using Network Neighborhood to Find Network Files," page 182.

For information about *mapping network drives,* see "Mapping a Network Folder to a Drive Letter," page 187.

For information about *using the Control Panel,* see Chapter 3, "Personalizing Your Workspace," page 85, and Chapter 11, "Customizing Windows," page 279.

For information about *working with printers,* see Chapter 9, "Installing, Configuring, and Using Your Printers," page 223.

For information about *dial-up networking,* see "Using Dial-Up Networking," page 372.

Network Neighborhood

Opening the Network Neighborhood icon provides a folder window displaying the names of each server or computer in your own workgroup. In addition, the Network Neighborhood folder includes an Entire Network icon, which you can use to access other workgroups on your network. Figure 1-5 on the next page shows how the Network Neighborhood folder might appear on a system that's part of an 11-member workgroup. In this illustration, the computer icons—Acadia, Arches, and Badlands, for example—represent computers in the workgroup.

Network Neighborhood
File Edit View Help
Entire Network
Acadia
Arches
Badlands
Biscayne
Denali
Glacier
Olympic
Sequoia
Voyageurs
Yellowstone
Yosemite
12 object(s)

FIGURE 1-5. The Network Neighborhood icon opens into a folder window showing all members of your own workgroup.

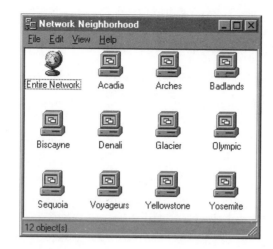

NOTE: If your computer isn't part of a network, the Network Neighborhood icon won't appear on your desktop.

The Recycle Bin

The Recycle Bin provides temporary storage for files that you delete. If you change your mind after deleting a file, you may be able to recover the file by retrieving it from the Recycle Bin. As Figure 1-6 shows, the Recycle Bin records the name, original location, date deleted, type, and size of each object you delete. A simple menu command lets you restore (undelete) any item.

Recycle Bin
File Edit View Help
Name
Original Location
Date Deleted
Type
Size
Copy #1 of help C:\WINDOWS\Des... 12/10/94 7:40 PM Bitmap Image 137KB
Delta C:\WINDOWS\Prog... 12/11/94 1:03 PM Shortcut 2KB
DELTA C:\WINDOWS 12/11/94 1:06 PM Configuration Settings 1KB
f01-02 C:\GPBETA 12/11/94 3:43 PM Bitmap Image 151KB
f01-02.rle C:\GPBETA 12/11/94 3:43 PM RLE File 151KB
f01-03t C:\RW95 12/11/94 11:15 AM Bitmap Image 26KB
f01-04-g C:\RW95 12/27/94 5:01 PM Bitmap Image 29KB
LabelPro (DOS) C:\WINDOWS\Prog... 12/11/94 1:03 PM Shortcut 2KB
logon C:\WINDOWS\Des... 12/10/94 7:40 PM Bitmap Image 151KB
22 object(s)
959KB

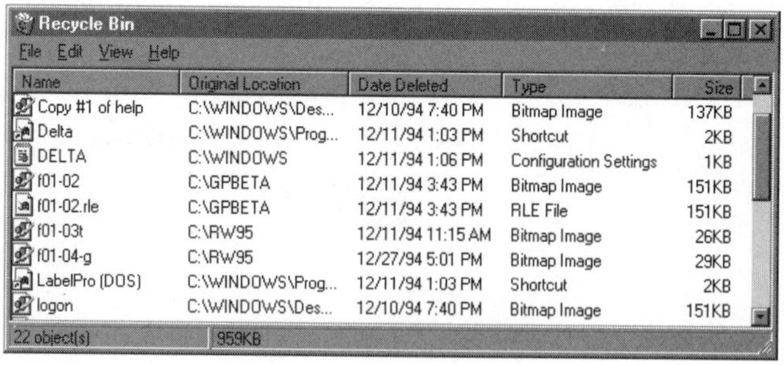

FIGURE 1-6. The Recycle Bin provides a safety net against accidental deletions.

For more information about *using the Recycle Bin*, see "Restoring Deleted Folders, Files, and Shortcuts," page 150.

Shortcuts

A shortcut provides easy access to some object on your system, such as a program, a document, a printer, a local hard disk, or a network server. For example, opening the shortcut labeled Writing in Figure 1-2 on page 9 opens a folder window containing files stored in the Writing folder. Opening the shortcut labeled Paint runs the Windows Paint program, and so on. You can create shortcuts for just about any object you use frequently.

For more information about *shortcuts*, see "Using Shortcuts to Run Programs and Open Documents," page 71.

Working with Windows

All Windows-based applications run within rectangular frames called windows. As shown in Figure 1-7 on the next page, these features are common to nearly all windows:

Borders. The four edges that define the perimeter of a window are called borders. You can drag the borders of most windows to change their size.

Title bar (caption). Directly below the top border is a region that includes the window's name. This is called the title bar, or caption. You can move a window by dragging its title bar.

Control-menu icon. At the left edge of the title bar is the Control-menu icon. You can click here to get a menu of basic commands for sizing and positioning the window. These commands all have mouse-action equivalents, so you may never need to use the Control menu.

Close button. At the right edge of the title bar is a square containing an *X*. You can click here to close a document or folder, or to terminate an application.

FIGURE 1-7.

Nearly all Windows-based applications run in windows that include these elements.

Control-menu icon

Title bar

Close button

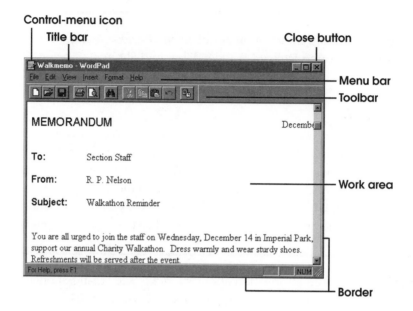

Menu bar

Toolbar

Work area

Border

 Another way to close an application window, folder window, or dialog box is to press Alt-F4.

Minimize, restore, and maximize buttons. To the left of the close button, you will find other buttons that look like this:

Minimize

Restore

Maximize

Clicking the minimize button causes a window to collapse into its taskbar button. The window is still open, and the program inside it continues to run. But the window no longer takes up space on your desktop. You can reopen a minimized window by clicking its taskbar button or by using the Alt-Tab "cool switcher."

Clicking the maximize button causes a window to occupy all of the desktop. While you're using an application, you may want to keep its window maximized most of the time, so that you have as much screen real estate as possible to work with.

Clicking the restore button causes a window to assume an intermediate amount of space—neither maximized nor minimized. With windows restored, you can keep two or more applications in view at the same time. You can adjust the size of a restored window by dragging its borders. (See "Sizing and Moving Windows," below.)

 Another way to maximize a window is to double-click its title bar. If the window is already maximized, you can restore its intermediate size by double-clicking the title bar.

Menu bar. Directly below the title bar is the menu bar. The menu bar provides access to most of an application's commands.

Toolbar. Many windows include a toolbar, which is a row of icons and buttons that provide mouse-click shortcuts for an application's commonly used commands.

Work area. The inside of a window is called the work area or client area.

Sizing and Moving Windows

To change a window's size, drag its borders. For example, to make the window wider, drag either the left or right border. To make a window both wider and taller, you can drag one of the corners.

To move a window, drag its title bar.

 Dialog boxes sometimes get in the way of underlying applications. To see what's under a dialog box, move it—by dragging its title bar.

Switching Between Windows

When two or more application windows are open at once, the one lying on top has what's called the *focus*. The window with the focus is the one

Mouse Terminology

To *click* an object, position the mouse pointer over that object and press the primary mouse button once. To *double-click*, position the pointer and press the primary mouse button twice in quick succession.

The *primary* mouse button is ordinarily the left button, the one that lies under the index finger of your right hand. If you're left-handed, you may want to make the right button your primary button. You can do that by choosing Settings from the Start menu, choosing Control Panel, and then double-clicking the Mouse icon. For details, see "Setting Preferences for Your Mouse," page 111.

In this book, as in most other writing about Windows, to *right-click* means to press the secondary mouse button, whichever button that happens to be.

To *drag* an object, click it, and then while holding down the primary mouse button, move the mouse. When the object is where you want it to be, release the mouse button. Use the same method—except hold down the secondary mouse button—to *right-drag* an object.

To *select* a block of text with the mouse, click the beginning of the block, and hold down the mouse button while you move the mouse to the end of the block. Then release the mouse button. To *right-select*, follow the same procedure but use the secondary mouse button.

that will respond to your next keystrokes. (The window that has the focus is sometimes also called the *foreground* or *active* window.) To switch the focus to another window, you can use any of the following techniques:

- Click anywhere on or in the window that you want to switch to.

- Click the taskbar button for the window you want to switch to.

- Press and hold the Alt key. Then press Tab to bring up the Windows "cool switcher." The cool switcher displays an icon for each running application and draws a box around the icon whose window currently has the focus. Continue holding Alt and pressing Tab until the window you want to switch to has the focus.

 If you're ever in doubt about which window has the focus, check your windows' title bars. The active window's title bar is normally displayed in one color, while the title bars of all inactive windows are displayed in another color. In addition, the taskbar button for the active window appears to be pressed in.

Arranging Windows on the Screen

If you have a lot of windows open at once, it may be hard to see what's going on. Windows provides some handy commands for making all your windows visible. To put all the windows in a neat stack, with each window's title bar visible, do the following:

1. Right-click the taskbar. (Press Ctrl-Esc first if you can't see the taskbar.)

2. Choose the Cascade command.

With your windows in a cascade, you can easily switch focus by clicking any title bar—as well as by clicking the taskbar.

If you want to see a portion of the contents of each open window, choose one of the tiling commands. Right-click the taskbar and choose either Tile Horizontally or Tile Vertically.

To minimize all open windows, right-click the taskbar and choose Minimize All Windows.

 After cascading, tiling, or minimizing all windows, you can restore your windows to their previous positions by right-clicking the taskbar. The menu that appears includes a new command that reverses your previous action. For example, if you have just minimized all windows, the new command will read Undo Minimize All.

Keeping Windows on Top

Some windows are designed to stay on top, even when they don't have the focus. Windows that contain help information, for example, often behave this way, allowing you to read their helpful text even while you're working in a maximized application.

Most programs that stay on top give you the option of disabling this behavior. If a stay-on-topper becomes a visual nuisance, look in its menu system for a command such as "Always On Top" or "Stay On Top." Often you'll find it on the program's Control menu. (For information about the Control menu, see "The Control Menu and the Menu Bar," page 25.) These commands are usually *toggles;* you choose them once to turn the feature on and a second time to turn it off.

 The taskbar itself is a stay-on-top window. In its default display mode, it remains visible even when the foreground application is maximized. You can defeat this behavior by right-clicking an unoccupied part of the taskbar, choosing the Properties command, clicking the Taskbar Options tab, and deselecting the check box labeled Always On Top. (To get back to the taskbar when it's not visible, press Ctrl-Esc.)

Window Panes

Some programs use windows that are split vertically, horizontally, or even both vertically and horizontally. The resulting window divisions are called *panes.* Figure 1-8 shows an example of a window divided vertically into panes.

In most cases, when a window has been divided into panes, you can change the relative sizes of the panes by dragging the pane divider. In Figure 1-8, for example, you could make the left pane wider by dragging the divider to the right.

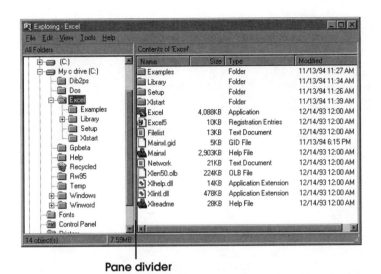

FIGURE 1-8.

This window is divided into a left pane and a right pane. You can change the size of the panes by dragging the pane divider.

Pane divider

Working with Document Windows

Windows come in two varieties, called application windows and document windows. Application windows house programs or folders, can be moved freely around the desktop, and can be maximized to fill the screen or minimized to taskbar buttons. All the windows illustrated thus far in this chapter are examples of application windows.

Document windows live inside application windows. As their name implies, they are designed to hold documents, not programs. Document windows can be maximized, restored, minimized, moved, and sized, but they must remain within the confines of an application window. Figure 1-9 on the next page shows an application window containing four open and three minimized document windows.

Notice that the title bar for one of the document windows (the one in the front of the cascade stack) is the same color as the title bar for the application window. That document window currently has the focus. Also notice that document windows, when minimized, become miniature title bars.

FIGURE 1-9.

This application window contains four open document windows and three minimized document windows.

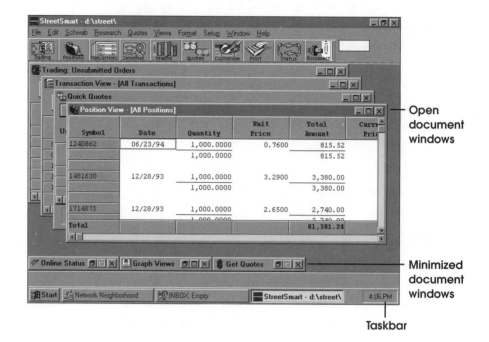

Open document windows

Minimized document windows

Taskbar

 You can close the current document window by pressing Ctrl-F4. In many programs, you can move from one document window to the next document window by pressing Ctrl-F6.

Working with Folders

A folder is a container for computers, disk drives, printer queues, other folders, and files. The most common kind of folder is exemplified by Figure 1-10. It's a place where programs, document files, and perhaps additional folders are kept. Such a folder is directly analogous to a directory in MS-DOS and in earlier versions of Windows. Your computer's hard disks, as well as those of your network's servers, are organized into hierarchies of folders.

At the top of a disk hierarchy in MS-DOS is a directory called the root directory. The Windows 95 folder corresponding to the root directory

FIGURE 1-10.

This Excel folder contains the Excel program file, seven Excel worksheet documents, two help files, a few other documents, and four additional folders.

goes by the volume name assigned to the disk on which it lives. If you have named your C drive George, for example, its top-level directory is a folder named George.

Your computer itself is a folder called My Computer. Your network workgroup is a folder called Network Neighborhood.

Windows 95 uses two different types of windows to display the contents of folders. One type is shown in Figure 1-10. This book refers to windows of this type as *folder windows*. The other type, shown earlier in Figure 1-8, is called a *Windows Explorer window*. Folder windows and Windows Explorer windows provide alternative ways of looking at the same information—the contents of a folder. Both are ordinary application windows.

Windows 95 uses *system folders* to hold items that are related to your system. For example, you can install and configure printers by opening a system folder called *Printers*, view and install fonts in a system folder called *Fonts*, and customize Windows in a variety of ways using a system folder called *Control Panel.*

The Desktop Is Also a Folder

At the top of the Windows 95 hierarchy is a folder called the desktop. This mother of all folders has some special characteristics. In particular, you don't need a folder window to see its contents. The desktop underlies all other windows and is fully visible when all your windows are minimized.

If you do want to see the desktop displayed in a folder window, don't try to get to it by opening My Computer and asking to see My Computer's parent. The desktop *is* the parent of My Computer, but its information is stored elsewhere. If you're using profiles, you'll find the desktop folder for your profile in C:\Windows\Profiles\Profilename\Desktop, where *Profilename* is the name under which you log on. If you're not using profiles, the desktop information is stored in C:\Windows\Desktop.

See Also:

For more information about *folder windows*, see Chapter 4, "Working with Folders," page 115.

For more information about *Windows Explorer windows,* see Chapter 5, "Managing Folders and Files with Windows Explorer," page 163.

For more information about *printers*, see Chapter 9, "Installing, Configuring, and Using Your Printers," page 223.

For more information about *fonts*, see Chapter 8, "Installing and Using Fonts," page 205.

For more information about *Control Panel*, see Chapter 3, "Personalizing Your Workspace," page 85, and Chapter 11, "Customizing Windows," page 279.

Working with Menus and Dialog Boxes

In virtually all Windows applications, commands are chosen from *drop-down menus*—sets of options that emerge from a menu bar at the top of the application window. When a program needs additional information from you before it can carry out your command, it presents a *dialog box*—a smaller window with places for you to fill in blanks or choose between preset options. These devices behave in a consistent and predictable way in all Windows-based programs.

The Control Menu and the Menu Bar

The two main elements of a Windows-based application's menu system are the *Control menu* and the *menu bar*. The Control menu emerges from the icon at the left side of the title bar. The menu bar is the row of commands directly below the title bar.

The Control menu provides a set of generic commands common to all applications. With few exceptions, each program's Control menu includes the same commands.

The menu bar includes commands specific to the current application. Each word on the menu bar opens a drop-down menu of related commands. For example, a program's File menu includes commands for opening and saving files, the Edit menu has commands for changing the contents of a document, and so on.

Choosing Commands with the Mouse

To get to the menu system with the mouse, simply click the desired word in the menu bar. To open the File menu, for example, click the word *File*. To open the Control menu, click the icon at the left edge of the title bar. To choose a command from a drop-down menu, simply move the mouse down until you reach the desired command, and then click.

To get out of the menu system without choosing a command, click the mouse anywhere outside the drop-down menu.

Choosing Commands with the Keyboard

To choose any command with the keyboard, begin by pressing the Alt key. (You can also access the menu system by pressing F10.) When you do that, Windows highlights the first command on the menu bar. At this point, you can use the Left arrow and Right arrow keys to move around the menu bar. To open a particular menu, move to that menu and press the Down arrow or Up arrow key.

To leave the menu system without choosing a command, press the Alt key, or click the mouse anywhere outside the menu system.

Accelerator Keys and Other Shortcuts

A more direct way to open a particular drop-down menu is to press Alt, followed by the menu's *accelerator key*—the under-lined letter in the menu's name. The accelerator key is often, but not always, the first letter of the menu name. In Microsoft Word, for example, you can open the File menu by pressing Alt-F, but to get to the Format menu, you need to press Alt-O.

Some menu commands have shortcuts assigned to them. These are single keystrokes or simple keystroke combinations that execute a command directly. In many programs, for example, pressing Ctrl-S is equivalent to executing the File menu's Save command. When a keyboard shortcut is available, it usually appears to the right of the command name on the menu.

Object ("Right-Click") Menus

In many parts of Windows 95, as well as in many Windows-based applications, pressing the secondary mouse button brings up a small menu appropriate to the currently selected object (or the one the mouse is pointing to). For example, if you right-click the taskbar, you get a menu of commands relating only to the taskbar. If you select a block of text in Microsoft Word and then right-click, you get a menu that includes commands for formatting, moving, and copying the selected text. These right-click menus go by various names in various applications. Some programs call them "property inspectors," others call them "shortcut menus," still others identify them as "context menus." In this book, they're called *object menus*.

Whatever they're called, they often provide the quickest route to a needed menu command.

 When you right-click certain objects in Windows 95, the object menu includes one command in boldface type. The boldface command is the one that would have been executed had you simply double-clicked the object instead of right-clicking it.

 For information about *using the keyboard to perform mouse functions*, see "Using the Keyboard Instead of the Mouse," page 435.

Gray Commands, Checks, and Cascading Menus

Here are some other menu conventions observed by most Windows-based applications:

- A command that appears in gray letters on a menu is one that's not available in the current context. In Microsoft Excel, for example, the Window menu's Unhide command remains gray until at least one window has been hidden.

- A check mark beside a command indicates that a certain condition has been turned on. Choosing such a command turns the condition off and removes the check mark.

- An arrowhead to the right of a command means that this command brings up a cascading submenu. The Start menu on the taskbar, for example, has four such commands: Programs, Documents, Settings, and Find. Choose any one of these commands, and another menu unfurls.

Quick Viewing and Property Inspection

Two commands that appear on many object menus are particularly important and useful. The Quick View command lets you look at the contents of a file without opening the application that created the file. For example, by right-clicking the icon for a text file, you can read the text without opening WordPad or any other text editor. Not all files can be quick-viewed, but many can. To see if a file can be quick-viewed, open the folder in which the file is stored, and then right-click the file's icon or name. If a viewer is available for this file type, the Quick View command appears on the object menu. For more information about the Quick View command, see "Inspecting Documents and Programs with Quick View," page 67.

Objects such as files and folders have properties, such as type, size, creation date, and location. The Properties command, which appears at the bottom of an object's object menu, lets you inspect those properties. For example, to find out when a file was last changed, you can right-click that file's icon or name in a folder window, choose Properties, and then read the "Modified" item in the property sheet that appears. To find out how much space is taken up by all the files in a folder, you can right-click the folder icon and choose Properties.

In some cases, you can not only inspect but also change an object's properties by choosing the object menu's Properties command. For example, right-clicking the taskbar and choosing Properties takes you to a dialog box in which you can customize the appearance and behavior of the taskbar and the Start menu. Right-clicking the desktop and choosing Properties lets you customize the appearance of the desktop.

Using Dialog Boxes

An ellipsis (...) is a punctuation symbol signifying an incomplete sentence. In a Windows menu, an ellipsis following a command name indicates an incomplete command. Such a command brings up a *dialog box*, which is a device used by Windows to get more information from you.

Dialog boxes come in all sizes and shapes. Some are simple, others quite complex. But nearly all dialog boxes have the following components:

- One or more places for you to enter information or choose options

- One or more command buttons

Most dialog boxes have a command button that you click after you've filled out the dialog box to your satisfaction and another that you click if you want to back out of the dialog box without making an entry. In many cases, these buttons are marked OK and Cancel, respectively. Many dialog boxes also have a button labeled Help or a button with a question mark on it; you can click this kind of button if you're not sure what some of the dialog-box options mean.

Pressing Esc or Alt-F4 in a dialog box is usually equivalent to clicking the Cancel button. It dismisses the dialog box without taking any further action. Still another way to dismiss a dialog box is to click the Close button on its title bar.

Accelerator Keys in Dialog Boxes

Like menu commands, the names of dialog box elements often have underlined letters that you can use for quick keyboard access. These accelerator keys provide a quick way to select dialog box options using the keyboard. In Figure 1-11 on the next page, for example, F is the accelerator key for the Formula Bar check box; S is the accelerator for the Status Bar check box, and so on.

To use accelerator keys in a dialog box, hold down the Alt key while you press the accelerator key.

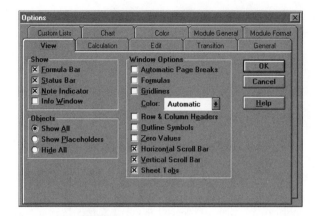

Dialog Box Tabs

The dialog box shown in Figure 1-11 actually includes ten "pages" of options. You select the page you're interested in by clicking its tab at the top of the dialog box. For example, the portion of the dialog box shown in the figure offers viewing options; to select editing options, click the Edit tab—and so on. Press Ctrl-Tab to flip through the pages with the keyboard.

If the current tab has a dotted marquee around it, as the View tab does in Figure 1-11, you can also move between tabs by pressing the arrow keys.

Dialog Box Elements

In the section of a dialog box where you enter information or select options, you'll encounter the following kinds of elements:

- Text boxes
- List boxes
- Drop-down list boxes
- Option buttons
- Check boxes
- Spinners
- Sliders

A *text box*, sometimes also called an *edit box*, is a place for you to type something. The rectangles containing dates, near the center of the following illustration, are examples of text boxes.

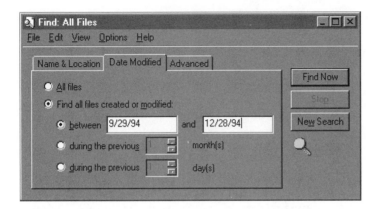

To fill out a text box, click in the box. You'll then see a flashing vertical line, which is called an *insertion point*. If the text box is empty, the insertion point appears at the left side of the box. If the box already contains text, the insertion point is located at the spot where you clicked the mouse. In either case, the insertion point marks the place where the characters you type will appear.

A *list box* presents a set of options in the form of a list, like this:

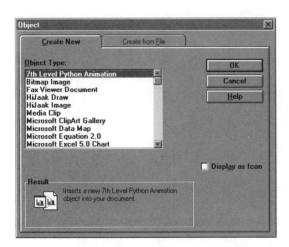

In most list boxes, you can choose only one item at a time, but in some you can choose two or more. If a list box allows you to choose more than one option at a time, hold down the Ctrl key while you click each item you want to choose.

If the list contains more items than can be displayed at once (as the list shown on the previous page does), you will find a *scroll bar* at the right side of the list box. The scroll bar helps you move quickly from one part of the list to another. (For more information about scroll bars, see "Using Scroll Bars," page 36.) You can also move through a list box by pressing the Up arrow or Down arrow key, PgUp, or PgDn.

When you're scrolling through a list, the keyboard is often quicker than the mouse. In most newer applications, including the "applets" included with Windows 95, simply type the first few letters of a list item to move the highlight to that item. (If the highlight moves as you type each letter to the next item that *begins* with that letter, the application is using the older, Windows 3.x method of navigating through lists. Such applications consider only the first letter of each list item.)

A *drop-down list box* looks like a text box with a downward-pointing arrow to the right of it. The Of Type line in the following illustration is an example.

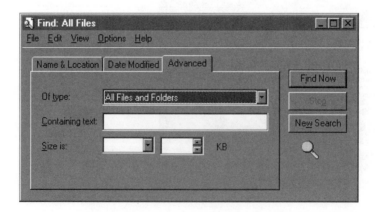

When you click the downward-pointing arrow (or press Alt-Down arrow), an ordinary-looking list box unfolds, like this:

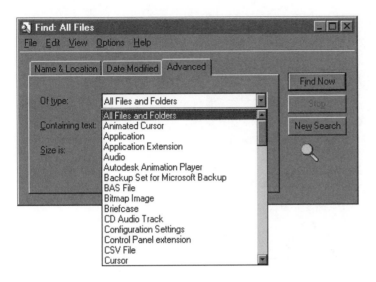

 You can use the arrow keys to move through a drop-down list without first opening the list box. You can also type the first few letters of an item to move directly to that item. (In Windows 3.x–style applications, pressing a letter key moves to the next item that *begins* with that letter.)

 You can move from one item to another in a dialog box by pressing the Tab key (or Shift-Tab to go backwards).

Option buttons (sometimes called *radio buttons*) present a set of mutually exclusive options. In the following dialog box, for example, the Browsing Options section has an option-button group with two buttons.

You may choose either option, but not both. To express your preference, click a button—or anywhere in the text next to a button.

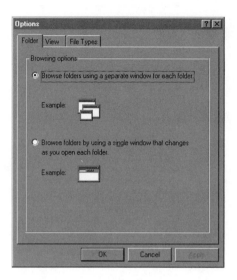

Option buttons always come in groups of two or more. The buttons may be either round or diamond-shaped. Either way, they look quite different from check boxes, which are always square.

Check boxes come either in groups or one at a time. Each check box is independent of all others in the dialog box. Figure 1-12 includes two check-box items in the Energy Saving Features group, labeled Low-Power Standby and Shut Off Monitor. You may select either, both, or neither. To check (select) a check-box item, click the box or anywhere in the text next to the box. To uncheck (deselect) the item, click again.

A "yes" vote for a check box may be marked by either an *X* or a check mark.

Some check boxes have three states—checked, unchecked, and solid. Usually, a solid check box means that a certain condition applies to some of a selection, but not all of it. For example, in Figure 1-13, some of the selected cells in a Microsoft Excel worksheet have been given the "Strikethrough" effect. The rest of the cells have not. In the Format Cells dialog box, therefore, the Strikethrough check box is solid.

A *spinner* is a pair of arrows used to increment or decrement the value in a text box. In Figure 1-12, the arrows to the right of the three

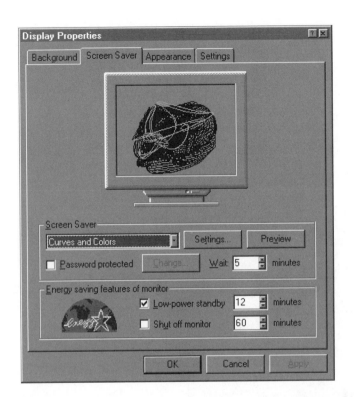

FIGURE 1-12.

The white squares in this property sheet are check boxes. Click one to check it.

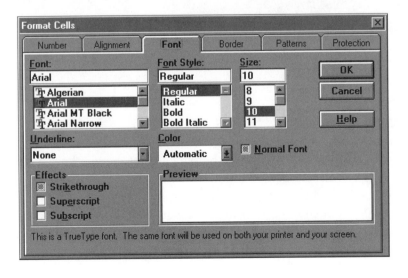

FIGURE 1-13.

When the Strikethrough effect applies to part of the selected text, its check box is solid.

boxes labeled "minutes" are examples of spinners. To increase the value in the text box, click the up arrow; to decrease, click the down arrow.

Just because a text box has a spinner next to it doesn't mean you can't type directly into the text box. Typing may be quicker, particularly if you want to change the value by a significant amount.

A *slider* works like the darkness setting on your toaster. Move it one direction to increase some value, move it the other to decrease the value. The three rate and delay settings in the following illustration are examples of sliders.

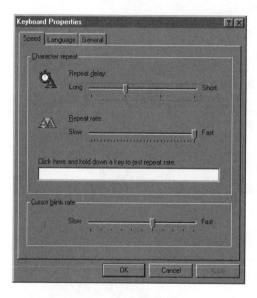

Using Scroll Bars

If a window is not long enough to display its contents completely, Windows adds a *vertical scroll bar* to the right side of the window. If the window is not wide enough, Windows adds a *horizontal scroll bar*. If it's neither long enough nor wide enough, Windows adds both kinds of scroll bars. Figure 1-14 shows a window with vertical and horizontal scroll bars.

Scroll bars offer an easy way to navigate through a window with the mouse. They also provide useful information about the contents of the window.

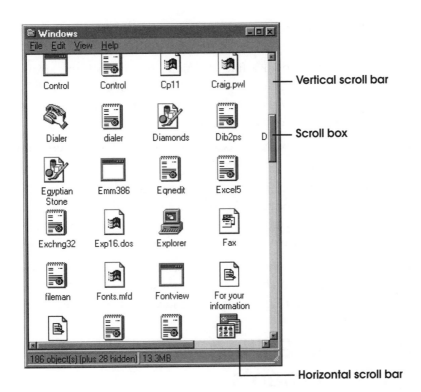

FIGURE 1-14.
Scroll bars provide information about the contents of a window and allow you to move quickly from one part of the window to another.

Vertical scroll bar

Scroll box

Horizontal scroll bar

In Figure 1-14, notice the rectangular *scroll box* in each scroll bar. The position of this box within the scroll bar tells you where you are in the window itself. In the vertical scroll bar, for example, the scroll box is situated about 20 percent of the way down the bar. That means that roughly 20 percent of the window's contents lie above your current position in the window. In the horizontal bar, the scroll box is all the way at the left edge, telling you that there's nothing more to be seen to the left of your current position.

Now notice the size of the scroll boxes relative to the length of the scroll bars. The vertical box is about 20 percent of the length of the scroll bar itself. That means that about one fifth of the window's vertical extent is currently visible within the window frame. The horizontal scroll box is about two-thirds as wide as the horizontal scroll bar, which means that about two-thirds of the window's horizontal extent is now visible.

For navigation purposes, you can use scroll bars in the following ways:

- To move up or down a line at a time, simply click the arrow at either end of the vertical scroll bar. To move side to side a character at a time (or by a small increment in a noncharacter display), click the arrow at either end of the horizontal bar.

- To move by approximately one windowful, click the mouse in the scroll bar itself, on either side of the scroll box.

- To continuously scroll a line at a time, click an arrow and hold down the mouse button. To continuously scroll a windowful at a time, click in the scroll bar itself and hold down the mouse button. When you arrive where you want to be, release the button.

- To move to a specific location, drag the box. To move halfway down a long document, for example, you could move the vertical scroll box to about the midpoint of the vertical scroll bar.

Entering and Editing Text in Documents

Unless you happen to be concerned only with visual images, you will probably spend much of your time in Windows entering and editing text. This is true whether your primary application is word processing, financial planning, database management, project management, or communications. Even though Windows is a graphical environment and uses your computer's graphics display modes, the information you work with consists primarily of letters and numbers—in other words, text.

Fortunately, a basic set of concepts and procedures applies to text in most applications for Windows.

The Insertion Point

The flashing vertical line that you see whenever you work with text in a Windows-based application is called the *insertion point*. It's analogous to the cursor in a character-based word processing program. The insertion point indicates where the next character you type will appear.

Toolbars, Speedbars, Button Bars, and Sushi Bars

Only kidding, of course. In this version of Windows, there are no sushi bars. But you will find icon bars aplenty. Most major applications for Windows have adopted the convention of augmenting their menu systems with palettes of icons. The icons are shortcuts that save you the trouble of pulling down menus and submenus. These palettes go by different names in different programs. Microsoft calls them toolbars. Other vendors refer to them as button bars, SmartIcon palettes, speedbars, tool boxes, or tool kits.

The row of icons underneath the menu bar in Figure 1-9 on page 22 is an example of an icon palette. In this example, each icon includes a text legend to help you understand its purpose. In many other cases, you won't find a legend on the icon itself, but if you point your mouse at an icon a legend will appear—directly below the icon, in a pop-up balloon beside the icon, or perhaps in a status area at the bottom or top of the window. (In Microsoft's programs, as in Windows itself, the icon legends appear in a small box next to the icon after you rest your mouse on an icon for about a half second.)

In many programs, the icon palettes are customizable. That is, you can set up the palette so that it includes icons for just those commands that you use most often. Customizable icon palettes can be a real convenience. If your program includes an icon palette, check its documentation to see if you can tailor the palette to suit your preferences.

Of course, icon palettes may not be your kettle of sushi. If that's the case, check your program's documentation to see if the palette can be removed. Most likely it can, and getting rid of it will give you a bigger window to work in.

There's one difference between the insertion point and the cursor used in most MS-DOS–based programs. The insertion point is always positioned *between* two characters, *before* the first character in a block, or *after* the last character in a block. It never appears directly under a character. That's because characters are always *inserted* at the insertion point.

In the following illustration, for example, the insertion point is located between the *i* and the *n* in the word *tiny*.

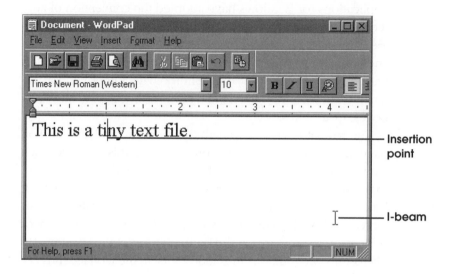

To replace existing text with new characters that you type, Windows uses a different concept, called *selection*. More about that in a moment.

The I-Beam

When you work with text, Windows changes your mouse pointer from an arrow to something that looks like a lanky capital *I*. The pointer is then usually called an *I-beam*. In the illustration above, you can see the I-beam in the lower right corner of the window.

The I-beam provides a way to relocate the insertion point. In the tiny text file above, for example, if you want to move the insertion point to the beginning of the line, simply use the mouse to position the I-beam before the capital *T,* and then click. (You can also use the keyboard to move the insertion point, as we'll see in a moment.)

The Selection

To *select* something in Windows means to highlight it—with the keyboard or the mouse. In the following illustration, for example, the word *tiny* has been selected. The object that you select is called the *selection*.

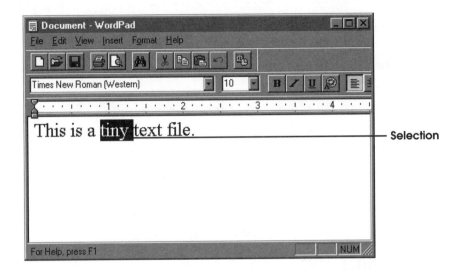

You might select a block of text for any of several reasons:

■ To apply a formatting change to the entire block (In the illustration above, for example, if you click WordPad's Underline tool after selecting the word *tiny*, the entire word is underlined.)

■ To *copy*, *cut*, or *delete* the entire block

■ To replace the entire block

Notice that there's no insertion point in the illustration above. The insertion point disappears when you make a selection, because the next character you type *replaces* the entire selection.

Positioning the Insertion Point

As mentioned before, the easiest way to move the insertion point is with the mouse. Simply put the I-beam wherever you want the insertion point, and then click.

41

You can also use the keyboard. The following keystroke combinations apply to most Windows-based applications that work with text:

- The Right arrow and Left arrow keys move the insertion point forward or backward a character at a time. Ctrl-Right and Ctrl-Left move it forward or back a word at a time.

- End moves the insertion point to the end of the line. Home moves it to the beginning of the line.

- The Up arrow and Down arrow keys move the insertion point up or down a line at a time.

- PgUp and PgDn move up or down a windowful at a time.

- Ctrl-End moves to the end of the document. Ctrl-Home moves to the beginning of the document.

Some applications use additional keystroke combinations for moving the insertion point. In Microsoft Word, for example, pressing Ctrl-Down takes you to the first word in the next paragraph, and Ctrl-Up takes you to the beginning of the previous paragraph.

Selecting Text

To select text with the mouse, put the I-beam at one end of the block you want to select. Then hold down the mouse button, move to the other end, and release the mouse button. In other words, simply drag the mouse across the text you want to select. You can select a word by double-clicking anywhere in it.

To select text with the keyboard, first put the insertion point at one end of the block you want to select. Then hold down the Shift key and *extend* the selection to the other end of the block. The same keystrokes you use to move the insertion point extend the selection.

For example, to select three characters within a word, put the insertion point before the first character, and then hold down the Shift key while pressing the Right arrow key three times. To select an entire word, position the insertion point to the left of the word, hold down the Shift key, and press Ctrl-Right. To select from the insertion point position to the end of the line, hold down the Shift key and press End—and so on.

Deleting Characters

To delete a few characters, put the insertion point where you want to make the deletion. Then use the Backspace or Del key to make your corrections. Backspace deletes characters to the left of the insertion point; Del deletes characters to the right of the insertion point.

Deleting Blocks of Text

To delete a block of text, first select the block. Then do one of the following:

- Press Del or Backspace.
- Choose the Edit menu's Delete or Clear command (if your application's menu has such a command).
- Choose the Edit menu's Cut command.

Pressing Del or Backspace deletes the selected text. Choosing Delete or Clear from the Edit menu does exactly the same thing. Choosing the Cut command, however, does something quite different. It deletes the text from your document but stores it in an area of memory called the Clipboard. After the selection has been stored on the Clipboard, you can *paste* it somewhere else—in either the same or another document (even a document created by a different application).

Undoing a Deletion

Many applications include an Undo command on their Edit menus. This command gives you the opportunity to change your mind about a deletion. The Undo command usually can reverse only your most recent edit, however. So for example, if you delete a line of text, and then apply a formatting command to a different block of text, you won't be able to use the Undo command to reverse your deletion; at this point the Undo command is poised to undo the formatting change, not the deletion. (Some programs do have multiple-level Undo commands, however.)

Copying and Moving Text

The Clipboard makes it easy to copy or move text from one place to another. Follow these steps:

1. Select the text you want to move or copy.

2. To move, choose the Edit menu's Cut command. To copy, choose the Edit menu's Copy command.

3. Move the insertion point to the place where you want to move or copy your text.

4. Choose the Edit menu's Paste command.

This simple procedure can be used to move or copy text from one place to another in the same document, from one document to another created by the same application, or from one application to an entirely different application.

See Also: For more information about *using the Clipboard*, see Chapter 10, "Exchanging Information: The Clipboard and OLE," page 251.

Getting Help

Most Windows programs include a Help menu as the rightmost item on the menu bar. Any time you're unsure how a feature or command works, you can pull down the Help menu and find useful information. In many cases, the help window stays on top of all other windows by default, so you can continue reading the help text as you work. If a help window does not stay on top, or you find it inconvenient to keep it on top, you can switch back and forth between your program and the help text by pressing Alt-Tab. One Alt-Tab takes you to the help window; the next Alt-Tab returns you to your work, and so on.

In your travels through Windows you are likely to find two basic kinds of help systems—a simpler system introduced with Windows 95 and a more complex hypertext system that was introduced several years earlier with Windows 3.0. Along with newer applications, the "applets" (accessory programs) supplied with Windows 95 mostly use the newer help system. Most older programs use the Windows 3.x hypertext system.

Figure 1-15 shows the Contents view of a typical Windows 95 help document—in this case, the document that appears when you choose Help from the Start menu. Notice that the Help window has three tabs, labeled Contents, Index, and Find. These tabs offer three different ways to get at the information in your program's help file.

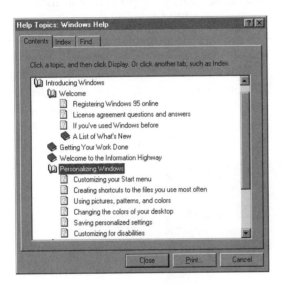

FIGURE 1-15.

The Contents view is an outline of main headings, subheadings, and displayable topics.

- The Contents tab presents general topics in the form of an outline.

- The Index tab presents more specific topics, listed alphabetically.

- The Find tab lets you search for particular words or phrases in a help topic.

Most of the time, you'll find what you need in either the Contents tab or the Index tab. These components of the help system work exactly like their analogues in a printed book. When you're looking for information about a broad topic, such as personalizing Windows, you'll want to go first to the table of contents. When you need information about a more specific topic, such as changing the clock from a 12-hour format to a 24-hour format, you'll save time by going straight to the index.

Like the table of contents in many books, the help system's Contents tab is an outline structure. The book icons indicate headings that can be expanded or collapsed. The question-mark icons indicate topics that can be displayed. To display a help topic, double-click it, or select it and click the Display button.

 At any level of the Contents outline, you can print the help text by clicking the Print button. If you select an item marked with a book icon, your printout will include all pages under the selected heading.

To find an entry in the Index tab (see Figure 1-16), simply begin typing the first few characters of the entry in the top line of the dialog box. When you see the topic you want in the list below, double-click it. Or select it and click the Display button.

FIGURE 1-16.

The Index view's topics are more specific than those of the Contents view.

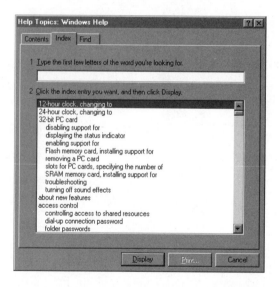

If you can't locate what you're looking for in either the Contents tab or the Index tab, try the Find tab. Where the Index tab lets you search through an alphabetical list of topics, the Find tab lets you search by the actual contents of the help messages. If you want to read all the help messages that include the word *color*, for example, you can do that by specifying *color* in the Find window.

Before you can use the Find window, you have to let the help system create a "word list" from all the messages in the current help file. When you click Find for the first time in a particular help file, the "wizard" shown in Figure 1-17 appears. (A wizard is a sequence of dialog boxes that help you complete a process, such as creating a word list for a help file.) To create the word list, choose one of the three option buttons offered by this wizard, click Next, and then follow the instructions in the subsequent dialog boxes.

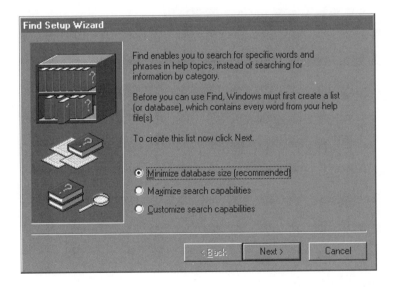

FIGURE 1-17.

The Find Setup wizard assists you in creating a list of all searchable words in the messages contained in a help file. You can then use the help system's Find tab to search for messages containing particular words or phrases.

Once you've created the word list for a particular help file, you'll be able to search for messages in that file that contain particular words or phrases. When you click the Find tab, you'll see a dialog box similar to the one shown in Figure 1-18 on the next page. Type the word or phrase that interests you in the top line of this dialog box. The help system responds by displaying the titles of messages containing your text. You can then display a message by selecting its name and clicking the Display button.

FIGURE 1-18.

The Find tab lets you search for help based on the contents of the help topics.

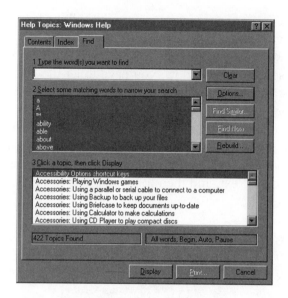

"Hot" Zones in Help Text

In the help text for some topics, you may find words or phrases underscored with dots. These are glossary terms; to see a definition, click the underscored item.

In many topics, you will find square gray buttons. When you position your mouse pointer over one of these buttons, the pointer changes shape—typically to a hand with an extended index finger. Click the button to display a related topic.

In some help topics, you may find text displayed in contrasting color (typically green) and underscored with a solid line. Click the underscored text to display a related item.

Some help windows, such as the one shown in Figure 1-19, include one or more shortcut buttons. A click on a shortcut button takes you directly to the area of Windows that is discussed in the help topic.

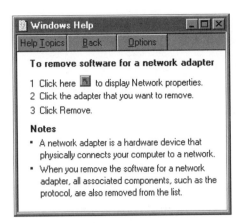

FIGURE 1-19.

Some help windows include handy shortcut buttons that take you straight to the area of Windows you're reading about.

Retracing Your Path Through the Help System

The help system uses hypertext techniques to link related information. That means that you can often wander from topic to related topic, just by clicking hot zones in help messages. To help you find your way back to messages you've read earlier, the topic window includes a Back button. (See Figure 1-19.) Clicking Back returns you to the last topic you read. Clicking Back repeatedly lets you retrace your passage through the help file.

If instead of returning to a prior topic, you want to return to the index or table of contents, click the Help Topics button.

Printing and Preserving Help Text

The help system provides ways to print or save its messages. You can copy a portion of any help topic, or the entire topic, to another application as follows.

To copy a portion of a topic:

1. Drag your mouse across the text to select it.

2. Press Ctrl-C to copy the selected text to the Windows Clipboard.

3. Activate the application into which you want to paste the text.

4. Use the application's Paste command (or press Ctrl-V, the keyboard shortcut for Paste).

To copy all of a topic:

1. Click the Options button at the top of the topic window.

2. Choose Copy from the menu that appears.

3. Activate the application into which you want to paste the topic.

4. Use the application's Paste command (or press Ctrl-V).

To print a topic, follow these steps:

1. Click the Options button.

2. Choose Print Topic from the menu that appears.

3. In the Print dialog box, make sure the printer you want to use appears on the Name line. (If it does not, choose the printer you want to use by clicking the drop-down arrow at the right side of the Name line.)

4. Click OK.

 See Also: For more information about *copy and paste*, see Chapter 10, "Exchanging Information: The Clipboard and OLE," page 251.

For information about *printing*, see Chapter 9, "Installing, Configuring, and Using Your Printers," page 223.

Annotating a Help Topic

You can add your own comments to any help message. Simply display the message, click the Options button, and choose Annotate from the menu that appears. An Annotate window will appear. Type your comments in the Annotate window, and then click the Save button. Windows displays a paper-clip icon beside the title of the help message. To redisplay your comments, click the paper clip.

Getting Help in Dialog Boxes

In theory, all Windows dialog boxes are entirely self-explanatory, so you'll never pause in puzzlement over what a particular button or check box means. To accommodate the divergence between theory and reality, many applications include invaluable Help buttons in their dialog boxes. If you're stumped, call for help.

In many dialog boxes, you will also see a question-mark icon right beside the close box. That's the "what's-this?" button. If you're not sure what some element of the dialog box means, click the what's-this button, and then click the element in question. An explanatory message will pop up. When you've finished reading, click inside the message box to make it go away.

Ending a Windows Session

WShen it's time to quit Windows, open the Start menu and choose Shut Down. You'll see the dialog box shown in Figure 1-20. (If you're not part of a network and aren't using profiles, the dialog box includes only the first three options.) Choose Shut Down The Computer. Windows closes any running applications, and in a moment or two, you will see another message, notifying you that it is safe to turn off your computer.

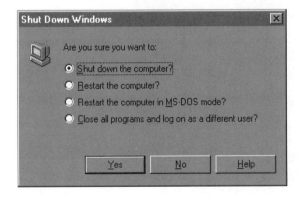

FIGURE 1-20.

At quitting time, use the Start menu's Shut Down command and choose the first option in this dialog box.

If for any reason your system is not ready to be shut down, you will be advised. For example, if you have unsaved work in an application, that program displays a prompt, giving you the opportunity to save before quitting. A program may also display a "can't quit" message if it objects to being closed for any other reason. This can happen, for example, if the program is in the middle of a communications session or if it's displaying a dialog box and waiting for you to respond.

If you've been a Windows NT user, you may appreciate the fact that you can also shut the system down by pressing Ctrl-Alt-Del and clicking the Shut Down button. This sequence of steps is equivalent to choosing the Start menu's Shut Down command and selecting the first option in the Shut Down Windows dialog box.

If you respond promptly to a "can't quit" message, Windows stops trying to shut down your system. Then you can respond to your program or wait until it's no longer busy, and then use the Shut Down command again.

If you do not respond to the "can't quit" message within a certain period of time, however, Windows displays the message shown in Figure 1-21. Your choices are spelled out in the text of the message. The safest thing to do is click Cancel, return to your program, and then either respond to its needs or wait until it has finished whatever it's doing.

FIGURE 1-21.

This message appears if you do not respond to a program's "can't quit" message or if a program is "hung."

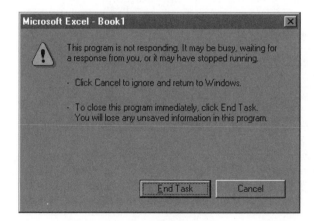

The message shown in Figure 1-21 also appears if an application has stopped responding to the operating system. You can use the End Task button to terminate such a "hung" program. You should not use this button capriciously, however. If a program is not hung but is simply busy, terminating it against its will may have adverse consequences—such as the loss of any work you've created since the last time you used the program's Save command.

Shutting Down If You Have Shared Resources

If you have made any of your computer's local resources—folders or printers, for example—available to other users on your network, you may see an advisory message when you shut down. The message tells you how many users are connected to your shared resources and warns you that shutting down will disconnect those users. If you know that no one will be needing the shared resources until you return to work, it's fine to go ahead and shut down. If you're not sure, or if you want to quit without disconnecting your colleagues, you can log off without quitting Windows.

For information about *sharing resources*, see "Sharing Folders with Other Users," page 190, and "Sharing a Printer," page 248.

Logging Off Without Quitting

The fourth option in the dialog box shown in Figure 1-20 shuts down all running programs and logs you off your network, but does not shut down Windows. You may want to use this option at quitting time if someone else will be using your computer.

When you log off without quitting, any resources shared by your computer remain available to other users on the network. Thus, for example, you might want to quit in this manner if others will be printing to a printer attached to your computer.

When you log off without quitting, Windows presents the same logon dialog box that you saw at the beginning of your current session, allowing you or another user to log back on.

2

Running Programs and Opening Documents

One of the things you'll like about Windows 95 is that there's usually more than one way to accomplish a given task. In many cases, there are a multitude of ways.

Take the act of running a program, for example. You can run most of the programs you need by making simple picks from the Start menu. But if you prefer using an MS-DOS–style command line, you can certainly do that as well. If you're a Windows 3.x veteran and are most at home with Program Manager, Windows 95 will be happy to accommodate your preference; simply bring a copy of Program Manager to your desktop, and you can run all your programs from there. (You might want to put Program Manager in the Startup folder. Then it will arrive on your desktop automatically each time you start Windows 95.)

One of the most useful innovations of Windows 95 is the *shortcut*. A shortcut is a pointer to a program, to a document, or to some other object. By creating shortcuts for programs or documents and placing them on the desktop, you can make everything you need accessible with a simple double-click.

In short, when it comes to running programs and opening documents, Windows gives you choices. You can find the working style that best suits you.

 See Also: For information about *installing programs*, see "Installing Applications," page 342.

Running Programs from the Start Menu

Figure 2-1 on the next page shows the Start menu for a typical user's system. At the top of this menu are the names of four programs and one folder this user works with every day. This area of your own Start menu may include more or fewer items—or perhaps none at all. To run a program whose name appears in the top part of the Start menu, click the Start button or press Ctrl-Esc to open the Start menu. Then move the mouse until the desired program's name is highlighted, and then click.

The Windows Setup program does not ordinarily put anything in the top part of the Start menu. That's because this part of the menu is

FIGURE 2-1.

The top part of the Start menu may be used for your most frequently needed programs, documents, and folders.

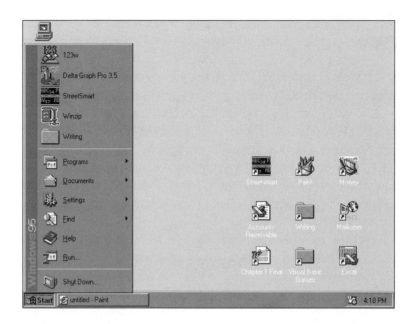

intended to give you access to the items you need most often, and the Setup program has no way of knowing what those items are. If your system was set up by an administrator, that person may have configured the top part of the Start menu for you. In any case, if you don't find the items you need here, you can easily add them, and you can just as easily get rid of items you don't need. (See "Customizing the Start Menu," page 81.)

 You can put document and folder names, as well as program names, in the top part of the Start menu. For details, see "Customizing the Start Menu," page 81.

To run a program that's not listed at the top of your Start menu, move the mouse pointer to the item labeled Programs. A submenu will appear, as shown in Figure 2-2.

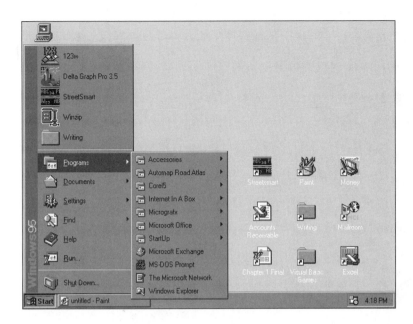

FIGURE 2-2.

The Programs submenu may include more program names, grouped by category.

Along with a few program names, your Programs submenu is likely to include several folders, each for a category of programs. The submenu in Figure 2-2, for example, includes a folder for accessories, folders for various applications, and a folder for startup programs (programs that run automatically at the beginning of each Windows session). Each of these folders opens another submenu, as Figure 2-3 on the next page shows. As you move through this tree of submenus, you eventually will come to the name of the program you want to run. When you do, give your mouse a click and your program will appear.

If you installed Windows 95 over a previous version of Windows, you'll find that each of your previous version's Program Manager groups has become a folder on the Programs submenu, and that programs that were listed in your StartUp program group are now listed in the Windows 95 StartUp folder. When you install new programs in Windows 95, those programs generally appear somewhere on the Start menu as well.

Like the top of the Start menu, the Programs submenu is customizable. If the bill of fare doesn't suit you, you can change it. (See "Customizing the Start Menu," page 81.)

FIGURE 2-3.

A tree of submenus leads eventually to the program you want to run.

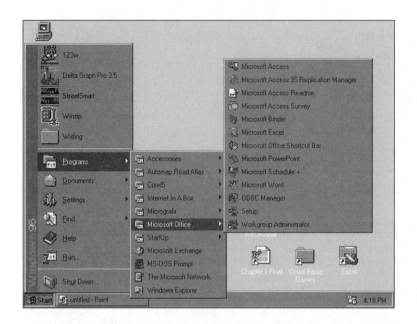

Running MS-DOS–Based Programs

You can run MS-DOS–based programs from the Start menu, just as you can run Windows-based programs. Alternatively, if the MS-DOS–based program you want to run doesn't appear on any part of the Start menu, try running the MS-DOS Prompt item. This opens an MS-DOS window and presents you with the familiar MS-DOS command prompt. From this prompt, you can type the name of the program you want to run (with the path if needed).

Yet another way to run an MS-DOS–based program is by using the Start menu's Run command. (See "Running Programs and Opening Documents with the Run Command," page 70.) Type *command* on the Run line to open an MS-DOS window, and then type your program's name at the MS-DOS prompt that appears.

For more information about running MS-DOS–based programs, see Chapter 12, "Running MS-DOS–Based Programs," page 301.

Running Programs with Program Manager

If you're accustomed to using an earlier version of Windows, you might want to run programs from Program Manager, at least for a while. To do that, you need to run a program called *progman*. If you don't find Program Manager anywhere on the Start menu, choose the Start menu's Find command and choose Files Or Folders. In the Named text box of the dialog box that appears, type *progman.exe*. Then click Find Now. In a moment an entry for Progman will appear in the bottom part of the Find dialog box. Double-click this entry to run Program Manager.

If you run Program Manager frequently, you might want to add it to the Start menu, using the customizing procedures described later in this chapter. If you run it all the time, you can add it to the StartUp menu (a submenu of the Start menu). Programs listed in the StartUp menu run automatically whenever you begin a session in Windows 95.

Opening Recently Used Documents from the Start Menu

As you work with programs and create documents, Windows keeps track of your 15 most recently used documents and makes those files available on the Documents submenu of the Start menu. You can reopen a recently used document, complete with its parent application, by clicking Start, selecting Documents, and choosing the name of the document you want to work with.

For example, suppose your Documents submenu includes an item called Letter of Introduction, and that this item is the name of a file created in Microsoft Word. When you choose Letter of Introduction on the Documents submenu, Windows 95 runs Word, and Word opens your letter.

Once your Documents submenu contains 15 document names, newly arriving items replace least-recently-used items. If you find that most of the items on the menu are old, you might want to clear the entire menu so that you can more easily find the new arrivals. To clear the Documents

Documents saved from applications written for earlier versions of Windows do not automatically appear on the Documents menu. For example, if the version of your word processor dates from the days of Windows 3.x, the files you save from that word processor will not automatically show up on the Documents menu. You can make them appear there, however. Any document that you open by double-clicking its entry in a folder or Windows Explorer window (or a shortcut to that entry) will appear on the Documents menu, regardless of the vintage of its parent application. For details, see "Running Programs and Opening Documents from Folders," below.

submenu, choose Settings from the Start menu. From the Settings submenu, choose Taskbar. In the Taskbar Properties dialog box, click the Start Menu Programs tab. Then click the button labeled Clear.

Running Programs and Opening Documents from Folders

Another way to run a program or open a document is to double-click its icon or name in a folder or Windows Explorer window. The window shown in Figure 2-4, for example, displays the contents of a folder named Excel. The fourth item in the first row of this window is the icon for the program Microsoft Excel. To run Excel from this window, you can simply double-click that icon. Alternatively, you can right-click the icon and choose the Open command. Or, if you prefer working with the keyboard, you can use the arrow keys to select the Excel icon, and then press Enter.

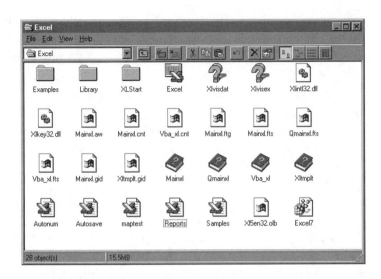

FIGURE 2-4.

You can run Microsoft Excel by double-clicking the fourth icon in the first row of this folder window.

In the fourth row of the folder are several icons that represent Excel documents. Double-clicking one of these—the icon labeled Autonum, for example—opens the associated document within Excel.

See Also: For more information about *folders and folder windows*, see "Working with Folders," page 22, and Chapter 4, "Working with Folders," page 115.

What to Do When Windows Can't Open Your Documents

Windows maintains a store of information about your system, called the *registry*. Along with many other details, the registry includes a list of applications installed on your computer, as well as information about the types of documents each application can create. It is this information that enables Windows to run the appropriate application when you select a document on the Documents submenu or double-click a document icon in a folder.

How does Windows tell one document type from another? By its file-name extension. When you install an application, the application tells the registry the default extensions it uses for its documents. Thus, for example, Microsoft Excel "reserves" the extension .XLS for its workbook files, .XLA for add-in files, .XLC for chart documents created in versions of Excel prior to 5.0, and so on. (By default, folder and Windows Explorer windows do not display the extensions of document filenames that are associated with registered applications. But Windows "sees" the extensions even if it doesn't show them to you.)

Chances are, most of the documents you use are associated with some application. But now and then you may try to open a document whose application "parent" is unknown to Windows. For example, WinCIM, the Windows version of the CompuServe Information Manager, routinely assigns the extension .LOG to transcript files created during CompuServe sessions. WinCIM does not, however, register the document type .LOG with itself. (That makes sense, because .LOG files are files of plain text, and WinCIM does not include a text viewer/editor.) If you try to open a .LOG file by double-clicking it in a folder window, you will see the Open With dialog box, shown in Figure 2-5.

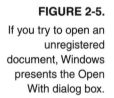

FIGURE 2-5.

If you try to open an unregistered document, Windows presents the Open With dialog box.

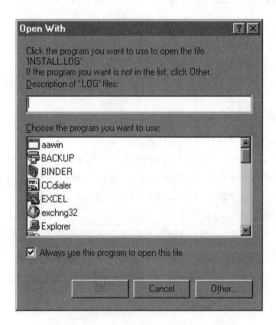

The Open With dialog box lets you create either a temporary or permanent association between a document type and a program. To create a one-time association between a document and a program, deselect the check box at the bottom of this dialog, and then choose a program from the list in the center. To create a permanent association, enter a description of the document type on the line at the top, and then select the program you want from the list in the middle of the dialog box. (The description line does not appear if the document you're trying to open has no filename extension.)

Note that you need to fill out the Description line only if you're making a permanent association, and on that line you can type whatever suits you. For example, you could describe .LOG files as "CompuServe transcripts," "Logs of CompuServe sessions," or simply "Log files."

If the application list doesn't include the program you want, click the Other button. That will take you to the dialog box shown in Figure 2-6.

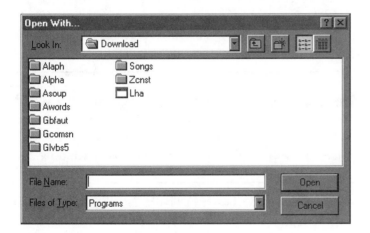

FIGURE 2-6.

Clicking the Other button displays the contents of the current folder. If the program you need is not shown here, you can navigate to it.

For example, the Open With dialog box in Figure 2-6 shows that the current folder, Download, contains one program file (Lha) and nine additional folders. If Lha is the program you want, you can double-click it, or click it once and then click the Open button. This will return you to the dialog box shown in Figure 2-5, with Lha added to the program list.

The Open With command presents a list of registered applications. To see a list of all document types known to the registry, and the application with which each is associated, choose the Options command on the menu bar of any folder or Windows Explorer window. Then click the File Types tab. For more information about file types, see "Working with the File Types List," page 155.

You can associate a document type with only one application. If you sometimes want to open a particular kind of document with one application and sometimes with another, try using the Send To command. For example, if you usually want to open .DBF files in dBASE for Windows, but occasionally you like to import them into Excel, create a Send To shortcut for Excel. For details, see "Customizing the Send To Menu," page 146.

Browsing Through Folders to Find the Program You Want

The dialog box shown in Figure 2-6 shows only the contents of the current folder. To make this window display a different folder, use the same navigation techniques that you would use in a normal folder window.

The dialog box shown in Figure 2-6 shows folders and filenames in List view, by default. To see the items displayed another way, right-click within the browse dialog box and choose View.

For information about *navigating in folder windows*, see "Moving from Folder to Folder," page 119.

Running Programs and Opening Documents with the Find Command

Double-clicking an icon in a folder window is a fine way to run a program that doesn't happen to be on your Start menu—provided the folder is at hand or easy to get to. If that folder is more than a few mouse-clicks away, however, a quicker solution may be to use the Start menu's Find command. The Find command is a powerful tool for locating just about anything on your own computer or on a network server.

The Find command displays its results in a window that behaves much like any folder window. That means you can run a program or open a document by simply double-clicking it within a Find window. (Alternatively, you can right-click an item and choose the Open command, or select the item with the keyboard and then press Enter.)

 See Also: For more information about *the Find command*, see Chapter 7, "Using the Find Command," page 193.

Inspecting Documents and Programs with Quick View

With thousands of files on your hard disk, it's not always easy to know which is the document or program you need. Wouldn't it be handy to be able to peek at a document before going to the trouble of opening it and its parent application? With Quick View, you can do just that.

To use Quick View, simply right-click a document, program, or shortcut anywhere you see it—in a folder window, in a Windows Explorer window, on your desktop, or in a Find window. If the item you've selected is viewable, the Quick View command appears near the top of the object menu. Table 2-1 on the next page shows some of the file types that can be inspected with Quick View. In addition to these file types, others on your system may also be viewable.

TABLE 2-1.

You can use Quick
View to examine
these file types.

File Type	Extension
Ami or Ami Pro document	.SAM
Bitmap image	.BMP, .RLE
CompuServe GIF image	.GIF
Configuration settings	.INI
CorelDRAW drawing	.CDR
Encapsulated PostScript file	.EPS
Freelance Graphics presentation	.PRE
Lotus 1-2-3 spreadsheet or chart	.WKS, .WK1, .WK3, .WK4
Micrografx Draw drawing	.DRW
Microsoft Excel worksheet or chart	.XLS, .XLC
Microsoft PowerPoint presentation	.PPT
Microsoft Word document	.DOC
Microsoft Works spreadsheet	.WKS
Microsoft Works word processing document	.WPS
Multiplan spreadsheet	.MOD
Quattro Pro spreadsheet	.WB1, .WQ1, .WQ2
Rich Text Format document	.RTF
Setup information	.INF
Text file	.TXT, .ASC
Tiff graphics image	.TIF
Windows Metafile	.WMF
WordPerfect document	.DOC, .WPD
Write document	.WRI

Font files cannot be inspected with Quick View. But you can display a sample of any TrueType font simply by double-clicking its icon. For more information about inspecting fonts, see "Viewing and Printing Font Samples," page 212.

Figure 2-7 shows a Quick View window for a text document. Notice that the window includes a menu bar and toolbar, just like those found in other applications. The window also includes ordinary horizontal and vertical scroll bars, allowing you to see any part of the document.

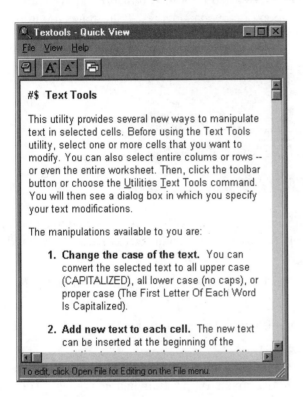

FIGURE 2-7.

Quick View displays a document without opening the document's application.

Quick View gives you a read-only peek at your document. If you want to edit or print the document, you'll need to open it in its parent application. You can do that from within Quick View, by choosing Open File For Editing from the File menu or by clicking the first icon on the toolbar. Other menu and toolbar options let you do such things as change the font used to display your document (but not the fonts used by the document in its parent-application setting) and "zoom-out" for a full-page view of your document.

Running Programs and Opening Documents with the Run Command

The Start menu also includes a handy Run command that you can use to launch programs and open documents. Figure 2-8 illustrates the Run command.

FIGURE 2-8.

The Start menu's Run command is handy for running items that aren't on your Programs menu.

You can use the Run command to launch any program, open any document, or even open a folder. The command is particularly handy in the following situations:

- When you want to rerun or reopen a recently used program or document

- When the program you want to run needs a command-line parameter

As Figure 2-8 shows, the Open line in the Run dialog box presents, as a default, whatever document or program name you last specified. Rerunning that item, therefore, is as simple as choosing Run on the Start menu and clicking OK. Moreover, the Open line is actually a drop-down list. Clicking the arrow at the right side of the line reveals a scrollable list of more than 20 of your most recently used Run commands. Thus if you use this command regularly for a particular group of programs or documents, you will nearly always be able to pick any of those items from the list.

Windows-based programs seldom need command-line parameters, but MS-DOS–based programs sometimes do. One way to run an MS-DOS–based program that needs a parameter is to open an MS-DOS Prompt window. That technique takes you to an MS-DOS command prompt, where you can type the name of your program and any required parameters. (For more information, see Chapter 12, "Running MS-DOS–Based Programs," page 301.) Another way you can do this is by using the Start menu's Run command.

For example, suppose you want to use the MS-DOS DiskCopy command to duplicate a diskette. You can choose the Run command and type *diskcopy a: a: /v.*

You can also use the Run command to open folder windows without actually running any programs. To open a window for the folder C:\Writing\PCMag, for example, simply type that string of characters on the Run command line.

If you're not sure what to put on the command line, enter the name of the folder you're interested in, and then click the Browse button. For example, if you want to run an installation program on drive B, but you aren't sure about the name of that program, you can type *b:* on the Run line. You will then see a dialog box similar to the one shown in Figure 2-6 on page 65. In that dialog box, you can find or navigate to the program or document you want to use.

Using Shortcuts to Run Programs and Open Documents

Yet another way to run programs and open documents is to create shortcuts for them. A shortcut is a tiny file that's linked to a program, document, or folder. The file is represented by an icon that includes a black arrow in its lower left corner, like this:

The item to which a shortcut is linked can be anywhere—on a local hard disk or CD-ROM drive, on a floppy disk, or on a network server. The

Sometimes it can be handy to store a shortcut for a folder inside another folder. For example, suppose your spreadsheet's default data directory is C:\Office95\Excel\Worksheets, but you occasionally need to open files stored in C:\Personal. If you create a shortcut to C:\Personal and store that shortcut in C:\Office95\Excel\Worksheets, you'll save yourself a lot of folder-traversing when you need a personal worksheet. Your shortcut to Personal will appear as a normal folder inside your Worksheets folder. To simplify your return to the Worksheets folder, you might also want to create a shortcut for that folder and put it in C:\Personal.

item to which the shortcut is linked can even *be* a local hard disk or CD-ROM drive, a floppy drive, or a network server.

Like any other kind of file, a shortcut may be stored in any folder, including your desktop. If you store shortcuts for programs and documents you use often on your desktop, you can get to them easily at any time. For example, if you use a half dozen or so programs nearly every day, why not simply add shortcuts for them to your desktop? Whenever you want to run one of those programs, you can simply double-click the appropriate shortcut icon.

A shortcut is a *pointer* to an object, not the object itself. That means that you can create and delete shortcuts without in any way affecting the underlying object. It also means that you can create a shortcut to a major application without duplicating the large file that actually runs that program. Shortcuts themselves use less than 2 KB (kilobytes) of disk storage, so a proliferation of shortcuts is not likely to run you out of hard-disk space.

If you've used an earlier version of Windows, you will probably recognize that a shortcut behaves like a program item in Program Manager. You can even assign a shortcut key to a shortcut, so that you can "run" the shortcut without using your mouse. (See "Assigning a Shortcut Key to a Shortcut," page 76.) There is one important difference between shortcuts and Program Manager program items, however: a shortcut is more versatile. You can assign it to folders, as well as to programs and documents.

Figure 2-9 shows a desktop with eight shortcuts, in addition to the standard desktop objects (My Computer, Network Neighborhood, and Recycle Bin). One shortcut on the left side points to a printer. One near the right edge points to a document (Accounts Receivable), two point to folders (Fonts and Writing), and the remaining four point to applications. In this example, the Writing folder actually resides on a network server; Windows makes no visual distinction between local and remote resources.

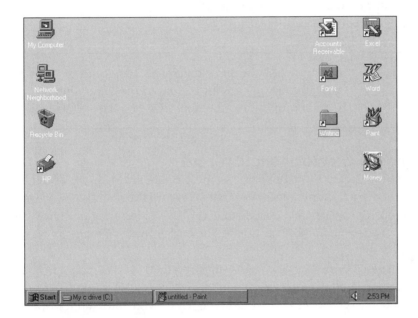

FIGURE 2-9.
You can identify shortcuts by the little arrow in their icon.

Creating a Shortcut

There are two easy ways to create a shortcut: by dragging and dropping and by visiting the Create Shortcut wizard.

Creating a Shortcut with Drag and Drop

If the item for which you want to create a shortcut is visible in a folder or Windows Explorer window, right-drag that item to wherever you want the shortcut to appear. Then, from the object menu, choose Create Shortcut(s) Here.

For example, suppose you want to create a shortcut for the WordPad accessory and put that shortcut on your desktop. Start by opening the folder containing WordPad. After locating the WordPad icon, drag that icon with the right mouse button, and release the button when the mouse pointer is positioned somewhere over the desktop. When you release the button, Windows displays a short object menu, from which you choose Create Shortcut(s) Here.

Alternatively, you can simply right-click an object and choose Create Shortcut from its object menu. Windows creates your shortcut in the same folder in which the underlying object is stored. You can then drag the new shortcut to another location.

 You can use the Find command to locate the item for which you want a shortcut. From the Find window, you can then right-drag the item to create the shortcut.

Using the Create Shortcut Wizard

To use the Create Shortcut wizard, start by right-clicking in the folder where you want your shortcut to appear. (If you want the shortcut to be on your desktop, right-click the desktop.) From the object menu, choose New. Then choose Shortcut. The Create Shortcut wizard appears, as shown in Figure 2-10.

If you know the command line required to run your program or open your document, simply type it and click the Next button. (The command line is whatever you would type to run your program or open your document if you were using the Run command, described earlier in this chapter.) If you don't know the command line, or if Windows gives an error message when you click Next, click the Browse button. This summons a dialog box similar to the one shown in Figure 2-6 on page 65. (The only difference is that the dialog box's title bar says "Browse," instead of "Open With.") Use this dialog box to locate the item for which you want to create a shortcut. Then click the Open button.

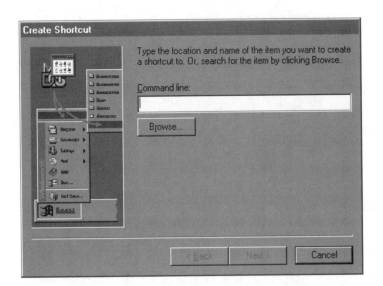

FIGURE 2-10.

The Create Shortcut wizard makes it easy to populate your desktop—or any other folder—with shortcuts.

After you click the Open button, the wizard returns you to its initial dialog box (shown in Figure 2-10), with the command line filled in. Click Next, type a name for your shortcut, click Finish, and your shortcut will appear.

 Some shortcuts can be used as drag-and-drop "targets." For example, if you put a shortcut for a printer on your desktop, you can print files by dragging them from folder windows to the printer shortcut. If you create a shortcut for a floppy disk drive or the top-level folder on a hard disk, you can copy files by dragging them from folder windows to the shortcut. For more information about copying files, see "Moving or Copying Folders, Files, and Shortcuts," page 142. For more information about drag-and-drop printing, see "How Do I Print Thee? (Let Me Count the Ways)," page 227.

Renaming a Shortcut

When you first create a shortcut, Windows gives it a default name based on the underlying object. You're not obliged to live with that name. To rename the shortcut, follow these steps:

1. Right-click the shortcut.

2. From the object menu, choose Rename.

3. Type the name you want to use.

 You can also rename any object by selecting it, pressing F2, and typing the new name.

Assigning a Shortcut Key to a Shortcut

A shortcut key is a keystroke combination that runs a shortcut—that is, it runs the program or opens the dialog to which the shortcut is linked. For example, you might assign Ctrl-Alt-P as a shortcut key for a shortcut linked to Paint. Then, instead of double-clicking your Paint shortcut to start a copy of Paint, you could simply press Ctrl-Alt-P.

 Shortcut keys assigned to shortcuts take precedence over any shortcut keys used by applications. For example, all Windows-based programs use Alt-F4 as a shortcut for their Exit command. If you happen to assign Alt-F4 as a shortcut for launching a copy of Paint, you will no longer be able to quit programs by pressing this combination. Instead, no matter where you are, pressing Alt-F4 will get you another copy of Paint. You might want to keep this in mind as you choose keystroke combinations for your shortcuts.

To assign a shortcut key to a shortcut, follow these steps:

1. Right-click the shortcut and choose Properties from the object menu.

   Alternatively, you can hold down the Alt key and double-click the shortcut.

2. In the Properties dialog box, click the Shortcut tab.

   A dialog box similar to the one shown in Figure 2-11 appears.

3. On the Shortcut Key line, type the keystroke combination you want to use.

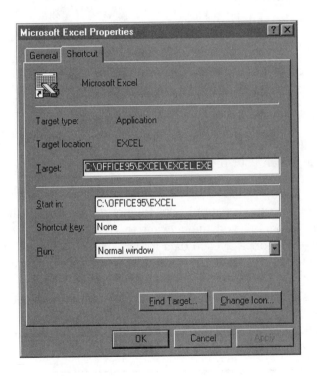

FIGURE 2-11.

With this dialog box, you can set a variety of properties for a shortcut, including its shortcut key and the type of window the shortcut should open.

NOTE: If you type a keystroke combination in the Shortcut Key box, and you've already assigned that combination to another shortcut, Windows runs the other shortcut! Don't be alarmed; simply return to the shortcut properties dialog box, and choose a different combination.

Using Shortcut Properties to Set a Program's Data Folder

On the Start In line of the dialog box shown in Figure 2-11, you can specify a program's default data folder. This is the folder to which the program will save new document files, unless you tell it to do otherwise. So, for example, if you want Excel to use C:\Budgets as its default data folder, do as follows:

1. Right-click the shortcut.

2. From the object menu, choose Properties.

3. Click the dialog box tab labeled Shortcut.

4. On the Start In line, type *c:\budgets*.

   NOTE: Some programs use their own menu commands to set a default data folder, overriding anything you specify on the Start In line.

If you leave the Start In line blank, your default data folder will normally be the one in which your program's executable files are stored.

If you use two or more data folders regularly with the same program, you might want to create two or more shortcuts—one for each data folder. To create a copy of a shortcut, right-click the first shortcut and choose Create Shortcut. The new shortcut will be linked, not to the first shortcut, but to the first shortcut's underlying object. Thus you can set properties for each shortcut independently. By repeating this process you can create as many shortcuts as you need for the same underlying object.

Specifying the Type of Window a Shortcut Opens

The Run line of the dialog box shown in Figure 2-11 lets you indicate what kind of window you want your shortcut to open—a maximized window, a "normal" window (one that's open but not maximized), or a minimized window. If you choose minimized, your shortcut's underlying object opens as a taskbar button. To specify a window type, follow these steps:

1. Right-click the shortcut.

2. From the object menu, choose Properties.

3. Click the dialog box tab labeled Shortcut.

4. Click the drop-down arrow on the Run line. From the list that appears, select the window type you want.

Changing a Shortcut's Icon

Normally a shortcut uses the same icon as its underlying object, except that the shortcut icon includes a pointer arrow to help you recognize it as a shortcut. To choose a different icon for a shortcut, follow these steps:

1. Right-click the shortcut.

2. From the object menu, choose Properties.

3. Click the dialog box tab labeled Shortcut.

4. Click the Change Icon button. As Figure 2-12 shows, the dialog box that appears presents whatever icons are made available by the file to which the shortcut points. With the help of the horizontal scroll bar, you can choose a different icon for your shortcut.

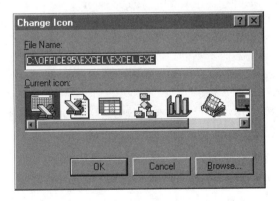

FIGURE 2-12.

The Change Icon dialog box initially presents all the icons that are stored in the file to which your shortcut points.

With some applications, document shortcuts initially use the same icon as the application with which the document is associated. You can choose a different icon to help you recognize that the shortcut is for a document.

You are by no means limited to using one of the icons provided by the shortcut's underlying object. You can use any icon from any file. To search for other icons, type a different filename in the File Name text box, or choose the Browse command in the Change Icon dialog box and select a different file.

Repositioning Shortcuts on the Desktop

You can change the positions of your desktop shortcuts at any time. Simply drag them. You can also get Windows to help you keep your shortcuts neatly aligned. Follow these steps:

1. Use your mouse to bring your shortcut icons into approximate alignment.

2. Right-click the desktop.

3. From the object menu that appears, choose Line Up Icons.

If you want all your desktop shortcuts organized in columns starting at the left side of the desktop, right-click the desktop, choose Arrange Icons, and then choose Auto Arrange. With Auto Arrange turned on, your icons always stay neatly aligned, even if you try to drag them out of place.

Whether you choose Line Up Icons or Auto Arrange to tidy up your desktop, Windows aligns the icons to an invisible grid that evenly spaces the icons. If you want the icons to be closer together or farther apart, you can adjust the grid spacing. To do so, follow these steps:

1. Right-click the desktop.

2. From the object menu, choose Properties.

3. In the Display Properties dialog box, click the Appearance tab.

4. Open the Item drop-down list and select Icon Spacing (Horizontal) or Icon Spacing (Vertical).

5. Adjust the setting in the Size box. (A larger number increases the space between icons.)

NOTE: In addition to controlling the desktop icons, changing the icon spacing affects the spacing of icons in folders when you use Large Icon view.

Deleting a Shortcut

To remove a shortcut, simply select it and press the Del key. Or right-click it and choose Delete from the object menu. Either way, Windows asks you to confirm your intention—thereby protecting you from an accidental deletion. Note that deleting a shortcut does not delete the program or document that the shortcut points to; doing so deletes only the shortcut itself.

Customizing the Start Menu

Two sections of the Start menu—the top of the menu and the Programs submenu—are completely customizable. You can put whatever folders, programs, or documents you want in either of those places, or you can remove anything that's already there.

Adding Items to the Start Menu

Adding items to the Start menu is a matter of creating shortcuts and putting them in the proper folders. Fortunately, Windows makes this all very easy to do.

To add items to either the top of the Start Menu or the Programs submenu, follow these steps:

1. Right-click an unoccupied area of the taskbar.

2. Choose Properties from the object menu.

3. Click the Start Menu Programs tab in the dialog box that appears.

4. Click the Add button.

This sequence takes you straight to the Create Shortcut wizard, which you have already encountered earlier in this chapter. (See Figure 2-10 on page 75.) Type the command line for the item you want to add to the menu. Or click the Browse button to locate the item, just as you would if you were creating a shortcut to put on the desktop or in another folder. When you have the command line filled out, click Next. You'll see a dialog box similar to the one shown in Figure 2-13.

FIGURE 2-13.

In this dialog box, you tell the wizard where you want your new menu item to appear.

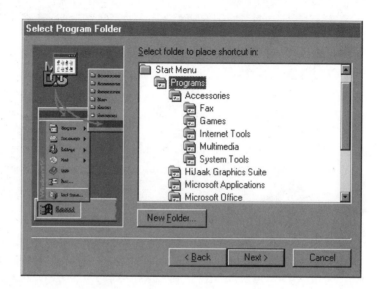

Here the wizard presents an outline of the Programs section of your Start menu. If you want your new menu item to appear at the top of the Start menu (rather than as part of the Programs submenu), simply select Start Menu (the first folder in the outline diagram) and click Next. If you want your new item to appear somewhere within the Programs submenu, first select the heading under which you want it to appear, and then click Next.

For example, suppose you're adding a menu item for the program Microsoft Money, and you want that item to appear within the Microsoft Applications section of the Programs submenu. In the dialog box shown in Figure 2-13, you would select Microsoft Applications, and then click the Next button.

 To make a program or document available at the beginning of every Windows session, create a Start Menu item for it and put that item in the StartUp section of the Programs submenu.

After clicking Next, you'll be asked to name the menu item. If the document, folder, or program you're adding to the menu has a long name, you might want to choose a shortened version of that name for the menu. In any case, either accept the name proposed by the wizard or modify it, and then click the Finish button to install your new menu item.

Tip An alternative way to add an item to the top of the Start menu is to drag it and drop it on the Start menu button. For example, suppose you have a shortcut on your desktop for a document you use every day. Having this item on the top section of your Start menu might make it easier to open the document while you're working in a maximized application. To create the Start menu item, simply drag the desktop shortcut and drop it onto the Start button. Now you'll have easy access to your document from two places, the desktop *and* the Start menu.

What if you want to create a new heading on the Programs submenu and add a program, document, or folder under that heading? In that case, start by creating the shortcut for your program, document, or folder, following the procedures just described. Then, when the wizard asks where you want the new item to appear (the step shown in Figure 2-13), click the New Folder button. (If you want your new folder to be a subfolder of an existing folder, select that folder before you click New Folder.) A default-named folder entry will appear on the outline. Type the name you want to use for your menu heading, and then click Finish. Windows will create the new menu heading and put your new menu item under that heading.

Removing Items from the Start Menu

To remove an item from the Start menu, follow these steps:

1. Right-click an unoccupied area of the taskbar.

2. Choose Properties from the object menu.

3. Click the Start Menu Programs tab in the dialog box that appears.

4. Click the Remove button.

These steps summon the Remove Shortcuts/Folders dialog box, similar to the one shown in Figure 2-14.

FIGURE 2-14.

You can remove items from the Start menu by navigating to them in this outline.

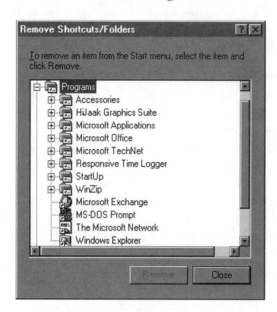

Navigate to the item you want to remove, and then click the Remove button. Note that items on the top of your Start menu appear at the bottom of this outline diagram, after all the items on all the branches of the Programs submenu. You might need to use the scroll bar to find those items.

Notice the plus signs in the outline shown in Figure 2-14. These denote headings that can be expanded—that is branches of the Programs submenu that contain menu items (or further branches) within them. To open a heading and reveal its menu items, simply click the plus sign. To remove an entire limb of the Programs submenu—that is, a heading plus all menu items subsumed by that heading, select the heading name and click Remove. The wizard prompts you to confirm your intentions.

The Start menu is designed to be extremely malleable. With these few simple mouse actions, you can keep the menu trim and efficient, so that it always contains the items you currently need—and none of the ones you don't.

3

Personalizing
Your Workspace

When you first install Windows 95, the Setup program provides a standard configuration for your desktop, your keyboard, and your mouse. You get a fine color arrangement, a "normal" screen resolution, appropriately sized buttons and icons, a default layout of desktop objects, and a keyboard and mouse that behave as Windows' designers think the typical user wants them to behave.

But because one size does not fit all, Windows provides you with a great range of choices regarding the appearance and behavior of your working environment. You can control the amount of information that fits on your screen (within the limits of your display hardware), change the colors used by the various elements of the Windows user interface, change the sizes of window borders and title bars, reposition the taskbar, and decide whether or not the taskbar should remain visible while you work in maximized applications. You can add a textured background to your desktop or drape the desktop with a graphic image, increase or decrease the size of the characters Windows uses for menus and messages, or change the size of all type fonts used on your system. You can speed up or slow down the movement of your mouse pointer and adjust the repeat speed of your keyboard.

 Microsoft Plus! provides many additional options for customizing the sights and sounds of your Windows landscape. For details, see Appendix A, "Using the Power of Your 486 or Pentium with Microsoft Plus!," page 727.

 For information about *other customizing options*, see Chapter 11, "Customizing Windows," page 279.

Taking Advantage of User Profiles

User profiles allow two or more users to share a Windows system and maintain their own preferences with regard to display colors, the organization of the Start menu, and other settings. Each time a user logs on to a

Windows system that is set up for user profiles, Windows restores the working environment that was in place when that user last logged off.

If you're not the only person who uses Windows at your computer, you might want to ensure that your system is set up for user profiles before you make any of the changes described in this chapter. To see whether Windows is set up for user profiles, follow these steps:

1. From the Start menu, choose Settings, then Control Panel.

2. In Control Panel, double-click the Passwords icon.

3. In the Password Properties dialog box, click the User Profiles tab.

This takes you to the dialog box shown in Figure 3-1.

FIGURE 3-1.

You can turn user profiles on or off by visiting the Passwords icon in Control Panel.

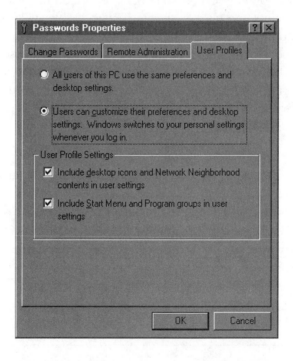

If the second option button (Users Can Customize . . .) in this dialog box is selected, the user-profile feature is turned on and you can customize away without risking the wrath of others who use your machine. If the first option button (All Users . . .) is selected, you can turn user profiles on by simply selecting the second button and clicking OK.

After you select the option button to turn user profiles on, read the text beside the two check boxes at the bottom of the dialog box. These govern the degree to which individual users at a machine can establish personal settings. For maximum "personalizability," select both check boxes.

 Even if you're the only user of your machine, you might still want to set up different profiles for different ways in which you use Windows. Simply use different logon names (with or without different passwords) and tailor each "user's" settings to suit your purposes.

Personalizing the Taskbar

The default location of the taskbar is along the bottom edge of your desktop. If you're accustomed to earlier versions of Windows, which put icons for minimized applications at the bottom of the screen, you may be quite at home with this arrangement. But you're not obliged to accept it. To move the taskbar to another screen edge, simply put your mouse on an unoccupied part of the taskbar, and then drag the taskbar to its new location.

By default, the taskbar shows one row of buttons (or one column, if your taskbar is docked against the left or right side of the desktop). As you open more programs and folders, Windows squeezes more and more buttons into this limited space, truncating the buttons' captions more and more as the button population grows. At some point it may become difficult to know which button is which, and you may long for another row or two. No problem. Simply position the mouse along the inner boundary of the taskbar (the edge closest to the center of the screen). When the mouse pointer becomes a two-headed arrow, drag toward the center of your screen to expand the taskbar.

Other Ways to Make More Room on the Taskbar

You can also increase button space by removing the clock from the taskbar. If you don't need Windows to tell you the time of day, for example, you can probably squeeze at least one more button onto the bar by unloading the clock.

To remove the clock, right-click the taskbar and choose Properties from the object menu. Choose the Taskbar Options tab and then deselect the Show Clock check box.

 You can also make room for more buttons by switching to a higher-resolution display. See "Controlling the Amount of Information That Fits On Screen," page 92.

You can make room for more text on each taskbar button by reducing the point size of the text. You can do this by choosing a smaller size for the Inactive Title Bar item in the Appearance tab of the Display Properties dialog box. To get there, right-click the desktop, choose Properties, and choose Appearance. (For more information, see "Changing the Colors, Fonts, and Sizes of the Windows User Interface," page 98.)

To decode an overcrowded taskbar, rest your mouse pointer for about a half second on each button. If a button's caption is truncated, Windows displays its full text in a pop-up window. If you rest your mouse pointer on the clock, Windows displays the date in a pop-up window.

If the Taskbar Gets in Your Way

By default, your taskbar is a stay-on-top window. That means it remains visible even when you're working in a maximized application. If that's inconvenient for any reason, you can tell it to get out of the way. Simply right-click any unoccupied part of the taskbar, choose Properties from the object menu, and click the Taskbar Options tab. Windows displays the Taskbar Properties dialog box shown in Figure 3-2.

Deselect the Always On Top check box and click OK. Now you'll be able to see the taskbar at all times *except* when a window is maximized.

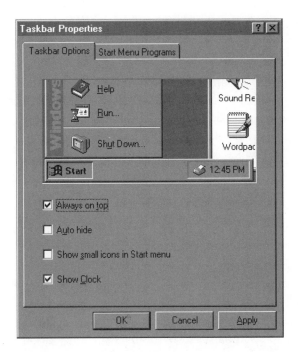

FIGURE 3-2.

The Always On Top and Auto Hide check boxes in this dialog box provide ways to keep the taskbar out of your hair.

 Regardless of how you set options in the Taskbar Properties dialog box, you can make the taskbar visible at any time by pressing Ctrl-Esc.

Another way to make the taskbar less obtrusive is to select the Auto Hide check box shown in Figure 3-2. With this option on, Windows hides the taskbar as soon as you open any window. To get back to the taskbar, you can minimize all windows, press Ctrl-Esc, or move the mouse pointer to the edge of the screen where the taskbar is located.

 For information about *stay-on-top windows*, see "Keeping Windows on Top," page 20.

Controlling the Amount of Information That Fits On Screen

The default Windows screen configuration is standard VGA, which provides 640 pixels in the horizontal dimension by 480 pixels in the vertical dimension, along with a palette of 16 colors. (A *pixel* is the smallest point of light that your screen can display.) This default resolution is also the minimum resolution under which Windows can run.

As Figures 3-3 and 3-4 show, switching from 640×480 to a higher resolution dramatically increases the amount of information you can see on your screen. At 640×480 (Figure 3-3), a Microsoft Excel spreadsheet with standard column widths and row heights can display cells A1 through I16 (assuming the taskbar is also visible). At 800×600 (not shown), your "viewport" onto this spreadsheet extends three columns and seven rows further, to cell L23. Bumping the resolution up to 1024×768 (Figure 3-4) gives you three more columns and ten more rows. Notice, too, that increasing the resolution gives you room to add new tools to customizable toolbars. At 1024×768, the standard Excel toolbars are only about two-thirds full.

Most important, perhaps, at higher resolutions it's much easier to work with two or more open windows at once, because each window can show more information without covering its neighbors.

But higher resolutions have disadvantages as well. At higher resolutions, your computer has to work harder to manage the display, because it has more pixels to process. Therefore, you may notice some degradation in performance. (The load on your computer also varies with the color depth of your display. See "Changing the Color Depth of Your Display," page 97.)

Also, the more pixels you put into a given display area, the smaller the pixels must be. Fortunately, when you change to a higher resolution, Windows gives you the option of increasing the relative size of your fonts. This option can help you maintain readability at high resolutions. Nevertheless, depending on the size of your monitor and the nature of the programs you use, you may find that certain display elements become vanishingly small at very high resolutions.

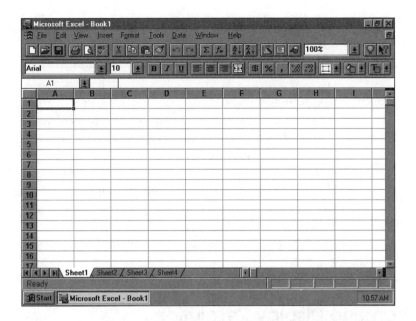

FIGURE 3-3.

At standard VGA resolution, 640×480, toolbars are full and maximized applications can display a limited amount of information.

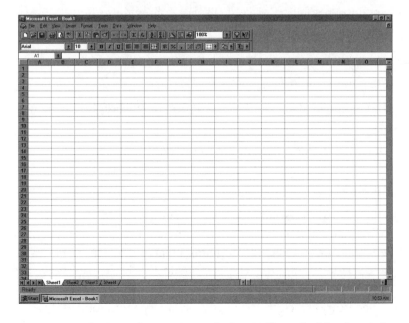

FIGURE 3-4.

Moving from standard VGA to 1024×768 lets you see almost three and a half times as many default-sized spreadsheet cells.

Your choice of screen resolution will probably depend on several factors—the size of your screen, the kind of work you do, the acuity of your eyesight, and the quality of your display adapter and monitor. Experiment to see what works best for you.

> Many Windows-based applications include Zoom commands that let you magnify or reduce the size of on-screen text and graphics. With these commands, you may be able to tailor your environment to give you the best of both worlds. For example, if you like working with graphics programs at 1024×768 but find writing impossible at this resolution, check to see if your word processor has a Zoom command. Zooming the word processor to about 150 percent makes it emulate a lower resolution, allowing you to work with text at one level and graphics at another.

Changing Display Resolution

To change the resolution of your display, follow these steps:

1. Right-click the desktop.

2. Choose Properties from the object menu.

3. Click the Settings tab.

   The Settings tab of the Display Properties dialog box is shown in Figure 3-5.

4. Drag the Desktop Area slider to the right to increase resolution or to the left to decrease it.

5. Click OK.

The available resolutions depend on your display hardware—the type of monitor and video adapter your computer is using. When you installed Windows, the Setup program detected the type of hardware you have and made the appropriate settings available. To see what it determined your monitor type and adapter type to be (and correct these settings if necessary), click the Change Display Type button.

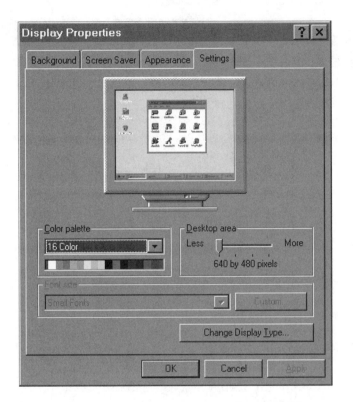

FIGURE 3-5.

In this dialog box, you can change the resolution and color depth of your display.

 You can also get to the Display Properties dialog box by choosing Settings on the Start menu, choosing Control Panel on the Settings menu, and then double-clicking the Display icon in Control Panel.

 For information about *installing new display hardware*, see "Installing a Legacy Peripheral," page 349.

When Display Changes Go Awry

The Settings tab of the Display Properties dialog box lets you change the number of displayed colors (with the Color Palette drop-down list), the resolution (with the Desktop Area slider), and the font size. In most cases, when you make such a change, Windows makes the change immediately and you can go on about your business. (With certain changes, Windows asks you to restart your computer before it can implement the change.)

If you select a combination that your display adapter or monitor is incapable of handling properly, your display might look like a snowstorm video after the change rather than what you intended. If Windows made this dreadful change without restarting the computer, just wait. In a few seconds, Windows reverts to its previous display settings unless you approve the new settings by clicking a button. (And if you can't see the button, you're not likely to approve, right?)

The solution to a scrambled display is a little more complex if the new settings took effect only after you restarted your computer. You'll need to restart your computer again. (Press Ctrl-Esc to open the Start menu, press U to choose the Shut Down command, press Alt-R, and then press Enter.) When your computer restarts—before the Windows logo screen appears—press F5 to boot in "Safe mode." In this mode, you can go back to the Display Properties dialog box and restore your old settings—the ones that worked.

Changing the Font Size

If text at a particular resolution is hard to read, you might want to experiment with the Font Size setting in the Settings dialog box. (See Figure 3-5.) This drop-down list has two entries, Small Fonts (the default) and Large Fonts. In addition, you can click the Custom button, to the right of the Font Size drop-down, and specify smaller, larger, or intermediate sizes.

If you choose Large Fonts, Windows increases the displayed size of all fonts on your system—those that Windows uses for menus, dialog boxes, and messages, as well as all fonts that you use in your documents. However, the point size of those fonts does not change. If you created a document in 10-point Times New Roman, it will still be formatted in the same font at the same point size, and it will look exactly the same on paper with either Small Fonts or Large Fonts in effect. But the letters will be larger on screen.

For text-based work, the effect of switching to Large Fonts is about the same as switching to a lower resolution. A spreadsheet at 800×600 in Large Fonts will look nearly the same as it would at 640×480 in Small Fonts. But at 800×600 in Large Fonts you will still be able to display graphic images that are 800 pixels wide by 600 pixels deep. In 640×480, you would need to scroll to see all parts of an image that size.

 You can also adjust the font size used for particular types of text, such as menus or window title bars, without changing the font size for all text. See "Changing the Size of Particular Display Elements," page 103.

Changing the Color Depth of Your Display

As Figure 3-5 shows, the Settings tab of the Display Properties dialog box also includes a drop-down list labeled Color Palette. This list includes all the color-depth options available for your display hardware in its current resolution. To choose a different color depth, select from the list and click OK.

As with the choice of resolution, the selection of color depth involves tradeoffs. A 256-color setting lets you display certain bitmap images that you can't display correctly in 16 colors. With a 16.8-million-color display (the so-called "true color" setting), you can see images on screen that are as true to life as a high-quality color slide. But the more colors your display can handle, the more information it must process.

If you regularly run multimedia or other graphics applications, you will almost certainly want to use at least a 256-color display. If you work primarily with word processors, spreadsheets, and databases, 16 colors may be quite adequate.

Fortunately, you can switch from one color depth to another at any time as easily as you can change display resolutions. Simply right-click the desktop, choose Properties from the object menu, and click the Settings tab in the Display Properties dialog box. Then select from the Color Palette drop-down list.

Changing the Colors, Fonts, and Sizes of the Windows User Interface

When you first install Windows 95, it uses a combination of colors, fonts, and sizes called Windows Standard. It's a fine arrangement, but you can also choose from a number of alternative schemes. And if you don't like any of the formatting combinations that Windows offers, you can design your own. Once you've found a pleasing arrangement of colors, fonts, and sizes, you can name and save the arrangement. You can design as many custom formatting schemes as you want, adding each to the menu that Windows supplies. As mood or necessity dictates, you can switch from one scheme to another by choosing from a simple drop-down list.

To see what the supplied formatting schemes look like, choose Properties from the object menu that appears when you right-click the desktop, and click the Appearance tab. Windows presents the dialog box shown in Figure 3-6. The upper part of this dialog box is a preview window, showing you a sample of each screen element whose color, font, or size you can modify.

Click the drop-down list labeled Scheme, and then use the Up arrow and Down arrow keys to scroll through the list of named formatting schemes. As you highlight the name of each scheme, Windows displays a sample of that scheme in the upper part of the dialog box. You can apply any formatting scheme to your Windows environment by highlighting its name and clicking OK.

 You can get a larger sample of the current color, font, and size settings without leaving the dialog box. Simply make your selections and then click Apply.

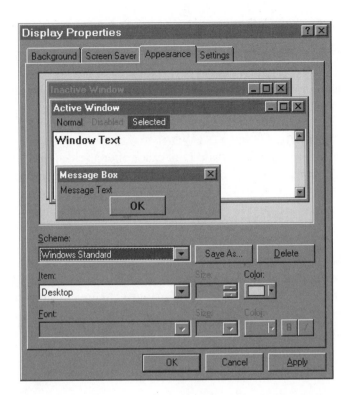

FIGURE 3-6.

As you select from the supplied formatting schemes or create your own, the upper part of this dialog box provides a preview of your selections.

Modifying the Supplied Formatting Schemes

To modify one of the supplied formatting schemes, select its name in the Scheme drop-down list. In the sample window, click the screen element you want to change. Then use the drop-down lists and buttons at the bottom of the dialog box to make your color, font, and size selections.

For example, suppose you want to modify the Windows Standard color scheme, making the active window's title bar yellow, with black text in 12-point bold italic MS Serif. To assign this admittedly garish combination, you would do as follows:

1. Select Windows Standard in the Scheme list.

2. In the preview area of the dialog box, click the title bar labeled Active Window. (Or select Active Title Bar in the Item list.)

3. In the Font list, select MS Serif.

4. In the Size list directly to the right of the Font list, select 12.

5. Click the *I* button to the right of the font-size list.

6. Open the Color drop-down list to the right of the Item list and select yellow.

7. Open the Color drop-down list to the right of the Font list and select black.

If You Don't See the Color You Want

The drop-down lists for Item Color and Font Color offer a selection of 20 colors. If you don't see the one you're looking for, click the button labeled Other. Windows then displays a larger menu, consisting of 48 colors. Should you fail to find exactly the shade you want in this expanded offering, you can define your own custom colors.

Defining Custom Colors

To add your own colors to the ones offered by Windows, open the Color drop-down list for the screen element you want to change. (That is, if you want to customize a text element, open the Font Color drop-down list. If you want to customize a nontext element, open the Item Color drop-down list.) Then click the Other button. Windows opens the custom color selector, shown in Figure 3-7.

FIGURE 3-7.

You can add custom colors to the Windows user interface by designing them in this dialog box.

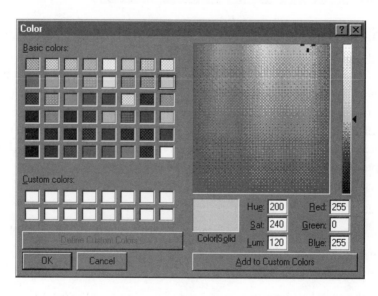

To set a custom color with the mouse, adjust the position of two pointers—the cross hair in the big square grid and the arrowhead to the right of the vertical scale. As you move these pointers, Windows displays a sample of the selected color in the box near the center of the dialog box. If you prefer using your keyboard, you can enter numbers for either or both of the two scales in the boxes at the lower right corner of the dialog box.

The sample box actually comprises two halves because your system might not be capable of displaying every possible color. For colors that your system can't display directly, Windows creates a patterned mixture of two or more colors that it can display directly—a process called *dithering*. The left half of the sample box (the one marked Color) displays the dithered color; the right half (marked Solid) displays a closely related color that your system can display without dithering. (For information about color parameters, see "How Colors Are Defined," on the next page.)

Experimenting with Color

In the Color dialog box, the vertical scale on the right controls luminosity (brightness). As you move its pointer higher, the color becomes lighter. Putting the pointer at the top of the scale creates pure white, no matter where the cross-hair pointer may be in the grid; putting the pointer at the bottom of the luminosity scale produces black.

The square grid controls hue and saturation. Moving the cross hair from side to side changes the hue; moving it higher increases the saturation.

To see the range of "pure" colors available, start by putting the luminosity pointer about halfway up the vertical scale. Then put the cross hair at the upper left corner of the square grid. This combination gives you a fully saturated red of medium luminosity. Now slowly drag the cross hair across the top of the grid; as you do so, you'll move from red through yellow, green, blue, violet, and back to red again. (Alternatively, you can enter a value in the Hue box to step the Hue parameter from 0 to 239.)

To see the effect of luminosity on color, double-click the Solid half of the sample box or press Alt-O. This moves the cross-hair pointer to the nearest position where you see a pure color in both sample boxes. Then move the luminosity pointer up and down the scale (or change the value in the Lum box).

How Colors Are Defined

Colors in Windows are recorded as a combination of three parameters: hue, saturation, and luminosity. Roughly speaking, the basic quality of a color—its redness, blueness, or whatever—is defined by its *hue*. The purity of a color is defined by its *saturation*; a lower saturation value means more gray is mixed in. The brightness or dullness of a color is defined by its *luminosity*.

Hue, saturation, and luminosity are the parameters that Windows uses internally, but your video display hardware lives by a different set of numbers. Images on a color monitor are formed by a combination of dots, or *pixels*. To make each pixel visible, a beam of electrons is fired at three tiny spots of phosphor—one red, one green, and one blue. The result is three points of distinctly colored light so close together that they're perceived as a single light source. The apparent color of that light source is determined by the relative intensities of its red, green, and blue components.

Every combination of hue, saturation, and luminosity, therefore, is translated by Windows into varying levels of energy directed at those spots of red, green, and blue phosphor.

Thus there are two boxes in the lower right corner of the custom color dialog box—one for the parameters used by Windows, the other for the relative red, green, and blue intensities. You can define a custom color by modifying the numbers in either box—or by simply dragging the mouse pointers until you see the color you're looking for.

To see the effect of saturation, put the luminosity pointer back in the middle of the scale and drag the cross hair straight up and down in the square grid (or change the value in the Sat box).

Adding Custom Colors to Your Palette

When you find a color you like, you can add it to your Custom Colors palette by clicking Add To Custom Colors. (If you prefer to add the solid color, double-click the Solid half of the sample box or press Alt-O first.) Windows adds the color to the first available Custom Colors box. If you want to add it to a specific box in your custom palette (for example, if you want to replace a custom color), select that box with the mouse before clicking Add To Custom Colors.

When you've filled out the custom palette to your satisfaction, click OK. Now you can assign your custom colors to the screen elements exactly as you did the basic colors.

Changing the Size of Particular Display Elements

You can make certain elements of the Windows user interface—such as title bars, caption (title bar) buttons, and window borders—larger or smaller by using the Size box to the right of the Item list. If a number appears in this box, the element shown in the Item list can be sized.

Windows automatically adjusts the size of elements that contain text. For example, if you increase the font size for your active title bars, Windows adjusts the size of the title bar itself to accommodate the larger text. But you can override Windows' judgment by manipulating the spinners next to the Size box.

Saving a Formatting Scheme

If you hit upon a pleasing new combination of colors, fonts, and sizes, it's a good idea to name and save it before leaving the dialog box. That way, you'll be able to switch back and forth between your own custom formats and the ones supplied by Windows—or between several of your own making.

To save a scheme, simply click the Save As button and supply a name. Windows adds the name you provide to the list.

If you tire of your new scheme, you can easily remove it. Simply select its name, and then click the Delete button.

Assigning Sounds to Events

If you have a sound card installed in your computer, you can customize the various beeps, squeals, squeeks, and other exclamations emitted by Windows as you go about your workday. Or you can opt for golden silence instead. You can even create named sound schemes, comparable to your named color schemes, for easy reuse and recall.

To change the sounds used by Windows, follow these steps:

1. Choose the Settings command from the Start menu.

2. Choose Control Panel.

3. In the Control Panel folder, double-click the Sounds icon.

   You will see the Sounds property sheet, shown in Figure 3-8.

FIGURE 3-8.

The Sounds property sheet lets you assign sound files to events and create named sound schemes.

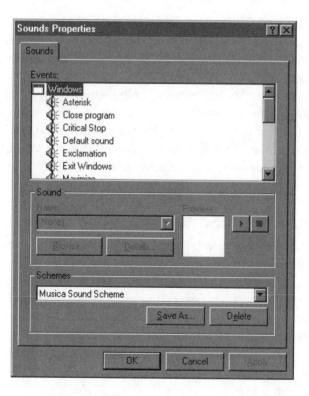

The Events list box in the Sounds property sheet lists all the different system events to which you can attach (or from which you can detach) sounds. The list is structured as a two-level hierarchy. The first top-level item is Windows itself. The events subordinate to the Windows heading have to do with such things as opening and closing programs, maximizing and minimizing windows, starting and ending a Windows session, and so

104

on. If you scroll downward through the Events list, you will find another top-level heading for Windows Explorer and, possibly, additional headings for other applications installed on your computer.

 If a sound icon appears in your taskbar's notification area (next to the clock), you can click that icon to change the volume at which sounds are played. You can also temporarily disable sounds by selecting the Mute check box. For more information about controlling the playback volume, see "Controlling Sound Volume," page 554.

Directly below the Events list box is a drop-down list labeled Name. This lists all the sound files (files with the extension .WAV) that are available in the current folder.

Near the bottom of the dialog box is another drop-down list labeled Schemes. Here you will find all the named combinations of sounds and events that are currently available. You can switch from one sound scheme to another by choosing from this list.

To hear what sound is currently assigned to an event, select the event in the Events list. The name of the assigned sound appears in the Name drop-down, and an icon appears in the Preview box, to the right of the Name drop-down. Click the Play icon (the right-pointing arrow beside the Preview box) to sample the current sound.

To assign a new sound to an event, select the event, and then choose a different item from the Name drop-down list. Click the Play button to be sure you've chosen the sound you want. If the sound you're looking for isn't listed in the Name drop-down, click the Browse button. This takes you to the file-and-folder browser, where you can hunt for a different sound file.

To remove all sound from an event, select the event in the Events list. Then choose (none) in the Name drop-down.

Once you've hit upon a combination of sounds and events that pleases your ear, you can name it and add it to the Schemes drop-down. Simply click the Save As button and enter a name for your new sound scheme.

Using Patterns, Wallpaper, and Screen Savers

Windows provides several additional options for personalizing the appearance of your desktop:

- You can cover your desktop with a repeating pattern—one you create yourself or one that Windows supplies. Doing this is somewhat like throwing a tweed tablecloth over your screen; just the ticket, perhaps, if you get bored with solid colors or grays.

- For a more pictorial backdrop, you can add "wallpaper" to your desktop. The wallpaper can be a small image repeated as many times as necessary to fill the screen (like conventional wallpaper), a single image centered on the desktop, or a single image that covers the entire screen.

- To protect your screen while your computer is idle, and to hide what you were working on while you're away from your desk, you can install a screen saver.

Adding Patterns

To apply a background pattern to your desktop, right-click the desktop and choose Properties from the object menu. Then click the Background tab to get to the dialog box shown in Figure 3-9. Select one of the patterns in the Pattern list, and click OK.

Editing a Background Pattern

If you want to modify an existing pattern or create a new one, select a pattern name and then click Edit Pattern. When the Pattern Editor dialog box appears, press the Up arrow or Down arrow key to step through the list and see an enlarged sample of each pattern. Figure 3-10, for example, shows what the Thatches pattern looks like.

Modifying an Existing Background Pattern The big square on the left side of the Pattern Editor dialog box represents the "cell" from which the selected background pattern is made. The cell is an eight-by-eight grid of dots; each dot is either dark or light. You can edit the background pattern

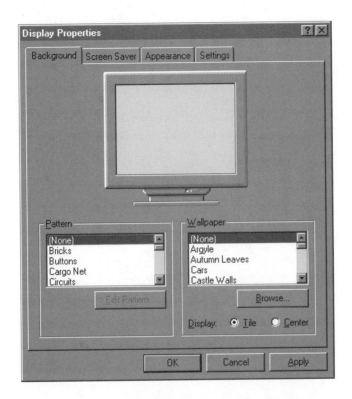

FIGURE 3-9.
The Background tab of the Display Properties dialog box lets you add a pattern or picture ("wallpaper") to your desktop.

FIGURE 3-10.
The Pattern Editor lets you modify or create background patterns for your desktop.

by changing one or more dots from light to dark or dark to light. To do that, click the mouse on the dots you want to change. (There is no keyboard equivalent for this procedure.)

As you make changes in the dot pattern in the cell, you can see the effect of those changes in the Sample box in the center. When you're satisfied with your editing, click Change to save the revised pattern. Then click OK to select it.

Creating a New Background Pattern   The easiest way to create a background pattern is to edit an existing one, as explained above, and give it a new name by replacing the text in the Name text box in the Pattern Editor dialog box. Windows grays out the Change button and activates the Add button. Click Add, and your new pattern joins the list of existing patterns. You can then apply it to your desktop by clicking Done in the Pattern Editor dialog box and then clicking OK in the Display Properties dialog box.

Adding Wallpaper

To drape your desktop with something livelier than a simple dot pattern, try the wallpaper option. Follow these steps to display a picture as a backdrop to everything you do in Windows:

1.   Right-click the desktop.

2.   Choose Properties from the object menu.

3.   Click the Background tab. This takes you to the dialog box shown in Figure 3-9.

4.   Select an image file from the Wallpaper list. (If you don't find the file you're looking for, click the Browse button.)

 When you click the Browse button in the Background dialog box, Windows displays filenames with the extension .BMP or .DIB. You can use files with either extension as wallpaper. You can also use graphics files with the extension .RLE.

Some wallpaper files produce a single image that covers your entire desktop. Others produce smaller images that can either be displayed once, in the center of the desktop, or repeated as many times as necessary to fill the screen. If you want the image to appear only once, select the Center option button; otherwise, select Tile.

You can also use commands on Paint's File menu to apply wallpaper to your desktop. For more information about Paint, see "Making Wallpaper," page 513.

Using a Screen Saver

Cathode-ray-tube (CRT) displays used by desktop computers create images by firing electron beams at phosphor-coated screens. If the same picture or text remains on a screen for a long period of time, the phosphor coating can be damaged, leaving a faint but permanent image on the screen. Screen savers reduce this hazard by monitoring screen activity. Whenever your screen remains unchanged for a specific length of time, the screen saver displays its own constantly varying image. As soon as you press a key or (with most savers) move the mouse, the screen saver restores the original image.

That's the ostensible purpose of a screen saver, at any rate. In truth, with current display technology, the probability that you'll damage your screen with a burned-in image is remote. But screen savers have other virtues, as well. They're fun to watch, and they're one way to prevent others in your office from prying while you're away from your machine. Many screen savers have "save now" and password options. The save-now option lets you display the saver pattern on demand, either by pressing a certain keyboard combination or by moving the mouse to a particular corner of the screen. The password option ensures that only you are able to restore the original image. If your screen saver has these features, you can display the saver image any time you walk away from your computer and be reasonably confident that no one will invade your privacy.

To install one of the Windows-supplied screen savers, right-click the desktop and choose Properties from the object menu. Then click the Screen Saver tab to get to the dialog box shown in Figure 3-11 on the next page.

To apply a screen saver, select from the Show drop-down list. Then use the Wait spinners to specify how long a period of inactivity Windows should allow before displaying the screen saver.

FIGURE 3-11.

The Screen Saver
tab of the Display
Properties dialog
box offers a choice
of customizable
screen savers.

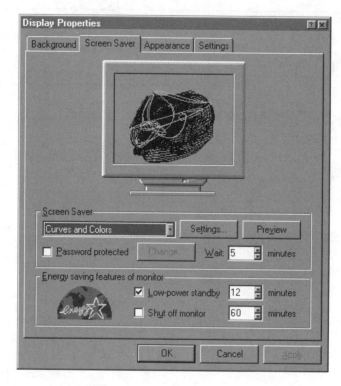

All the Windows-supplied screen savers (except for Blank Screen) include options that you can set. These options let you adjust colors, speed, and other display preferences. Figure 3-12 shows the settings dialog box for the Curves And Colors screen saver.

FIGURE 3-12.

After choosing a
screen saver, you
can click the
Settings button to
specify display
options.

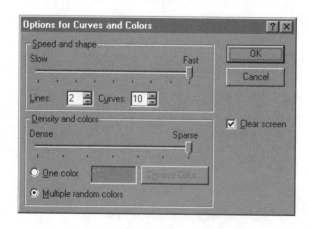

Taking Advantage of Your Monitor's Energy-Saving Features

If your monitor complies with the Energy Star standard, Windows can automatically power it down following a specified period of inactivity. To take advantage of this capability, go to the Screen Saver tab of the Display Properties dialog box. (See Figure 3-11.) Then select either or both of the two check boxes at the bottom of the dialog. Adjust the spinners to the desired time settings, and then click OK.

If you check Low Power Standby, your monitor switches to a low-power setting after the specified interval has elapsed. Simply press a key or move the mouse to restore full power. If you check Shut Off Monitor, your monitor powers itself down after the interval has elapsed.

 If the Low Power and Shut Off Monitor check boxes are gray, Windows doesn't know that you have an Energy Star–compliant monitor. To correct this situation, go to the Settings tab of the Display Properties dialog box. In the Settings dialog box (see Figure 3-5 on page 95), click the Change Display Type button. Then select the Monitor Is Energy Star Compliant check box.

Setting Preferences for Your Mouse

Windows lets you tailor the behavior of your mouse or other pointing device to suit your personal tastes. The options available depend on what kind of device you're using, but for most pointing devices you can adjust the pointer size, as well as the pointer-movement and double-click speeds, and you can swap the functionality of the left and right mouse buttons. You might find it handy to swap mouse button functions if you're left-handed, so you can put the mouse on the left side of your keyboard and still use your index finger for most mouse commands.

To make mouse adjustments, choose Settings on the Start menu, and then choose Control Panel. In Control Panel, double-click the Mouse icon. (Or select the Mouse icon, pull down the File menu, and choose Open.) If you're using a Microsoft Mouse, you'll see a dialog box similar to the one shown in Figure 3-13.

FIGURE 3-13.

The Mouse Properties dialog box lets you swap mouse-button functionality, adjust double-click speed, and set other mouse preferences.

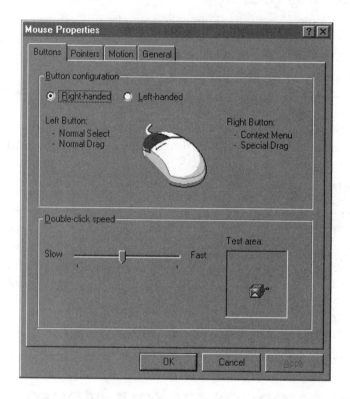

In the top part of this dialog box, you can swap mouse-button functionality. In the lower part, you can adjust the double-click speed. (The double-click speed specifies the time interval within which two mouse clicks are interpreted as a double-click.)

Other sections of your Mouse Properties dialog box may allow you to adjust the pointer size and pointer speed. The pointer speed refers to the relationship between movement of the mouse on your desk and movement of the pointer on screen. If you often find your mouse pointer overshooting its target as you select commands or objects in Windows, you may find it helpful to decrease the pointer speed. On the other hand, if you find yourself "rowing"—picking up the mouse, bringing it back through the air, and then sliding it over the mouse pad again merely to get the pointer from one side of the screen to the other—try increasing the pointer speed.

Your Mouse Properties dialog box may also include a Pointer Trail option. If selected, this option causes your mouse to leave a temporary trail of pointer images (mouse droppings?) as it moves across the screen. This trail can help you keep track of the pointer's location on some displays.

If you run Windows on a portable computer and sometimes have trouble finding the mouse pointer, try increasing the pointer size and turning on a pointer trail.

For information about *using the keyboard to perform mouse functions*, see "Using the Keyboard Instead of the Mouse," page 435.

Adjusting the Keyboard Repeat and Cursor Blink Rates

Unless you have disabled the "typematic" behavior of your keyboard to take advantage of Windows 95's accessibility features, Windows repeats a character after you have held its key down for a certain length of time. You can adjust both the repeat speed and the interval that Windows waits before beginning to repeat. To do this, choose Settings from the Start menu and Control Panel from the Settings submenu. In Control Panel, double-click the Keyboard icon to get to the dialog box shown in Figure 3-14 on the next page.

To shorten the delay before repeating begins, drag the Repeat Delay slider to the right. To increase the repeat speed, drag the Repeat Rate slider to the right. Putting both these sliders as far as they'll go to the right makes your keyboard as responsive as Windows will allow. If you find yourself occasionally getting unwanted repeated characters, move the Repeat Delay slider, or both sliders, to the left. You can use the text box to test your settings before clicking OK.

FIGURE 3-14.

The Keyboard Properties dialog box lets you adjust your keyboard's repeat speed, the speed at which the cursor blinks, and a variety of other preferences.

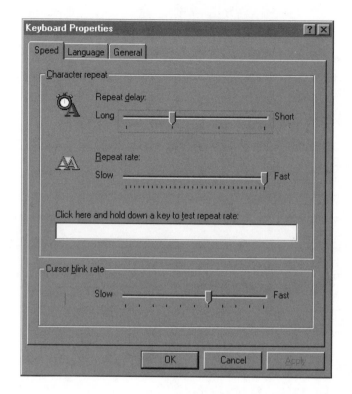

In the lower part of the dialog box shown in Figure 3-14, you'll find another slider, for adjusting the rate at which the cursor blinks. If you're not happy with the default blink rate, you might want to experiment with moving this slider. The blinking line to the left of the slider shows your new cursor blink rate.

The Keyboard Properties dialog box also allows you to install keyboard support for a variety of languages.

See Also: For more information about *international language support,* see "Installing Language Support and Using Keyboard Layouts," page 296.

For more information about *controlling or disabling the keyboard repeat rate,* see "Controlling the Keyboard Repeat Rate with FilterKeys," page 429.

4

Working with Folders

A hard disk is a mansion with many wings, branches, halls, ballrooms, libraries, salons, alcoves, closets, and crannies. A typical computer system today comprises at least one such estate and often two or more. With the help of networking technology, moreover, many users are connected to virtual cities of palatial storage spaces.

Organizing one's local disks effectively and keeping track of where needed resources lie on the network used to be a daunting task, requiring mastery of arcane path syntax and networking commands. It's far simpler in Windows 95, thanks to Windows' unified "namespace" and comfortable browsing methods.

Windows 95 provides two distinct methods of navigating through local and remote resources. You can browse with folder windows, or you can use Windows Explorer. The choice is yours. In this chapter, we'll survey the folder method.

Windows 95 also includes a powerful search facility to help you find folders and files anywhere on your own system or your network. Getting to a particular item "out there somewhere" is often quicker via the Find command than by any other method.

 See Also: For information about *Windows Explorer*, see Chapter 5, "Managing Folders and Files with Windows Explorer," page 163.

For information about *the Find command*, see Chapter 7, "Using the Find Command," page 193.

The Windows 95 Namespace

The term *namespace* refers to the universe of storage entities accessible from your computer system. Figure 4-1 on the next page shows a schematic diagram of a typical workstation's namespace, and the following paragraph provides a quick review of the namespace's organization.

Your desktop is where all the action in Windows originates, so the top of the namespace hierarchy is called *Desktop*. At the next organizational level are three folders, called *My Computer, Network Neighborhood,* and *Recycle Bin*. My Computer is the parent folder for all disks attached to

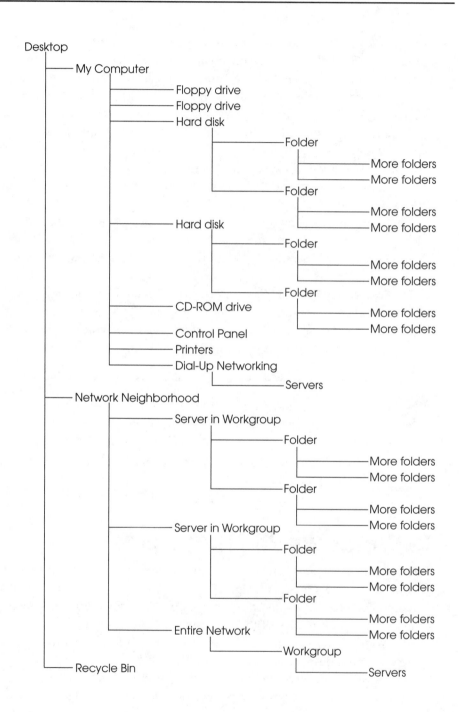

your own computer, including hard disks, floppy drives, and CD-ROM drives. Network Neighborhood is a folder comprising all network servers in your immediate workgroup. Through Network Neighborhood, you can also get to network servers beyond the immediate workgroup. Recycle Bin is where deleted folders, files, and shortcuts go—until you dump the trash, at which point such items are gone for good.

In this chapter, we'll concentrate on local folder operations, reserving network-specific issues for Chapter 6, "Using and Sharing Files on the Network." But bear in mind that folder navigation and housekeeping are essentially the same throughout the Windows namespace. Moving from folder to folder in a network server, for example, is just like moving between folders on your own hard disk.

See Also: For information about *Network Neighborhood*, see Chapter 6, "Using and Sharing Files on the Network," page 179.

For information about *Recycle Bin*, see "Restoring Deleted Folders, Files, and Shortcuts," page 150.

Moving from Folder to Folder

A folder is a bin for storing files and other folders. For example, suppose that on drive C of your computer you have a folder named Office95, into which you have installed the various applications that make up the Microsoft Office application suite. Inside this folder, you would likely have other folders with names such as Excel, Word, PowerPoint, and perhaps Access. Within each of these subfolders, you'd have additional folders. In the Excel folder, for example, you might have folders named Examples, Library, and XLStart. Inside each member of this group, you might have a collection of Excel workbook files.

Because your copy of Microsoft Office is installed on drive C, all of these folders would be contained within the drive C folder. And because C is a local disk, the drive C folder would be contained within My Computer, the master folder of local resources.

To move from one point to another within this structure, you can simply double-click My Computer and then double-click each subfolder in turn. Depending on how you've set Windows' browsing options, your screen might then display a proliferation of folder windows, as shown in Figure 4-2.

FIGURE 4-2.

You can move from folder to folder by double-clicking icons or by selecting icons and choosing the File Open command.

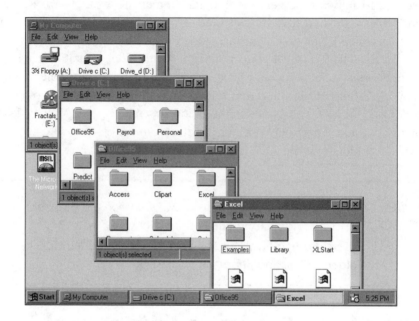

The Anatomy of a Folder Window

A folder window is simply a window that displays the contents of a folder. Like a miniature application, it includes a title bar, buttons for sizing and closing the window, a Control-menu icon, a menu bar, an optional toolbar, and an optional status bar. The title bar of any folder window, by default, contains exactly the same text that appears beneath the folder's icon.

Folder windows behave exactly like other kinds of program windows. You can make them bigger or smaller by dragging the borders, you can maximize and minimize them using the buttons at the right side of the title bar, and so on. All folder windows share a common set of menu commands.

To run a program, open a document, or open a subfolder, simply double-click the item you're interested in. Alternatively, select the item and choose the File menu's Open command. You can select the item with the mouse or by using cursor keys. If you prefer to use the keyboard, you can sometimes select an item quickly by pressing its first few letters. (For details, see "Selecting Folders and Files in a Folder Window," page 136.)

 If you find yourself regularly navigating to a particular folder, make a shortcut for that folder and put it on the desktop. For more information about desktop shortcuts, see "Using Shortcuts to Run Programs and Open Documents," page 71.

Many Windows or One?

By default, when you double-click a folder icon in a folder window, the newly opened folder appears in a separate window, and the window for the *parent* folder (the one containing the newly opened folder) remains open. This separate-window browsing mode is shown in Figure 4-2.

The advantage of the separate-window mode is that it lets you see the parent folder and the new folder at the same time. To return to the parent folder, you can simply click back in that folder window or press the Backspace key. (Or close the new window; in most cases, when you do that, the parent window will once again have the focus.) You can also reselect the parent window by pressing Alt-Tab.

The disadvantage of this mode is that it tends to clutter up your screen when you travel through several layers of subfolders. If the proliferation of windows becomes bothersome, you can switch to the single-window browsing mode, in which a newly opened folder window *replaces* its parent window.

To switch browsing modes, open any folder window's View menu and choose Options. You will see the dialog box shown in Figure 4-3. Select the option button for the browsing mode you want. You can switch between browsing modes at any time. Your selection applies to all folder windows you open thereafter.

 If you hold down the Shift key while clicking a folder window's Close icon (or while choosing its File Close command), Windows closes the current folder plus all of its "ancestor windows" (parent, grandparent, and so on). Thus, for example, you could close all four windows shown in Figure 4-2 by holding down Shift and clicking the Excel folder's Close icon.

FIGURE 4-3.

When you open a subfolder in the default browsing mode, the parent folder window remains visible. In the single-window mode, the subfolder window replaces the parent folder window.

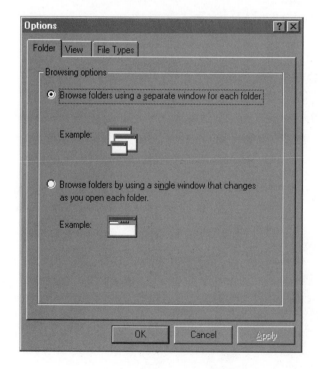

Reselecting the Parent Folder in Single-Window Mode

As mentioned earlier, in the separate-window browsing mode, you can re-select a parent folder window by clicking that window. In the single-window mode, you can't do that because the subfolder replaces the parent window. Instead, you simply press Backspace to redisplay the parent folder window. Or, you can use the Up One Level button on the toolbar, as described below.

 To see the full pathname of the current folder window, choose the View menu's Options command, select the View tab, and then select the check box labeled "Display the full MS-DOS path in the title bar." This option may be particularly handy if you have many levels of subfolders and prefer the single-window approach to browsing.

Displaying and Using the Toolbar

To display the toolbar, if it's not currently visible, open the folder window's View menu and choose Toolbar. The toolbar is shown in Figure 4-4. Because the Toolbar setting is window-specific, you will need to choose this command in each folder window in which you want the toolbar displayed.

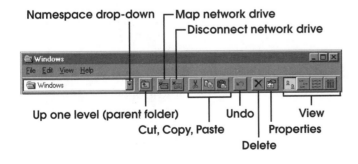

FIGURE 4-4.

The folder window toolbar includes a handy "up one level" tool to help you retrace your steps.

The toolbar is the same in all folder windows that display disk directories. Table 4-1 on the next page provides a brief description of what each tool does.

Table 4-1. Folder Window Toolbar

Toolbar Icon	Description
Windows	Allows you to move directly to a folder in a different drive or server
	Moves to the parent of the current folder
	Allows you to make a network folder behave as though it were a drive on your own computer—or breaks that connection (For details, see "Mapping a Network Folder to a Drive Letter," page 187.)
	Shortcuts for operations that move or copy files or folders (For details, see "Moving or Copying Objects with Menu Commands," page 144.)
	Reverses the last action you took, if possible (For details, see "Reversing Moves, Copies, and Name Changes with the Undo Command," page 148.)
	Deletes the selected item(s) (For details, see "Deleting Folders, Files, and Shortcuts," page 149.)
	Displays the property sheet for the selected item(s) (For details, see "Inspecting Folder and File Properties," page 137.)
	Shortcuts for View-menu commands that provide alternative ways to display folder information (For details, see "Folder Viewing Options," page 128.)

Using the Status Bar to Learn About Folder Contents

At times it's helpful to have a summary of a folder's contents. You can get that by opening the View menu and choosing Status Bar. As Figure 4-5 shows, the status bar can tell you how many items a folder contains, how many of those items are hidden, and how much disk space the items use. (Hidden items are items contained in the folder but not displayed by the folder window. Typically such items are files that your system needs in order to run, as opposed to documents or programs. The View menu's Options command, discussed later in this chapter, lets you decide whether or not to display such items in your folder windows.)

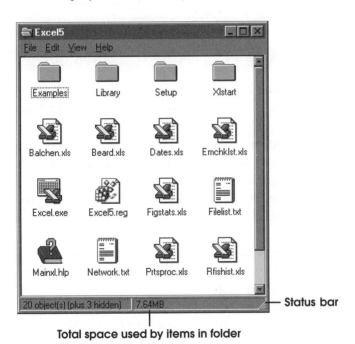

Total space used by items in folder

FIGURE 4-5.

The status bar can tell you how many items a folder contains and how much disk space those items use.

In Figure 4-5, the status bar reports the total size of the items contained in a folder. You can also use the status bar to find out how much space is used by a particular item or group of items:

■ To have the status bar report the space used by a particular item, simply select that item.

- To have the status bar report the space used by a group of items, hold down the Ctrl key and click each member of the group.

- To have the status bar report the size used by all items in the folder, including the hidden items, click on any of the folder window's "white space"—that is, anywhere but on an item. (The total includes all the items in the folder, but does not include the contents of any of its subfolders.)

 You can also learn the size of a particular item by right-clicking the item and choosing Properties from the object menu.

Navigating in the File Open and File Save Dialogs

Many Windows-based applications use a common set of dialog boxes for their File Open, File Save, File Save As, and Print commands. These dialog boxes are supplied by Windows and are known as the "common dialogs." Windows-based programs are not obliged to use them, but the fact that a great many programs do helps make it easier for you to master new programs. Thanks to the common dialogs, the process of saving a new file is likely to be very much the same in nearly every program you use.

Also, as the following illustration shows, the common dialogs that have to do with file management look a lot like ordinary folder windows. A drop-down list at the top of the dialog box shows the name of the current folder—the one that Windows is now prepared to save your file to or open a file from—and lets you navigate to distant folders on the same or other disks. The big window in the center of the dialog box, meanwhile, shows you all the subfolders and files contained in the current folder. You can move to a subfolder here exactly as you would in an ordinary folder window—by simply double-clicking the folder's name.

Navigating in the File Open and File Save Dialogs

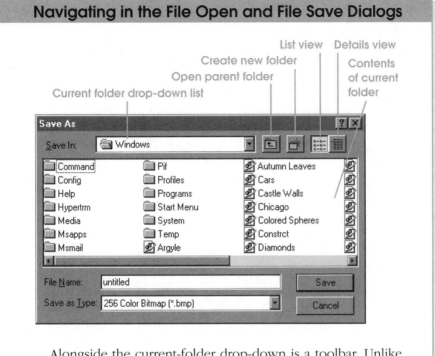

Alongside the current-folder drop-down is a toolbar. Unlike the folder window toolbar, this one is not optional. Using tools here, you can switch the large window between list and details views, or you can back up to the parent folder.

The toolbar also includes a handy tool not found on the folder window toolbar. The Create New Folder tool lets you do just that—create a new folder within the current folder. You'll find this tool invaluable when you want to save a file in a folder that you haven't created yet.

For more information about *files and properties*, see "Inspecting Folder and File Properties," page 137.

Folder Viewing Options

Windows gives you several ways to view the contents of your folders. You can choose from four display styles, sort folder entries in a number of ways, and decide whether to keep your folder entries in tidy columns or not. Each of these options can be applied separately to any of your folders.

Big Icons or Small?

By default, Windows displays a folder's contents as a set of "large icons." Three other display styles are available, and you may choose the style you prefer with commands on the View menu or tools on the toolbar. Those alternatives to large-icon display are small icons, list, and details. (See Figure 4-6.)

The small-icon view has the virtue of letting you see more file and subfolder names without enlarging the window. The list view is identical to the small-icon view except that the folder's contents are arranged vertically instead of horizontally. In the details view, the folder's contents are also arranged vertically, but the folder includes information about each entry's size, type, and the date of the most recent edit.

Because your choice of display style applies only to the current folder, you can vary your choice depending on the contents of the folder. You might, for example, prefer the large-icon view for most folders but adopt small-icon or list view for folders containing an unusually large number of files.

 You can also change the font that's used for text that accompanies each icon in a folder window. Right-click the desktop and choose Properties from the object menu. In the Display Properties dialog box that appears, click the Appearance tab. Select Icon in the Item drop-down list, and then select a font and size.

 **Large icons**

FIGURE 4-6.

The View menu lets you choose between four display options.

 **Small icons**

 **List**

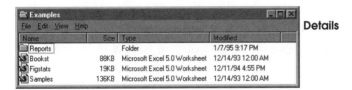 **Details**

 To change the width of columns in details view, drag the column boundaries in the headings row. For example, to make the Size column wider, drag the vertical line between the Size and Type headings.

To adjust a column's width automatically, so that it's just wide enough for the column's widest entry, double-click the right boundary of the column. For example, to adjust the Name column automatically, double-click the line between the Name and Size headings.

The details view tells you when a file was last edited. To find out when it was created and when it was last accessed, right-click the filename or icon and choose Properties from the object menu. For more information about properties, see "Inspecting Folder and File Properties," page 137.

Sorting Options

In details view, you can sort the contents of a folder by clicking a column heading. For example, to arrange a folder's contents by file size (smallest to largest), click the Size heading. Click the column heading again to reverse the sort order (largest to smallest).

In the other views, you can sort the contents by choosing Arrange Icons from the View menu, and then selecting a sort key (name, file type, file size, or date) from the submenu. You can also choose the Arrange Icons command from the object menu that appears when you right-click in any unoccupied area of the folder window.

Neatly Arranged or Casual?

In large-icon and small-icon views, you can have Windows automatically preserve an orderly arrangement of folder contents. To do this, open the View menu and choose Arrange Icons. If the Auto Arrange command, at the bottom of the Arrange Icons submenu, is not checked, select it. With Auto Arrange on, any icon you add to a folder (by creating a new file, for example) automatically falls in line with the rest of the folder's contents. If you delete an icon, the remaining icons automatically close ranks. If you drag an icon out of position, Windows snaps it back into place.

If you don't like this regimentation, you can turn it off—by opening the View menu, choosing Arrange Icons, and then deselecting the Auto Arrange command. With Auto Arrange off, you can drag your icons anywhere you please. (See Figure 4-7.)

The Auto Arrange option applies only to the current folder, so you can use it for some of your folders and not for the rest.

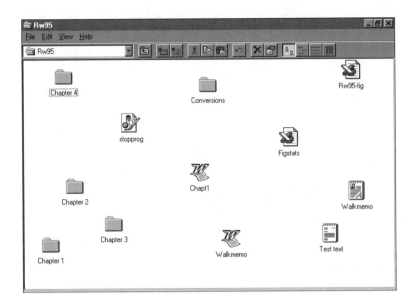

FIGURE 4-7.

Turning Auto
Arrange off gives
you the freedom to
drag icons out of
their orderly rows
and columns.

Turning Auto Arrange off has the advantage of letting you create ad hoc groupings. For example, you can put all the items that you're currently working with together at the top of the folder. But with this freedom comes some hazard: if you're too casual with your ad hoc arrangements, you can lose track of items. For example, if you drag an icon so far from its comrades that you have to scroll a long distance to see it, you might forget you have it.

 When Auto Arrange is off, you can choose any of the sorting commands (By Name, By Type, By Size, or By Date) to return your icons to orderly rows and columns.

 To turn Auto Arrange on or off for your desktop icons, right-click anywhere on the desktop and choose Arrange Icons.

If your folder icons are lined up neatly in rows and columns, but they don't use the full width of the window, check to see if Auto Arrange is on. With Auto Arrange off, icon positions are not adjusted when a window's size is changed.

Deciding What to Include in a Folder Window

Windows gives you some choices regarding what to include in a folder window. By default, you see all files and folders except the following:

- Hidden files
- Dynamic-link libraries (.DLL files)
- System files (.SYS files)
- Device drivers (.VXD, .386, or .DRV files)

All these files are crucial to the operation of applications and of Windows itself. They're not normally included in folder windows because accidental deletion or relocation of one of them can have serious adverse consequences—possibly requiring the reinstallation of an application or of Windows. Therefore, unless you need to work with these types of files, it's a good idea to leave them out of sight.

To make these files (and all others) visible in your folder windows, choose the View menu's Options command, and then click the View tab. You will see the dialog box shown in Figure 4-8. Select the Show All Files option button.

Note that this option setting applies to all folders, not just to the folder in which you select it.

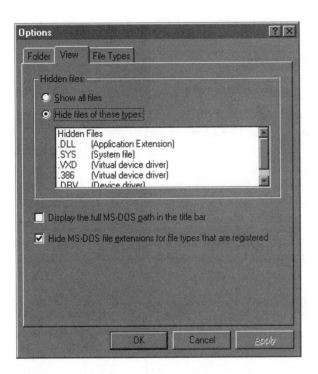

FIGURE 4-8.
The View tab of the Options dialog box gives you choices about what should be included in folder windows.

 File types not shown in folder windows are also invisible to the Find command. If you want to be able to search for particular types of files with the Find command, be sure to make those file types visible in your folders.

 For more information about *hidden files,* see "Setting Attributes for Folders, Files, and Shortcuts," page 154.

Displaying Filename Extensions

A *filename extension* is any group of characters that appears after the final period in a filename. As you may know, earlier versions of Windows, as well as the versions of MS-DOS on which they were built, allowed filenames to have extensions of up to three characters. Such extensions provided a means of categorizing files. All batch files, for example, had the extension .BAT; all graphics files in the Windows bitmap format had the extension .BMP, and so on.

Windows 95 has done away with the three-character extension limit—as well as the onerous eight-character limit that applied to the main part of a file's name. Windows 95 filenames can consist of up to 255 characters, including as many periods as you like and as many characters as needed after the final period.

These emancipations notwithstanding, Windows 95 and Windows-based applications still use filename extensions to categorize files. Many applications, for example, automatically append an extension to any filename you supply, even though you may not see the extensions in the entries that appear in your folder windows.

Windows 95 Filename Restrictions

Names of folders and files used by programs written for Windows 95 can include as many as 255 characters. Thus, there's no need to be cryptic or overly compact in your choice of a filename. Instead of naming that departmental budget worksheet EBUD96-1, you can call it Editorial Budget for 1996—First Draft.

Programs designed for earlier versions of Windows and not yet updated for Windows 95 still adhere to the old limit of eight characters plus an optional three-character extension. If a program you're using rejects long filenames, check with the vendor to see if an updated version is available.

In any filename, long or short, certain characters are prohibited. These characters are:

* | \ < > ? / " :

Spaces and the following additional characters are prohibited in MS-DOS (short) filenames:

+ , . ; = [ ]

These characters are reserved for use by the operating system.

Windows 95 uses the *registry*—its central depository of information about applications, their documents, and your system—to determine what kind of icon to display next to names in folder windows. Excel documents get Excel-style icons, text files get icons that look like notepads, and so on.

Document files for which no registry entry exists get a "miscellaneous" icon—something that looks like a Windows logo on a page with a dog-ear in its upper right corner. By default, only files of such unregistered types have their extensions displayed in folder windows.

If you'd like to see extensions for all filenames, choose the View menu's Options command and click the View tab. In the dialog box that appears (see Figure 4-8 on page 133), deselect the check box labeled "Hide MS-DOS file extensions for file types that are registered." You might want to make this change if you're having difficulty determining which icon represents which kind of file. You can, of course, switch back to the default display mode at any time.

By default, filename extensions are displayed in folder and Windows Explorer windows only for unregistered file types. However, you can display all extensions or extensions for particular registered file types. To display all extensions, use the View tab in the folder window's Options dialog box, as described above. To display extensions for particular registered file types, use the File Types tab of that same dialog box. (For more information about the File Types tab, see "Specifying Display of Extensions," page 158.)

Refreshing the Contents of a Folder Window

The Refresh command, on the folder window's View menu, ensures that a folder window's display reflects any changes to the folder's contents that may have taken place since you opened the window. For example, if you're looking at a folder on a network server, other users may be adding, deleting, or renaming files on that folder while your window is open. To

> ### Sharing Windows 95 Files with Systems That Don't Allow Long Filenames
>
> If you need to share documents with users of earlier versions of Windows or MS-DOS, you might be concerned that those users will not be able to read files with long names. Fortunately, there is no need to worry. When you save a file with a long filename, Windows 95 also records an alternative short name. You can find out what the short version of any filename is by inspecting the file's properties. (See "Inspecting Folder and File Properties," page 137.) On the property sheet, the short name is identified as the "MS-DOS Name." Thus, you don't need to constrain your filenames for the sake of other users.

be sure that what you see matches what's out there, choose the View menu's Refresh command—or type its keyboard shortcut, F5.

Selecting Folders and Files in a Folder Window

The first step in many operations in Windows—opening, copying, or moving a document, for example—is to *select* the folder or file you want to use. When a folder or file is selected, its icon and title appear in a color that's different from unselected items. You can select a folder or file in a folder window in any of the following ways:

- Click its icon or title. (Note that in details view, you must click only the icon or title to select an object—not the other parts of the description line.)

- Type the first few letters of the title.

- Use the arrow keys to move the highlight.

You'll often want to select more than one item at a time. Here are some ways to select a group of objects:

- "Lasso" them. Hold down the mouse button while you drag a rectangle around all members of the group.

- Hold down the Ctrl key while you click each item in the group.

- If the items are next to one another in the window, click the first. Then hold down the Shift key while you click the last.

- Choose Select All from the Edit menu—or use its keyboard shortcut, Ctrl-A—to select all the items in the window.

 Two commands on the folder window's Edit menu can be useful when you need to select groups. If you need to select everything in a folder, choose Select All (or press Ctrl-A). If you want to select nearly all items, select those that you do *not* want to select. Then choose the Invert Selection command. This action deselects what you've already selected and selects everything else.

Inspecting Folder and File Properties

Windows 95 provides you with a simple way to learn a folder or file's size, creation date, and other vital statistics. Simply right-click a folder or file and choose Properties from the object menu. (If the folder window's toolbar is visible, you can click the Properties tool to get to the property sheet directly.) Figure 4-9 on the next page and Figure 4-10 on page 139 illustrate the property sheet for a folder and a file.

 To read the property sheet for an open folder, right-click anywhere within the folder's unoccupied space, or right-click the Control-menu icon at the left edge of the title bar. Then choose the Properties command.

FIGURE 4-9.

This folder's
property sheet
shows that the folder
includes 45 files and
3 subfolders,
occupying a total of
12.3 MB
(megabytes).

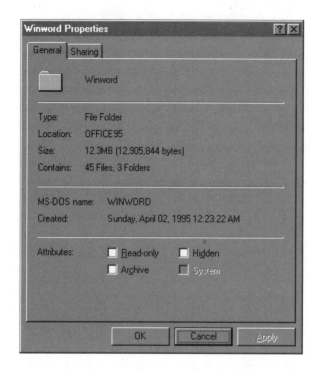

Notice that the folder property sheet shows how many subfolders the folder contains as well as the number of files. The number of folders and files, along with their cumulative size, includes the contents of the folder and all its subfolders. (As mentioned earlier, the statistics in a folder window's status bar do not take into account the contents of subfolders.)

If your computer is part of a network and your system has been set up to allow file sharing, the folder property sheet includes a Sharing tab. By clicking here, you can make the folder available to others on your network (or stop making it available).

The file property sheet (see Figure 4-10) includes three dates—the date the file was created, the date it was most recently changed, and the date that it was most recently opened. If the file is a document created by an OLE application, it may include additional information. Property sheets for Excel documents, for example, include a Summary tab and a Statistics tab (see Figure 4-10), which provide a revision number, keywords, comments, and other details. If the file is an MS-DOS–based application, the property sheet includes tabs that let you set operating parameters for the program.

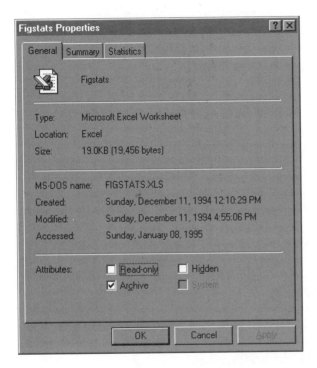

FIGURE 4-10.

Along with other details, the property sheet for this 19.0-KB (kilobyte) document file shows when the file was created, when it was last modified, and when it was last accessed. The Summary and Statistics tabs provide more details about the content of the file.

The Accessed date on a file's property sheet can help you determine whether a file might be a good candidate for deletion. If it hasn't been accessed any time during the last two years, perhaps you no longer need it.

You can use the Find utility to locate all files that have not been modified within some specified period of time. Then by inspecting the properties of each such file, you can weed out the files that not only haven't been modified but also haven't even been looked at recently. You can inspect the properties of a file directly in the Find window by right-clicking the filename or icon. For more information about the Find command, see "Finding Files and Folders," page 195.

See Also: For information about *sharing folders*, see Chapter 6, "Using and Sharing Files on the Network," page 179.

For information about *setting properties for MS-DOS–based applications,* see Chapter 12, "Running MS-DOS–Based Programs," page 301.

Inspecting Properties for Groups of Objects

By selecting two or more folders or files, and then right-clicking, you can inspect properties for groups of objects. The resulting property sheet tells you the total size of the selected objects, whether they're all of the same type, and whether they're all located in the same folder. Figure 4-11 shows a property sheet for a group of files.

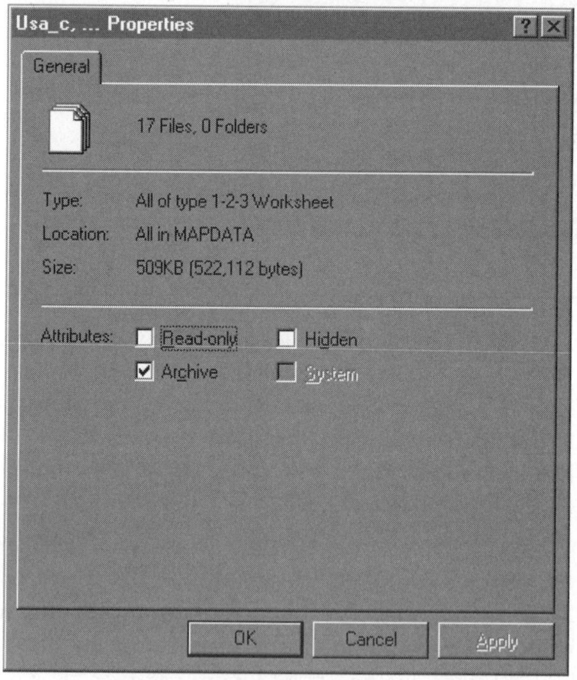

FIGURE 4-11.

This property sheet indicates that the 17 selected files are all 1-2-3 worksheets stored in the Mapdata folder, and that together they occupy 509 KB.

Usa_c, ... Properties	? ☒

General

📄 17 Files, 0 Folders

Type: All of type 1-2-3 Worksheet
Location: All in MAPDATA
Size: 509KB (522,112 bytes)

Attributes: ☐ Read-only   ☐ Hidden
              ☑ Archive   ☐ System

| OK | Cancel | Apply |

To select a group of folders or files, hold down the Ctrl key while clicking on each object. Or, if the objects are adjacent to one another, click the first, and then hold down the Shift key while you click the last. When you have selected the objects you're interested in, right-click to get to the property sheet.

To select a group of folders or files that are not all in the same folder, use the Find command to collect the objects in a Find window. Then Ctrl-click (hold down Ctrl while you click) each object you're interested in.

Inspecting a Disk's Properties

The property sheet for a disk's top-level folder is different from all others. It uses a large pie graph to show how much of the disk is in use and how much remains available. Figure 4-12 shows an example.

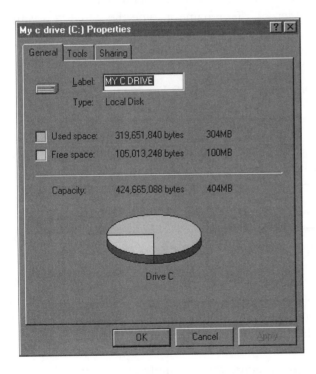

FIGURE 4-12.

The property sheet for a disk's top-level folder lets you see how much space is available.

To get to the top-level folder for a disk, begin by double-clicking My Computer. Then right-click the icon for the disk you're interested in. That icon may look like a disk instead of a folder, but the object it represents is still a folder—as you can see by double-clicking it.

Creating New Folders

Folders in Windows 95 can be nested to any level. That is, you can have folders within folders within folders—to whatever degree of complexity you want.

To create a new folder, begin by displaying the folder in which you want the new folder to reside. Right-click anywhere within this parent folder's unoccupied space, and then choose New from the object menu. When the submenu appears, choose Folder. (Alternatively, you can choose New from the folder window's File menu, and then choose Folder from the submenu.)

Your new folder will begin with a default name, such as "New Folder" or "New Folder #2." To rename it, type the name you want and press Enter.

If you click away from the new folder before renaming it, simply right-click it and choose Rename from the object menu. (Alternatively, choose Rename from the folder window's File menu.)

 See Also: For more information about *renaming folders,* see "Renaming Folders, Files, and Shortcuts," page 148.

Moving or Copying Folders, Files, and Shortcuts

To move or copy an object in a folder window, right-drag it from its current position to its destination. When you release the mouse button, an object menu appears. From this object menu, you can choose Copy Here, Move Here, or Create Shortcut(s) Here. Make the appropriate selection, and you're done.

To move or copy an entire folder, simply display the folder's parent folder. Then right-drag the folder icon (or the folder entry, if you're working in list or details view). Be aware that this action moves or replicates not only the folder but everything within the folder as well.

If you copy an object to a new destination in the same folder, Windows gives the copy a default name, such as "Copy of Myfile." While the object is still selected, you can give it a new name by typing and pressing Enter. Alternatively, right-click it and choose Rename.

If you prefer to drag with the left mouse button, you can do so, but in this case you need to know the following:

- If you left-drag a program file from one folder to another or to the desktop, Windows leaves the program in its source folder and creates a shortcut to the program in the destination folder. (Note that Windows ignores this "rule" if more than one file is selected when you drag.)

- If you left-drag any other file type from one folder to another on the same disk, Windows performs a move.

- If you left-drag from a folder on one disk to a folder on a different disk, Windows performs a copy.

- If you left-drag a folder or any file other than a program file from a folder to the desktop, Windows performs a move—provided the source folder resides on the disk where you installed Windows. If the source folder is on a different disk, Windows performs a copy instead of a move.

 You can force Windows to *copy* the selected objects—regardless of file type and destination—by holding down the Ctrl key as you drag. You can force Windows to *move* objects by holding down the Shift key as you drag. You can force Windows to create a shortcut by holding down Shift and Ctrl as you drag.

Moving or Copying Objects to Unopened Folders

In many cases, you can move or copy an object to a new folder without opening the destination folder. For example, suppose the file Rough Draft is stored in the folder PMFeature and you want to move it to the folder Outtakes, which is also stored in PMFeature. Simply grab Rough Draft with your mouse, drag it to the folder icon for Outtakes, and then release the mouse button.

As you drag an object from one folder to another or to the desktop, Windows displays a ghost image of the object you're dragging. If you're dragging with the left mouse button, you can look at the lower right corner of this image to see what action Windows will perform when you release the button. If Windows is going to create a copy, you'll see a plus sign in the lower right corner. If Windows is going to create a shortcut, you'll see a shortcut arrow. If Windows is going to move the object, you won't see anything in the lower right corner.

If you don't like the proposed action, click the right mouse button before you drop the object on the destination to cancel the drag operation in process.

If the destination folder is minimized, you can move or copy an object to it by dragging the object to the folder's taskbar button. Hold the object over the button for a moment while holding down the mouse button, and the folder window will open.

 If you have a shortcut for a folder on your desktop, you can move or copy items to that folder by dragging them to the shortcut.

Moving or Copying Objects with Menu Commands

If dragging and dropping is not convenient, you can move or copy objects using the Edit menu's Copy, Cut, and Paste commands (or their toolbar shortcuts).

 It's often quicker to use the keyboard shortcuts for Copy, Cut, and Paste than it is to visit the Edit menu. Press Ctrl-C to copy or Ctrl-X to cut, and then press Ctrl-V to paste.

- To move an object, select it and choose Cut from the source folder's Edit menu. Then choose Paste from the destination folder's Edit menu. (If the desktop is your destination, right-click the desktop and choose Paste from the object menu.)

- To copy an object, select it and choose Copy from the source folder's Edit menu. Then choose Paste from the destination folder's Edit menu. (If the desktop is your destination, right-click the desktop and choose Paste from the object menu.)

 When you cut an item, that item is not removed from its source folder until you paste it somewhere. If you change your mind in midstream, simply press Esc.

Moving or Copying Groups of Folders and Files

To move or copy a group of folders or files, select all members of the group, and then follow the same procedure you would use to move or copy a single item. To select a group, hold down the Ctrl key while you select each member. Alternatively, if the items are located next to one another in the folder window, you can select the first, and then hold down the Shift key while you select the last.

 For more information about *selecting a group of folders or files*, see "Selecting Folders and Files in a Folder Window," page 136.

Moving or Copying Objects with the Send To Command

When you right-click a folder or file, the object menu includes a Send To command. In response to this command, Windows displays a submenu of destinations, typically including any floppy drives on your system, as well as various other destinations. You can use the Send To command as a quick and easy way to copy or move a folder or file to any destination. You can also customize the Send To menu so that it includes destinations you frequently use.

> **NOTE:** When you use the Send To command with a folder destination, Windows treats the object just as if you dragged the object to the folder using the left mouse button. That is, if the destination and source folders are on the same disk, Windows performs a move; if the destination and source folders are on different disks, Windows performs a copy.

Customizing the Send To Menu

The contents of the Send To menu are determined by the contents of a folder named SendTo. On a system that does not use profiles, the SendTo folder is located within the Windows folder. On a system that uses profiles, each user has his or her own SendTo folder. To locate yours, use the Find command.

To add destinations to the Send To menu, simply create shortcuts for those destinations and store the shortcuts in the SendTo folder. For example, suppose you want to create a Send To menu item for a folder named Budgets, which is a subfolder of C:\Msoffice\Excel. Here is one way you can accomplish this addition:

1. Choose Run from the Start menu, type *c:\windows\sendto*, and click OK.

2. Right-click any unoccupied space in the SendTo folder, choose New from the object menu, and choose Shortcut.

3. In the command line text box in the Create Shortcut wizard, type *c:\msoffice\excel\budgets.* Then click Next.

4. In the wizard's next dialog box, accept or modify the wizard's proposed name for your new shortcut. Then click OK.

Of course, you can also use any other technique for creating a shortcut to your new destination folder.

See Also: For more information about *creating shortcuts*, see "Creating a Shortcut," page 73.

Using Applications and Other Kinds of Destinations on the Send To Menu

Your Send To menu may include applications, printers, and other types of "destinations," as well as folders. If you select a document and then choose an application from the Send To menu, Windows launches the application and attempts to open the selected document. If you select a document and choose a printer, Windows tries to print your document using that printer. In all cases, Windows does what it would have done had you dragged the selected document to a shortcut for the destination object. In other words, the Send To command is a menu alternative for a drag-and-drop operation.

NOTE: If you try to drag a folder to an application on the Send To menu, you'll get an error message. You'll also get an error message (a different one) if you try to drag multiple documents to an application that can't handle multiple documents. No harm is done in either case.

 Putting a shortcut for Notepad in your SendTo folder gives you a way to inspect plain text files that may not be identified in the registry as quick-viewable. For example, suppose you have a file named READ.ME, and your registry knows nothing about .ME files. With Notepad on your Send To menu, you can simply right-click and send the file to Notepad for easy viewing and printing.

To add an application to the Send To menu, simply create a shortcut for that application in your SendTo folder, in the same way as you would add a folder destination to the Send To menu.

Renaming Folders, Files, and Shortcuts

The simplest way to rename an object is to right-click it, choose Rename from the object menu, and then type a new name. But other methods are also available:

- Select the object and choose Rename from the folder window's File menu.

- Select the object. Then click the object's name. When a rectangle appears around the object's name, type a new name or edit the current name.

   When you use this method, you need to pause a moment between selecting the object and clicking the object's name. Otherwise, Windows interprets your action as a double-click and opens the selected object.

- Select the object and press F2. Then type a new name or edit the current name.

Windows preserves the case (capital and lowercase) for objects you name, with one exception: file or folder names that are eight characters or shorter and typed in all capitals or all lowercase. Windows displays such names with an initial capital and the rest of the name in lowercase. (This is done to "beautify" standard MS-DOS file and directory names.)

> If you make a mistake while changing a name, simply press Esc to cancel the process.

Reversing Moves, Copies, and Name Changes with the Undo Command

If you change your mind after moving or copying something, you can reverse your action by choosing the Undo command from any folder window's Edit menu. (If the toolbar is visible, you can simply click the Undo tool.) Be aware, however, that you must use the Undo command right

If you've chosen not to display extensions for registered files, be careful not to type the extension when you re-name a file. For example, suppose you have a file named My Picture.bmp, and your folder window displays that file's name as simply My Picture. If you change the name to Your Picture, be sure to type *Your Picture*, not *Your Picture.bmp*. Otherwise, the file's name will be recorded as Your Picture.bmp.bmp.

away. As soon as you perform some other action, Undo will reverse that action, not your move or copy.

Deleting Folders, Files, and Shortcuts

To delete an object or a group of objects, select what you want to delete and press the Del key. If you prefer a more complicated method, try one of these:

- Right-click an object and choose Delete from the object menu.

- Select an object or group of objects, pull down the folder window's File menu, and then choose Delete.

- Select an object or a group of objects, and then drag it to the Recycle Bin icon on your desktop—or to a shortcut for Recycle Bin.

However you do the deed, Windows presents a prompt and asks you to confirm your intent. This protects you from accidental deletions.

 If you don't want Windows to prompt for confirmation when you delete folders or files, clear the Display Delete Confirmation Dialog check box at the bottom of the Re-cycle Bin's property sheet.

As further protection, items you delete from hard disk folders or the desktop are automatically transferred to the Recycle Bin, from whence you can retrieve them if you change your mind.

If you change your mind right away about a deletion, you can restore whatever you deleted by choosing the Undo Delete command from the folder window's Edit menu.

Restoring Deleted Folders, Files, and Shortcuts

Have you ever deleted one file when you really meant to delete a different one? Wiped out a whole directory by mistake? Or simply trashed a document you thought you were finished with, only to discover the following week that you desperately needed it back?

Windows 95 provides a way to recover gracefully from accidents such as these. For a period of time after you delete an object, that object remains accessible via the Recycle Bin. If you change your mind, a simple menu command or mouse action restores selected items to the folders from which they were deleted.

The Recycle Bin is like that large trash barrel outside your house or the dumpster in the alley behind your office. Until the big truck comes to empty that container, anything you've tossed out can still be retrieved. (For information about when the big truck arrives in Windows, see "Setting Your Recycle Bin's Capacity," page 152.)

When you double-click the Recycle Bin icon, Windows displays the names of recently deleted items in an ordinary folder window. (See Figure 4-13.) By default, the window appears in details view and includes columns to show when each item was deleted and which folder it was deleted from. As in other folder windows, you can click column headings to change the sort order, and you can use toolbar icons or commands on the View menu to switch to list view or large- or small-icon view.

To restore an item from the Recycle Bin, simply select it and choose the File menu's Restore command (or right-click the item and choose Restore from the object menu). The Restore command puts the item back in the folder from which it was deleted. If that folder doesn't currently exist, Windows asks your permission to re-create it.

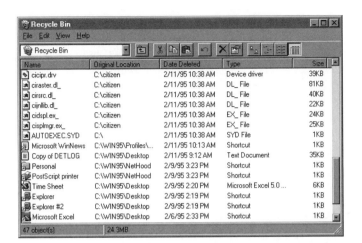

FIGURE 4-13.

Opening the Recycle Bin reveals an ordinary folder window in details view.

You also have the option of restoring a deleted item and putting it in a different folder. To do this, select the item and choose Cut from the File menu or object menu. Go to the folder in which you want the item to be restored, and then choose the Paste command on that folder window's Edit menu.

Here are three other important things to know about the Recycle Bin:

- Items deleted from floppy disks or network servers are not stored in the Recycle Bin. When you delete such an item, Windows asks you to confirm the deletion.

- Some application programs provide their own commands for deleting files. If you use an application's delete command your deleted file may not be transferred to the Recycle Bin.

- If you delete a folder, Windows stores all of the folder's files, but not the folder itself, in the Recycle Bin. When you restore an item that was deleted from a deleted folder, Windows (with your permission) re-creates the deleted folder.

To restore all files from a folder that was accidentally deleted, sort by Original Location to group all the files from that folder. Then select those files and choose Restore from the File menu.

The Find command cannot be used to locate items in the Recycle Bin. To search for items in the Recycle Bin, sort the Recycle Bin display on the column heading of interest. For example, to find an item when you know its name, click the Name heading so that all deleted items' names appear in alphabetical order. To find items that were deleted on a particular day, click the Date Deleted column heading.

Setting Your Recycle Bin's Capacity

Although you have only one Recycle Bin icon (plus any shortcuts to that icon that you've created), Windows actually maintains separate recycle bins for each hard disk on your system. The default size of each recycle bin is 10 percent of the capacity of the hard disk on which it's stored. When a recycle bin exceeds that limit, Windows begins removing files permanently, starting with the files that have been in the Recycle Bin the longest.

You can make your recycle bins larger or smaller by right-clicking the Recycle Bin icon and choosing Properties. (If the Recycle Bin is already open, you can get to the object menu by right-clicking the window's Control-menu icon.) You'll see a dialog box similar to the one shown in Figure 4-14, with a tab for each of your system's hard disks.

To adjust the size of all recycle bins on your system, select the Use One Setting For All Drives option button, and then adjust the slider on the Global tab. To adjust the size of recycle bins individually, select the Configure Drives Independently option button, and then adjust the sliders on each disk drive tab. To turn off recycle bin functionality globally, select the check box labeled "Do not move files to the Recycle Bin; remove files immediately on delete." To do this only for a particular hard disk, select the Configure Drives Independently option button, and then select the "remove files immediately" check box on the appropriate disk tab.

 To delete a file without moving it to the Recycle Bin, hold down the Shift key while you press Del.

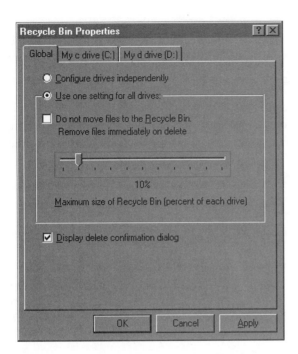

FIGURE 4-14.

The Properties command lets you configure each hard disk's recycle bin.

Purging the Recycle Bin

A deleted file sitting in your Recycle Bin takes up just as much space as it did before it was deleted. If you're deleting files in order to free up room for new programs and documents, simply transferring them from ordinary disk folders to the Recycle Bin folder won't do you much good. You need to get the old files off your system permanently. The safest way to do this, of course, is to move the files to a removable medium, such as a floppy disk. That way, you can always get your files back if you change your mind.

If you're sure you'll never need a particular file again, however, you can delete it in the normal way, and then purge it from the Recycle Bin. To delete an item from the Recycle Bin, simply display the Recycle Bin, select the item, and then press the Del key. Be aware as you answer the confirmation prompt that this deletion removes your selection permanently.

To delete a group of items from the Recycle Bin, hold down the Ctrl key while you select each one, and then press the Del key. (If the files are located next to one another in the Recycle Bin window, you can select the first member of the group, and then hold down the Shift key while you select the last member.)

> You can check the properties of a file before deleting it by double-clicking the file's icon in the Recycle Bin window.

To empty the Recycle Bin in one fell swoop, simply right-click the Recycle Bin icon and choose Empty Recycle Bin from the object menu. Or, if you're already in the Recycle Bin window, choose this command from the File menu.

Setting Attributes for Folders, Files, and Shortcuts

Attributes are markers that file systems employ to identify certain characteristics of files. In the Windows 95 file system, folders, files, and shortcuts can have no attributes or any combination of the following attributes: archive, hidden, read only, and system. The property sheet (see Figure 4-9 on page 138 and Figure 4-10 on page 139) lets you see an item's current attributes and change them if necessary.

The *archive* attribute indicates that an item has been modified since it was last backed up. Each time you create a new file or change an old one, Windows assigns the archive attribute to that file. Backup programs typically remove the archive attribute when they back up a file. If you change the file after backing it up, the file again gets the archive attribute so your backup program can recognize it as needing to be backed up again.

A few programs use the *hidden* and *system* attributes (either, but usually both) to mark important files that must not be modified or deleted because they are critical components of the program or Windows.

You can open a file with the *read-only* attribute, but you can't save it unless you first rename it. Some programs—and many users—set this attribute to prevent accidental changes to a file.

In many contexts, the read-only attribute not only prevents an item from being altered, but also keeps it from being deleted. For example, the MS-DOS Erase and Del commands refuse to delete files that are marked read-only. (You'll get the error message "Access denied" if you try.) If you select a read-only file in a folder window and press the Del key, Windows presents a confirmation prompt, reminding you that the file is read-only.

Assigning the read-only attribute to important files makes it less likely that you will delete those files accidentally. To assign this attribute, right-click the file, choose Properties in the object menu, and then select the Read Only check box. Note, however, that you will need to remove this attribute (by deselecting the check box) if you want to edit the file without changing its name.

You can assign attributes to entire folders as well as to individual files. Making a folder read-only does not alter the attributes of files or folders contained within the read-only folder, but it does afford some protection against accidental deletion of the folder.

Working with the File Types List

If you choose Options on the folder window's View menu, and then click the File Types tab, Windows displays a list of all registered file types. A sample of this list is shown in Figure 4-15 on the next page.

Working with this list, you can do a number of things:

- Decode the icons in your folder windows

- Change a file type's icon

- Add or remove quick-view capability for a file type

- Change the registered name of a file type

- Specify whether the file type's extension should be displayed in folder and Windows Explorer windows

- Remove a file type from the registry

- Change the actions carried out by commands on the file type's object menu

- Add or delete commands on the file type's object menu

- Create new file types

FIGURE 4-15.

The File Types tab in
the View menu's
Options dialog box
lists all file types
known to the
registry, provides
details about how
they're associated,
and allows you to
change document
icons or add quick-
view capability.
Stepping through the
File Types list may
help you sort out
what all those icons
in your folder
windows represent.

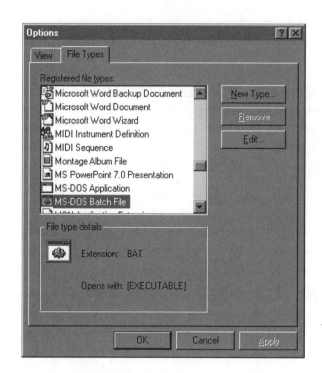

Decoding Document Icons

As you've undoubtedly noticed, document files are marked by icons shaped like pages with a dog-ear in the upper right corner. Icons for registered documents resemble those of their parent applications, and icons for unregistered documents bear the generic Windows emblem. But if you open your Windows folder or its System subfolder, you'll probably find dozens of files with icons that may not be familiar. What do all these icons signify?

One way you can find out is by stepping through the File Types list. As you select each file type in the list, a full-size version of the file type's icon appears in the bottom of the dialog box along with the file type's extension and the icon used by its parent application (if it has one). You will learn, for example, that an icon that looks like a folder window with a big gear stands for an MS-DOS batch file (see Figure 4-15), that .COM files are marked by plain window icons without the big gear, and so on.

Changing a File Type's Icon

Just as you can change the icons used by your programs (see "Changing a Shortcut's Icon," page 79), you can also reassign document icons. To do this, open a folder window's View menu, choose Options, and click the File Types tab. In the Registered File Types list, find the file type you want to modify, and then click Edit. Click the Change Icon button at the top of the ensuing dialog box, and then choose a new icon from the Change Icon gallery.

If you don't see a suitable icon in the Change Icon gallery, you can specify a different program in the File Name text box—and then "borrow" an icon from that program.

Adding or Removing Quick-View Capability

The Quick View facility lets you look at many types of files, including both text and graphics files, without invoking the applications that created them. If a file type's object menu does not include the Quick View command, you can add it as follows:

1. Select the file type in the File Types list.

2. Click the Edit button.

3. Select the Enable Quick View check box and click OK.

If Windows doesn't have a viewer specific to the selected file type, it uses the plain-text viewer. This may or may not produce an edifying display. If it doesn't, no harm is done. You can go back to the File Types list and deselect the Enable Quick View check box.

 See Also: For information about *Quick View*, see "Inspecting Documents and Programs with Quick View," page 67.

Changing the Registered Name of a File Type

The names that appear in the File Types list may show up in menus used by your applications. For example, if you use the Insert Object command in WordPad (or in another program that supports OLE), you'll see a list of embeddable objects. This list is derived from the File Types list. You can change what you see on the menus by changing the names in the File Types list. There's probably no compelling reason to do this, unless you simply object to the length of some of the names.

For example, suppose you tire of seeing the name *Microsoft* before every file type created by a Microsoft application. To reduce Microsoft Access Database Application to something a bit simpler, such as Access Application, you could do as follows:

1. In the File Types list, select the Microsoft Access Database Application entry.

2. Click the Edit button.

3. In the Description Of Type box, type the short name you prefer, and then click OK.

Specifying Display of Extensions

By default, folder and Windows Explorer windows do not show extensions for registered file types. You can turn the extension display on for all file types using the folder window's Options command. Using the File Types list, you can also show extensions for a particular file type, while suppressing the extensions for other registered file types. Here's how:

1. Select the file type in the File Types list.

2. Click the Edit button.

3. Select the Always Show Extension check box and click OK.

See Also: For information about *the Options command*, see "Displaying Filename Extensions," page 133.

Removing a File Type from the Registry

If you use the Add/Remove Programs wizard to uninstall Windows-based programs that you no longer need, you should not have to "unregister" the file types used by those applications. The wizard should take care of that detail for you. But if the wizard lets you down, or if you remove a program without the wizard's assistance, you may want to visit the File Types list to clean up. You can remove a file type from the registry as follows:

1. Select the file type in the File Types list.

2. Click the Remove button and reply to the confirmation prompt. Then click OK.

 For information about *the Add/Remove Programs wizard,* see "Installing Applications," page 342.

Modifying a File Type's Object Menu

If you know what you're doing, you can change the contents of a file type's object menu or modify the behavior of commands on the menu. To see what commands are on the object menu, select a file type and click the Edit button. To see what a particular command does, select that command in the Actions section of the ensuing dialog box, and then click Edit in that dialog box. To make changes, modify the next dialog box that appears.

> **NOTE:** Unless you're completely sure of your ground, this part of the File Types list is best seen but not touched. If you make mistakes here, you may need to reinstall the affected application.

Creating New File Types

The New Type button in the File Types list allows you to add new file types to the registry. Normally, you should have no reason to use this button. Instead, if you want to create an association between an unregistered file type and an application, simply double-click an instance of that file type in a folder window. Then fill out the Open With dialog box.

 For information about *the Open With dialog box,* see "What to Do When Windows Can't Open Your Documents," page 63.

Formatting Disks

To format a disk, right-click an icon or entry for it in a folder window, and then choose Format from the object menu. Windows displays a dialog box similar to the one shown in Figure 4-16.

FIGURE 4-16.

To format a disk, right-click its icon and choose Format from the object menu.

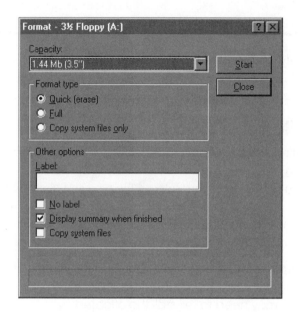

First choose the capacity of the disk you're about to format. Next, choose the type of format you want. If you choose a full format, Windows checks the disk for bad sectors after completing the format. If you go for a quick format, Windows skips the media check and simply erases everything on the disk. This option can't be used with disks that have never been formatted.

The Copy System Files Only option turns a floppy disk that's already been formatted into a "boot disk"—a disk that you can use to boot your computer. If you want to format a disk *and* make it a boot disk, choose Full or Quick in the Format Type section of the dialog box, and also select the Copy System Files check box.

NOTE: You cannot use the Format command to format the hard disk on which your Windows files are stored. You can use it to format other hard disks, though.

Windows can also make a "startup disk" that is not only a boot disk, but also includes several utility and diagnostic programs. To make a startup disk, double-click the Add/Remove Programs item in Control Panel. Click the Startup Disk tab, and then click Create Disk.

Copying Floppy Disks

To copy a floppy disk, right-click its icon in a folder window and choose Copy Disk from the object menu. Make sure the Copy To and Copy From sections of the dialog box are correctly filled out, and then click Start. When the copy is complete, the dialog box remains on screen. If you want to copy another disk, insert it and then click Start again.

5

Managing Folders and Files with Windows Explorer

Now that you're comfortable navigating with folder windows, you're ready to explore with Windows Explorer. Windows Explorer has been described by some early reviewers of Windows 95 as a souped-up version of the Windows 3.x File Manager—a "File Manager on steroids"—but it would be more precise to call it a folder window with an attachment. The attachment is simply an "org chart" of your computer and its network environment.

Figures 5-1 and 5-2 on the next page show a folder-window view of a folder and the same folder as seen through Windows Explorer. As you can see in Figure 5-2, Windows Explorer's window has a left pane and a right pane. The right pane looks just like an ordinary folder window and functions the same way. The left pane is an outline of your Windows namespace. It shows the directory structure of your local hard disks, plus any other resources attached to your computer—including floppy disks, CD-ROM drives, system folders, and network servers. The outline even provides access to printer queues, Control Panel, and the Recycle Bin.

Like an ordinary folder window, Windows Explorer includes a menu bar, an optional toolbar, and an optional status bar. The menu bar is exactly like a folder window's, except that it includes an additional menu called "Tools." Also like a folder window, Windows Explorer's right pane offers you a choice of four viewing modes: large icons, small icons, list, and details. By default, the right pane appears in details view. We've shown it in large-icon view in Figure 5-2 to emphasize the fact that Windows Explorer is merely an extension of the standard folder window—not a wholly new way of interacting with Windows.

The left pane in the Windows Explorer window confers three benefits: it makes it easy to move quickly between unrelated folders, it lets you see the structure of your folders at a glance, and it allows you to move and copy files by dragging them from the right pane to the left. On the other hand, the split window does make for a more complex display. If you prefer the simplicity of the standard folder window (or, should we say, if the divided window gives you a pane), you can ignore Windows Explorer. But if you experiment a bit with Windows Explorer, you may find its benefits substantial. In any case, the choice is yours. You can use Windows Explorer always, occasionally, or never.

FIGURE 5-1.

A folder-window
view of a Microsoft
Project folder.

FIGURE 5-2.

The same folder as
seen through
Windows Explorer.

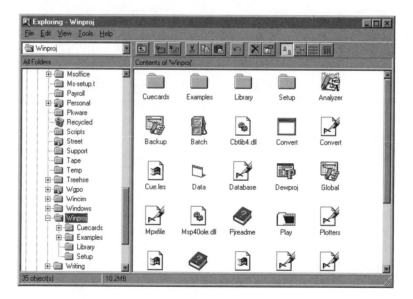

You can use the Windows 3.x File Manager as an alternative to Windows Explorer. To run File Manager, choose the Run command on the Start menu, type *winfile*, and press Enter. The version of File Manager that appears is the one that Microsoft shipped with Windows for Workgroups 3.11.

File Manager's chief virtue relative to Windows Explorer is that it offers a customizable toolbar. But if you're not already proficient with File Manager, you'll probably find it more difficult to learn and use than Windows Explorer.

Opening Windows Explorer

Windows Explorer normally is located on your Start menu—usually under Programs. If so, you can use the Start menu to get to Windows Explorer. Here are some additional ways to open Windows Explorer:

- Right-click My Computer or Network Neighborhood, and then choose Explore from the object menu.

- Right-click any folder icon, or any shortcut icon that points to a folder, and then choose Explore from the object menu.

- In a folder window, select any folder icon and then choose Explore from the File menu.

- In a folder window, select any folder icon and then hold down the Shift key while double-clicking.

- In a folder window, select any folder icon and then hold down the Shift key while pressing Enter.

- In a folder window, right-click the Control-menu icon (at the left edge of the title bar), and then choose Explore.

You can make Windows Explorer your default browsing tool. To do so, open any folder in a folder window or in Windows Explorer. Choose Options from the View menu and click the File Types tab. Select Folder in the File Types list and then click the Edit button. In the Actions list, select Explore and then click the Set Default button. (This should make Explore appear in boldface type.) Click Close twice.

Now whenever you double-click My Computer or any other folder, Windows Explorer will appear.

An Overview of Windows Explorer

Figure 5-3 shows a Windows Explorer window in its default display mode, with toolbar and status bar visible and the right pane in details view. Directly below the toolbar are legends for the two panes, which read "All Folders" for the left pane and "Contents of 'My c drive (C:)'" for the right pane. To make the legends appear in your own Windows Explorer (if they don't already), choose Options from the View menu, click the View tab, and select the check box labeled "Include description bar for right and left panes."

Notice that the right pane includes column headings—Name, Size, Type, and Modified. Besides telling you what each column is for, these headings are live buttons; you can sort the pane on any column by clicking its heading.

 To reverse the sorting order of a column, click the heading a second time.

**Drag the pane divider to
change the pane width**

**Drag column dividers to
change the column width**

Click heading buttons to sort

FIGURE 5-3.

By default, Windows
Explorer's right pane
appears in details
view.

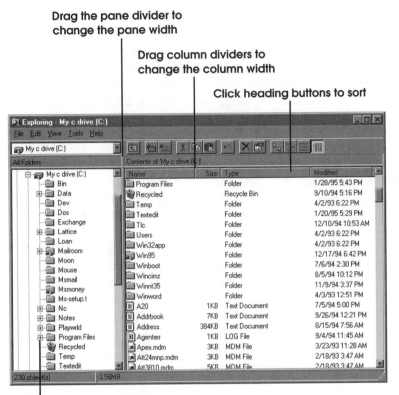

**Click plus or minus buttons
to expand or collapse the outline**

You can change the way Windows Explorer's window space is distributed as follows:

- To change the width of either pane, drag the dividing line between the panes.

- To change the width of any column in the right pane, position the mouse pointer on the divider line to the right of the column heading. When the mouse pointer changes to a two-headed arrow, drag the divider line.

- To adjust the width of a right-pane column so that it just accommodates the column's longest entry, double-click the divider line to the right of the column heading.

169

■ To hide a right-pane column, drag its divider line to the left until the column disappears. To restore a hidden column, position the mouse pointer on the divider line for the column heading to the left of the hidden column. When the mouse pointer changes to a split two-headed arrow (as opposed to a solid two-headed arrow), drag to the right, and the hidden column will reappear.

The headings in the right pane change, depending on the contents of the Windows Explorer window. When Windows Explorer is showing the contents of a disk folder, the headings appear as shown in Figure 5-3. However, if you use Windows Explorer to examine My Computer, Network Neighborhood, Recycle Bin, or a system folder, you will see different column headings.

For a quick overview of the total space available on each of your hard disks, right-click My Computer and choose Explore. The third and fourth columns in the right pane will tell you the total capacity of and available space on each local hard disk. (If you don't see this information, pull down the View menu and choose Details.)

For information about *Network Neighborhood*, see "Using Network Neighborhood to Find Network Files," page 182.

For information about *the Recycle Bin*, see "Restoring Deleted Folders, Files, and Shortcuts," page 150.

Working in the Right Pane

Working in the right pane of a Windows Explorer window is exactly like working in an ordinary folder window. You can run programs or launch documents in the right pane, move from folder to folder, copy and move files between folders, and do anything else that you might do in a folder window.

To open a folder window for any folder shown in the right pane, right-click the folder and choose Open from the object menu.

 See Also: For more information about *using Windows Explorer's right pane*, see Chapter 4, "Working with Folders," page 115.

Navigating in the Left Pane

Moving from one folder to another using Windows Explorer's left pane is easy, provided you remember three things:

- To move to another folder, click the folder's name—not the plus or minus sign next to the name, but the name itself. The folder you click becomes the current folder, and its contents appear in the right pane.

- To expand or collapse an outline entry in the left pane, click the plus or minus sign to the left of the folder name. The contents of the right pane do not change when you do this, but the level of detail shown in the left pane does.

- To move to another folder and at the same time expand or collapse its outline entry, double-click the folder name—not the plus or minus sign next to the folder, but the name itself. The folder you click becomes the current folder, and its contents appear in the right pane. At the same time, the level of detail shown in the outline changes.

That's all there is to it. Here are some examples.

In Figure 5-3 on page 169, the current folder is "My c drive (C:)." To switch to drive D, click once on the entry "My d drive (D:)" in the left pane. Figure 5-4 on the next page shows how Windows Explorer would appear after this action.

The plus sign next to the entry "My d drive (D:)" in the left pane of Figure 5-4 indicates that this folder contains subfolders. (Of course, you can also tell that it does by looking at all the folder icons in the right pane.) To display the subfolders in the left pane, click the plus sign next to the entry "My d drive (D:)." Figure 5-5 shows the result.

FIGURE 5-4.

Clicking the "My d drive (D:)" entry in the left pane displays the contents of "My d drive (D:)" in the right pane.

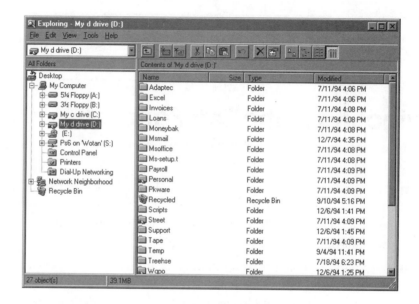

Notice that when you expand the entry "My d drive (D:)," its plus sign changes to a minus sign. When you're ready to collapse that entry, click the minus sign.

Now suppose that you want to move to the Excel folder, one of the subfolders of "My d drive (D:)." Because there's a plus sign beside the Excel entry, you can expand the Excel entry at the same time that you switch to that folder. Double-clicking Excel does the trick, and Figure 5-6 shows the result.

172

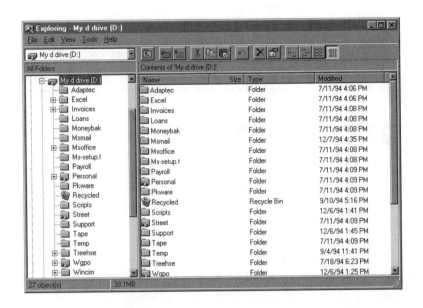

FIGURE 5-5.

Clicking the plus sign to the left of the "My d drive (D:)" entry expands the entry in the left pane but leaves the right pane unchanged.

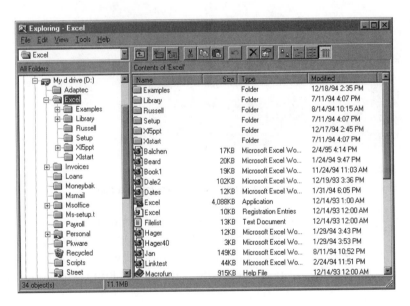

FIGURE 5-6.

Double-clicking the Excel entry in the left pane switches to the Excel folder and at the same time expands the Excel outline entry.

Whether you're working in a folder window or any part of Windows Explorer, pressing Backspace always takes you to the parent of the current folder.

Going Places with the Go To Command

The Tools menu includes a handy Go To command, whose dialog box is shown in Figure 5-7. As its name implies, the Go To command is a navigational instrument. You can hop directly from one folder to another by typing the folder's name and path in the Go To Folder dialog box. For example, to get directly from C:\Windows to D:\Excel\Examples, without fussing with either window pane, you can simply pull down the Tools menu, choose Go To, and type *d:\excel\examples*.

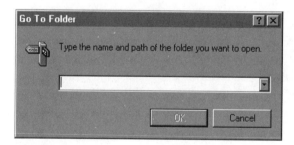

FIGURE 5-7.

Windows Explorer's Go To command can quickly take you to a folder.

If you've used the Run command on the Start menu, the Go To command may look familiar. Clicking the drop-down arrow at the right side of the dialog box reveals the same list of command entries that you would see by opening the drop-down on the Start menu's Run command. Unlike the Run command, however, the Go To command merely lets you hop to a new folder. If you enter the name of a program or a document in the Go To Folder dialog box, Windows Explorer displays an error message—but doesn't open the program or document.

See Also: For more information about *the Run command,* see "Running Programs and Opening Documents with the Run Command," page 70.

Using Windows Explorer for Housekeeping Chores

All the housekeeping operations described in Chapter 4—copying, moving, deleting, creating, and renaming objects, and working with file types—are available in Windows Explorer as well. Windows Explorer simply provides an extra convenience—the ability to use outline entries in drag-and-drop maneuvers.

For example, suppose that after studying the folder outline shown in Figure 5-6, you decide that the Invoices folder really should be a subfolder of Excel. You could carry out this reorganization as follows:

1. Right-drag the Invoices entry in the left pane and drop it on the Excel entry in the left pane.

2. From the object menu, choose Move Here.

You can drag objects from either pane to the other, as well as from one location to another in the same pane. As in folder windows, it's best to drag with the right mouse button, and then choose the action you want from the object menu. That way, you'll never inadvertently ask Windows to copy an object when you meant to move it, or vice versa.

See Also: For more information about *copying and moving objects*, see "Moving or Copying Folders, Files, and Shortcuts," page 142.

For information about *deleting objects*, see "Deleting Folders, Files, and Shortcuts," page 149.

For information about *creating new objects*, see "Creating New Folders," page 142.

For information about *renaming objects*, see "Renaming Folders, Files, and Shortcuts," page 148.

For information about *file types*, see "Working with the File Types List," page 155.

Using Command Lines to Open Windows Explorer and Folder Windows

With command-line expressions you can open Windows Explorer and make it display a particular folder, display a folder and select a particular object in that folder, or limit its display to a subset of your namespace. You can use these command lines with the Start menu's Run command, assign them to a shortcut, or store them in an MS-DOS batch file. (By entering command strings in an MS-DOS batch file, you can open two or more Windows Explorer windows.) You can also use command-line strings to open folder windows.

The syntax is as follows:

```
explorer [/n][/e][,/root,object][[,/select],subobject]
```

/n	always opens a new window, even if the specified folder is already open.
/e	opens the folder in Windows Explorer. If you omit /e, a folder window is opened.
/root,*object*	restricts Windows Explorer to *object* and all folders contained within *object*.
/select,*subobject*	gives initial focus to the parent folder of *subobject* and selects *subobject*. If /select is omitted, *subobject* specifies the folder that gets the initial focus.

Here are some examples:

```
explorer /e,/root,C:\Windows
```

opens a Windows Explorer view restricted to C:\Windows (and all folders contained in C:\Windows).

```
explorer /e,/select,C:\Windows\Win.ini
```

opens a Windows Explorer view of C:\Windows, with the Win.ini file selected.

```
explorer C:\Windows
```

opens a folder-window view of C:\Windows

```
explorer
```

opens a Windows Explorer view of C:\ (or the disk on which your Windows 95 files are stored). Note that when no arguments are given, you don't need to include /e to get a Windows Explorer view.

6

Using and Sharing Files on the Network

Windows 95 was designed from the start as a networking operating system. In many other networking environments, the networking functionality is superimposed on a single-user-oriented operating system. In Windows 95, networking features are fully integrated into every aspect of the system.

Windows 95 provides support for networks from a number of vendors, including Microsoft, Novell, Artisoft, Banyan, Digital Equipment Corporation, and IBM. In addition, the system supports the simultaneous use of multiple networking protocols. This means that, assuming your network administrator has set up your system properly, you should be able to work successfully in a heterogeneous network environment, making use of servers that run Windows NT, Windows 95, Windows for Workgroups, Novell NetWare, and other operating systems.

Best of all, using network resources and sharing your own resources with other network users is almost as simple and straightforward as using your own local resources. Browsing a network folder is just like browsing a folder on your own hard disk. Sending a document to a network printer is just like printing at your own machine. The procedures for interacting with one kind of server (say, a Windows NT server) are identical to the procedures for working with another kind (for example, a NetWare server). You don't have to learn network commands to use your network's resources.

In this chapter, we'll look at the steps involved in working with programs and documents stored on network servers, as well as at what you need to do to share your own folders and files. Other networking topics may be found in other parts of this book.

See Also: For information about *using network printers,* see "Printing to a Network Printer," page 233.

For information about *remote access,* see "Using Dial-Up Networking," page 372.

For information about *direct cable connections between computers,* see "Transferring Files with Direct Cable Connection," page 360.

Using Network Neighborhood to Find Network Files

Network Neighborhood is your gateway to all available network resources, just as My Computer is the gateway to resources stored on your own system. Double-clicking the Network Neighborhood icon opens a folder window containing icons for all workstations and servers in your immediate workgroup (as defined and configured by your network administrator). Figure 6-1 shows the Network Neighborhood folder for a typical small local-area network.

FIGURE 6-1.

The icons in the Network Neighborhood folder represent workstations in your workgroup.

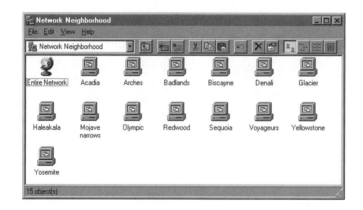

 To browse your network using Windows Explorer, right-click the Network Neighborhood icon and then choose Explore from the object menu.

 If you're not sure what kind of files are contained on a server, right-click its icon and choose Properties from the object menu. On the property sheet, you may find a comment (entered by the person who shared the folder) that describes the contents of the server.

In addition to entries for each workstation in your workgroup, the Network Neighborhood folder includes an entry labeled Entire Network. Double-clicking Entire Network opens a folder that displays a top-level view of your entire corporate network. If your network is particularly complex, you might find it helpful to view its structure in a Windows Explorer window. To do that, right-click the Entire Network icon and choose Explore. Figure 6-2 uses Windows Explorer to show the "entire-network" view of the network shown in Figure 6-1.

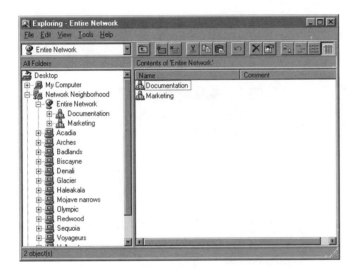

FIGURE 6-2.

The Documentation icon in this window represents the workgroup shown in Figure 6-1.

If you frequently need access to a network server that isn't included in your Network Neighborhood, create a shortcut for it, and put the shortcut in your Network Neighborhood folder. To do this, simply open Entire Network, find the server you need, right-drag it to the Network Neighborhood icon, and then choose Create Shortcut(s) Here from the object menu.

Connecting to a Network Server

A *server* is a remote source of shared files. Because the Microsoft networking services are "peer-based," a server can be a computer that acts solely as a repository for shared files (a "dedicated" server), or it can simply be a shared folder on a computer used by one of your colleagues.

In either case, to interact with a server, simply double-click the icon for that server in your Network Neighborhood folder or Windows Explorer window. This opens a new folder window, in which you can see all the folders and printers on the selected server to which you have been granted access. Figure 6-3 shows such a window. Double-clicking a folder icon reveals all folders and files stored in that folder, and so on.

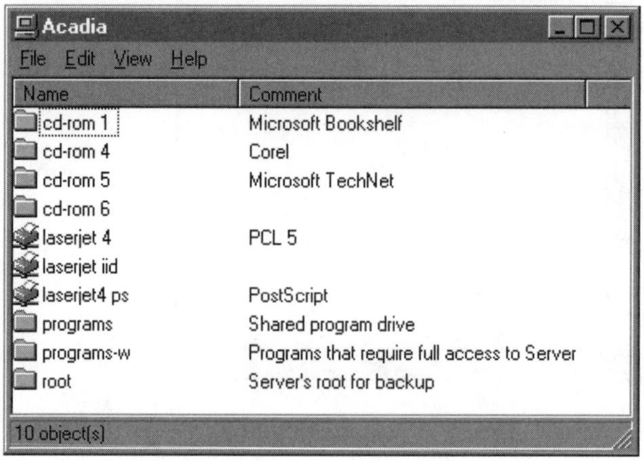

FIGURE 6-3.

Details view of a folder window for a server that includes a comment for each shared resource. The comment is provided by the person who shared the resource.

Your Network Neighborhood folder also includes an icon for your own computer. By double-clicking this icon, you can see the names of all folders and printers on your own system that have been made available to other network users.

When you double-click a server-based folder, you may be asked to supply a password. If so, you will see a dialog box similar to the one shown in Figure 6-4. Before typing in your password, you might want to make sure the check box at the bottom of the dialog box is selected. That way Windows will add your password to a list of passwords associated

FIGURE 6-4.

When you open a password-protected folder for the first time, Windows presents this dialog box. If you select the check box, you won't have to reenter the password the next time you open the folder.

with your name, and you won't have to reenter the password the next time you open this folder.

 Create desktop shortcuts for the network folders you use regularly. That way, you won't have to travel through the Network Neighborhood each time you want to read or save a server-based file. To create a desktop shortcut for a network folder, simply right-drag its icon to the desktop, and then choose Create Shortcut(s) Here.

If you don't want to clutter your desktop, but you still want to avoid traveling down the Network Neighborhood path to find a folder, you can drag its icon to the Network Neighborhood folder (or any other convenient folder) instead of to the desktop.

 You can use the Find command to locate network servers, server-based folders, and individual server-based files. For details, see Chapter 7, "Using the Find Command," page 193.

Access Levels

Folders can be shared with full access or read-only access. If a folder is shared with read-only access, you can work with the folder's programs and documents, but you can't save documents to that folder. To save a document that you retrieved from a read-only network folder, specify a local folder (or a network folder for which you have full-access privileges) as the document's destination.

If a folder is shared with full access, you can do anything with its documents and programs that you can do with files stored in local folders. In the absence of file-specific restrictions, you can read, write, rename, delete, move, and copy files in full-access folders, just as though they were on your own computer. (Individual files can also have access restrictions, such as password protection or read-only access.)

Some folders are shared as *either* full-access or read-only, depending on the password you supply. For example, a network administrator may want to give some users unrestricted access while limiting others to read-only use. In such cases, if you've been entrusted with both passwords, you might want to limit your full-access use to times when you actually need to change files on the server. Operating in read-only mode at other times will protect you against accidental changes to or deletions of critical documents.

Connecting to a Server from the Common Dialog Boxes

If the program you're working with uses the Windows 95 common File Open, File Save, and File Save As dialog boxes, you can retrieve or save files on servers without going through your Network Neighborhood icon. Simply open the Look In or Save In drop-down list at the top of the dialog box and then choose Network Neighborhood. The big window in the center of the dialog box then displays the names of your servers, allowing you to navigate to the folder of your choice.

See Also: For more information about *common dialog boxes,* see "Navigating in the File Open and File Save Dialogs," page 126.

Mapping a Network Folder to a Drive Letter

"Mapping" a network folder makes it appear to Windows as though the folder is part of your own computer. Windows assigns the mapped folder a drive letter, just as if it was an additional local hard disk. You can still access a mapped folder in the conventional manner, by navigating to it through folder windows or Windows Explorer. But mapping gives the folder an alias—the assigned drive letter—that provides an alternative means of access.

Folder mapping offers the following benefits:

■ It makes the network folder available to programs that don't use the Windows 95 common dialog boxes.

  With programs that use the Windows 95 common dialog boxes, you can navigate to network folders just as you would with Network Neighborhood. But to read a document from or save a document to a network folder using other programs, you will probably need to map the folder to a drive letter.

■ It makes the network folder accessible from the My Computer icon.

  Because a mapped folder becomes a "virtual" disk on your local computer, an icon for the folder appears in the My Computer folder, right alongside your real local disks. If you do most of your work with files stored locally but occasionally need access to particular servers, you might find it convenient to map them. That way, you won't have to bother opening the Network Neighborhood icon to find the servers you need.

■ Windows can automatically reconnect to your mapped network folders at startup.

When you navigate to a server using Network Neighborhood, you might experience momentary delays while Windows locates and opens a channel to the selected server. If you map the folder and choose the Reconnect At Logon option, any connection delays will occur at the beginning of your work session, and you'll be less likely to find them intrusive.

■ Mapped folders become part of My Computer for file-search purposes.

When you use the Find command to search for files stored on My Computer, the search encompasses not only your real local disks but also any mapped network folders. If you sometimes need to search for items that may be stored *either* locally or in a particular network folder, you can save yourself a search step by mapping the network folder.

To map a network folder, follow these steps:

1. Navigate to the folder in Network Neighborhood.

2. Right-click the folder icon and choose Map Network Drive from the object menu.

   The dialog box shown in Figure 6-5 appears.

FIGURE 6-5.

Right-clicking a network folder icon and choosing Map Network Drive allows you to turn the folder into a virtual local hard disk.

3. Choose a drive letter in the Drive drop-down.

   Windows proposes the first available drive letter, but you can choose any letter that's not already in use. You might want to pick one that's mnemonically related to the content of the folder—for example, R for Reports.

4. Select the Reconnect At Logon check box if you want Windows to
    connect to this server automatically at the start of each session.

"Unmapping" a Mapped Network Folder

If you change your mind about mapping a network folder, simply right-
click the folder's icon in your My Computer folder. As Figure 6-6 shows,
you'll see a Disconnect command in the resulting object menu. Choose this
command, and the tie will be severed.

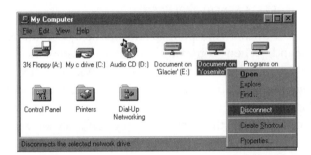

FIGURE 6-6.

To "unmap" a
network folder, right-
click the folder's icon
in My Computer and
choose Disconnect
from the object
menu.

Opening Network Folders
with the Run Command

In Windows 95, you do not have to memorize path specifications to use
network folders. Instead, you can simply navigate to the folders you need,
using either folder windows or Windows Explorer. But every network folder does, in fact, have a path specification, and you're welcome to use those
path specifications wherever you find it convenient.

A network folder's path consists of two backslash characters, followed by a server name, another backslash, and a *share* name. The share
name is the name assigned to the folder by the person who made the
folder available on the network. (For more information about share
names, see "Sharing Folders with Other Users," page 190.) So, for example, the network path for the folder selected in Figure 6-6 is

    \\YOSEMITE\DOCUMENT

because this folder's share name is Document and it's stored on a server
named Yosemite.

If the server in question is part of a Windows NT *domain* (a collection of computers that share a common domain database and security policy), you may need to include the domain name in the path. For example, a folder named Fafner, stored on the Budgets server in the Marketing domain would have the following path:

```
\\MARKETING\BUDGETS\FAFNER
```

Additionally, a network path may include subfolder names. To get to the December folder on Fafner, for example, you could specify

```
\\MARKETING\BUDGETS\FAFNER\DECEMBER
```

The most likely use for network path specifications is in conjunction with the Run command. When you want to get to a network folder quickly, without traversing a sequence of folder or Windows Explorer windows, you can simply pop up the Start menu, choose Run, and type the path for the folder you need.

Note that you can also use this technique to open a folder window for the server itself, from which you can then choose any available subfolder. For example, to display all the shared folders on the server named Wotan, you can choose the Run command and simply type *wotan*.

Remember, too, that the Run command keeps a list of your most recently used commands. Thus, if you often need to use a particular server or network folder, you can type its path once on the Run command line, and then choose its path from the drop-down list the next time you need it.

Sharing Folders with Other Users

To share a folder on your own system so that other network users can access it, begin by displaying the folder's icon in its parent's folder window. Right-click the icon, and then choose Sharing from the object menu. This takes you to the Sharing pane of the folder's property sheet, as shown in Figure 6-7.

Choose the Shared As option button, and then either accept or amend the proposed share name. The share name is the name that will appear under the folder icon when others access this folder via their own Network Neighborhood icons. It's also the name that will be used in the folder's network path specification. By default, the share name is the same

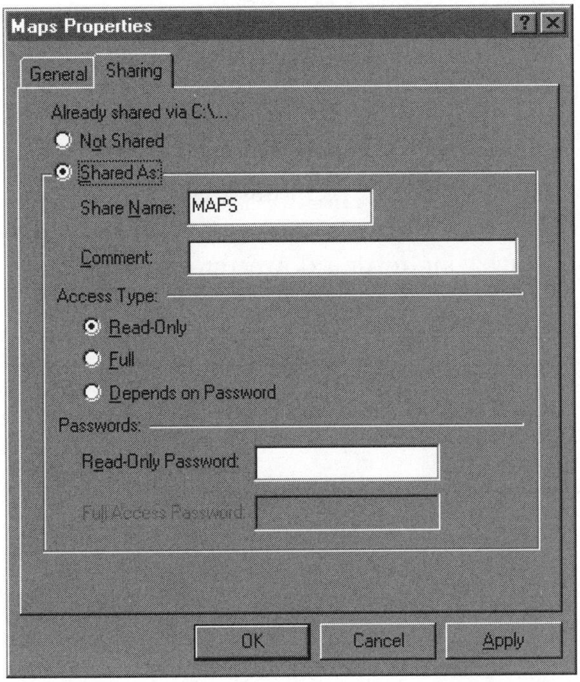

FIGURE 6-7.

To share one of your own folders, choose the Sharing command on the folder's object menu.

as the folder name. In most cases that's an ideal name, but you're not obliged to use it. You might want to change it, for example, if your workgroup already is using a shared folder with the same name.

In the Comment line, you can type a description of the folder's contents. Other users will see this description when they inspect the folder's property sheet in their Network Neighborhood folders.

As mentioned earlier, a folder can be shared in any of three modes— Read Only, Full, and Depends On Password. If you choose either Read Only or Full, you can specify a password, but you are not required to do so. If you choose Depends On Password, you *must* specify two passwords, one for read-only access and one for full access.

Note that when you share a folder, you also make any of that folder's subfolders available on the network. If the access mode you choose for the folder would not be appropriate for any of its subfolders, you should either reconsider your choice of access mode or restructure your folders to avoid the problem.

You can separately share a subfolder of a folder that you've already shared. In this case, the Sharing pane of the folder's property sheet will indicate that the folder is already shared, by way of its parent (or another ancestor further removed). For example, the line "Already shared via C:\...," near the top of Figure 6-7, indicates that the Maps folder is already available to network users. Sharing Maps in this case may still be a good idea, however, because it gives network users a way to go directly to a folder of interest without having to drill down through layers of folders and subfolders.

 See Also: For more information about *access*, see "Access Levels," page 186.

7

Using the Find Command

Scooting around your hard disk or network with folder windows and Windows Explorer is dandy when you know where you're going. But it's less dandy when all you know about the item you need is that it's "out there somewhere." In that all-too-common circumstance, you'll want to use Windows 95's versatile Find command.

The Find command can quickly locate documents, programs, folders, and even entire computers, anywhere on your own computer or amongst the shared resources of your network. You can find what you're looking for by name, creation date, size, file type, content, or any combination of these. For example, you can ask the Find command to locate all 1-2-3 for Windows documents created within the last month that are at least 30 megabytes in size and contain the word "xenon." Or you can use it to generate a list of all applications on a particular server. Or to find all files that are larger than 100 kilobytes and haven't been modified during the last six months. And so on.

After you've found an item or group of items that you're looking for, you can work with the search results directly in the Find window, just as if it was an ordinary folder window. Alternatively, you can select any item in the Find window and use a File-menu command to go directly to the item's containing folder.

If you plan to reuse a set of search criteria, you can use a simple menu command to save the criteria on your desktop. When you do this, you can either save or discard the current search results (the files and folders that currently meet the search criteria), as you choose.

Finding the Find Command

The Find command is a permanent fixture of the Start menu, so you can always invoke it there. Alternatively, you can get to the Find command by right-clicking any folder icon or folder shortcut and choosing Find on the object menu.

To search for something in a particular folder, display the folder and press F3.

When you choose Find from a folder's object menu, Find proposes to conduct its search beginning at the current folder. Thus, if you know that the items you're looking for are in a particular folder (or one of its subfolders), and if that folder is at hand, it's more efficient to choose Find from the folder's object menu, saving you the effort of specifying a starting point for the search. Otherwise, it's probably simpler to open the Start menu.

Finding Files and Folders

When you choose Find from the Start menu, the submenu shown in Figure 7-1 appears. Your choice here determines the type of object Find will search for. Because most of the time you're likely to be hunting down files and folders, we'll begin with an overview of that branch of the Find facility. Later in the chapter we'll look at the use of Find for locating computers.

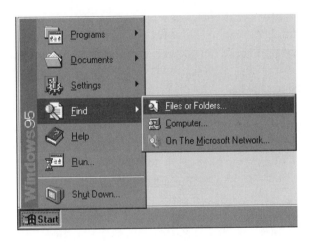

FIGURE 7-1.

When you choose Find from the Start menu, it first asks you to tell it what kind of object you're looking for.

Telling Find Where to Search

After you choose Files Or Folders from the submenu shown in Figure 7-1, the dialog box shown in Figure 7-2 on the next page appears. Notice there are two text boxes with associated drop-down arrows here. The second of these, marked Look In, is already filled out with the name of the disk on which your Windows system files are stored. This is the default search area for a file-and-folder search initiated from the Start menu.

FIGURE 7-2.

When you choose Find from the Start menu, the program proposes to search the disk on which your Windows system files are stored.

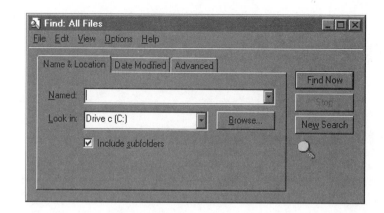

To change the contents of the Look In line, click the drop-down arrow at the right side of that line. The list that emerges includes My Computer, an entry for each local hard disk, an entry for each local floppy disk, an entry for each local CD-ROM drive, and an entry for each network drive that you have mapped to a local drive letter. These are all local resources, and they're also all top-level options. That is, if you choose drive D from this list, Find searches all of drive D.

If you want to search an unmapped network server or restrict the search to a particular folder, click the Browse button instead of the Look In drop-down arrow. Find then displays an outline of your entire namespace, exactly as you might see in the left pane of a Windows Explorer window. Select the folder where you want to begin the search, and then click OK.

By default, Find searches the disk or folder specified on the Look In line, plus all the subfolders of that disk or folder. If you don't want to search the subfolders, deselect the Include Subfolders check box.

For information about *mapping network drives*, see "Mapping a Network Folder to a Drive Letter," page 187.

For information about *namespace*, see "The Windows 95 Namespace," page 117.

Telling Find What to Search For

You can use any of the following criteria, singly or in combination, when searching for files and folders:

- Name
- Most recent modification date
- File type
- File size
- File content

If you use a combination of criteria, Find ferrets out only those items that meet *all* criteria.

Tip When you finish a search, Find retains your search criteria in case you want to perform another search based on similar criteria. If you want to start a brand new search, it's a good idea to click the New Search button. That way you won't inadvertently reuse a criterion from your previous search.

Searching by Name

To specify a search by name, click the Name & Location tab (if this tab isn't already selected) and enter the appropriate text on the Named line. If the name you're looking for is one you've recently used in a search, you can save yourself some typing by clicking the drop-down arrow at the right side of the Named line and selecting the text from the ensuing list.

You can search by name without knowing exactly how the item you want is spelled. If you know any part of it, enter that part on the Named line. Find locates all items whose names include the letters you type. For example, if you simply type *Sales* on the Named line, Find locates items with names such as Quarter 1 Sales, Quarter 2 Sales, Sales Forecast, Salespersons, and Sales Tax.

Using Wildcards A *wildcard* is a character used as a proxy for one or more other characters. If you're an MS-DOS veteran, you may be accustomed to using wildcards in directory searches. You'll be glad to know the same wildcards also work with filename searches conducted by the Find command. The two wildcards recognized by Find are ? and *.

The question mark represents any single character. For example, specifying

```
199?
```

would get you any file or folder that included any year from 1990 to 1999 in its name, as well as files and folders that included 199 followed by any other character. You can use as many question-mark wildcards in a specification as you want.

The asterisk represents any single character or combination of characters. For example, searching for

```
1*4
```

might turn up 123r4, 1994, 1024, and so on. The most common use for the asterisk wildcard is to find all files with a common extension. For example, to find all files with the extension .XLS, you can enter

```
*.xls
```

on the Named line. If you simply entered *xls* without the wildcard and period, you would get, in addition to all the files with the extension .XLS, all files with "xls" anywhere else in their names. An alternative way to find all files with a certain extension is to use the search-by-file-type option. But the search-by-file-type option is useful only for file types that are recorded in your Windows registry. For extensions that are not in the registry, the wildcard approach is ideal.

 See Also: For information about *the search-by-file-type option*, see "Searching by File Type," page 200.

For information about *the registry*, see "Working with the File Types List," page 155.

Searching by Most Recent Modification Date

To use the most recent modification date as a search criterion, click the Find dialog's Date Modified tab. That takes you to the dialog box shown in Figure 7-3. Note that all the options here apply both to files that were *created*

Interrupting a Search

Once the item or items you're looking for appear in the Find window, there's no need to sit on your hands while Find continues searching. You can halt the search at any time by clicking the Stop button.

Alternatively, you can begin working with an item in the Find window while the search goes on. Simply select any item in the window and use it any way you like. You can right-click the item to get its object menu, double-click it to open it (if it's a document) or run it (if it's a program), drag it somewhere if you want to copy it or make a shortcut from it, and so on.

within a particular time interval and to files that were last *modified* during that interval. Find does not have the ability to locate files that were most recently accessed (but not modified) within a certain timeframe.

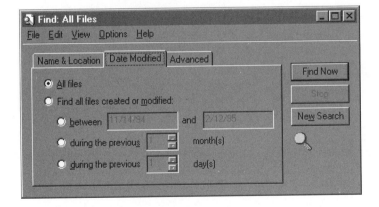

FIGURE 7-3.

You can search for files or folders last modified during a particular time interval.

The modification-date options are commonly used in conjunction with other specifications. For example, if you want to locate all Microsoft Word documents that were created or modified within the last seven days, you can select Microsoft Word Document in the Advanced tab (see "Searching by File Type," on the next page) and also select "during the previous 7 days" in the Date Modified tab. To set the latter criterion, click the "during the previous day(s)" option button (the one with the under-lined *d*), and then use the day spinner to enter the number 7.

Note that when you tell Find to locate all objects last modified dur-ing the previous *n* days, that means the previous *n* days plus all of today. For example, if you ask Find to locate all files modified during the previ-ous 1 day, it finds everything that was changed yesterday plus anything that was changed today.

Searching by File Type

To search for a particular kind of file, or to restrict the search to folders only, click the Advanced tab. That brings up the dialog box shown in Fig-ure 7-4.

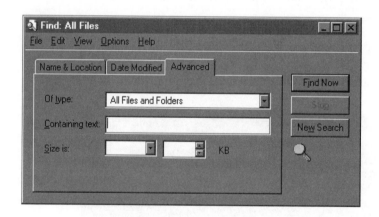

The default type specification, shown in Figure 7-4, is All Files And Folders. To narrow the search to a particular type, click the drop-down arrow on the Of Type line, and select from the ensuing list. Note that the drop-down list includes some general categories, as well as the various document types known to your registry. For example, to search for pro-grams, choose Application. To search for folders, excluding documents and programs, choose Folders, and so on.

Searching by File Size

To search for files and folders that are larger than or smaller than a partic-ular size, click the Advanced tab. Then, in the dialog box shown in Figure 7-4, click the drop-down arrow on the Size Is line. A two-item list unfolds, giving a choice of At Least and At Most. If you're looking for files smaller than some threshold amount, choose At Most. Otherwise, choose At Least. Finally, type the size threshold in the KB text box, or manipulate its spinner to indicate the size you're interested in.

Searching by File Content

To search for files containing some particular text, click the Advanced tab. Then type the text you're looking for on the Containing Text line. Note that the text you type is treated literally—that is, you cannot use wildcards on the Containing Text line. Also be aware that searching for files by their content takes much longer than searching by name, modification date, type, or size. To avoid unnecessarily lengthy searches, restrict the search as much as is practical. For example, if you're looking for a Microsoft Excel spreadsheet with a particular number or phrase in it, restrict the file type to Excel documents and, if all the likely possibilities are stored in a certain folder, enter that folder name on the Look In line.

Making a Search Case Sensitive Content searches ignore case by default. If you're sure how the text you're looking for is capitalized, you might want to make the search case sensitive. To do that, simply pull down the Options menu and choose Case Sensitive. A check will appear beside the command name, indicating that the next search will be case sensitive.

If you turn on the case-sensitive option, all your searches will be case sensitive until you turn the option off again. Also be aware that, although you can turn this option on or off while Find is searching, your change doesn't take effect until the next search.

Finding a Network Server

To look for a particular computer on the network, right-click the Network Neighborhood icon and choose Find Computer. Or choose Find on the Start menu and Computer on the submenu that appears. Either way, you'll come to the dialog box shown in Figure 7-5 on the next page.

Note that the Find Computer dialog box does not include a Look In line. That's because Find assumes that when you're looking for a particular server, you want to scan your entire network.

FIGURE 7-5.

The Find command can help you locate a server in the vast expanse of your network.

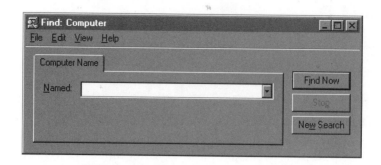

Working with Search Results

As the Find command searches, it presents its findings in the bottom half of an expanded window, as shown in Figure 7-6. Here you can work with found items exactly as though they were in an ordinary folder window. For example, you can click the column headings (Name, In Folder, Size, and so on) to change the sorting order of the found items, or use commands on the View menu to switch from the default details view to an icon or list view. You can also right-click any item and then choose Properties to inspect the item's property sheet or choose Quick View to take a peek at the item without opening its parent application (if a quick viewer is available for that file type). You can double-click an item to open it, or right-drag an item to the desktop or to another folder to copy, move, or create a shortcut for the selected item.

In addition, the Find command's File menu includes one handy command not found in folder windows: Open Containing Folder. By selecting an item and choosing this command, Windows opens the selected item's folder window, allowing you to navigate immediately to the folder in which the item is stored.

 See Also: For more information about *working with items in a folder window,* see "Running Programs and Opening Documents from Folders," page 62, and Chapter 4, "Working with Folders," page 115.

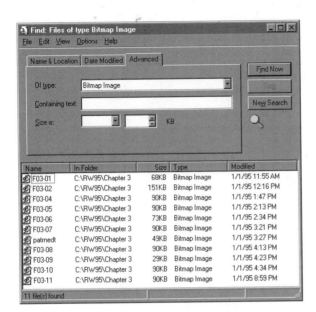

FIGURE 7-6.

The Find command presents its findings in the lower part of an expanded Find window.

Saving Search Results

To preserve the criteria used in a Find operation for reuse after you close the Find dialog box, pull down the File menu and choose Save Search. To preserve the current search results as well as the criteria, first choose Save Results from the Options menu. Then choose Save Search from the File menu. With results or without, Find creates an icon on your desktop and assigns that icon a default name. For example, if you ask Find to locate all folders whose names include the word *personal*, and then save the results of that search, your new desktop icon will be called something like *Files of type Folder named personal*. Because the default name is long and not always completely descriptive (it will not, for example, include modification-date specifications), you'll probably want to assign your own name to the new icon. You can do that by right-clicking and choosing Rename.

The Save Search command puts an icon on your desktop, regardless of whether you invoked the Find command from the Start menu or from the object menu of a folder. But the icon itself represents an ordinary document file, and you may copy it, move it, or create a shortcut to it, just as you can any other document file.

To reuse a saved set of search criteria, double-click the desktop icon and click Find Now.

8

Installing and Using Fonts

ne of the great advantages of creating text documents in a graphical operating environment such as Windows 95 is that you can employ a variety of fonts and typographical styles and judge their impact before committing your work to paper. Within limits, and with some exceptions, what you see on screen is what you'll get from any output device, whether it be a dot-matrix printer, a laser printer, a plotter, or a fax machine.

Windows puts typography at your disposal. Using it well, however, can be a challenge. To help you meet this challenge, this chapter begins with an overview of basic terminology. Then we'll look at the procedures for adding and deleting fonts, getting better acquainted with the fonts you have, using them in your documents, and using some of the special characters—accented letters, commercial symbols, and so on—that are included with most fonts but can't be accessed with normal typewriter keystrokes.

Terminology

A *font* is a complete set of characters in one size and one typeface. For example, all the letters, numbers, punctuation marks, and other symbols available in 12-point Courier New bold italic constitute one font. The same set of characters in another size constitutes another font.

Fonts are identified by their size, typeface family, weight, and style. In the name "12-point Courier New bold italic," for example, 12-point is the size, Courier New is the typeface family, bold is the weight, and italic is the style. When the weight is "normal" and the style is "roman," these terms are usually omitted.

Font Size

A font's size is usually measured in points and expressed as a "point size." A *point* is a printer's measurement, equal to $\frac{1}{12}$ of a *pica*. (A pica, in turn, is approximately $\frac{1}{6}$ of an inch, so there are about 72 points in an inch.) A font's point size is approximately the distance in points from the top of its highest character to the bottom of its lowest character, as shown in Figure 8-1 on the next page. (This definition applies to a font's printed size only. On screen, point size has no absolute significance at all because of the differences in screen size and resolution. For example, a 10-point font on a

16-inch screen at 640×480 resolution will probably be larger than a 12-point font on a 14-inch screen at 800×600 resolution.)

FIGURE 8-1.

A font's point size is a measure of its height—from the top of its highest character to the bottom of its lowest.

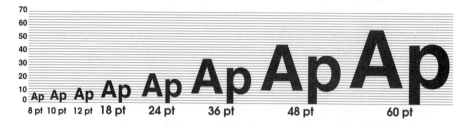

Point size is a rough measure of a font's height but says nothing about its width. Many font families come in *compressed* and *expanded* variants, as well as normal width. Some programs, such as desktop publishing programs and sophisticated word processors, allow you to squeeze characters closer together without changing their individual widths. This process, called *kerning*, can change the apparent width of a font, creating a denser look and allowing you to put more words on a line. Some programs also allow you to add extra increments of space between characters, a process called *letterspacing*.

Style and Weight

The most common *style* variants for fonts are roman and italic. Roman characters are the "normal" kind, with vertical strokes predominating. Italic characters, which are forward slanting and often more rounded, are used for emphasis, for book titles, and so on.

The term *weight* refers to the thickness of a font's strokes. The most common weights are normal (also called regular) and bold, but some font families also include other weights, such as thin, light, heavy, ultra, and black.

Serif and Sans Serif Fonts

Most fonts fall into one of two categories—*serif* or *sans serif*. Serif fonts have fine lines that finish off the main strokes—for example, at the bottom of a capital *T* and the ends of the *T*'s crossbar. These "finishing strokes," called serifs, are absent in sans serif fonts. Serif fonts, such as Times New Roman, are generally considered more suitable for conventional text, such as that in a newspaper or book. Sans serif fonts, such as Helvetica and Arial, have a more modern appearance and are often used in headlines, tabular material (such as spreadsheet reports), and advertising.

Monospaced and Proportionally Spaced Fonts

Fonts in which every character takes up the same amount of space are called *monospaced*. Fonts in which some characters (such as *m* and *w*) are wider than others (*i* and *t*, for example) are called *proportionally spaced*. (See Figure 8-2.) Proportionally spaced fonts produce a more typeset appearance and are generally considered easier to read. Monospaced fonts are often preferred for such things as legal documents, which have traditionally been produced on typewriters.

**Microsoft
Windows 95**

Proportionally
spaced

`Microsoft
Windows 95`

Monospaced

FIGURE 8-2.
In proportionally spaced fonts, characters have different widths. In monospaced fonts, all characters have the same width.

Arial and Times New Roman are examples of proportionally spaced fonts. The most commonly used monospaced font is Courier.

Keep in mind that although the widths of letters in a proportionally spaced font vary, the widths of numerals are usually all the same so that numbers can be aligned in tables.

Scalable and Nonscalable Fonts

Fonts can also be described as *scalable* or *nonscalable*. Scalable fonts are those for which a single master can produce any point size. Nonscalable fonts are designed for use at particular sizes; enlarging or reducing them generally produces unattractive distortions, such as serrated diagonal lines and jagged curves.

Nonscalable fonts are also sometimes called *bitmap fonts* because the form in which they're stored on your hard disk (or in a printer's read-only memory) records the relative position of each dot comprising each character. For example, a capital *I* might be stored as a column of 12 dots plus two 6-dot crossbars. To generate a character from a bitmap font, your screen or printer simply reproduces the bitmap at the desired location.

Scalable fonts are sometimes called *outline fonts* because they are stored as a collection of outlines; an outline is a mathematical description of each character. To generate a character from an outline font, font-management software uses a process called *scan conversion* to convert the outlines to bitmaps, which are then reproduced on your screen or printer. To avoid jagged lines and other distortions in the final rendering, particularly at smaller point sizes, the font-management software employs *hints*— algorithms that modify the scan-conversion process to produce optimal-looking characters.

Because outline fonts are stored as mathematical descriptions, they can be scaled to a wide range of point sizes. They can also be slanted, rotated, compressed, extended, inverted, and otherwise manipulated. Their *metrics* (character-width specifications) can also be modified to produce kerned or letterspaced typography. The one small disadvantage of outline fonts is that the scan-conversion process takes a modest amount of processing time. The first time you use an outline font at a given point size, therefore, you might encounter a slight delay while your system performs the calculation required to convert the font's outline into the appropriate set of bitmaps. After the bitmaps have been rendered, however, they're stored in an area of memory called a *cache*. When you need to reuse the font, Windows simply grabs the bitmaps out of the cache, thereby avoiding the original calculation delay.

Fonts Supplied with Windows

Incorporated into Windows 95 is a scalable font technology called True-Type. Along with this font-management technology, Windows includes five TrueType typeface families—Arial, Times New Roman, Courier New, Symbol, and Wingdings. Arial is a sans serif typeface similar to Helvetica. Times New Roman is a serif face similar to Times Roman. Courier New is a mono-spaced serif face. Symbol is a serif face consisting of the Greek alphabet plus a few mathematical and phonetic symbols. Wingdings is a collection of icons, symbols, and "dingbat" characters that you can use to enliven your documents.

In addition to the five TrueType families, Windows also includes three sets of bitmap fonts—MS Serif, MS Sans Serif, and Courier—to provide compatibility with earlier versions of Windows. (MS Serif was previously known as Helv, and MS Serif is the former TmsRmn.) They're available only in certain point sizes, and you can't use them with laser printers.

Along with this assortment of font resources, you might find additional fonts on your system, courtesy of particular applications that you have installed. Some Microsoft applications, for example, use a nonscalable font called Small Fonts for generating print previews. Any font installed by an application is available not only in that program but also in any other Windows-based program you run.

Your Printer's Own Font Resources

In addition to the fonts that Windows supplies and any additional fonts that you install in Windows, you can use your printer's internal fonts. Your printer driver tells Windows which fonts the printer provides, and those fonts appear in the Font dialog boxes used by your applications.

When you use your printer's internal fonts, Windows doesn't have to download font information or turn each page of your document into a bitmap (a time-consuming process), so printing is likely to be quicker. In exchange for this speed increase, however, you might have to sacrifice some degree of correspondence between the appearance of your document on screen and its appearance on paper.

When you format a document with an internal printer font, Windows displays the same font on screen if it can. If Windows does not have a screen font to match the printer font you select, it gives you the closest match that it can. For example, if you choose the Courier font that's built into your printer, Windows formats your text on screen using its own True-Type Courier font (Courier New). If you select your PostScript printer's Avant Garde font (and you have not installed Adobe Type Manager and the Avant Garde screen font), Windows uses Arial, the nearest TrueType equivalent, on screen.

Even when the screen font used by Windows doesn't exactly match the printer font you select, Windows-based applications attempt to show you where your lines will break on the printed page. The correspondence of line endings on screen to line endings on paper might not always be perfect, however, and some applications do a better job of this than others. If precise text positioning is critical, it's always best to avoid printer fonts that don't have equivalent screen fonts.

See Also: For information about *printer drivers*, see "Installing a New Printer," page 237.

Viewing and Printing Font Samples

To see samples of the fonts installed in your system, start by opening the Fonts folder, which is stored in your Windows folder. The easiest way to open the folder is to double-click its shortcut in Control Panel. To open Control Panel, choose Settings from the Start menu, and then choose Control Panel. Figure 8-3 shows an example of a Fonts folder.

FIGURE 8-3.

To see samples of your fonts, install new fonts, or delete fonts, open your Fonts folder.

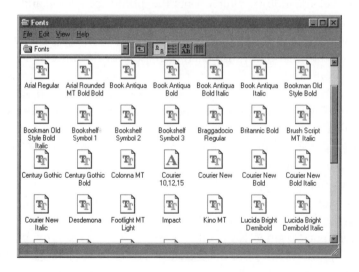

NOTE: PostScript fonts rendered by Adobe Type Manager do not appear in your Fonts folder. To see samples of these fonts, use Adobe Type Manager.

The icons with two *T*s represent TrueType fonts; those with an *A* represent nonscalable fonts. The point sizes for which these nonscalable fonts were designed are usually included with the font name.

To see a sample of any font, simply double-click its icon—or right-click the icon and choose Open from the object menu. As Figure 8-4 shows, the ensuing window displays the font at various point sizes.

To print the font sample, click the Print button.

FIGURE 8-4.

Double-clicking a font icon produces a printable sample of the font at various point sizes.

Viewing Options in the Fonts Folder

Like an ordinary file folder window, the Fonts folder offers icon, list, and details views of your font library. You can choose these options from the toolbar or the View menu. In addition, the Fonts folder offers two other viewing options: List Fonts By Similarity and Hide Variations. These options are also available on the View menu.

The List Fonts By Similarity option lets you find all the fonts in your library that are similar to some other font. As Figure 8-5 on the next page shows, when you choose this option, a drop-down list of your fonts appears below the toolbar. Your font library appears in the window listed in order of decreasing similarity to the font selected in the drop-down list.

FIGURE 8-5.

In this "similarity" view, fonts are listed in order of decreasing similarity to Arial Italic.

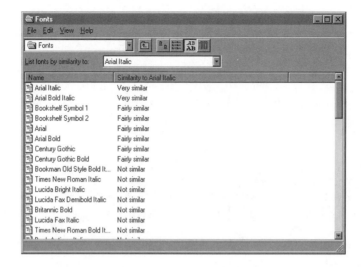

If you choose Hide Variations, Windows displays only one font from each font family. For example, suppose your Fonts folder includes Arial, Arial Bold, Arial Italic, and Arial Bold Italic. If you choose Hide Variations, the list shows only Arial. This option, which you may use in any viewing mode, is particularly handy when you have a large font library.

Adding Fonts

Scalable TrueType fonts, in addition to the ones supplied with Windows, are available from Microsoft and numerous other vendors. You can also download fonts from electronic bulletin boards and information services such as CompuServe. When you acquire an additional font, you need to install it so that Windows knows it's available.

To install a new font, simply open the Fonts folder and choose Install New Font from the File menu. You'll be greeted by the Add Fonts dialog box, shown in Figure 8-6.

Use the Drives and Directories sections of this dialog box to indicate where the fonts you want to install are currently stored. For example, if your new fonts are on a floppy disk in drive A, choose drive A in the Drives list. The names of all fonts available for installation will then appear in the top section of the dialog box. Choose Select All if you want

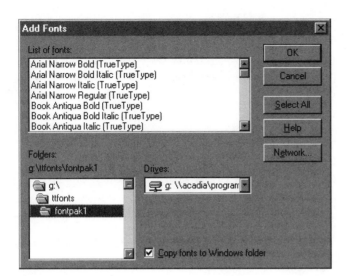

FIGURE 8-6.

The Add Fonts dialog box makes it easy to expand your font library.

to install the whole lot. To install particular fonts, hold down the Ctrl key while you select the fonts you want.

When you're finished selecting fonts, click OK. In a moment your new fonts will appear in your Fonts folder and will be available for use in your applications.

 You can also use drag and drop to add fonts to your system. For example, if you have a new font stored in a folder named Download, you can install that font as follows: Display both the Download folder and the Fonts folder. Then drag the font icon from the Download folder to the Fonts folder.

To Copy or Not to Copy?

If you're installing fonts from a floppy disk, be sure to select the Copy Fonts To Windows Folder check box in the Add Fonts dialog box. Windows then copies your font files to the Fonts folder, a hidden subfolder of your Windows folder. If the fonts you're installing are already stored in another folder on your hard disk, Windows will duplicate your font files in the Fonts folder.

If you prefer to keep your fonts in other folders (for example, in a folder that you use for downloading files from an information service), you can do so. Simply deselect the Copy Fonts To Windows Folder check box. Windows will remember which folder you installed your fonts from, and, provided you don't rename or move that folder, your fonts will still be available to your applications.

 It's always a good idea to select the Copy Fonts To Windows Folder check box. That way, you're unlikely to delete font files inadvertently.

Deleting Fonts

To "deinstall" a font, simply remove it from your Fonts folder. You can do that by deleting the font icon or by moving the icon to another folder. If you delete a font icon, Windows stores the font in your Recycle Bin, so you can restore it if you change your mind.

Using Fonts in Documents

To use fonts in your documents, simply follow standard Windows editing procedures: select the text you want to format, and then choose your application's Font command. (You'll find it on the Format menu in most applications.) In many programs you can also select fonts by right-clicking the selected text and choosing Font from the object menu that appears, or by clicking icons on a toolbar.

In many programs, choosing the Font command brings you to a dialog box similar to the one shown in Figure 8-7. This dialog box, shown here in the form used by WordPad, is one of the Windows "common dialogs," so you can expect to see close approximations of it in many of the newer applications for Windows. Notice that you can use it to choose color and two special effects, strikeout and underlining, in addition to typeface, style, and point size.

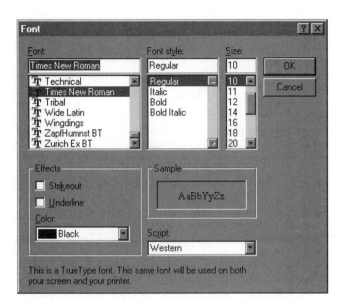

FIGURE 8-7.

The Font common dialog box lets you choose typeface, style, point size, color, and special effects.

For information about *the Script drop-down in the Font dialog box*, see "Installing Language Support and Using Keyboard Layouts," page 296.

Embedding TrueType Fonts

If you create documents that will be read on other computers, it's a good idea to stick with fonts that all your readers are likely to have. The safest ones to use are Arial, Courier New, and Times New Roman—the sans serif, monospaced, and serif faces shipped with Windows.

What happens if a reader's system does not have one of the fonts used by your document? For example, suppose you've formatted your entire report in Bozo Bold, but you're the only one in your company who's installed the Bozo family? In that case, Windows substitutes a closely related font on your reader's system. For example, assuming Bozo is a serif face, your reader will probably see Times New Roman on his or her computer. (You can get an idea what fonts Windows considers "similar" by opening your Fonts folder and using the View menu's List Fonts By Similarity command.)

If it's crucial that all readers see your document in the exact fonts you've used, check to see if the application you used to create the document supports TrueType font embedding. If the program can embed the TrueType fonts your document uses, your document will include a copy of the font file for each TrueType font you use. Your readers will then see your document with its original fonts. And, unless the document has read-only status, they'll be able to edit with those fonts as well.

Note that embedding TrueType fonts adds greatly to the size of your document. A 5-KB report, for example, might easily grow to 50 KB with only one font embedded. If you use italics and boldface, along with regular roman, your document could swell another 100 KB or so. Although most TrueType fonts can be embedded, font manufacturers can disable that capability. Therefore, always check to make sure a font is embeddable before you do any work that depends on this capability. (You can tell if your font is being embedded by comparing the size of the same document saved with and without embedding.)

If you're using Microsoft Word 6.0 or 7.0, you can turn embedding on by choosing the Options command from the Tools menu, clicking the Save tab, and selecting the Embed TrueType Fonts check box. Note that this setting is file-specific—that is, changing it for one document does not affect other documents.

 To see if a program offers TrueType embedding, use the program's Help facility's Search command to search for "TrueType."

Note that TrueType embedding has nothing to do with OLE. A program that supports OLE may or may not offer TrueType embedding, and one that offers TrueType embedding may or may not support OLE.

Fonts and Character Sets

Most Windows fonts use a common character layout known as the eight-bit American National Standards Institute (ANSI) character set. This is simply a table in which each character in the font is mapped to a particular number from 0 through 255. Because characters in your documents are recorded using their ANSI numbers, and because most fonts use the ANSI scheme, switching text from one font to another usually produces no change in the identity of the characters.

You should be aware, however, that the ANSI character set used by most Windows fonts is not the same as the "extended ASCII" character set used by most MS-DOS–based applications. The letters *A* through *Z* in uppercase and lowercase, the numerals 0 through 9, and the common punctuation symbols are mapped to the same values in both ANSI and extended ASCII. But the two systems diverge widely for accented letters and other special symbols.

When you copy text to the Clipboard from most Windows-based programs, the text is stored on the Clipboard in at least two formats, called Text and OEM Text. The inclusion of the OEM Text format, in most cases, allows you to copy symbols from a Windows-based application to the Clipboard, and then to paste those symbols (unchanged) into an MS-DOS–based application.

For example, if you copy the letter *a* with a circumflex accent from Word for Windows to the Clipboard, and then paste this character into an MS-DOS–based program, you will still get an *â* in your MS-DOS–based application—even though this character is mapped to the value 226 in the ANSI character set and the value 131 in the extended ASCII set. Windows takes care of the translation for you. A similar conversion process takes place automatically when you copy text via the Clipboard from an MS-DOS–based program to a Windows-based program.

For more information about *using the Clipboard to copy text,* see "What the Cut, Copy, Paste, and Paste Special Commands Do," page 257.

Using Character Map

Character Map, one of the accessory programs included with Windows, is a utility that shows you the character set of each of your fonts. You'll find Character Map invaluable when you need to work with a non-ANSI font (such as Symbol or Wingdings), and when you need accented letters, commercial symbols, and other characters that are not available on the standard typewriter keys of your keyboard. Character Map's initial display is shown in Figure 8-8.

FIGURE 8-8.

Character Map helps you find and use special characters in any font.

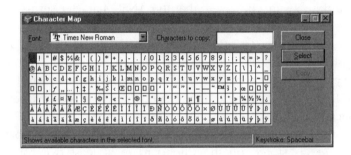

> **NOTE:** If Character Map has not been set up on your computer, double-click the Add/Remove Programs item in Control Panel, click the Windows Setup tab, select Accessories, and click the Details button. Select Character Map and click OK two times.

In the top left corner of the window is a drop-down list in which you can select any font available on your system. Below the list is a table displaying all the characters available in the selected font. You can't change the size of the Character Map window (other than to minimize it), but you can get an enlarged view of any character by selecting it with the mouse or the keyboard.

To select a character with the mouse, simply click the character. To select a character with the keyboard, press Tab until the highlight is in the character grid. Then use the arrow keys to move the highlight. Figure 8-9 shows how Character Map looks when the copyright symbol in the True-Type font Times New Roman is selected.

The panel in the lower right corner of the Character Map window tells you how you can produce any character using the keyboard. For example, in Figure 8-9, the panel reads "Keystroke: Alt+0169." This means

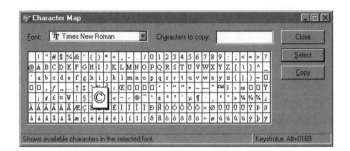

FIGURE 8-9.

To get an enlarged view of any character, simply select it.

that in most Windows-based applications, you can get a copyright symbol in Times New Roman by doing the following:

1. Use your program's formatting commands to specify Times New Roman as your font.

2. Hold down the Alt key.

3. Type *0169* on the numeric keypad (not on the row of numbers at the top of your keyboard).

4. Release the Alt key.

If you don't want to type Alt-key sequences, you can generate special characters with the help of Character Map's Select and Copy commands. For example, you can enter a copyright symbol or another character in your document by doing the following:

1. Be sure the Characters To Copy box (in the upper right corner of the Character Map window) is blank. If it is not blank, clear it by selecting whatever is currently there and pressing the Del key.

2. Use the mouse or keyboard to select the copyright symbol or other character in the main part of the Character Map window.

3. Click the Select button or press Enter.
   As an alternative to steps 2 and 3, you can simply double-click the copyright symbol.

4. Click the Copy button to copy the contents of the Characters To Copy box to the Clipboard.

5. Activate your word processor or other application and use its Paste command.

You can use this method to copy more than one character at a time. Each time you click the Select button, Character Map adds the current character to the end of the character sequence in the Characters To Copy text box.

9

Installing, Configuring, and Using Your Printers

A check of your printer's properties may reveal options and features you didn't know you had.

When it comes to translating your work from the computer screen to the printed page, Windows 95 provides a wealth of support. The operating system's printing features let you (or your system administrator) do the following things, among others:

- Print in the background to any local or shared network printer

- Print in the background from MS-DOS–based applications as well as from Windows-based applications

- Examine the print queues for any local or shared network printer so that you can choose the printer that's likely to get your job done soonest

- Control the position of documents in print queues, or remove documents from queues

- Create multiple logical printers for any physical output device, assigning different characteristics to each logical printer

In this chapter, we'll explore these and other features.

 See Also: For information about *faxing*, see Chapter 24, "Using Microsoft Fax," page 641.

Goodbye Print Manager, Hello Printers Folder

Unlike earlier versions of Windows, Windows 95 does not include a Print Manager. In its place is a system folder called *Printers*. All the functionality that was provided by the Windows 3.x Print Manager is now available via the Printers folder.

To get to the Printers folder, choose Settings from the Start menu. Then choose Printers. (Alternatively, open the My Computer folder and double-click the folder icon labeled Printers.) Figure 9-1 on the next page shows an example of a typical Printers folder.

The Printers folder looks and acts like any other folder window. You can choose to display or not display the toolbar and status bar, display

FIGURE 9-1.

You can find out anything you need to know about your printing resources by opening the Printers folder.

printers as icons or list entries, select browsing and viewing options from the View menu, and use standard navigation techniques to move from this folder to any other folder on your system.

Within the Printers folder, you'll find entries for each printer you've installed, including local printers and printers attached to network servers. If you or your system administrator chose to have the Windows Setup program install the Microsoft Fax service, you'll find an icon for that service alongside your printer icons. And, finally, your Printers folder includes an icon labeled Add Printer, which you can use to install new printers.

Windows uses the following icons to distinguish various kinds of printers from one another:

   A printer attached to your own computer

   A printer attached to a network server

   A printer attached to your computer but made available to other network users

   A printer attached to your computer but set up to redirect output to a disk file

To view or change the properties of any printer, right-click its icon and choose Properties.

To inspect or modify the contents of a printer's queue, double-click the printer's icon, or right-click it and choose Open.

See Also: For information about *folders*, see Chapter 4, "Working with Folders," page 115.

For information about *printer properties*, see "Inspecting and Setting Printer Properties," page 244.

For information about *print queues*, see "Inspecting and Managing a Print Queue," page 236.

How Do I Print Thee?
(Let Me Count the Ways)

In Windows, there is nearly always more than one way to accomplish a task. Printing is no exception. Here are three ways to transport information from an application to your printer:

- Use your application's Print command.

- Drag a file and drop it on a printer icon.

- Right-click a file and use the Send To command.

Printing from an Application

If the document you want to print is already open, the simplest way to print it is to pull down the File menu and choose Print. Or simply click the Print icon on the application's toolbar—if it has a toolbar with a print icon. The toolbar approach typically bypasses all dialog boxes and sends your entire document to the current default printer. The *default printer*, as its name suggests, is the one that Windows uses unless you tell it to do otherwise.

What if you want to print to a different printer? In that case, you have a couple of choices. You can change the default printer (see "Setting or Changing the Default Printer," page 235), or you can use a menu command to select a different device.

Selecting a Printer

Figure 9-2 shows the dialog box for the Print command used by most applications. (This is one of the "common dialogs" that are part of Windows 95.) This dialog box, or something very similar to it, is what you are most likely to see when you print from a newer Windows-based application. The drop-down list near the top indicates the name of the printer that will be used when you click OK. The Status line below the drop-down tells you whether this printer is the default device and whether it is ready. Opening the drop-down reveals a list of all installed printers. Simply select the name of the printer you want to use from this list.

FIGURE 9-2.

The common Print dialog box lets you select a printer and set options without changing system defaults.

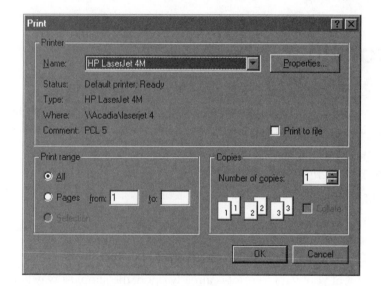

 The Status line in the common Print dialog box provides useful information about the printer selected in the Name list. In Figure 9-2, for example, the Status line reports that the printer named HP LaserJet 4M is ready. If HP LaserJet 4M were busy, the Status line would tell you how many jobs were currently in its queue. By scrolling through the Name list and checking the status of each printer, you can determine which one has the shortest queue.

In some programs, you might find the list of printers in a dialog box labeled Choose Printer, Printer Setup, or something similar. Sometimes this dialog box is accessible via a button in the Print dialog box; in other cases, you get to it via a separate File-menu command. In any event, most Windows programs provide some mechanism for selecting a printer other than the default printer.

A few programs, particularly simple applications that handle unformatted text only, do not allow you to select a printer. To print to a different device from an application such as this, you'll need to visit the Printers folder and change the default. (See "Setting or Changing the Default Printer," page 235.)

How Much to Print?

In addition to letting you select a printer, the common Print dialog box lets you set options for that printer. For example, you can specify whether you want to print all of your document, only a range of pages, or only the portion of your document that's currently selected.

Printing Multiple Copies

The common Print dialog box also lets you indicate the number of copies you want and whether you want multiple copies collated. If you don't collate, Windows prints all copies of your first page, followed by all copies of your second, and so on. If you collate, you'll get all pages of your first copy, followed by all pages of your next copy, and so on.

 In earlier versions of Windows, it was considerably quicker to print multiple copies uncollated than collated. In Windows 95, uncollated printing is still quicker but often insignificantly so. In any case, the difference in printing time is trivial compared to the amount of time it takes to collate copies by hand. Therefore, it's usually best to select the Collate check box when printing multiple copies.

NOTE: Some applications and drivers for some printers do not support multiple copies and collating.

Switching Between Portrait and Landscape Orientation

The common Print dialog box does not include an orientation option. In many applications you can switch between portrait orientation (in which the printed sheet is taller than it is wide) and landscape orientation (the opposite) by choosing a Page Setup command from the File menu. This command (or something similarly named) also typically allows you to set margins and choose paper size and source.

You can also change orientation by modifying your printer's property sheet. You can view the property sheet by clicking the Properties button in the common Print dialog box. When you change the property sheet, however, your change affects all subsequent printouts. If you want just a particular document printed in landscape instead of portrait orientation, it's better to use your program's Page Setup command.

 See Also: For more information about *property sheets*, see "Inspecting and Setting Printer Properties," page 244.

Changing Resolution

Resolution is a measure of the density at which a printer puts dots on paper. High resolutions, such as 300 or 600 dots per inch (dpi), produce smoother, higher-quality output but require longer printing times. Lower-resolution settings, such as 75 dpi, produce draft-quality output. Generally speaking, resolution is an issue associated with graphics printing; therefore, you probably won't find an option for setting resolution anywhere within your word processor's printing and page-layout dialog boxes. Your graphics programs may offer such an option, however.

You can also change resolution by modifying your printer's property sheet. A change here affects all future printouts.

Drag and Drop Printing

If the document you want to print is not open, you can double-click its icon in a folder or Windows Explorer window, and then use the Print command in its parent application. But you don't need to do this. Another way to print that document is to grab its icon and then drag it to a printer icon. However, this method works only with documents that are associated with

While a print job that you initiate remains in a print queue, a printer icon is displayed in the taskbar notification area, just to the left of the clock. When that icon disappears, you know that all your print jobs have finished. If you want to check the status of your print jobs, you can double-click that printer icon to open the folder for the printer you're using and inspect that printer's queue. For more information about print queues, see "Inspecting and Managing a Print Queue," page 236.

their parent application in your Windows registry. If you try it with an unregistered document type, you'll get an error message.

To print a document, you can drag it to the printer icon with either mouse button. (If you drag with the right button, choose Print Here from the object menu that appears when you release the button.) As you reach the drop zone, the printer icon darkens and your document icon sprouts a plus sign to indicate that you are copying data to the printer (as opposed to moving it there permanently).

When you drop a document onto a printer icon, Windows loads the parent application and executes its print command. Depending on the application, you may or may not have to respond to a dialog box before printing begins. As soon as the information has been transferred to the print queue, the application closes.

Although you can print by dragging a document icon to a printer icon in your Printers folder, you'll probably find it more convenient to create a desktop shortcut for each printer you plan to use this way. To create a desktop printer shortcut, open your Printers folder, right-drag the printer's icon, and release the mouse button on your desktop. From the object menu, choose Create Shortcut(s) Here.

For information about the *registry and associating documents with applications*, see "Working with the File Types List," page 155.

Printing with the Send To Command

If you don't like cluttering your desktop with printer icons, or if you find it inconvenient to make those icons visible when you want to print, try using the Send To command. Simply right-click the icon for the document you want to print, choose Send To from the object menu, and then choose the name of the printer you want from the Send To menu. If the printer's name isn't on the Send To menu, you can put it there as follows:

1. Open your Printers folder.

2. Open your SendTo folder.

3. Right-drag the printer's icon from the Printers folder to the SendTo folder.

4. Choose Create Shortcut(s) Here from the object menu.

5. Right-click the new icon in the SendTo folder and choose Rename. Delete "Shortcut to" and then press Enter.

When you print with Send To, Windows first opens your document's parent application, just as it does when you drag the document to a printer icon.

For more information about *the SendTo folder,* see "Customizing the Send To Menu," page 146.

Printing from MS-DOS–Based Applications

To print from an MS-DOS–based application running under Windows, simply use that application's normal print procedures. Unless you are running your program in MS-DOS mode, Windows prints your document in the background, just as it would print any Windows document.

See Also: For information about *MS-DOS mode*, see "Running a Program in MS-DOS Mode," page 323.

Printing to a Network Printer

Printing to a network printer is just like printing to a local printer, provided the network printer has been shared (your network administrator should do that for you), you have been given access to it (also a task for your network administrator), and a copy of the printer's driver has been installed on your own computer (something you may need to do yourself). If access to the printer requires a password, you will be prompted for that password when you initiate the print job.

Once the network printer's driver is installed locally, you can print an open document to a network printer using your application's Print command, just as you would for a local printer.

 If your network printer is down, or if you just want to avoid traffic jams during times of peak usage, you can tell Windows to print offline. All your print jobs will then be stored locally. When rush hour is over, you can go back online and have your print jobs transferred to the printer. To print offline, open your Printers folder, right-click the icon for your network printer, and choose Work Offline. While the printer is offline, its icon in your Printers folder is dimmed. To go back online, right-click the printer again and choose Work Offline a second time.

Installing a Local Copy of a Network Printer Driver

If a network printer's driver hasn't been installed on your own system, the printer will not appear in your application's list of available printers. You have to install the driver before you can print an open document to that printer. You can do this with the Add Printer icon in your Printers folder. (See "Installing a New Printer," page 237.) Or you can use drag and drop.

Getting Notification from WinPopup

WinPopup is a little utility that enables network administrators to broadcast messages to network users. It also provides automatic notification to users when network printing jobs are complete. If you have WinPopup running on your system and you send a job to a network printer, WinPopup will pop up to let you know when you can fetch your printout. (Note that Win-Popup does not have to be running on the print server—only on your own machine.)

If you've installed WinPopup, you can run it by using the Start menu's Run command and typing *winpopup*. If you haven't installed it, use the Add/Remove Programs item in Control Panel, click the Windows Setup tab, select Accessories, and click the Details button. You'll find WinPopup among the optional accessory programs.

Drag and Drop Installation of a Network Printer

Here are two ways to install a network printer using drag and drop:

- Find the printer's icon in your Network Neighborhood folder. Then drag that icon to your own Printers folder.

- Find the printer's icon in your Network Neighborhood folder. Then drag a document icon (for a document you want to print) and drop it on the printer icon.

Either way, you'll be greeted by the Add Printer wizard and walked through the steps involved in setting up a local copy of the printer driver. If the computer to which the printer is connected is running Windows 95, these steps are very simple because Windows copies the driver across the network to your own computer. You still need to supply a few details (such as the name by which the printer will be known on your own computer), but most of the information Windows needs is transferred automatically from the network server.

If the computer to which the printer is connected is running Windows NT, Windows for Workgroups, or another operating system, the steps are almost as simple. But you may be prompted to insert one or more floppy disks, or a CD-ROM containing the necessary printer-driver files.

For more information about *installing printer drivers*, see "Installing a New Printer," page 237.

Setting or Changing the Default Printer

Your Printers folder itself does not show you which printer is the default. But you can find out whether any given printer is the default printer by right-clicking its icon. Near the middle of the object menu, you'll see a Set As Default command. (See Figure 9-3.) If a check appears beside that command, the printer you right-clicked is the default.

To change the default to a different printer, right-click the icon for the printer you want to make the default, and then choose Set As Default.

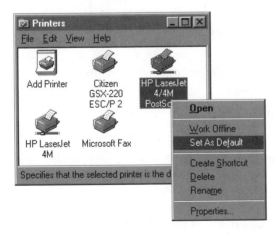

FIGURE 9-3.

To make a printer the default printer, right-click its icon and choose Set As Default. If a check mark appears beside this command, the printer you right-clicked is already the default.

Inspecting and Managing a Print Queue

When you print a document, Windows creates a temporary file, called a *spool file,* on your hard disk (if the printer is local) or the hard disk of the computer to which your network printer is attached. While this file is being created, your application is temporarily busy and unavailable. After the spool file has been created, the print job enters a print queue and you can return to your application while printing continues in the background. If no other jobs are in the queue, your document's spool file is "despooled" to the printer. Otherwise, it waits its turn.

You can check the status of a printer's queue by double-clicking the printer's icon in your Printers folder. Windows displays the print queue in a folder window similar to that shown in Figure 9-4.

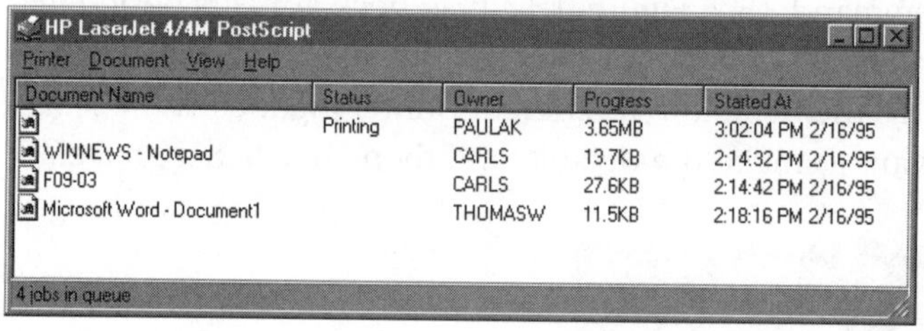

FIGURE 9-4.

Double-clicking a printer icon displays the printer's queue, allowing you to manipulate the flow of jobs to the printer.

Using commands on this folder window's Printer and Document menus, you can do the following:

- Pause and resume printing the entire queue
- Pause and resume individual documents in the queue
- Remove individual documents from the queue
- Purge the entire queue

Pausing and Resuming the Print Queue

To pause an entire print queue, choose the Pause Printing command on the Printer menu. The folder window's title bar then changes to include the word *Paused,* and a check mark appears beside the Pause Printing command. Choose the Pause Printing command a second time to resume printing.

Pausing a Particular Document

To suspend temporarily the printing of a particular document, select that document in the print queue window. Then choose Pause Printing from the Document menu. To resume printing, select the paused document and choose Pause Printing a second time.

If the paused document is at the top of the queue (that is, if Windows was actually printing it when you chose the Pause Printing command), the printer itself will be effectively paused until you resume printing of the document. If the paused document is somewhere else in the queue, lower-priority jobs will be printed ahead of it as long as the document remains paused.

Removing a Document from the Queue

To remove a document from the print queue, select it. Then choose Cancel Printing from the Document menu. Be aware that the print queue has no Undo command. If you change your mind, you'll have to begin the printing process anew.

Removing All Documents from the Queue

To remove all documents from a print queue, simply choose the Purge Print Jobs command from the Printer menu. Use this command with caution! The queue window has no Undo command!

 You can pause a local printer or remove all documents from its queue without opening its queue window. Simply right-click the printer's icon in the Printers folder, and then choose Pause Printing or Purge Print Jobs.

Installing a New Printer

What Windows 95 calls a *printer* is more precisely a constellation of settings applied to an output device. That device may be a traditional printer, a fax modem, a disk file, or perhaps something else altogether. Each combination of settings and output device constitutes a *logical* printer. Each logical printer is treated as though it is a separate device, and is displayed as a separate icon or list entry in your Printers folder. You can install as many logical printers as you like, and you can install multiple logical printers for the same physical output device.

The settings that make up a logical printer include the following:

- The name of the printer

- A *share* name, if the printer is available to other network users

- For shared printers, a description that network users will see when they browse Network Neighborhood in search of a printer (if they use details view)

- The *printer driver*—a software component that enables Windows to translate output into the language used by the physical printer

- Various properties, including the paper tray to be used, the paper size, the amount of memory in the printer, any font cartridges or soft fonts in use, and so on; the available properties vary from printer to printer

- Certain other defaults, such as orientation and resolution

- The port to which the printer is connected

- The name of a separator-page file, if one is to be used

- The length of time Windows should wait before notifying you in case of an error

You might find it useful to set up several logical printers for a single physical printer if you frequently switch among groups of settings. If you often switch between portrait and landscape orientations, upper and lower paper trays, or duplex and single-sided printing, for example, you can set up a logical printer for each. This way, you can simply select a different "printer" to change settings.

Installing a Plug and Play Printer

If the physical printer you want to install conforms to the Plug and Play standard, Windows should recognize it and know automatically what kind of printer it is, how much memory it has, what font cartridges are installed, what paper tray it's set up to use, and possibly other details as well.

If you connect a Plug and Play printer to your computer while Windows is not running, you might see a message similar to Figure 9-5 at the beginning of your next Windows session. You will then be placed in the benevolent hands of the Add Printer wizard, who will have only a few more questions to ask you.

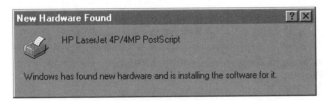

FIGURE 9-5.
If you attach a Plug and Play printer to your computer while Windows is not running, you'll see a message similar to this one the next time you start Windows.

 See Also: For more information about *Plug and Play*, see "Plug and Play: The End of the Hardware Blues?," page 346.

Installing a Non–Plug and Play Printer

To begin installing a printer that does not support the Plug and Play standard, or to create a new logical printer using a physical output device that's already installed, start by doing the following:

1. Open your Printers folder and double-click the Add Printer icon. This brings you to the Add Printer wizard.

2. Click Next to get to the wizard's second screen.

Alternatively, you can start installing a printer from Control Panel by following these steps:

1. Open Control Panel (choose Settings on the Start menu, and then choose Control Panel) and double-click the Add New Hardware icon. This takes you to the Hardware Installation wizard.

2. Click Next to get to the wizard's second screen.

3. In the device list, select Printer. Then click Next to get to the wizard's third screen.

By either of these routes, you will come to the screen shown in Figure 9-6. At this point, if the printer you're installing is physically connected to your own computer, choose the Local Printer option. Otherwise, choose Network Printer. Then click Next again.

FIGURE 9-6.

Windows provides a wizard to assist you with printer installation.

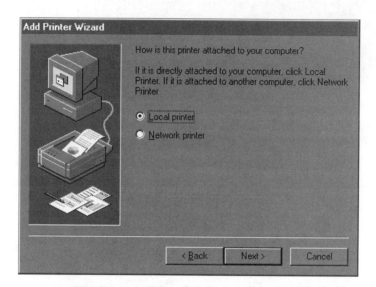

NOTE: The term *network printer* means a printer attached to some other computer. If the printer is attached to the machine you're typing at, that's a local printer—even if the printer is to be shared with others.

If your choice was Local Printer, the next thing you see will be the screen shown in Figure 9-7.

If your choice was Network Printer, you will be asked for the location of your network printer and whether you intend to use this printer with MS-DOS–based applications as well as Windows-based applications. (If you answer Yes, the wizard lets you assign a port to this printer, something required by most MS-DOS–based applications.) For the printer location, you can either supply a network path specification or click the Browse button and find the printer server in a hierarchical diagram of your network. After you've supplied this information, if the printer server is a machine running Windows 95 or Windows NT, the appropriate printer driver will be copied from the server to your own computer. Otherwise, you will arrive at the screen shown in Figure 9-7.

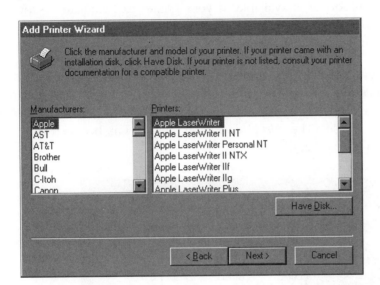

FIGURE 9-7.

Windows 95 supports hundreds of printers. Odds are you'll find your make and model in these two list boxes.

Choosing a Printer Driver

In the screen shown in Figure 9-7, you indicate the make and model of your printer so that Windows can install the appropriate driver for your printer.

After you've made your selections in the list boxes shown in Figure 9-7, Windows might prompt you to insert one or more floppy disks or a CD-ROM so that it can copy the necessary files to your system. If the required driver is already present on your hard disk, the wizard asks your permission to use it. (Knowing that your intention may be to install an updated version of the driver, the wizard does not assume it should use the existing driver.)

What to Do If Your Printer Isn't on the List If your printer isn't on the list of supported printers shown in Figure 9-7, you might want to contact the printer vendor to see if a driver for Windows 95 is available. If you can obtain a driver, repeat the steps that brought you to Figure 9-7. Then click

Have Disk and follow the prompts to direct the Add Printer wizard to your driver file.

If no driver is available, check your printer documentation to see if your printer emulates another printer make and model, one for which a Windows 95 driver is available. If your printer can emulate a supported printer, use the emulation mode and select the supported driver in the dialog box shown in Figure 9-7.

Specifying a Port for Your Printer

After you select a driver and supply the necessary source media, click Next. This takes you to the screen shown in Figure 9-8. Here you tell Windows what port to use. (The *port* provides the physical link between your computer and your printer.)

FIGURE 9-8.

After your printer driver is installed, the wizard needs to know which port your printer is connected to.

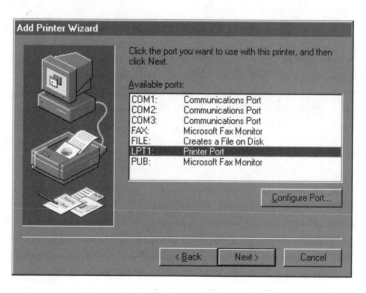

NOTE: If you're installing a network printer, you won't see the screen shown in Figure 9-8. Instead, you'll skip ahead to the printer-naming screen. See "Name That Printer," page 243.

The ports most commonly used for printing are LPT1: (or LPT with some other number) for a printer that uses a parallel cable and COM1: (or COM with some other number) for a printer that uses a serial cable. If you choose a COM port, you should also click the Configure Port button and make sure the communications settings (bits per second, data bits, parity, stop bits, and flow control) are correct for your printer. Consult your printer's documentation if you're not sure what settings to use. (Note: *bits per second* may be called *baud rate* in your printer's documentation.)

Printing to a Disk File To send your output to a disk file, choose FILE: for your printer port. Windows will prompt for a filename whenever you print. You can copy the resulting disk file to a physical printer at a later time by running MS-DOS Prompt. For example, if you have a physical printer attached to LPT1:, you can copy a print file to that printer by choosing MS-DOS Prompt from the Start menu's Programs submenu. Then, at the MS-DOS command prompt, type:

```
copy filename lpt1:
```

The print-to-file option is also useful if the machine on which you ultimately intend to print is not attached to your network—for example, if you plan to use a service bureau to generate high-resolution PostScript output.

 If you sometimes want to print to a physical printer and sometimes to a file, you can change the port setting as needed by visiting the property sheet for your printer. (See "Inspecting and Setting Printer Properties," page 244). Alternatively, you can set up two printers using the same driver. Assign one printer to a physical port and one to FILE:.

Name That Printer

After you choose a port and click Next, the wizard asks you to name your new printer. The name you choose here will appear under the printer icon in your Printers folder, as well as in your applications' Print dialog boxes.

Printing a Test Page

As a final step in the installation process, you can ask the wizard to send a test page to your new printer. This is a good idea. If you've made any incorrect choices in the wizard's dialog boxes (such as choosing the wrong port), it's better to find out now rather than when you're trying to generate some real output.

Inspecting and Setting Printer Properties

The most crucial questions regarding printer setup—the printer driver and the port to be used—get resolved at the time the printer is installed. The decisions you make in these matters are recorded in your printer's property sheet, which you may inspect by right-clicking the printer's icon in your Printers folder and choosing Properties. They're also recorded in your Windows registry so the information is available to inquiring applications.

The property sheet stores many additional choices, however, that affect the behavior of your printer. It's a good idea to visit the property sheet after installing a new printer to make sure all options are set as you want them. You may also have occasion to change properties as you work.

Many of the property options, such as the choice between portrait and landscape orientation, are merely defaults that you can override from within your applications. For example, if you normally print in portrait mode but occasionally need to generate a report in landscape, you don't need to change the property setting; you can simply select landscape mode using your application's Page Setup (or equivalent) command. Other matters, however, such as whether to use separator pages, can only be specified via the property sheet.

Property options vary from printer to printer. In the next several pages we will survey some of the most important options you're likely to find in your printer's property sheet.

Providing a Comment

On the General tab of most printer property sheets, you can enter a comment describing the printer. This information appears in the common Print dialog box, shown in Figure 9-2 on page 228. Figure 9-9 shows an example of the General tab.

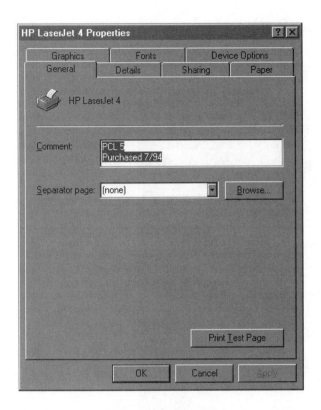

FIGURE 9-9.

On the General tab of a printer's property sheet, you can describe the printer, choose a separator page, and print a test page.

Using Separator Pages

A separator page is like a fax cover sheet. It separates one print job from the next and identifies the person who sent the job, the time it was sent, and the name of the document printed. On the General tab of a printer's property sheet, you can choose between two styles of separator pages: full and simple. The full page uses large type and is adorned with the Windows logo. The simple page provides the same information in humble 12-point Courier New.

 Separator pages are printed *before* each print job. If you're printing a special form, such as a sheet of checks, be sure your printer has a blank sheet of paper on top of the form.

Changing the Port

Should you ever need to change the port for a printer, you can do that on the Details tab of the printer's property sheet. (See Figure 9-10.)

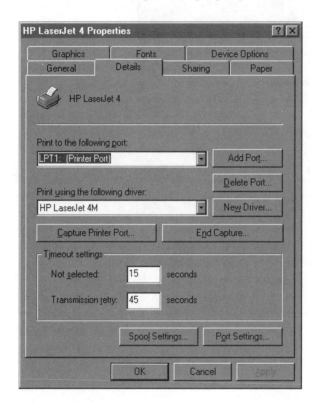

Changing Drivers

If by any chance you've installed the wrong driver for your printer, you can fix the problem by going to the Details tab of the printer's property sheet. Click the New Driver button, and Windows displays the list of printer manufacturers and models shown in Figure 9-7 on page 241.

Changing Timeout Settings

The Details tab of a printer's property sheet includes two timeout settings. These affect the behavior of your system when, for some reason, Windows is unable to communicate with your printer.

Printer vendors often update their printer drivers. To get the maximum functionality from your printer, be sure you're using the latest version of the driver. If you acquire a later version, install it by going to the Details tab of your printer's property sheet. Click the New Driver button, and then click Have Disk when the list of printer manufacturers and models appears.

The Not Selected value sets the length of time that Windows waits before notifying you that your printer is unplugged, turned off, or off line. The default value of 15 seconds is reasonable; it gives you a chance to switch the printer on if you notice after issuing a Print command that it's turned off.

The Transmission Retry value sets the length of time Windows waits if the printer is on line but "busy." Printers can't handle information as fast as computers can send it to them. They store data in memory buffers while they print, and when the buffer gets full, they send a signal to the computer to hold up until further notice. When they're ready for more, they send another signal, telling the computer to resume. The default Transmission Retry setting of 45 seconds means that Windows will give up and issue an error message if it doesn't get a resume signal from the printer after 45 seconds of waiting. This should be ample, except possibly under one of the following conditions:

- If you're using a serial port; serial ports don't transmit data as quickly as parallel ports

- If you're printing to a network printer and there's a lot of network traffic

- If you're printing complex graphics, which take longer to process than text

If you find yourself getting timeout error messages when nothing is wrong, try increasing the Transmission Retry setting.

NOTE: PostScript printers have a different set of timeout defaults. To adjust those timeout settings, click the property sheet's PostScript tab.

Sharing a Printer

The Sharing tab of a printer's property sheet lets you make a printer available to other network users. If you want, you can include a comment and a password on this part of the property sheet. The comment appears in details view when you use Windows Explorer or Network Neighborhood to view the printer. You can use the password to limit access to particular users.

 You can get directly to the Sharing tab by right-clicking the printer's icon in the Printers folder. Then choose Sharing.

Changing the Default Paper Size, Paper Source, Orientation, and Number of Copies

Most printers print 8½ -inch by 11-inch sheets of paper by default but can accommodate a variety of other sizes as well. To change paper size, go to the Paper tab of the printer's property sheet.

On the Paper tab, you can also specify the default paper source (upper tray or lower tray, for example) and the default orientation—portrait or landscape. Depending on the printer you use, you may find additional options here—such as the number of copies printed by default, duplexing (two-sided printing) control, and even the ability to shrink images to fit two or four pages on a single sheet of paper.

 Don't change the Copies option in your printer's property sheet unless you want multiple copies for all printouts. If you want only certain reports printed in multiple copies, use your application to specify the number you want.

Changing Default Resolution, Dithering Options, and Intensity

As mentioned earlier, most printers allow you to choose between two or more resolutions for printing graphics. These options are expressed in terms of the number of dots per inch (dpi) the printer creates. To change resolution, go to the Graphics tab of the printer's property sheet. (See Figure 9-11.)

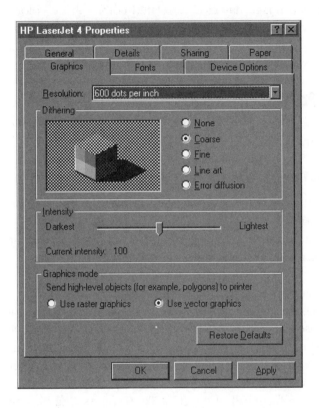

FIGURE 9-11.

The Graphics tab of a printer's property sheet lets you change resolution, dithering style, and intensity.

Some printers include a set of dithering options labeled None, Coarse, Fine, Line Art, and Error Diffusion. These settings govern the way Windows prints bitmap images on black-and-white printers.

Dithering is a process by which a device, such as a printer or video display, approximates colors that it cannot generate directly. When you print a color bitmap on a monochromatic printer, the printer driver uses dithering to translate colors other than black and white into shades of gray. The dithering options available with certain drivers govern the method by which these drivers do their dithering. The Rubik's cube in the center of the property sheet shows you what effect different options have.

In general, you'll probably want to avoid the None and Line Art choices, except in special circumstances. (You might choose None if you want to emphasize contrast in a printout at the expense of shades of gray.) When a bitmap image has closely related colors, those colors will usually be easiest to distinguish if you print with the Coarse setting. But the best policy is to experiment. Try all the options to see what generates the most satisfactory results with your images and your printer.

Specifying Font Cartridges

If your printer supports font cartridges, you can indicate which ones you're using by going to the Fonts tab of the printer's property sheet.

Printing TrueType Fonts as Graphics

The Fonts tab on the property sheet for many printers includes an option that lets you print TrueType fonts as graphics. Normally, Windows downloads TrueType font information to your printer's memory. This default setting lets your printer print documents in the shortest possible time. Under one circumstance, however, you might want to override the default and have your text printed as a page of bitmap graphics.

If your document includes graphic objects overlying text, downloading the fonts might cause the text to "bleed through" the graphics, producing a document that doesn't match what you see on screen. For example, if you print a Microsoft Excel document that includes a chart embedded on the worksheet, text that is not visible on screen might appear in your printout.

To correct this problem, select the Print TrueType As Graphics option on the Fonts tab of the printer's property sheet. Note that printing TrueType fonts as graphics slows your printer down considerably because Windows must compute a bitmap for the entire printed page (instead of relying on your printer's intelligence to render the text).

Specifying the Amount of Memory in Your Printer

If your printer supports different amounts of memory, it's important for Windows to know how much memory is installed. Otherwise, you might get unnecessary out-of-memory error messages when printing complex graphics. You can check, and change if necessary, the memory setting by visiting the Device Options tab of your printer's property sheet.

10

Exchanging Information: The Clipboard and OLE

n the bad old early days of desktop computing, transferring information from one application to another was a process beset with difficulties. In that time before Windows, users who wanted to build "compound documents"—documents with elements derived from two or more applications—often had to rely on clumsy TSR (terminate-and-stay-resident) utilities to act as data-moving intermediaries between applications. The dearth of file-format standards and the absence of treaties governing relations among programs that shared memory made the exchange of information frustrating and perilous. Single-application documents were the norm, and a compound document was usually something assembled by a pasteup artist.

Nowadays, compound documents have become so normal that the term itself has fallen into disuse. Windows users expect to be able to move text, graphics, sound, and video freely within and between documents and are seldom disappointed. In Windows 95, the process of generating what used to be called a compound document is easier than ever, thanks both to improvements in the Windows user interface and the growing prevalence of a standard called OLE (pronounced *olay*, with the stress on the second syllable) object technology.

In this chapter, we'll examine the methods and mechanisms for moving information between and within applications.

Data Exchange: A Symphony with Three Movements

Three forms of data exchange are common in Windows:

- Static moves and copies
- Embedding
- Linking

A static move or copy is a one-time transaction with a no-return policy. If you copy or cut a range of numbers from your spreadsheet and paste them statically into your word processor document, your word processor handles those numbers exactly as though you had typed them directly at the keyboard. You can format them, edit them, delete them, or

Servers, Clients, Sources, Destinations, Objects, Containers (and All That Jazz)

There are two parties to any OLE transaction. One party supplies the goods, the other receives them. For example, if you take a range from an Excel spreadsheet and embed it in a PowerPoint presentation, you have a supplying document (the Excel spreadsheet) and a receiving document (the PowerPoint presentation).

In OLE parlance, the supplying document is called the *source*, or *server*. The receiving document is known as the *destination*, the *client*, or the *container*. The goods, whatever they may be, are known simply as the *object*.

The terms *server* and *client*, of course, are also used in the context of networking. A server is a shared resource, typically a hard disk on a computer dedicated to storing files needed by many different users. A client is a computer that connects to a server. To minimize confusion in this book, we'll stick with *source* and *destination* when the subject is OLE, reserving *server* and *client* for their more traditional networking meanings.

stand them on their heads (if your word processor does that sort of thing), but they have no further relationship to the document and application in which they originated.

When you *embed* one document's data in a second document, the data remembers where it came from. If you want to edit that data, Windows lets you work in the data's original context. For example, suppose you copy a block of numbers from a spreadsheet and embed them in a word processing document. When you want to edit those numbers, the original spreadsheet application reappears, allowing you to use its commands, instead of your word processor's, to do your editing.

When you *link* one document's data to a second document, the data you link is not actually stored in the receiving document. Instead, the receiving application stores information about where the data came from. Continuing with our spreadsheet–word processor example, if you use a linking command to paste the spreadsheet numbers into your word processor document, the numbers look exactly as if you typed them in at the keyboard. But when you save that document to a disk file, the file does not include the numbers. Instead, it includes everything Windows needs to know in order to find those numbers again the next time you open the file. If you change the numbers in the spreadsheet, your changes also appear in your word processor document.

Embedding and linking also have one other important virtue: they allow you to incorporate material into your documents that your documents cannot render directly. For example, you can embed or link a sound annotation or a video clip into documents created by most word processors, database managers, and spreadsheet programs. Those programs display an icon to indicate where the sound or video has been embedded or linked. When you want to hear the sound or see the video, you simply double-click the icon. Windows then renders the object, using the sound or video application in which the object originated. (For more information about working with sound and video, see Chapter 21, "Using the Multimedia Accessories," page 539.)

 Many programs give you the option of displaying embedded or linked data as an icon, even if the program *can* render the data. For example, your word processor might permit you to embed a block of text but display it as an icon. The readers of your document can then skip over the embedded material if they're not interested in it. If they are interested, they can double-click the icon and read the embedded text.

The linking component of OLE is an extension of an earlier data-exchange technology called DDE (the letters stand for *dynamic data exchange*). In some applications, you might still encounter the term *DDE*, but unless you are a programmer, you will probably never need to concern yourself with the details about how DDE works. You can simply use your programs' Paste Link commands (as described later in this chapter) to create links and let Windows worry about what's going on under the hood.

See Also: For more information about *embedding*, see "How to Embed," page 263.

For more information about *linking*, see "How to Link," page 266.

OLE Is a Many-Flavored Thing

OLE object technology is Microsoft's ever-evolving standard for building documents from disparate sources. In the beginning, its formal name, Object Linking and Embedding, described everything it did. It allowed documents in supporting applications to embed data objects from other supporting applications, or to create links to such objects.

Subsequently, a second iteration of OLE, called OLE 2, appeared. OLE 2 introduced new facilities for integrating documents across applications, some of which had little to do with either embedding or linking. Therefore, official Microsoft literature now downplays the spelled-out form of the acronym—as well as the differences between OLE 1 and OLE 2.

If you follow the computer press at all, however, you will often see products described in terms of their degree of OLE support. Some programs support OLE 1 but not OLE 2. Others support certain, but not all, features of OLE 2, while still others offer the full range of OLE support. Here in a nutshell is what the jargon means:

OLE 1 means embedding and linking, as described in this chapter. (See "Data Exchange: A Symphony with Three Movements," page 253.) OLE 2 refers to linking and embedding *plus* any or all of the following:

In-place editing. When you edit an embedded object in a program offering in-place editing, the containing program's menus and toolbars are temporarily replaced by those of the object's

> ### OLE Is a Many-Flavored Thing
>
> source program. For example, if a Microsoft Excel chart is embedded in a Microsoft Word document, double-clicking the chart causes the Excel menus and toolbars to appear in place of the Word menus and toolbars. When you finish editing, the Word interface reappears. (For more information about in-place editing, see "How to Embed," page 263, and "Working with Embedded Objects," page 268.)
>
> **Cross-application drag and drop.** Some OLE 2 programs allow you to move or copy data between applications or between an application and a folder by dragging the data with the mouse.
>
> **OLE Automation.** Certain OLE 2 programs, such as Microsoft Excel, allow themselves to be "driven" by cross-application programming languages, such as Microsoft Visual Basic and Visual Basic for Applications. This level of OLE 2 support is called *OLE Automation.* With OLE Automation and a bit of programming skill, you can create "scripts" or "macros" that move data between two or more applications.

What the Cut, Copy, Paste, and Paste Special Commands Do

As you probably know, the universal method for moving or copying an item from one place to another is as follows:

1. Select whatever it is you want to move or copy—a block of text, a region within a graphical image, a range of spreadsheet cells, a file in a folder window, or whatever.

2. Choose the Cut command if you want to move the selected object. Choose the Copy command if you want to copy it. In virtually all Windows-based applications, these commands can be found on the Edit menu. In many applications, you can right-click and choose these commands from the object menu.

3. Move to the place where you want the data transferred and choose Paste or Paste Special. Like Cut and Copy, these commands can be found on programs' Edit menus. If you're pasting something onto the desktop or into a folder window, right-click and choose Paste from the object menu.

 You can save a lot of time by using keyboard shortcuts for Cut, Copy, and Paste. Use Ctrl-X for Cut, Ctrl-C for Copy, and Ctrl-V for Paste.

Now that many programs support moving and copying via drag and drop, this cut-and-paste (or copy-and-paste) sequence is no longer the only way to relocate data in Windows documents. But it's probably still the most commonly used method, so let's take a look at what happens when you use these commands.

 You can use Copy, Cut, and Paste with MS-DOS–based applications as well as Windows-based applications. For more information, see "Using Copy and Paste," page 315.

 For information about *selecting part of a document*, see "Selecting Text," page 42.

For information about *selecting files and folders*, see "Selecting Folders and Files in a Folder Window," page 136.

The Clipboard, Windows' Invisible Transfer Agent

When you select data and use an application's Cut or Copy command, the selected data is stored on the Clipboard, an area of memory used to hold data in transit. When you use an application's Paste command, the Clipboard's data is copied into the application.

Data on the Clipboard usually remains there until new data arrives to replace it. That means that you can copy or cut something to the Clipboard, and then paste it as many times in as many places as you please. But as soon as you use another Cut or Copy command, the data you were previously pasting disappears from the Clipboard.

CAUTION: Some applications clear the Clipboard "behind the scenes." Microsoft Excel, for example, often erases the Clipboard on its own initiative. This is uncommon behavior, however, and you're not likely to see it in most of the programs you use.

 To move information without disturbing the current Clipboard contents, drag it with the mouse. (Or hold down the Ctrl key as you drag to copy information.) Many Windows-based programs offer some level of "drag and drop" support (within a document, between documents, or even between applications), and this form of data movement bypasses the Clipboard.

Be careful with the Cut command. In most programs, the data you cut disappears from its source document as soon as you use this command. If you get distracted between cutting and pasting and happen to put another item on the Clipboard before pasting the first, you may lose the first item. If you change your mind between cutting something and pasting it, simply paste it back where you cut it. (If the cut item is one or more files or folders in a folder window, the selected files or folders remain in place until you paste them in another folder.)

Controlling the Outcome with Paste Special

When you cut or copy information from an application, the application supplies the information to the Clipboard in as many formats as it can. If you cut a paragraph in a Microsoft Word document, for example, Word transfers that paragraph to the Clipboard in both text and graphics formats. If you copy a spreadsheet range from Microsoft Excel, the Clipboard receives your selection in a large assortment of formats, including some that allow the data to be exported to other spreadsheet programs.

This multiple-format arrangement allows an application to receive Clipboard data in whichever format best suits it. For example, the fact that a Microsoft Word paragraph is stored on the Clipboard in both graphics and text formats means that you can paste it into Notepad, a program that accepts only text, as well as into other programs that accept only graphics.

The multiple-format arrangement also means that you often have choices about how to paste your data. When you simply use an application's Paste command, you get whatever format the program thinks you're most likely to want. But in many programs, you can use a Paste Special command and choose an alternative format. Figure 10-1 shows an example of a Paste Special dialog box. In this example, the source data is a range of spreadsheet cells. If you want to paste a picture of those cells, rather than the text contained in the cells, you can choose either Picture or Bitmap, both of which are graphics formats.

FIGURE 10-1.

The Paste Special command lets you choose what format to paste, as well as whether to link, embed, or paste statically.

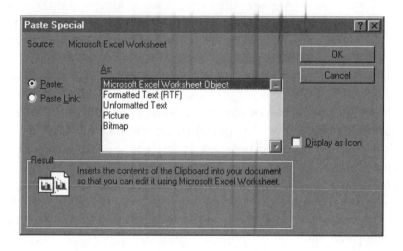

Table 10-1 describes some of the data formats you might encounter in your programs' Paste Special dialog boxes.

As we'll see, Paste Special also can be used to control whether Clipboard data is embedded, pasted statically, or linked.

Data Format	Description
Text	Unformatted character information (without style attributes, such as boldface and italics), using the ANSI standard character set used by all Windows-based programs.
Formatted Text (RTF)	A text format that uses embedded codes to store style information, such as boldface and italics. Microsoft Excel, Microsoft Word, and a growing number of other programs support rich text format.
Unicode Text	A 16-bit text-encoding format that allows for both Latin and non-Latin alphanumeric characters, plus an assortment of commercial, mathematical, and scientific symbols.
Bitmap	A graphic format in which each pixel in an image is represented by one or more data bits. Unlike a picture or metafile, bitmap data is specific for a given output device. If you display a bitmap on a device with resolution or color capability different from the one on which it was created, you're not likely to be pleased with the result. Also, although bitmap images can be resized or reshaped, this process generally introduces gross distortions.
Picture	A graphic format in which image elements are stored as a sequence of commands. An image in picture format can be reproduced without gross distortion at different sizes or shapes, as well as on different kinds of output devices. But a bitmap image might display more quickly because it doesn't have to be re-created from programmatic instructions. An image in picture format is also sometimes called a metafile (although the terms are not precisely equivalent).
DIB	A device-independent bitmap. This is a newer bitmap format (introduced with OS/2 version 1.1) that eliminates some, but not all, of the device specificity of the standard bitmap format by including information about the color palette and resolution of the originating device.
Link, OwnerLink, ObjectLink	Formats used to establish OLE links between documents.

TABLE 10-1.

The Clipboard can store data in these formats (among others), which you might see listed in a Paste Special dialog box.

To view the current contents of the Clipboard, you can use an application called Clipboard Viewer. With commands on Clipboard Viewer's Display menu, you can see what the current Clipboard contents look like in various display formats. If Clipboard Viewer has been installed on your system, you'll probably find it in the Accessories section of your Programs menu.

The ClipBook Viewer program that was included with Windows for Workgroups and Windows NT is not part of Windows 95. To create and share files of Clipboard objects ("clipbook pages," in Windows for Workgroup parlance), use the "scrap" feature. For details, see "Creating Scrap Files," page 273.

To Link, to Embed, or Merely to Paste?

Should you embed, should you link, or should you do neither? Here are a few guidelines:

Embedding's advantages are permanence and portability. Because the embedded data actually resides in the receiving application, you don't have to worry about what will happen if the source document becomes unavailable. Thus, for example, you'll want to choose embedding, not linking, if you plan to move the receiving document somewhere where it won't have access to the source document.

Linking's advantages over embedding are two. First, the resulting compound document is smaller because it stores "pointers" only, not the actual source data. Second, changes in the source data can be reflected automatically in the receiving document. You should use linking when you want your compound document to stay current with its component sources over time.

What about plain old-fashioned static pasting? If the documents involved do not support OLE, of course, that is your only choice. For example, if you paste a paragraph from a Notepad document into your word processor, that paragraph arrives as static text because Notepad is a simple program that does not support OLE. Even with OLE applications, though, there may be occasions when a straightforward static paste is more suitable than a fancy embedded object. Offsetting the convenience of editing an object in its source application, for example, is the time required for Windows to launch that application—or the component of it needed to provide in-place editing. If that delay is vexing, don't embed. OLE is a service, not an obligation.

How to Embed

In most cases you can embed an object simply by selecting it in its source document and pasting it into its destination document. That's because, when multiple formats are available on the Clipboard, the format that produces an embedded object is usually the default. It is not *always* the default, however. So if you want to be certain that you're embedding something and not simply pasting it statically, it's a good idea to use the Paste Special command. In the list of available formats presented by the Paste Special dialog box, the one that does the embedding will typically have the word *object* somewhere in its name. When you select that option, the explanatory text at the bottom of the dialog box will probably include words such as "so that you can edit it using," followed by the name of the source application.

Embedding a New Object

The previous paragraph assumes that the object you want to embed already exists somewhere in its source document. But what if it doesn't? Suppose, for example, that you're working in a WordPad document and you want to embed a graphic that doesn't exist yet. In that case, you can go to the Start menu, launch your graphics application, create the object, copy it to the Clipboard, and so on. Alternatively, you can simply use the Object command on WordPad's Insert menu. Figure 10-2 on the next page shows the dialog box you will see.

The Object Type list in this dialog box enumerates all the embeddable data types known to the Windows registry. Choose the type of object you want to embed, select the Display As Icon check box if you want the embedded object to appear as an icon, and click OK. Windows then either starts the application that's appropriate for the object type you selected or simply displays that application's menus and toolbars. At that

FIGURE 10-2.

To embed an object that doesn't exist yet, you can use the Insert Object command.

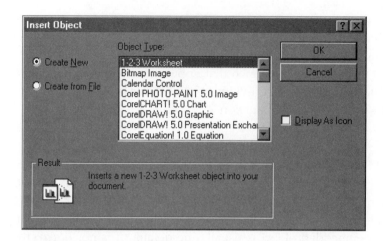

point, you can create the object you want to embed. For example, if you are working in WordPad and choose Bitmap Image as the object type, Windows replaces WordPad's menus with those of Paint, the application with which the Bitmap Image object type is associated. Figure 10-3 shows what you would see.

FIGURE 10-3.

If you use the Object command on WordPad's Insert menu, and then choose the Bitmap Image object type, Windows replaces WordPad's menus and toolbars with those of Paint, allowing you to create a new object.

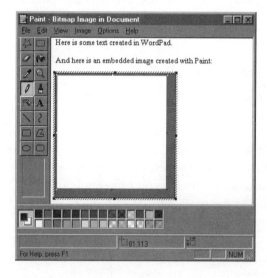

The word *Paint* now appears in Figure 10-3's title bar, and the menus and tools shown are those of Paint. The frame below the text is a Paint frame, embedded within a WordPad document. As long as the frame is selected, you can use Paint's menus and tools to create a bitmap image. When you finish, you can return to WordPad by simply selecting any part of the document outside the Paint frame.

If you choose to have the embedded object displayed as an icon, or if the program you're working with does not support in-place editing, clicking OK in the Insert Object dialog box causes Windows to launch the application that creates the object, rather than simply displaying that program's menus and toolbars within the containing document. In that case, when you finish creating the object, you can embed it by choosing the Exit & Return To Document command, at the bottom of the File menu. Figure 10-4 shows what you see if you choose WordPad's Insert Object command, select Bitmap Image as the object type, and also select the Display As Icon check box.

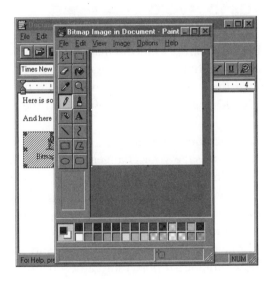

FIGURE 10-4.

If you choose to display a new embedded object as an icon, or if your program does not support in-place editing, Windows launches a full copy of the program with which the object type is associated.

The copy of Paint shown in Figure 10-4 is exactly like what you get by running Paint directly from your Start menu, except for its title bar and File menu. The title bar reveals the fact that this instance of Paint was launched for the purpose of creating (or editing) an embedded object, and the File menu includes two new commands—one to quit Paint and update the containing document and one to update the containing document without leaving Paint.

How to Link

To link an object, follow these steps:

1. Select the object in its source document.

2. Activate the destination document and place the insertion point where you want the linked object to go.

3. Choose the Edit menu's Paste Link command.

This creates a link to the source document and displays the source object in the default format. If you prefer a different format, choose Paste Special instead of Paste Link. In the Paste Special dialog box, select the format you want and then choose Paste Link.

Two Linking Hazards to Avoid

When you create a link, a visible change occurs in the destination document: new data arrives. At the same time, Windows makes a change in the source document, but this change is not visible. The reason for the change in the source document is that the source document now has a new "responsibility": it must notify the destination document whenever the linked object changes.

If you close the source document immediately after performing a paste link, you will be prompted to save your changes, even though you may not have done any editing in that document since your most recent save. Windows wants you to save your changes because the document has assumed the responsibility of supplying a link. If you ignore the prompt, the data in the destination document will be correct (for the time being), but the link may be broken. To avoid this mishap, be sure to save the source document after paste-linking an object into a destination document.

Another hazard arises when the source document is a spreadsheet. In a typical spreadsheet link, the source data is identified in the destination document by its cell coordinates. However, what happens to the link in this situation if someone working with the source document decides to add a few new rows or columns? Any such worksheet rearrangement can change the cell coordinates of the linked object and thereby invalidate the link—or worse, the link can remain valid as far as Windows is concerned, but it no longer contains the data you're interested in.

To avoid this trap, do the following:

1. In the source document, name the cell or range you want to link.

2. After you paste-link the object into your destination document, use the destination application's Edit Links command to verify that the link is recorded by your worksheet range name, not by absolute cell coordinates.

3. If the link is not identified by the range name, edit the link, replacing the cell coordinates with the range name.

The exact procedure for editing the link depends on the destination application. In WordPad, for example, the Edit Links dialog box includes a Change Source command button. Clicking this button brings up a "browser" dialog box, in which you can change the name of the source file or the description of the source object. As Figure 10-5 shows, the source object is described on a line marked Item Name. To replace cell coordinates with a range name, simply edit the Item Name line.

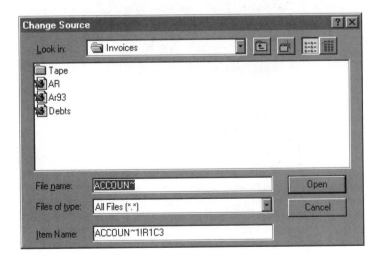

FIGURE 10-5.

In WordPad, by choosing Links from the Edit menu and then clicking the Change Source button, you can change the description of the linked object. In other applications, the procedure may be slightly different.

Embedding or Linking a File

In all our examples so far, the source object to be linked or embedded has been a part of a file—for example, a range of spreadsheet cells, a paragraph in a word processing document, or a selection from a graphic image. You can also link or embed entire files. Depending on the type of file involved and your preferences, the destination document either displays the contents of the file or an icon representing the file.

To embed or link a file, choose the Object command (in many applications it's called New Object) from the containing application's Insert menu, and then select the Create From File option button. The object type list in the center of the dialog box is replaced by a File text box and a Browse button, as shown in Figure 10-6.

FIGURE 10-6.

If you choose the Create From File option button in the dialog box shown in Figure 10-2, the dialog box changes to let you type a filename or browse through your folders to find the file you want to embed or link.

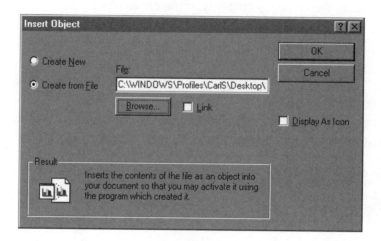

Working with Embedded Objects

The simplest way to edit an embedded object is to double-click it. Depending on whether the object is fully visible or shown as an icon, and depending on the level of OLE support provided by your applications, either you are transported to a copy of the object's source application or the source application's menus and toolbars appear at the top of your document. In either case, you edit the object using the facilities of the object's source application.

If you're editing in a copy of the source application, choose the last command in that application's File menu when you are finished editing. This command closes the source application and returns you to the document in which the object is embedded.

If the menus and toolbars of the object's source application have simply replaced those of the destination program (that is, you are editing in place), simply select another part of the destination document when you are finished editing the object. The original menus and toolbars then reappear.

Alternatively, you can edit an embedded object by selecting it and looking for an editing command at or near the bottom of the Edit menu. Figure 10-7 shows what you see on WordPad's Edit menu when you select an embedded bitmap image.

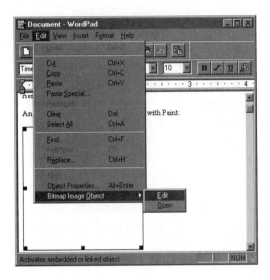

FIGURE 10-7.

To edit an embedded object, simply double-click it. Or select it and look for an editing command on the Edit menu.

Playing an Embedded Sound or Video Object

To play an embedded sound or video object, select the embedded object and choose the "Object" command on your application's Edit menu. This command identifies the type of object you selected. If you select a sound clip created in Sound Recorder, for example, the command says *Sound Recorder Document Object*. When you choose this command, a submenu appears. Choose Play on the submenu to play the embedded object.

Modifying the Properties of an Embedded Object

Like just about everything else in Windows 95, embedded objects have properties that can be inspected and modified. To get to the property sheet for an embedded object, you can do any of the following:

- Right-click the object and choose Object Properties from the object menu.

- Select the object and press Alt-Enter.

- Select the object and choose Object Properties from the Edit menu (if you're working in a context where there is an Edit menu).

On the property sheet, you might be able to do such things as switch between a rendered and an iconic display of the object or change the object's display size.

 If the selected object is displayed as an icon, you can use the object's property sheet to change the icon, the icon's caption, or both. Even if you're content with the default icon, you might want to replace the default caption with something descriptive. "Picture of Mom," for example, might serve your needs better than "Bitmap Image." To do so, click the Change Icon button in the property sheet, and then modify the Label text.

Working with Links

When a data object is linked to a document, changes to the object are reflected in the destination document. Whether they're reflected automatically or only on demand is up to you. Most (but not all) programs create automatic links by default. In any case, you can switch between automatic and manual linking by opening the property sheet for the link in question. To open the property sheet, select the linked object and choose the Object Properties command on the containing application's Edit menu. Figure 10-8 shows an example of a linked object's property sheet.

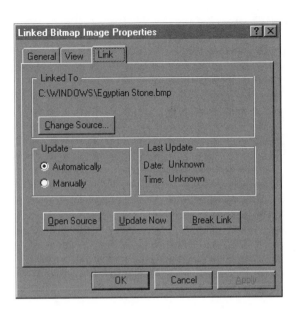

FIGURE 10-8.

On the Link tab of a linked object's property sheet, you can switch between automatic and manual linking, open the object's source document for editing, sever the object from its source document, or specify a different source document.

 If your destination program does not include an Object Properties command, look for a Links command on the Edit menu. That command displays a list of all links in the current document. By selecting an item in the list and choosing command buttons in the Links dialog box, you can switch between automatic and manual linking, open the source document for editing, break the link, or re-specify the source document.

To switch between automatic and manual linking, go to the Link tab of the property sheet and choose the appropriate option button in the Update group. If you choose Manually, you can refresh the containing document by clicking the Update Now button. If you choose Automatically, the containing document is refreshed any time the source document changes.

Another Linking Hazard

Under certain circumstances, it is possible for an automatic link *not* to reflect the current state of the source document. Here's how it can happen:

1. You double-click the linked object to edit it in the source document.

2. You change the object in the source document, and the link is updated appropriately.

3. You close the source document without saving changes.

After this sequence, the source document reverts to its original state (because you didn't save your changes), but the destination document does not revert to its former state. The two documents are now out of step with one another.

To be absolutely sure that all links in a destination document, both automatic and manual, are up-to-date, follow these steps:

1. In the destination document, choose the Edit menu's Links command.

2. In the Links dialog box, select the first link listed. Then scroll to the bottom of the list and hold down the Shift key while selecting the last link listed. (This selects all links in the list.)

3. Click the Update Now button.

Breaking a Link

If you no longer want a linked object to reflect changes in the object's source, visit the Link tab of the object's property sheet, and then click the Break Link button. If it can, Windows converts the item to an embedded object.

What to Do If the Source Document Is Moved or Renamed

If the source document for a link is renamed or relocated, the link becomes invalid. When you open a destination document containing such an invalid link, you might or might not receive a warning from the destination application. (It depends on the application.) If you know the link has become invalid, choose Links on the Edit menu. Then click the Change Source (or equivalent) button and follow your application's procedures for editing the link.

If you're not sure whether or not the link is valid, choose the Edit menu's Links command. Select the link in question (or all links) and click the Update Now (or equivalent) button. The destination application should then tell you if any source object is unavailable. If you have invalid links, you can click the Change Source (or equivalent) button to edit them.

Creating Scrap Files

Windows Explorer is an OLE program. That means you can embed data objects in folders or on your desktop. So, for example, if there's a particular image you want to use repeatedly, you can drag it out of a Paint window and drop it onto your desktop. To reuse it in your word processor, simply drag it again and drop it into the receiving document.

OLE objects in folders or on the desktop are called *scrap files*. When you create such an object, Windows gives it a default name based on its contents or source, such as "WordPad Document Scrap 'Now is the time ...'" You can assign your own name by pressing F2 and typing.

A scrap file must originate in a program that supports OLE as a source. If the program also supports OLE drag and drop, you can create the scrap by simply dragging the object. If not, select the object in its source program, choose the Copy command, and then move to your folder or to the desktop and choose Paste.

Sharing and Using OLE Objects Across the Network

By storing scrap files in a shared folder, you can make OLE objects on your system available to other network users. Similarly, by opening a shared folder on a server, you can access OLE objects stored on that server. To embed a server-based scrap file, for example, simply open the network folder in which the scrap resides, using Network Neighborhood or a mapped folder. Then drag the object to wherever you want it to go. Alternatively, select the object in the network folder, and then paste it into an application or local folder.

To activate a network scrap object's parent application, either for editing purposes or to render an object that's embedded as an icon, you must have a local copy of the parent application.

See Also: For information about *using shared folders,* see Chapter 6, "Using and Sharing Files on the Network," page 179.

Making
Windows Work
for You

11

Customizing
Windows

n Chapter 3, we looked at some of the ways in which you can tailor your working environment to meet your preferences. Specifically, that chapter explored options for personalizing the appearance of your desktop, the responsiveness of your mouse and keyboard, and the various utterances offered up by your computer's speakers. In this chapter we'll address a few more ways in which you can customize Windows. Here we'll look into procedures for doing the following:

- Resetting the date and time

- Changing passwords

- Reconfiguring your modem

- Changing dialing locations so that automatic dialing programs can distinguish local from long-distance calls

- Setting the volume levels for your speakers, microphone, and headphones

- Setting the window size for video-clip playback

- Specifying "regional" settings, such as date and time formats, the default symbol for currency, and the symbol for a decimal point

- Setting up different keyboard layouts, such as the Dvorak layout or a layout for a different language

- Using Windows' support for multiple languages

Introducing Control Panel

Your key to nearly all customizing options in Windows—everything except options relating to your taskbar and Start menu—is a system folder called Control Panel. The easiest way to get to this folder is to choose Settings from the Start menu, and then choose Control Panel from the submenu that unfolds. Figure 11-1 on the next page shows what the Control Panel folder looks like on one of the systems used to create this book.

On your own computer, Control Panel may not look exactly like Figure 11-1. You may have additional icons not shown in the figure, and you may lack certain icons that are shown. When Windows was installed, the Windows Setup program populated Control Panel with items appropriate

FIGURE 11-1.

The Control Panel folder contains property sheets and wizards that help you customize Windows.

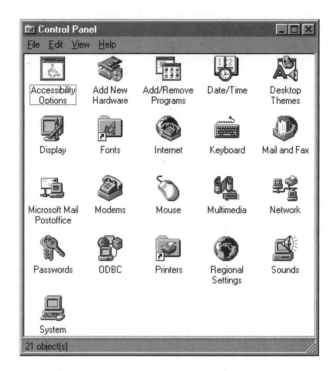

for your hardware, and possibly also for the access privileges accorded to you by your system administrator.

In this chapter, we'll investigate the following items, which are common to most Windows 95 systems: Date/Time, Modems, Multimedia, Passwords, Regional Settings, and Keyboard. Table 11-1 shows the icons for Control Panel items that are discussed elsewhere in this book.

 You can create shortcuts for any item in Control Panel or for the Control Panel folder itself. Follow the same procedures you would use to create any other kind of shortcut. For example, to create a desktop shortcut for Control Panel's Passwords icon, simply right-drag the icon to your desktop, and then choose Create Shortcut(s) Here from the object menu.

Icon	For Information, See
Accessibility Options	Chapter 17, "Using the Accessibility Features," page 423
Add New Hardware	"Installing a Legacy Peripheral," page 349
Add/Remove Programs	"Adding or Removing Parts of Windows," page 339, and "Installing Applications," page 342
Desktop Themes	Appendix A, "Using the Power of Your 486 or Pentium with Microsoft Plus!," page 727
Display	"Controlling the Amount of Information That Fits On Screen," page 92, "Changing the Colors, Fonts, and Sizes of the Windows User Interface," page 98, and "Using Patterns, Wallpaper, and Screen Savers," page 106
Fonts	Chapter 8, "Installing and Using Fonts," page 205
Keyboard	"Adjusting the Keyboard Repeat and Cursor Blink Rates," page 113
Mail and FAX	Chapter 23, "Using Microsoft Exchange," page 587, and Chapter 24, "Using Microsoft Fax," page 641
Mouse	"Setting Preferences for Your Mouse," page 111
Printers	Chapter 9, "Installing, Configuring, and Using Your Printers," page 223
Sounds	"Assigning Sounds to Events," page 103
System	"Uninstalling a Legacy Peripheral," page 353, and Chapter 15, "Optimizing and Troubleshooting," page 375

TABLE 11-1.

These Control Panel items are described in other chapters of this book.

Resetting the Date and Time

To change your computer's date or time setting, double-click the Date/Time icon in Control Panel. You'll see the Date/Time property sheet, shown in Figure 11-2.

FIGURE 11-2.

To change your system's date or time, double-click the Date/Time icon in Control Panel.

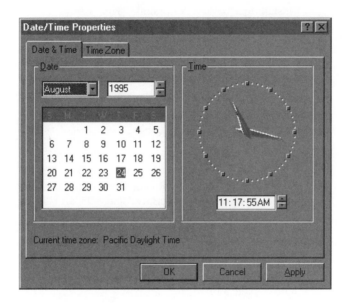

The Date/Time property sheet has two tabs. Use the Date & Time tab to adjust your system's clock or calendar. Use the Time Zone tab if you're moving to a different time zone, or to enable or disable Windows' automatic adjustment for daylight saving time.

 You can also get to the Date/Time property sheet by double-clicking the clock on your taskbar.

On the Date & Time tab, you can adjust the day of the month by clicking on the calendar. To choose a different month or year, select from the drop-down list and spinner above the calendar. To change the time of day, click the appropriate portion of the time edit box, and then use the spinners to the right of the edit box. For example, if the clock says 2:36 P.M., but it's really only 2:31, select the 36 and then click the downward arrow five times. (Unfortunately, you can't adjust the time by dragging the hands on the clock.) If the clock says A.M., but it's actually P.M., click on or beside the "AM" and then click either spinner arrow once. After you've set the time, click Apply or OK to start the clock running again.

 To change the display format used by the clock—for example, to change AM and PM to am and pm—use the Time tab of the Regional Settings property sheet. For more information, see "Specifying Regional (International) Settings," page 294.

You can also adjust the date and time by running MS-DOS Prompt and using the Date command or the Time command. Changes made this way have exactly the same effect as changes made via the Date/Time property sheet.

On the Time Zone tab, you can simply click your location on the world map. Alternatively, you can select a time zone from the drop-down list at the top of the dialog box. Windows uses this information to track time information for files saved on a network that operates across multiple time zones.

Windows can automatically adjust your system's clock when daylight saving time begins or ends. If you want to use this feature, select the Automatically Adjust Clock For Daylight Saving Changes check box, on the Time Zone tab of the Date/Time property sheet.

If your computer is connected to a Windows 95, Windows NT, or Windows for Workgroups network, you can set your computer's clock to match the time on another computer in your network. To do so, choose the Run command from the Start menu, and type *net time \\computer /set /yes*, where *computer* is the name of the computer you want to synchronize with. To synchronize your clock automatically each time you start Windows, create a shortcut with this command and place it in your StartUp folder.

Changing Passwords

If you get tired of using the same old password every day when you log on, you can trade that password in for a new one. Here's how:

1. Double-click the Passwords icon in Control Panel.

2. On the Change Passwords tab of the Passwords property sheet, click the Change Windows Password button.

3. In the dialog box that appears (see Figure 11-3), enter your current password, your new password, and then your new password again.

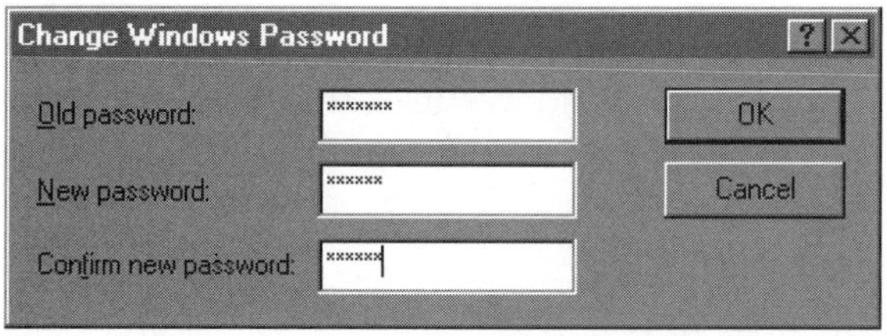

FIGURE 11-3.

You can change passwords by double-clicking the Passwords icon in Control Panel.

Change Windows Password		
Old password:	********	OK
New password:	******	Cancel
Confirm new password:	******	

To protect your privacy, Windows displays asterisks as you type your old and new passwords. You must type your new password twice to ensure that you've typed it accurately. If the New Password and Confirm New Password lines don't match, or if your entry on the Old Password line is incorrect, Windows rejects your new password.

If you use passwords to connect to other resources, such as Novell NetWare servers, you can change those passwords by clicking the Change Other Passwords button on the Change Passwords tab of the Passwords property sheet. When you click this button, Windows displays a list of the various types of passwords you use. Select the one you want to change, and then click the Change button.

See Also: For information about *using the Passwords property sheet to enable or disable user profiles*, see "Taking Advantage of User Profiles," page 87.

Changing Modem Settings and Dialing Locations

If you have a modem connected to your computer when you install Windows, the Windows Setup program usually identifies the make and model of the modem and configures it to operate properly. You might want to adjust some of your modem's settings from time to time, however. For example, you might decide that you don't need to hear the modem's speaker every time it dials, or that you'd rather hear it at a lower volume level. You can make these and other adjustments via the Modems item in Control Panel.

You can also use the Modems section of Control Panel to let automatic dialing programs know the area code of the location in which you work. With this information, your programs can distinguish between local and long-distance calls, and dial appropriately. You can also set up multiple dialing locations, which are useful if you travel with your computer.

To change your modem or dialing-location settings, start by double-clicking the Modems icon in Control Panel. You will arrive at the Modems property sheet, shown in Figure 11-4 on the next page.

FIGURE 11-4.

The Modems property sheet lets you change the settings used by any modem attached to your system

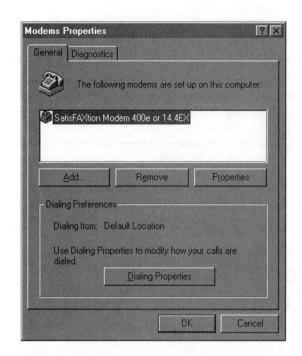

In the center of the property sheet, Windows lists all the modems currently attached to your system. To inspect or change the settings for a modem, select the modem and click the Properties button. You'll then see a property sheet for the selected modem. The options available on that sheet depend on the modem you're using. Figure 11-5 shows the choices for a SatisFAXtion 400e.

For this modem, the available options include the communications port, speaker volume, and maximum speed. Additional options on the Connection tab allow for adjustments to communications parameters—including data bits, parity, and stop bits. You might want to investigate all the tabs of your modem's property sheet to see what choices are available.

Be aware that the settings on the modem property sheet are merely defaults. Communications programs can override these defaults.

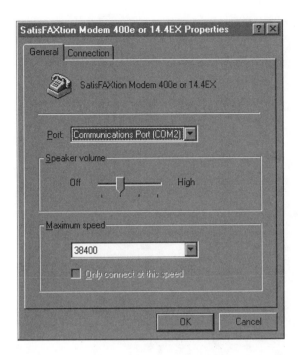

FIGURE 11-5.

The property sheet for a specific modem might let you adjust the communications port, the default speaker volume, maximum speed, and default communications settings (on the Connection tab, in this example).

For information about *setting up a new modem,* see "Installing a Legacy Peripheral," page 349.

Changing Dialing Locations

To change the settings for your dialing location, or to add new dialing locations, first double-click the Modems icon in Control Panel. Then, in the Modems property sheet (see Figure 11-4), click the Dialing Properties button. This brings you to the Dialing property sheet, shown in Figure 11-6 on the next page.

FIGURE 11-6.

The Dialing property sheet lets you specify the area code and country, as well as any access numbers required for local and long-distance calls.

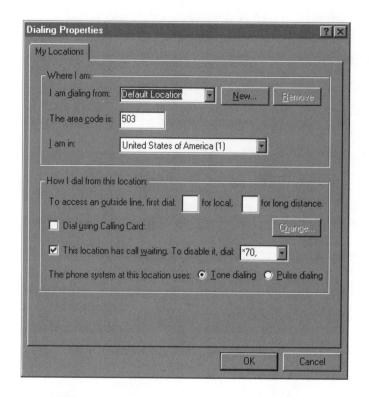

NOTE: Settings on the Dialing property sheet are used only by "TAPI-aware" applications—that is, programs that take advantage of Microsoft's telephony applications programming interface. All of the communications programs included with Windows 95—Microsoft Exchange, Dial-Up Networking, Phone Dialer, HyperTerminal, The Microsoft Network, and Microsoft Fax—are TAPI-aware. Most other communications programs written expressly for Windows 95 are also TAPI-aware.

This property sheet should already have settings in place for at least one location, identified as Default Location. If you have set up additional locations, you can see the settings for those locations by choosing from the I Am Dialing From drop-down list. Make sure the settings are appropriate for the location from which you call.

> If the phone line used by your modem has call-waiting service, be sure to indicate that on the Dialing property sheet, and also specify what code is used to disable the call-waiting feature. Otherwise, if an incoming call arrives while your modem is active, the call-waiting signal can disconnect the modem.

To add a new dialing location, click the New button. You'll then be asked to provide a name for the new location. After you do that and click OK, you'll be returned to the Dialing property sheet, where you can supply the area code and other settings for the new location.

NOTE: Make entries in the "local" and "long distance" text boxes only if you need to enter a number to get an outside line at this dialing location. The "long distance" box is *not* for entering a long-distance dialing prefix.

Setting Volume Levels

If your computer has a sound card, you can adjust the volume of sound sent from the sound card to your speakers, the volume level applied to the microphone jack, and the volume of sound sent out through the head-phone jack of your CD-ROM drive. To do any of these things, start by double-clicking the Multimedia icon in Control Panel. This action summons the Multimedia property sheet.

To change the speaker or microphone volume, click the Audio tab of the Multimedia property sheet. You'll see a dialog box similar to the one shown in Figure 11-7 on the next page. Simply adjust the Playback and Recording sliders as needed.

If your computer has more than one playback and recording device, you can specify the one that Windows will use by choosing from the drop-down lists in the Playback and Recording sections of the dialog box. And if your system is capable of recording at more than one quality level, choose the level you prefer from the Preferred Quality drop-down in the Recording section of the dialog box. Be aware that higher-quality recording generates larger sound (.WAV) files.

FIGURE 11-7.

On the Audio tab of the Multimedia property sheet, you can set volume levels for your speakers and microphone.

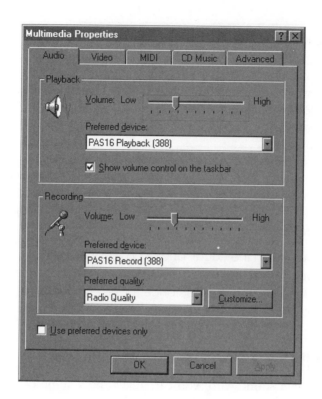

 If you select the Show Volume Control On The Taskbar check box, you can change the speaker volume level by clicking the sound icon in your taskbar's notification area. If you want to adjust the volume for a particular sound source (instead of the master speaker volume control), *double-click* the taskbar icon, which opens the Volume Control application. For more information about Volume Control, see "Controlling Sound Volume," page 554.

To set the volume level used by your CD-ROM when it's playing music CDs through the headphone jack, click the CD Music tab. In the ensuing dialog box you'll find another volume slider along with a drop-down list from which you can select the drive you want to adjust (in case your computer has more than one CD-ROM drive).

For information about *using the Volume Control program,* see "Controlling Sound Volume," page 554.

Setting the Video Playback Size

The Video tab of Control Panel's Multimedia property sheet lets you specify the size at which video (.AVI) files are played back. With the default setting in effect, .AVI files are played in a window at the same size at which they were recorded. This provides the smoothest playback and minimum graininess. But you might want to enlarge the playback size to see more detail. You can do that by double-clicking the Multimedia icon in Control Panel and then clicking the Video tab. You'll see a dialog box similar to the one shown in Figure 11-8.

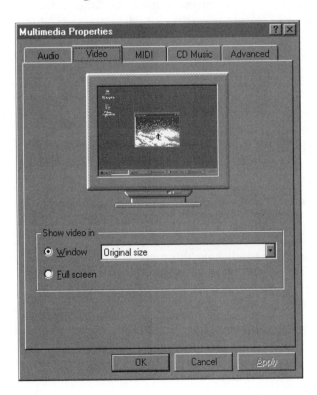

FIGURE 11-8.

The Video tab of the Multimedia property sheet lets you change the default playback size for video clips.

To choose a windowed playback size, open the Window drop-down list. To play your video clips in a full screen, rather than in a window, choose the Full Screen option button. You will probably get smoother playback in full-screen mode than you will in a maximized window.

 For information about *playing .AVI files*, see "Recording Sounds with Sound Recorder," page 557.

Specifying Regional (International) Settings

The Regional Settings icon in Control Panel allows you to adjust the way Windows displays dates, times, currency amounts, large numbers, and numbers with decimal fractions, as well as whether Windows should employ the metric or "imperial" system of measurement. This section of Control Panel corresponds to what was called International in earlier versions of Windows.

To modify any of Windows' regional settings, start by double-clicking the Regional Settings icon in Control Panel. You will see the five-tabbed property sheet shown in Figure 11-9.

On the first tab of the Regional Settings property sheet, you'll find a map of the world. If you're adjusting your system for a new country—for example, if you've just taken your portable computer overseas—start by clicking the new country on this map. In response, Windows applies the default settings for all adjustable items—numbers, currency, times, and dates—all at once. In most cases, you won't need to make any further changes. As an alternative to clicking the map, you can select a country from the drop-down list.

Control Panel does not change the keyboard layout when you choose a different country in the Regional Settings property sheet. To specify a different keyboard layout, use the Keyboard property sheet. For details, see "Installing Language Support and Using Keyboard Layouts," page 296.

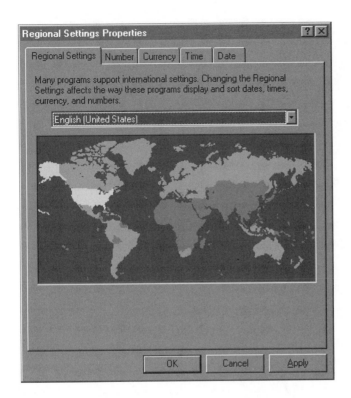

FIGURE 11-9.

You can change many regional settings at once, simply by clicking the world map in the Regional Settings property sheet.

To override one or more default settings for a country, click the appropriate tab of the Regional Settings property sheet and fill out the dialog box that appears. Figure 11-10 on the next page shows the dialog box you'll see if you click the Number tab. Note that the Measurement dropdown, near the bottom of this dialog box, lets you switch between the metric and "imperial" measurement systems. (The latter is called U.S. on the property sheet.)

Be aware that all the settings in the Regional Settings property sheet are merely defaults. Windows makes your choices available to applications, but the applications are not required to use them. Some programs ignore the Windows default settings and instead maintain their own formatting defaults. If you ask for a particular display format style via Control Panel, but your application uses a different style, consult the documentation or help file for your application.

FIGURE 11-10.

On the Number tab, you can choose the display formats to be used for decimal points and large numbers, as well as choose a default system of measurement.

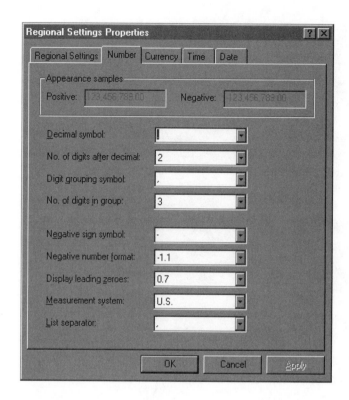

Installing Language Support and Using Keyboard Layouts

Windows 95 comes with support for a multitude of languages and keyboard layouts. If you work in more than one language or communicate with speakers of other languages, you might find it convenient to have two or more languages installed simultaneously. Then you can use simple mouse and keyboard procedures to switch from one language to another.

Languages and layouts are separate but related issues. When you activate another language, applications that have been written with language support in mind can provide appropriate services, such as using a different spelling checker or using special characters in TrueType fonts. For example, if you switch from English to Russian, WordPad automatically uses Cyrillic characters.

When you switch to a different language, you get the default keyboard layout for that language, but you can choose alternative layouts. For German, for example, Windows supplies a standard layout and an IBM layout. For Russian, there's a standard layout and a typewriter layout—and so on.

Even if you work only in English, you might want to check out alternative layouts. Typing letters with accents, for example, might be simpler if you use the United States–International layout. And if the standard QWERTY system of typing isn't your preference, you can opt for the United States–Dvorak layout.

Installing a New Language

You can install support for a new language as follows:

1. Double-click the Keyboard item in Control Panel.

2. Click the Language tab.

   These steps take you to the Language tab of the Keyboard property sheet, as shown in Figure 11-11 on the next page.

3. Click the Add button and select the language you want from the drop-down list.

   Windows might prompt you to insert one or more of your Windows 95 distribution diskettes or the Windows 95 CD-ROM.

 If the language you're looking for isn't in the drop-down list, double-click the Add/Remove Programs item in Control Panel. Click the Windows Setup tab and then select the Multilanguage Support check box and click OK. You'll be prompted for one or more diskettes or the Windows 95 CD-ROM. After you complete this process, return to the Keyboard item in Control Panel.

Before leaving the Keyboard property sheet, select one of the option buttons for switching languages. By default, you can switch from one language to another by holding down the Alt key on the left side of your keyboard and pressing the Shift key. If you prefer, you can opt for the

FIGURE 11-11.

In the Keyboard property sheet, you can add support for other languages or switch keyboard layouts.

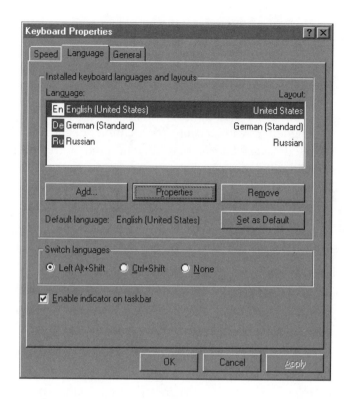

combination of Ctrl and Shift instead. Or you can turn off switching-by-keystroke altogether.

By default, Windows displays a two-letter symbol in the notification area of your taskbar whenever you have more than one language installed. You can use this symbol both as a reminder and as a switching mechanism. To switch languages, click the language symbol and then choose from the list that pops up. If, for some reason, you don't want this convenience, deselect the Enable Indicator On Taskbar check box at the bottom of the Keyboard property sheet.

 By right-clicking the language symbol in the notification area of your taskbar and choosing Properties from the object menu, you can go directly to the Keyboard property sheet without running Control Panel.

Switching Keyboard Layouts

To switch keyboard layouts, first go to the Language tab of the Keyboard property sheet in Control Panel, following steps 1 and 2 in the previous section. Select the language for which you want to switch layouts, and then click the Properties button. Then select the layout you want from the drop-down list that appears.

12

Running MS-DOS–Based Programs

L ike earlier versions of Windows, Windows 95 lets you run MS-DOS–based programs without leaving Windows. Subject to constraints imposed by the overall memory capacity of your system, you can run as many MS-DOS "sessions" (programs) simultaneously as you please. You can run most of your MS-DOS–based programs in windows that look and behave much like those of Windows-based programs. Or you can run MS-DOS–based programs in "full-screen" mode, so that they look the way they did when you ran them outside of Windows.

Windows provides multitasking services for MS-DOS–based programs, just as it does for Windows-based programs. That means, for example, that a lengthy macro in an MS-DOS–based spreadsheet program or a script in an MS-DOS–based communications program can continue to run while you focus your attention on another program. (You can disable the background processing of any MS-DOS–based program if you want.) Windows also manages resource contention among MS-DOS–based programs and between MS-DOS–based programs and Windows-based programs. So, for example, if you print a document from an MS-DOS–based word processor and your printer is busy, your document joins the printer queue just as though it had come from a Windows-based program.

If you were unable to run certain large MS-DOS–based programs under Windows 3.x, you may be pleasantly surprised to discover that your programs run fine under Windows 95. That's because Windows 95 stores more of its own essential "driver" files in extended memory, thereby making a smaller demand on the memory range used by MS-DOS–based programs. Unless your particular hardware requires one or more "real-mode" drivers, each of your MS-DOS sessions should be able to access considerably more memory than it could when running under earlier versions of Windows.

A smaller footprint in conventional memory is only one of the ways in which Windows 95 provides improved support for MS-DOS–based programs. Others include a streamlined interface for tailoring the way individual programs use memory and other resources (eliminating the need for the PIF Editor program supplied with earlier versions of Windows), the ability to run MS-DOS–based programs in scalable windows, the ability to tailor the MS-DOS environment on a program-by-program basis, and better support for graphics-intensive programs such as games.

In this chapter we'll survey the ins and outs of running MS-DOS–based programs under Windows 95. We'll also spend a few paragraphs looking at the MS-DOS prompt itself. If you're accustomed to using MS-DOS commands for tasks such as copying files, creating directories (folders), or running commands in batch mode, there's no requirement to change your ways. Fortunately, thanks to support for UNC pathnames at the MS-DOS prompt, even these kinds of housekeeping chores should be easier to perform under Windows 95 than under previous versions of Windows.

To work exclusively at the MS-DOS prompt, without going into the graphical environment of Windows, press F8 as your computer is booting. That is, turn on your computer. Then, when the message "Starting Windows 95" appears on your screen, press F8. From the startup menu that appears, choose Command Prompt Only by typing its number and pressing Enter. If later on you want to start a normal Windows session, type *win* at the MS-DOS prompt or reboot your computer.

If you're already running Windows and you want to work exclusively at the MS-DOS prompt, choose Shut Down from the Start menu. Then select Restart The Computer In MS-DOS Mode. To quit your MS-DOS–only session and restart Windows, type *exit* at the MS-DOS prompt. If you're quitting for the day, you can safely turn your computer off; Windows will then start normally at your next session.

Launching an MS-DOS–Based Program

You can start an MS-DOS–based program using any of the techniques you use to start Windows-based programs. To start a program, you can do any of the following:

■ Choose your MS-DOS–based program from the Start menu, if it's there.

- Double-click the icon for your MS-DOS–based program in a folder or Windows Explorer window.

- Choose the Start menu's Run command, and then type the name of your program in the Open text box.

- Run MS-DOS Prompt and then type the name of your program at the MS-DOS command prompt.

If you start your program from either the Run dialog box or the MS-DOS command prompt, you might need to include your program's path as well as its name. In other words, starting your program from either command prompt is exactly like starting it from the MS-DOS prompt in earlier versions of MS-DOS.

 If you want to maximize the amount of conventional memory available to your MS-DOS–based program, launch it by choosing it from the Start menu, by double-clicking its icon, or by using the Start menu's Run command. Running MS-DOS Prompt consumes several kilobytes of memory by loading part of the command processor.

In addition to all these methods, you can, of course, create shortcuts for any of your MS-DOS–based programs and run those programs by double-clicking a shortcut icon. Creating a shortcut for an MS-DOS–based program is exactly like creating a shortcut for a Windows-based program.

 For more information about *starting programs*, see Chapter 2, "Running Programs and Opening Documents," page 55.

For more information about *creating shortcuts*, see "Creating a Shortcut," page 73.

Of PIFs and Property Sheets

If you have installed Windows 95 as an upgrade to an earlier version of Windows, you may already have created Program Information Files (PIFs) for some of your MS-DOS–based applications. If so, Windows 95 will continue to use the settings in your PIFs as you run your applications in the new environment.

> **NOTE:** In a folder window's details view, the file type for a PIF is shown as "Shortcut to MS-DOS Program."

Windows also maintains information about popular MS-DOS–based programs in a file called APPS.INF. If you run a program for which no PIF exists, Windows looks for information about the program in APPS.INF. Windows uses any information it finds there to create a PIF for your program. If your program is not included in APPS.INF and Windows finds no PIF for it, Windows runs your program with default settings. In the majority of cases, these defaults allow your program to run effectively, so you don't need to concern yourself with property settings. If you want, however, you can adjust your program's settings by working with its property sheet. When you make any changes to the property sheet, Windows records your choices in a newly created PIF.

See Also: For information about *application property sheets*, see "Working with Your Programs' Property Sheets," page 318.

Terminating an MS-DOS Session

The best way to end any MS-DOS–based program is to use the program's normal Quit or Exit command. Doing so ensures that the program is terminated in an orderly manner and that you're given the option to save any work created in the program.

If you're running an MS-DOS–based program in a window, however, you can also close it by clicking the Close button at the right edge of the title bar, by choosing Close from the Control menu, or by double-clicking the Control-menu icon. Normally, it's not a good idea to use any of these methods for shutting your program down, however, because Windows cannot ensure that your program is ready to be terminated. You could lose work or damage open data files by using a Windows procedure for shutting down an MS-DOS–based program.

By default, when you use a Windows procedure to close an MS-DOS–based program, Windows displays a warning. You can then ignore the warning and go ahead with your program's termination, or you can go back to your program and use its own shut-down procedure. Normally, Windows also requires you to close all MS-DOS–based programs before shutting down Windows itself. (By changing a property-sheet setting, you can disable these safeguards for particular programs. For details, see "Allowing Windows to Close an MS-DOS–Based Program," page 331.)

Depending on how another option on the MS-DOS–based program's property sheet is set, the program may remain visible in a window after you shut it down. If it does, the title bar for the closed program's window will include the word *Finished*. A program marked *Finished* has already shut itself down, so it's perfectly safe to close its window by clicking the Close button or pressing Alt-F4. (The option to keep a closed program visible in a *Finished* window is handy at times because it allows you to see the program's final output, including any messages displayed by the program if it happens to terminate abnormally. For information about using this option, see "Keeping a Program's Final Screen Visible at Close," page 323.)

Windowed Versus Full-Screen Display

With few exceptions, you can run any MS-DOS–based program either in full-screen display mode or in a window. (The principal exceptions are graphics programs that use resolutions higher than 640×480.) If you run a program in full-screen mode, it looks exactly as it does if you run it under a pre–Windows 95 version of MS-DOS. If you run it in a window, it has a title bar, a Control menu, and all the other standard window paraphernalia. Figure 12-1 on the next page illustrates an MS-DOS–based program running in a window.

FIGURE 12-1.

In windowed display, an MS-DOS–based program has all the standard window equipment—a title bar, sizing buttons, a Control-menu icon, and so on.

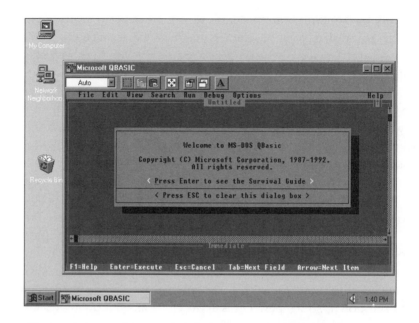

Advantages of Full-Screen Display

One advantage of running in full-screen mode is that your program gets the maximum amount of screen real estate—the same amount of display space you would have if you were running the program outside of Windows. If you run in a window, you can maximize the window but the presence of a window title bar means you'll still have something less than the full screen to work with.

> **NOTE:** "Maximizing" an MS-DOS window does not necessarily fill the screen, as it does with any resizable Windows-based application. The portion of the screen that the maximized window occupies depends on your Windows display resolution, the display mode used by the MS-DOS–based application, and the font size you select. (For information about changing the Windows display resolution, see "Changing Display Resolution," page 94. For information about font-size options, see "Font Options in a Windowed Display," page 312.)

Depending on the speed of your hardware, you might also enjoy faster screen performance in full-screen display. Particularly with graphics programs, this could be a compelling reason to choose full-screen mode.

If you're running in full-screen mode, you can switch to a different program by pressing Alt-Tab to invoke the "cool switcher," by pressing Ctrl-Esc to invoke the Start menu, or by first switching your program back to windowed display. When you switch away from a full-screen MS-DOS–based program, a button for your program appears on the taskbar. You can switch back to the full-screen program by clicking its taskbar button.

 If you have more than one full-screen MS-DOS session running and you want to switch from a full-screen MS-DOS session to the desktop, press Alt-Tab to invoke the cool switcher. This lets you switch between applications, but not to the desktop. Unless you *click* somewhere while the cool switcher is displayed, that is. Clicking anywhere on the screen takes you to the desktop.

You can also switch to the desktop by pressing Ctrl-Esc, which displays the desktop and opens the Start menu.

Advantages of Windowed Display

Windowed display, on the other hand, confers several benefits:

- You can keep several programs in view at the same time.

- You can more easily switch between programs.

- You can copy (but not cut) material from one program and paste it into another.

- You can read or modify your program's property sheet.

Switching Between Full-Screen and Windowed Display

Provided your MS-DOS–based program is not one of the few that run only in full-screen display, and provided you have not disabled the Alt-Enter shortcut key, you can switch from full-screen display to windowed display by pressing Alt-Enter. If you're running in windowed mode, you can use Alt-Enter to switch to full-screen display. Or, if the toolbar is visible, you can click the Full Screen tool—the fourth icon from the right.

 If you want to switch from full-screen to windowed display but you've forgotten which keystroke combination to use (Alt-Enter), press Alt-Tab or Ctrl-Esc to switch to another program. Then right-click the taskbar button for the program you switched away from. Choose Properties from the object menu, click the Screen tab in the property sheet, and select the Window option button.

Using the Toolbar

Like folder windows, the window that displays your MS-DOS–based program includes an optional toolbar. You can toggle this toolbar on or off by right-clicking anywhere on the window's title bar and choosing the Toolbar command from the ensuing Control menu. The toolbar slightly reduces the maximum amount of space that your application can use, but in return it offers the handy commands shown in Table 12-1.

All of these commands are also available via the Control menu, the menu that appears when you right-click the window's title bar (or click with either button on the icon at the left edge of the title bar), but you might find them more accessible with the toolbar in view.

Table 12-1. MS-DOS Window Toolbar

Toolbar Icon	Description
Auto	Font drop-down. Lets you choose between preset font options and an automatic mode in which the display font automatically adjusts as the program's window is resized.
	Mark. Use this to select text or graphics prior to copying. (If you have turned QuickEdit on, you do not need to use this command before selecting. For details, see "Mouse Options in a Windowed Display," page 313.)
	Copy. Copies the selection to the Clipboard.
	Paste. Pastes the Clipboard's contents into the MS-DOS–based application.
	Full-screen. Switches from windowed display to full-screen display.
	Properties. Displays the application's property sheet.
	Background. Allows a process in the application to continue running when you switch to other applications. Background processing is on if the toolbar icon appears to be pushed in.
A	Font. Displays the Font tab of the program's property sheet.

See Also: For information about *controlling the appearance of the toolbar whenever you start an application*, see "Displaying or Hiding the Toolbar," page 328.

Font Options in a Windowed Display

When you run an MS-DOS–based program in a window, Windows always displays its text in a monospaced font. That's because MS-DOS–based programs typically depend on uniform character spacing. You have choices about the size of the font to be used, however. To exercise your options, right-click the program's title bar, choose Properties from the Control menu, and then click the Font tab. You'll see the dialog box shown in Figure 12-2. The list box in the upper right quadrant of this dialog box presents the available font-size choices, while the two preview boxes below show the relative space occupied by the program's window and a sample of the selected font.

FIGURE 12-2.

Text in a windowed MS-DOS–based program is always displayed in a monospaced font of Windows' choosing, but you have options about font size.

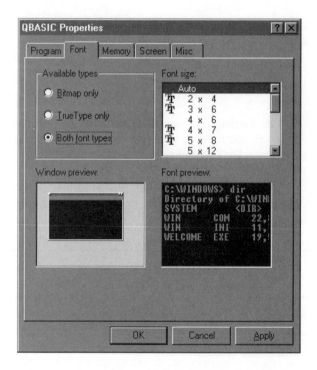

If you choose Auto (the default option), Windows automatically picks the optimal font and size whenever you change the dimensions of the program's window. If you select any of the other size options, Windows adjusts the dimensions of the window to fit the selected font size. With any size other than Auto in effect, you can't increase the size of the window. (You can click the Maximize button, but its only effect is to move the window to the upper left corner of the screen—without enlarging it.) You can decrease the window's size, but Windows then "clips" (truncates) the window's contents rather than adjusting the size of the text.

Note that the available font sizes (see Figure 12-2) are not listed as conventional point sizes. Instead, they're listed by the pixel dimensions of the font's character matrix. For example, 4 × 7 denotes a font in which each character occupies some portion of a box measuring four pixels wide by seven pixels tall. Some of the character matrix, of course, is actually "white" space. If you experiment with the various size options, you'll find several in which the vertical dimension is double or nearly double the horizontal dimension. These are not tall and skinny fonts; rather, they're options in which your text lines are more widely spaced. If you find the text in a windowed display hard to read, you might want to sample some of these options.

Fonts available for use in windowed MS-DOS–based programs come in two flavors: bitmap and TrueType. In the property sheet (see Figure 12-2), you can restrict the font choices to one type or the other, but it's unlikely you'll find a compelling reason to do so. For performance reasons, Windows uses a bitmap font when one happens to be available at the optimal size. Otherwise, it uses TrueType for scalability.

As you've seen, the toolbar includes a font-size drop-down list as well as a button that summons the property sheet. When all you want to do is make a size selection, and you don't care about seeing a preview of the selected size, the drop-down is a more direct way to get the job done.

Mouse Options in a Windowed Display

If your MS-DOS–based program supports the mouse, and you run the program in full-screen mode, the MS-DOS–based program "owns" the mouse. That is, you can choose commands, make selections, or do anything else with the mouse that you would be able to do if you were running your program outside of Windows.

If you run the program in a window, you have a choice about mouse ownership. You can continue to let the MS-DOS–based program own the mouse, or you can let Windows own it. If the program owns the mouse,

mouse, you will need to use the Mark command (on the toolbar or the Control menu) before copying anything to the Clipboard. If you let Windows own it, you can use your mouse to select information and copy it to the Clipboard, exactly as you would do in a Windows-based program. But you won't be able to use the mouse for choosing commands in the MS-DOS–based program.

Whichever mouse mode you elect to use, you can use the mouse to change the window's size or position, to choose commands from the toolbar, or to choose commands from the Control menu. In other words, the issue of who owns the mouse arises only when the mouse pointer lies within the client area of the program's window. On the borders, the toolbar, or the title bar, Windows always retains control of the mouse.

To switch from one mouse mode to the other, first display the program's property sheet—by clicking the Properties tool on the toolbar or by right-clicking the title bar and choosing Properties from the Control menu. Then click the Misc tab of the property sheet. You'll see the dialog box shown in Figure 12-3.

FIGURE 12-3.

On the Misc tab of the property sheet, you can tell Windows how your mouse should behave when its pointer lies within the MS-DOS–based program's client area.

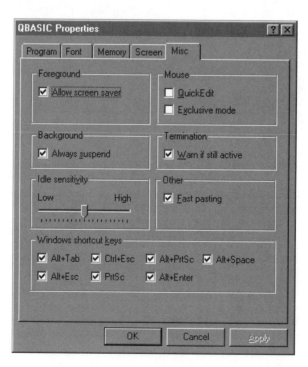

In the Mouse section, near the upper right corner of this dialog box, select the QuickEdit check box if you want to be able to select and copy window contents without first choosing the Mark command—that is, if you want Windows to have full control over your mouse. Leave this check box deselected if you want to be able to use your mouse to interact with the MS-DOS–based program.

The Mouse section of the property sheet's Misc tab also includes an Exclusive Mode option. If you select this option, the MS-DOS–based program will have sole dominion over the mouse as long as the MS-DOS–based program has the focus. That is, in exclusive mode, the mouse pointer will appear to be trapped within the client area of the MS-DOS–based program's window.

 If you turn exclusive mode on and then change your mind, you can return mouse control to Windows by pressing Alt-Spacebar to open the Control menu. Then click the Properties icon on the toolbar or choose Properties from the Control menu. Then you can click the Misc tab and deselect the Exclusive Mode check box.

 For information about *the other Misc-tab options*, see "Options on the Misc Tab," page 330.

Using Copy and Paste

Windows provides basic copy-and-paste services (without OLE) for MS-DOS–based applications, just as it does for Windows-based programs. The procedures for copying and pasting are nearly the same in both kinds of applications.

For more information about *copying and pasting*, see Chapter 10, "Exchanging Information: The Clipboard and OLE," page 251.

Copying from an MS-DOS–Based Application

To copy a block of data from a windowed MS-DOS–based application:

1. Click the Mark tool on the toolbar. Or right-click the title bar, choose Edit from the Control menu, and then choose Mark on the submenu that appears.

2. Drag the mouse to select the data you want to copy.

3. Press Enter or click the Copy tool on the toolbar.

4. Activate the document into which you want to paste, position the insertion point where you want the copied material to appear, and choose the Paste command.

If you have turned on the QuickEdit option for your MS-DOS–based application, you can omit step 1. (For more information about the QuickEdit option, see "Mouse Options in a Windowed Display," page 313.) How do you know if the QuickEdit option is on? You can go to the Misc tab of the property sheet and look at the QuickEdit check box. Or, more simply, you can drag with the mouse and see what happens. If QuickEdit is on, the word *Select* appears in the program's title bar as soon as you start dragging. If it does not, you are not in QuickEdit mode, and you need to click the Mark tool before making your selection.

Note one important difference between selecting text in an MS-DOS–based application and selecting text in a Windows-based application: In an MS-DOS–based application, your selection is always rectangular, even if that means that lines of text are truncated on the left side, the right side, or both. Figure 12-4 shows an example of a text selection in an MS-DOS window. In contrast, when you select text in a Windows-based application, your selection follows the flow of your text, whether or not that produces a rectangular block.

FIGURE 12-4.
When you select text in an MS-DOS–based application, your selection is rectangular, even if that means that lines are truncated.

 You can also select data in an MS-DOS–based application using the keyboard. Open the Control menu by holding down the Alt key while you press the Spacebar. Press E to open the Edit submenu, followed by K to choose the Mark command. You will see a rectangular cursor in the upper left corner of the application's window. This is your (unexpanded) selection. Use the Up, Down, Left, and Right arrow keys to position this cursor in one corner of the area you want to select. Then hold down the Shift key while you use arrow keys to expand the selection. When you have made your selection, press Enter to copy it to the Clipboard.

Pasting into an MS-DOS–Based Application

To paste data into an MS-DOS–based application, simply position your cursor where you want the pasted data to appear. Then open the Control menu, choose Edit, and choose Paste. Or click the Paste tool on the toolbar.

Note that the Paste command in an MS-DOS–based application is always active, even if the Clipboard is empty or contains data in a format that's not appropriate for your application. If you try to paste graphics data into a text-based application, you'll get an error message when you paste. A different error message appears if the Clipboard is empty when you try to paste.

Also be aware that when you paste text into an MS-DOS–based application, Windows feeds characters to the application exactly as if you had typed them yourself at the keyboard. That is, the program itself cannot tell that the characters aren't coming directly from the keyboard. If you paste into a program that performs some kind of syntax checking—for example, a spreadsheet that checks cell entries for correct formulation, or a program editor that verifies correct programming code—your paste may be interrupted by error messages from the application.

If you experience other kinds of problems pasting into an MS-DOS–based program, try disabling the Fast Pasting option. With this option on (as it normally is), Windows feeds character data to your program as fast as it can. Most, but not all, programs can accept this fast transfer. If yours cannot, open the Misc tab of your program's property sheet and deselect the Fast Pasting check box.

Working with Your Programs' Property Sheets

Each of your MS-DOS–based programs has a property sheet that spells out everything Windows needs to know to run your program. (As mentioned, Windows records your property-sheet settings in a Program Information File, or PIF.) You can use the property sheet to adjust such things as the amount of memory allocated to a program, the program's initial display mode (windowed or full-screen), the behavior of your mouse when the program is running in a window, and so on.

To get to a program's property sheet, do any of the following:

- If the program is already running, right-click its title bar or its taskbar button and choose Properties from the Control menu. (If the program is running in full-screen mode, first press Alt-Enter to switch to windowed mode.)

- If the program is already running and the toolbar is visible, click the Properties tool.

■ If the program is not running, right-click its entry in a folder or Windows Explorer window. Then choose Properties from the object menu.

If you open the property sheet while the program is not running, you'll see a tab called General that does not otherwise appear. This tab includes information about the size of the program, its creation and most-recent-access dates, and so on.

See Also: For more information about *the property sheet's General tab,* see "Inspecting Folder and File Properties," page 137.

Options on the Program Tab

Figure 12-5 on the next page shows the Program tab of an MS-DOS–based program's property sheet. Here you can do any of the following:

■ Change the name that appears on the program's title bar when the program is running in a window.

■ Add command-line parameters or otherwise modify the MS-DOS command line used to execute the program.

■ Specify a startup data folder.

■ Specify the name of a batch file that Windows will run prior to launching your program.

■ Specify a shortcut key that you can use to launch your program.

■ Indicate whether you want the program to start running in a maximized window, in a restored window, or as a minimized taskbar button.

■ Elect to keep the program's final display visible in a window after you quit the program.

■ Change the icon that appears on the program's title bar, on its taskbar button, and in folder and Windows Explorer windows.

FIGURE 12-5.

The Program tab lets you specify basic information about a program, such as its name and location.

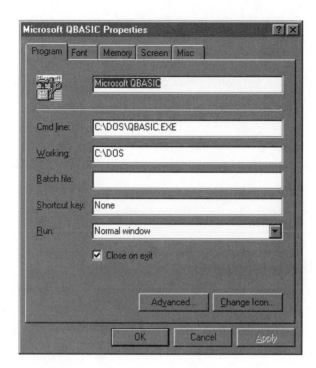

- "Hide" your program from Windows, so the program won't be able to detect the fact that you're running it under Windows.

- Run the program in MS-DOS mode.

- Have Windows recommend MS-DOS mode if Windows doesn't have enough resources to run the program normally.

If you decide to run your program in MS-DOS mode, the property sheet offers some additional options, discussed below.

Changing a Program's Title Bar Caption

To change the text that appears on a program's title bar, simply modify whatever appears in the first text box of the Program tab. For example, entering *QBasic* in the first text box of the property sheet shown in Figure 12-5 changes the title bar from "Microsoft QBASIC" to "QBasic."

Adding Command-Line Parameters

The second text box in the Program tab, the one marked Cmd Line, specifies the command line that MS-DOS uses to run your program. Many programs allow you to specify one or more command-line parameters following the name of your program's executable file. Depending on the program involved, parameters can be used for such things as loading a data file at the same time the executable is launched, modifying some aspect of the program's behavior, and so on. If you regularly want your MS-DOS–based program to use a particular command-line parameter, you can specify that parameter in the Cmd Line text box. Be sure to include a space character immediately after the name of the executable file, just as you would if you were entering the parameter at the MS-DOS command prompt.

 If you put a question mark as the program's parameter (that is, you follow the program name in the Cmd Line box with a space and a question mark), Windows pauses to ask for any command-line parameters whenever you start the program. This is useful, for example, for programs that use the name of the file you want to open as a command-line parameter.

Specifying a Startup Folder

The Working text box in the Program tab lets you specify an initial data folder ("directory" in MS-DOS parlance) to be used by the MS-DOS–based program. For example, if you enter *c:\mystuff* on the Working line for the QBasic property sheet, QBasic will initially be set to read files from and save files to the folder C:\MyStuff. This line is blank by default, which means the program makes its own choice about what default data folder to use. In most programs, the default data folder is the folder in which the program's executable file is stored.

Specifying the Name of a Batch File

If you enter the name of a batch file on the Batch File line of the Program tab, Windows always runs that batch file prior to launching the MS-DOS–based program. You can use this technique to launch a terminate-and-stay-resident (TSR) program that will share an MS-DOS session with your MS-DOS–based application. (If you run the TSR directly, instead of using this batch-file approach, the TSR will run in its own separate MS-DOS session, and your program will not have access to its services.) You can also use a batch file to modify some aspect of the MS-DOS environment. For example, when you run MS-DOS Prompt from the Start menu, you are running an MS-DOS session whose executable file is Command.com. If you want your MS-DOS Prompt sessions to use something other than the default pg (C:\>) prompt string, you can enter a Prompt command in a batch file and then specify the name of that batch file on the Batch File line of the Program tab for the Command.com property sheet. (For another way to modify the MS-DOS environment, see "Running a Program in MS-DOS Mode," page 323.)

Specifying a Shortcut Key

On the Shortcut Key line, you can specify a keyboard shortcut for switching to the MS-DOS–based program. For example, if you run the MS-DOS–based version of Systat 6.0 under Windows 95, you might want to supply Systat with the shortcut Ctrl-Alt-S. Note, though, that unlike a shortcut key assigned to a Windows-based program, the shortcut you give to an MS-DOS–based program cannot be used to launch the program. It works only for switching to the program after the program is already running.

See Also: For information about *assigning a shortcut key to a Windows-based program*, see "Assigning a Shortcut Key to a Shortcut," page 76.

Specifying the Initial Window State

You can use the Run line of the Program tab to indicate whether you want a program to open initially in a maximized window, in a restored window, or minimized. You might, for example, want to have a program open minimized if you include it with one or more other programs in your StartUp folder. That way, it will be unobtrusively available at the beginning of each Windows session.

Note that if you choose Minimized, the program will always start minimized, even if you also choose full-screen display on the Screen tab.

See Also: For information about *full-screen display*, see "Windowed Versus Full-Screen Display," page 307.

Keeping a Program's Final Screen Visible at Close

If an MS-DOS–based program terminates abnormally, it might be useful to keep the program's final screen output visible in a window after the program closes. That way you can read any error messages that the program may have displayed.

To exercise this option, clear the Close On Exit check box on the Program tab of the property sheet.

Changing a Program's Icon

Windows assigns a default MS-DOS icon to all MS-DOS–based applications. This icon appears on your program's title bar, on its taskbar button, and in your folder and Windows Explorer windows. If you'd like to choose a different icon, click the Change Icon button, near the bottom of the Program tab. A selection of alternative icons appears in the ensuing dialog box. If none of those suit you, specify an .ICO file (or the name of a .DLL or .EXE file containing icon resources) on the File Name line of that dialog box. Or click the Browse button and navigate to a file containing icon resources.

Preventing a Program from Knowing That It's Running Under Windows

Given adequate memory, nearly all MS-DOS–based programs are fully functional when running under Windows. In rare cases, however, a program might not run or might not run normally if it detects the presence of Windows. Should your program be one of those exceptional few, you can use a "stealth" feature to keep it from knowing that Windows is running. To do this, click the Advanced button near the bottom of the Program tab. Then select the check box labeled Prevent MS-DOS–Based Programs From Detecting Windows.

Running a Program in MS-DOS Mode

If an MS-DOS–based program won't run satisfactorily under Windows, no matter how you tweak its property sheet, you'll want to run it in MS-DOS mode. Before launching a program in MS-DOS mode, Windows closes all running programs and then removes most of itself from memory. The only part of Windows that remains is a stub that Windows uses to reload itself after you quit the MS-DOS–based program. In this mode, you can run only a single MS-DOS session; all other applications—whether Windows-based or MS-DOS–based—are closed before entering MS-DOS mode.

To set a program so that it always runs in MS-DOS mode, click the Advanced button on the Property tab. Then select the MS-DOS Mode check box. If you're not sure whether your program requires MS-DOS mode, click Advanced on the Program tab, and then select the check box labeled Suggest MS-DOS Mode As Necessary. Windows will then recommend MS-DOS mode if it appears that your program will not run without it.

Whether you run in MS-DOS mode by your own insistence or at Windows' recommendation, you also have the option of specifying CONFIG.SYS and AUTOEXEC.BAT settings tailored for the application you're planning to run. In other words, you can have default CONFIG.SYS and AUTOEXEC.BAT files that are applied to all your normal (non-MS-DOS-mode) MS-DOS sessions and different versions of CONFIG.SYS and AUTOEXEC.BAT for each program that you run in MS-DOS mode.

To modify the CONFIG.SYS and AUTOEXEC.BAT files used by a particular application running in MS-DOS mode, first click the Advanced button on the Program tab of the application's property sheet. Select the MS-DOS Mode check box on the Advanced page, and then click the option button labeled Specify A New MS-DOS Configuration. In the windows below this option button, you can edit the current CONFIG.SYS and AUTOEXEC.BAT files.

Going into MS-DOS mode can be disruptive because Windows has to shut down all running programs before it can do this. Therefore, by default, Windows displays a confirmation prompt before launching any program in MS-DOS mode. If you want to disable this prompt, click the Advanced button on the Program tab of the application's property sheet and deselect the check box labeled Warn Before Entering MS-DOS Mode.

Options on the Font Tab

The Font tab allows you to choose alternative display fonts to be used when an MS-DOS–based program is running in a window.

See Also: For more information about *the Font tab*, see "Font Options in a Windowed Display," page 312.

Options on the Memory Tab

The Memory tab, depicted in Figure 12-6, allows you to allocate to your applications particular amounts of memory in various categories. Those categories are as follows:

Conventional	Memory in the 0–640 KB range
Expanded (EMS)	Physical memory above 1024 KB that is "mapped" into ranges between 640 KB and 1024 KB
Extended (XMS)	Memory above 1024 KB
DOS Protected-Mode (DPMI)	Extended memory that is managed by the DOS Protected Mode Interface specification

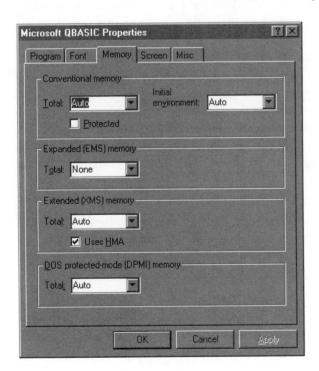

FIGURE 12-6.

Options on the Memory tab let you limit the amount of memory available to an application.

NOTE: If your CONFIG.SYS file invokes EMM386.EXE with the *noems* option, the EMS drop-down will not be available.

In all four cases, the default setting, Auto, should work for most programs.

For conventional memory, Auto means that Windows supplies your application with as much memory as it can. Unless you're running a particularly small-scale MS-DOS–based application and you need to conserve memory for other programs, it's unlikely you'll find a good reason not to choose Auto.

Auto also means "as much as possible" in the EMS and XMS drop-downs. In rare cases, an MS-DOS–based program may have trouble handling an unlimited amount of EMS or XMS memory. If your program is one of the exceptional few, use these drop-downs to reduce the available EMS or XMS memory.

In the case of DPMI, the Auto setting causes Windows to allocate an amount of memory based on your current configuration. Here, too, it's unlikely that you'll need to choose a different setting.

The Memory tab also provides a drop-down in which you can specify the size of your program's MS-DOS environment. The environment is an area of memory used by the MS-DOS command interpreter, Command.com, to store information about the current *path* (the set of directories that MS-DOS searches when you issue a command that does not include a path specification), the current prompt string, the location of a TEMP directory, and other similar variables. If you leave the Auto setting in place here, Windows allocates the amount of memory specified by the Shell statement in your CONFIG.SYS file (or the default amount, if there is no Shell statement). If you ever see "Out of environment space" errors in your MS-DOS sessions, try increasing this memory allocation.

Options on the Screen Tab

Options on the Screen tab allow you to do the following:

- Choose between full-screen and windowed display mode.

- Stipulate that a session should start with a 25-line, 43-line, or 50-line display.

- Display or hide the toolbar.

- Indicate whether Windows should remember your screen size, window position, and font at the end of the current session and restore it at the beginning of the next session.

- Disable a technique that Windows uses by default to achieve faster screen performance, in case that technique causes problems with your program.

- Disable a technique that Windows uses to allocate memory more efficiently, in case that technique causes problems with your program.

Figure 12-7 shows an example of the property sheet's Screen tab.

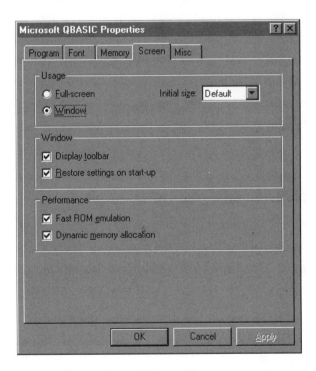

FIGURE 12-7.

On the Screen tab you can choose between windowed and full-screen display, opt for a 43-line or 50-line display, and override two of Windows' performance defaults.

Choosing Between Full-Screen and Windowed Display

As mentioned, you can switch a program between full-screen and windowed display at any time, simply by pressing Alt-Enter. Should you want to change the default display mode, you can do so by visiting the property sheet's Screen tab and selecting the Full-Screen or Window option button.

Specifying a 43-Line or 50-Line Display

Most MS-DOS–based programs display 25 lines of text per screen. Some also allow you to choose a 43-line or 50-line display. If your program supports these alternative display modes, you can use its property sheet to make either the default mode on startup. Click the Screen tab and select from the options listed in the Initial Size drop-down.

To let an MS-DOS–based program make its own decision about how many lines per screen to display, choose Default from the Initial Size drop-down.

Displaying or Hiding the Toolbar

The toolbar makes it easier to choose commands when an MS-DOS–based program is running in a window. In return for the favor, it slightly reduces the amount of screen real estate available for the program's display. You can suppress the toolbar (or reenable it) by means of the Display Toolbar check box on the Screen tab.

See Also: For information about *the toolbar,* see "Using the Toolbar," page 310.

Remembering or Forgetting Window Settings

By default, when you end a windowed MS-DOS session, Windows records the size and position of your window, as well as the current font size. At the start of your next session, those settings are restored. If for any reason you'd rather have Windows forget the current window settings, visit the Screen tab of the property sheet and clear the check box labeled Restore Settings On Start-Up.

> **NOTE:** Windows always records whether a program is running in full-screen or windowed display mode when you close the program—whether or not the Restore Settings On Start-Up check box is checked. The next time you run the program (unless you edit its property sheet in the meantime), it will start in the same mode—full-screen or windowed—in which you last closed it.

If you want to ensure that a program always starts in a particular display mode, regardless of its condition when you last closed the program, open the property sheet for its PIF from a Windows Explorer or folder window. (You can use the Find command to find the PIF. On the Name & Location tab, enter the name of the program. On the Advanced tab, in the Of Type drop-down, select Shortcut To MS-DOS Program.) Make all the settings you need, including the selection of Full-Screen or Window on the Screen tab. Then switch to the General tab and select the Read-Only check box. This prevents Windows from updating the PIF when you close the program.

Turning Off Video ROM Emulation

To achieve faster screen performance, Windows normally uses volatile memory (RAM) to emulate video routines that are stored in read-only memory (ROM). If you experience any abnormal screen behavior in an MS-DOS–based program, try turning this emulation off. Clear the Fast ROM Emulation check box on the Screen tab.

Turning Off Dynamic Memory Allocation

Programs use considerably less video memory when displaying text than when displaying graphics. When an MS-DOS–based program switches from a graphics display to a text display, Windows normally takes advantage of the "memory dividend" so that more memory will be available for other programs. When an MS-DOS–based program switches back to a graphics display, Windows reallocates memory to the MS-DOS session. If you experience any problems switching from text mode to graphics mode in an MS-DOS–based program, try turning off this "dynamic memory allocation." Clear the Dynamic Memory Allocation check box on the Screen tab of the property sheet.

Options on the Misc Tab

Figure 12-8 illustrates the Misc tab. With options on the Misc tab you can do the following:

- Disable your screen saver when an MS-DOS–based program has the focus.

- Specify how you want your mouse to behave when an MS-DOS–based program has the focus. (For information about QuickEdit and exclusive mode, see "Mouse Options in a Windowed Display," page 313.)

- Allow or disallow background processing of an MS-DOS–based application.

- Disable the warning that Windows normally displays when you use the Close icon to terminate an MS-DOS–based program, as well as the requirement that you close the MS-DOS–based program before quitting Windows.

FIGURE 12-8.

The Misc tab of an MS-DOS–based program's property sheet provides control over mouse behavior and several other matters.

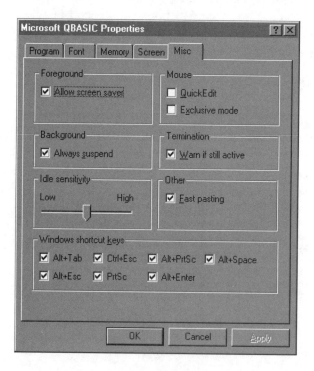

- Adjust the "idle sensitivity"—the amount of time Windows will wait before reducing the resources allocated to an idle MS-DOS–based program that has the focus.

- Adopt a slower pasting mode for an MS-DOS–based program that cannot accept data from the Clipboard as quickly as Windows normally supplies it.

- Disable certain keystroke combinations (such as Alt-Tab) that are normally used by Windows so that those combinations can be used by an MS-DOS–based program.

Disabling the Windows Screen Saver

Normally Windows starts the current screen saver after a specified amount of idle time has elapsed, regardless of what program has the focus. If your MS-DOS–based program has its own screen saver (and you want to use it instead of the Windows screen saver), or if for any reason the Windows screen saver interferes with your MS-DOS–based program's functionality, visit the Misc tab of the program's property sheet and clear the Allow Screen Saver check box.

Allowing an MS-DOS–Based Program to Run in the Background

If you want processing in an MS-DOS–based program to continue while you work in another program, clear the Always Suspend check box on the Misc tab. If the program doesn't need background processing, it's best to leave this check box selected.

Allowing Windows to Close an MS-DOS–Based Program

By default, Windows displays a warning if you try to quit a windowed MS-DOS–based program by using a Windows procedure—clicking the Close icon, double-clicking the Control-menu icon, or choosing Close from the Control menu. Windows also normally requires you to close all MS-DOS sessions before shutting down Windows itself. These safeguards protect you against accidental loss of data.

If your MS-DOS–based program is one that never creates data files, you can safely disable Windows' normal safety measures. To do this, clear the Warn If Still Active check box on the Misc tab of the program's property sheet.

Adjusting the Idle Sensitivity

When an MS-DOS–based program running in the foreground sits idle—for example, while it's waiting for your next keystroke—Windows makes some of the resources it normally allocates to that program available to other running programs. The Idle Sensitivity slider on the Misc tab gives you some control over how much idle time Windows tolerates before reallocating resources. If your program seems less responsive than you want it to be, move the slider to the left. If you want other programs to run more quickly while your MS-DOS–based program has the focus, move the slider to the right.

Slowing the Paste

If Windows doesn't correctly paste data from the Clipboard into an MS-DOS–based program, try clearing the Fast Pasting check box on the property sheet's Misc tab. This will slow the rate at which Windows feeds Clipboard data to the program.

See Also: For more information about *pasting*, see "Using Copy and Paste," page 315.

Disabling Windows Shortcut Keys

Windows normally reserves certain keystroke combinations for itself, even while an MS-DOS–based program has the focus. For example, if you press Alt-Enter while working in an MS-DOS–based program, Windows assumes that keystroke combination is intended for *it*, rather than for the MS-DOS–based program. The reserved keystroke combinations and their normal effects are as follows:

Alt-Tab	Lets you switch to a different program
Ctrl-Esc	Displays the Start menu
Alt-Print Scrn	Copies the current window, as a bitmap, to the Clipboard
Alt-Spacebar	Displays the current program's Control menu
Alt-Esc	Switches the focus directly to another program
Print Scrn	Copies the desktop, as a bitmap, to the Clipboard
Alt-Enter	Switches between full-screen and windowed display

To make any of these shortcuts available to your MS-DOS–based application, clear the appropriate check box in the Windows Shortcut Keys section of the Misc tab.

Entering Commands at the MS-DOS Prompt

Like previous versions of Windows, Windows 95 allows you to enter commands, run batch files, and run applications by typing commands at the MS-DOS prompt. If you're accustomed to performing file-management and disk-management operations at the command line, there's no need to change your ways in Windows 95.

 You can run Windows-based programs as well as MS-DOS–based programs from the MS-DOS prompt. To run a Windows-based program, simply type its name (along with its path, if needed), just as you would if you were running an MS-DOS–based program. Or use the Start command. (For information about the Start command, see "Running Programs with the Start Command," page 336.)

To get to the MS-DOS prompt, do any of the following:

- Choose MS-DOS Prompt from the Start menu.
- Choose the Run command from the Start menu and type *command*.
- Double-click the Command icon in your Windows folder, or any shortcut for Command.com.

To close an MS-DOS Prompt session, type *exit* at the MS-DOS prompt.

Differences Between the MS-DOS Prompt and the Start Menu's Run Command

The MS-DOS prompt and the Run command are similar in that they both accept traditional operating-system commands, with or without command-line parameters. The principal differences are the following:

- The MS-DOS prompt runs in a separate "virtual machine," and that virtual machine remains open after any MS-DOS command (other than Exit) is executed, allowing you to view the command's output or execute additional commands. The Run command does not maintain an open virtual machine after your command is executed. (A virtual machine is a session running in a processor mode that emulates a 640-KB computer running MS-DOS. Most processes running in a virtual machine cannot distinguish the virtual machine from a computer that is running *only* MS-DOS.)

- You cannot use the Run command to execute internal MS-DOS commands directly. To execute internal MS-DOS commands, you must use the MS-DOS prompt or precede the command in the Run dialog with *command /c*.

  The majority of MS-DOS commands are programs stored in files with the extension .EXE or .COM. These are the *external* commands of MS-DOS. A few commands are intrinsic, or *internal* to the operating system. (They're built into Command.com.) These commands can only be run from the MS-DOS prompt. The following commands are internal: Break, Call, CD, Chcp, ChDir, Cls, Copy, Ctty, Date, Del, Dir, Echo, Erase, Exit, For, LH, LoadHigh, MD, MkDir, More, Path, Prompt, RD, Ren, Rename, RmDir, Set, Time, Type, Ver, Verify, and Vol.

To display help for any MS-DOS command, run MS-DOS Prompt. Then type the command, followed by a space, followed by a slash and a question mark. For example, to read about all the ways in which you can use the Dir command, type *dir /?* at the MS-DOS prompt.

Differences Between MS-DOS Under Windows 95 and Earlier Versions of MS-DOS

The version of MS-DOS that is available to you under Windows 95 has been designed for maximum compatibility with previous versions. Much of the operating system has been rewritten in 32-bit code, and MS-DOS has been incorporated into Windows so that the two are now a single operating system. (Earlier versions of Windows were essentially an extension of MS-DOS. To run Windows 3.1, for example, you started MS-DOS and then executed an MS-DOS program called WIN.COM, which in turn loaded the rest of Windows.) But to your applications, nothing will appear to have been changed.

As you work at the MS-DOS command prompt, however, you will notice a few improvements:

- MS-DOS now supports long filenames.

- MS-DOS now lets you access network resources using the UNC path specification.

- You can now run Windows-based programs as well as MS-DOS–based programs at the MS-DOS command prompt, as well as incorporate commands to launch Windows-based programs in MS-DOS batch files.

- You can use a new Start command to launch one virtual-machine session from within another and to specify an application's initial window state.

To see long filenames in action, type *dir* at the MS-DOS prompt. MS-DOS displays traditional filenames (eight characters plus an optional three-character extension) on the left side of the directory listing and long filenames on the right side.

To access a network directory or file using a UNC path specification, type two backslashes, followed by a server name, another backslash, and a share name. Follow the share name by another backslash and the remainder of your path specification. For example, to display a directory listing for the Msoffice\Clipart directory, which is a subdirectory of the Programs share on the Acadia server, type:

```
dir \\acadia\programs\msoffice\clipart
```

If you map a network folder to a drive letter using Windows 95 commands, you can use that drive letter at the MS-DOS prompt. For information about mapping drives, see "Mapping a Network Folder to a Drive Letter," page 187.

Running Programs with the Start Command

You can run both Windows-based and MS-DOS–based programs simply by typing their names, with path specifications if necessary, at the MS-DOS prompt. You can also run them using the new Start command.

The principal advantage of using Start is that it provides a way to run an MS-DOS–based application in a new virtual machine, separate from the one in which you issue the Start command. For example, if you type

```
Start MyDOSPrg
```

at the MS-DOS prompt, you can continue working at the MS-DOS prompt and also use MyDOSPrg.

Start also allows you to specify your program's initial state—maximized, restored, or minimized. The syntax is as follows:

Start /m *MyProgram*	Starts *MyProgram* minimized
Start /max *MyProgram*	Starts *MyProgram* maximized
Start /r *MyProgram*	Starts *MyProgram* restored

If you do not include /m, /max, or /r, your program starts in a restored window.

13

Installing and Uninstalling Software and Hardware

Windows 95 has taken major strides toward making it easy for users to change components of their systems. The new Add/Remove Programs item in Control Panel, for example, simplifies the task of bringing new applications on board or helping old ones disembark. And thanks to Windows 95's implementation of Plug and Play technology, many of the potential frustrations and bewilderments associated with hardware changes have been eliminated. In many cases now, adding a new peripheral is truly as simple as hooking up the device and getting on with your work.

In this chapter, we'll survey the tools and wizards that Windows supplies to help you keep your system current as your hardware and software needs change.

Adding or Removing Parts of Windows

Windows 95 includes both essential and optional components. Among the latter are such things as screen savers, wallpaper images, accessory programs, and The Microsoft Network. When your system was first set up, chances are the person doing the setup installed many, but not all, of the optional components. As time passes you might find you need certain items that aren't currently installed. Alternatively, you might discover that some of the Windows accessories are merely taking up space on your hard disks without serving any useful purpose. In either case, it's easy to make the appropriate adjustments.

To add or remove an optional component of Windows 95, start as follows:

1. Choose Settings from the Start menu.

2. Choose Control Panel.

3. Double-click the item labeled Add/Remove Programs.

4. Click the Windows Setup tab.

These steps bring you to the Windows Setup tab of the Add/Remove Programs property sheet, shown in Figure 13-1 on the next page.

FIGURE 13-1.

To add or remove
components of
Windows, click the
Windows Setup tab
in the Add/Remove
Programs property
sheet.

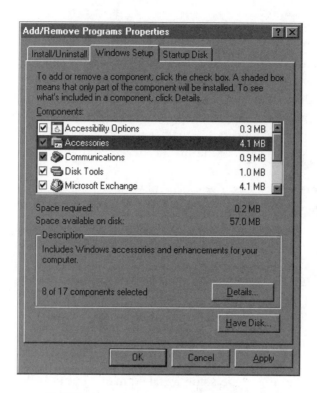

NOTE: The Windows Setup tab of the Add/Remove Programs
property sheet replaces the "maintenance-mode Setup
program" supplied with earlier versions of Windows.

In this dialog box, optional components of Windows are listed by
category. To the right of each category heading, you see the amount of
disk space used by those elements within a category that are currently
installed. Below, to the left of the Details button, the dialog box tells you
how many items in the selected category are currently installed. So, for
example, on the system depicted in Figure 13-1, 8 of 17 accessory programs are currently installed, and those 8 consume a total of 4.1 megabytes of hard-disk space.

Categories with all components installed are marked by a check mark
in a white check box. Categories in which some, but not all, components
are installed are denoted by a check mark in a gray check box. Figure 13-1

shows a system on which all components in the Accessibility Options, Disk Tools, and Microsoft Exchange categories, but only some components in the Accessories and Communications categories, are currently installed.

To add or remove a component, first select the component's category, and then click the Details button. This reveals a list of the items that make up the selected category, as shown in Figure 13-2.

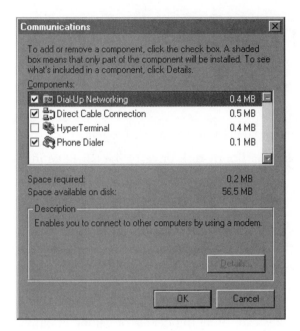

FIGURE 13-2.

To find out what's in a category, select it and click the Details button.

Here again, installed items are flagged with check marks. The system shown in Figure 13-2, for example, currently has three of the four communications items installed. The HyperTerminal program is not installed.

To install a component, put a check mark in its check box. To remove a component, remove its check mark. Then click OK twice—once to return to the property sheet shown in Figure 13-1 and a second time to close the property sheet. If you're installing an item, Windows might prompt you to insert a floppy disk or the Windows CD-ROM. (If you installed Windows initially from a network server, Windows looks on that server for the components it needs; be sure the network is available.)

NOTE: In most Windows dialog boxes, clicking the text next to a check box has the same effect as clicking the check box itself. This is not the case in the Windows Setup dialog box. Here selecting the text simply gives you an opportunity to read a description of the selected item. To change the state of the check box, you have to click the check box itself.

Installing Applications

To install an application from disk or a CD-ROM, follow these steps:

1. Choose Settings from the Start menu.

2. Choose Control Panel.

3. Double-click the item labeled Add/Remove Programs.

4. Insert the first disk in a floppy-disk drive or the CD-ROM in your CD-ROM drive.

5. Click the Install button.

6. Click the Next button.

NOTE: You can use this procedure for both Windows-based and MS-DOS–based programs.

Most original application disks include a program called Setup or Install. This program takes care of all the details of getting an application copied to your hard disk, updating the Windows registry, creating a new Start-menu item, and so on. When you click the Install button in Control Panel's Add/Remove Programs item, the Install wizard scans each of your floppy-disk drives in turn, followed by any CD-ROM drives, until it finds a program called Setup or Install. As soon as it locates such a program, the wizard presents a screen similar to the one shown in Figure 13-3. If the name of the installation program shown on the command line of this screen is correct, simply click the Finish button. In the unlikely event that the wizard has proposed the wrong installation program, you can click Browse instead of Finish, and then find the correct program from the ensuing dialog box.

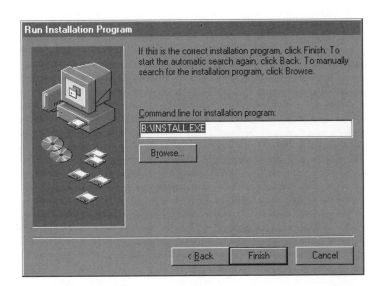

FIGURE 13-3.

The Install wizard automatically finds a program named Setup or Install and then asks you to confirm that it has found the correct installation program.

When you click Finish, Windows runs the installation program. At that point, the new application's installation program will probably ask you some questions about where you want the program installed, what optional components you want to install, and so on. If you're installing from floppy disks, you'll also be prompted to change disks from time to time.

Why Use the Install Wizard?

You don't *have* to use the Install wizard to set up a new application. Any technique that runs your program's Setup or Install routine will get the job done. The principal benefit of the Install wizard is not that it saves you the trouble of looking for Setup.exe. The wizard's real value is that it can save you time and trouble later on if you need to remove your new program. If your program comes with an uninstall utility, the Install wizard will "register" it—that is, add it to the list of programs that the wizard knows how to remove. Because you might not otherwise be aware that your program *has* an uninstall utility, it's a good idea to get in the habit of letting the Install wizard carry your bags. If and when it comes time to remove the new program, you'll be glad you did.

Uninstalling Applications

If you've ever tried to remove a Windows-based application from your system "by hand," you probably know that the task is anything but trivial. Getting rid of an unneeded program by simply deleting files is complex for the following reasons:

- Many Windows-based applications use .DLL files in addition to .EXE files. DLLs, *dynamic-link libraries*, are components that can be shared by two or more applications. Such components might or might not be stored in the same folder as the application's .EXE files. Even if you know exactly which DLLs a program uses, deleting them all might damage another application that relies on some of the same DLLs.

- Most Windows-based applications create entries in the registry, the database in which Windows records all vital information concerning your hardware and software. Even if you safely delete all executable components of your Windows-based application, if you don't also correctly modify the registry, the registry would no longer accurately describe your system. (And working directly with the registry is not advisable in any case.)

- Some Windows-based programs (in particular, many older ones) either create their own "private" configuration (.INI) files or create entries in a Windows configuration file called WIN.INI. Private .INI files might or might not be stored in the same folder as the rest of an application's files. Completely eradicating a Windows-based application means getting rid of its .INI files (or its entries in WIN.INI) as well as removing all of its other components.

For all of these reasons, but particularly because of the possibility of inadvertently deleting a DLL needed by some other application, it's best not to try removing Windows-based programs by simply going into a folder and deep-sixing its files. Instead, try the following steps (in order):

1. Check to see if the Install wizard knows how to uninstall the program for you.

   When you install a program using the Install wizard (see "Installing Applications," page 342), the wizard checks to see if the program includes an uninstall utility. If it does, the wizard registers the utility and adds the program to the list of programs that it knows how to uninstall. (See Figure 13-4.) If the program you want to remove is on this list, you can remove it by selecting it and clicking the Add/Remove button.

2. If Control Panel's Add/Remove Programs tool doesn't show your program as being uninstallable, check to see if there's an uninstall application in the folder where your program itself is stored.

It's possible your program has an uninstall utility, but the Add/ Remove Programs tool doesn't know about it. Look for something labeled "Remove" or "Uninstall." With most Microsoft applications, the Setup program also serves to uninstall the application. If you don't find an obvious uninstall utility, check your program's documentation to see if it provides any useful information.

3. If you're still not sure how to remove the program, give the program vendor's tech-support service a call. Ask them exactly what files you should and should not delete.

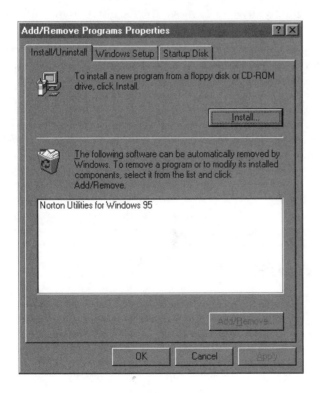

FIGURE 13-4.

Newer programs that were installed with the Install wizard can often be uninstalled automatically.

Before you delete or move a Windows-based application, it's a *very* good idea to back up any parts of your system that might be affected. At a minimum, this includes the folder in which the program is currently stored, all sub-folders of that folder, your Windows folder (on many systems, that's C:\Windows), and the System subfolder of your Windows folder. You can use the Windows 95 Backup program for this purpose. For information about Backup, see Chapter 16, "Protecting Your Data with Backup," page 405.

Moving Applications

The task of moving a Windows-based application from one disk or folder to another, like that of deleting an application, is seldom simple. The Windows-based program you want to move might rely on dynamic-link libraries (DLLs), which might or might not be stored in the same folder with the rest of the program's executables. And it might use a configuration (.INI) file in which (among other things) its current disk and folder are recorded. Simply packing up all the files in an application's folder and shipping them off to some other folder might work for the most rudimentary Windows-based applications, but more often than not it will fail.

If you must relocate a Windows-based application, the safest way to do it is to delete the program first, using whatever removal services are provided either by Windows 95 or your application. After you've deleted it, reinstall it in the appropriate folder.

Plug and Play: The End of the Hardware Blues?

Removing or relocating applications may be a pain sometimes, but it's a walk in the park compared to the travails that, until recently, have attended the installation of new hardware. Traditionally, the act of adding a new peripheral has been an exercise in frustration for many personal computer users, as well as a heavy expense for corporate support departments.

Hardware devices typically compete for a limited number of input-output (I/O) addresses, memory addresses, interrupt request (IRQ) lines, and direct memory access (DMA) channels. In order for your system to work properly, all of its pieces have to dance together without stepping on each other's toes. If your new sound card wants the same interrupt request line as your existing network adapter, something's got to give (in this case, the new sound card). Until recently, resolving a conflict of this kind has entailed some combination of the following: determining which resource is in contention, finding a nonconflicting alternative setting for the new peripheral, making a physical adjustment to the hardware (moving a jumper, for example), and modifying some aspect of the software that uses the new peripheral.

To alleviate these difficulties, Microsoft and other computer-industry firms developed the Plug and Play specification. Plug and Play, as its name implies, is intended to make adding a new peripheral to your computer as painless as installing a new toaster in your kitchen.

The full realization of this goal requires Plug and Play support from three elements of your system:

- The BIOS (*basic input-output system*)
- The operating system
- Any new peripherals you want to install

Because Windows 95 is a Plug and Play operating system, one of these elements is already in place on your computer. If your computer is quite new, it may incorporate a Plug and Play BIOS. (The BIOS, routines that manage the transfer of information between system components, is built into the computer's read-only memory, or ROM.) And by the time you read this, there should be a great variety of Plug and Play devices in all peripheral categories.

With all three elements in place, a newly installed hardware device announces its presence and resource requirements to the operating system. If necessary, the operating system restructures resource assignments on the fly (without requiring you to turn your computer off) to eliminate conflicts. The operating system then broadcasts a message to any running applications, letting them know about the change in your hardware setup so that they can take advantage of any new features. If a device is removed, the operating system hears about it from the BIOS and informs applications so that they can make any appropriate adjustments.

So, for example, a Plug and Play laptop computer that supports "hot-docking" can be connected to or disconnected from the docking station without first being turned off. If the docking station has access to a local or network printer, your applications will immediately know about any fonts or other resources offered by the printer, and Windows will begin despooling any print jobs that you have accumulated off line.

> **WARNING:** Even if your computer has a Plug and Play BIOS, always turn the computer off before adding or removing any device *inside* the system.

Provided a new device does not present an unresolvable resource conflict, the act of adding Plug and Play hardware to a Plug and Play BIOS computer running Windows 95 should indeed be toaster-transparent. And if an unresolvable conflict does arise, Windows identifies it for you, so that at least you'll know what options you have.

With a "legacy" computer (one that does not use a Plug and Play BIOS), Plug and Play still offers significant benefits, particularly if you're installing or removing a Plug and Play peripheral. By using the Add New Hardware wizard (see "Installing a Legacy Peripheral," page 349), you can make Windows aware that a new device is present. If the device supports Plug and Play, Windows can determine what type of device it is and what resources it requires. By consulting the registry (where current resource assignments for all your hardware are recorded), Windows can determine if the new device's default assignments create any conflicts. If a conflict exists, Windows can make adjustments to the new device (or another Plug and Play device already attached) to avoid the conflict.

When you attach a legacy peripheral, Windows 95 cannot adjust the new device's chosen settings, but if other of your peripherals support Plug and Play, it may be able to adjust their settings to eliminate conflicts. If not, and if conflicts exist, Windows advises you. You may then have to reset one or more jumpers on the peripheral yourself.

Getting the Maximum Benefit from Plug and Play

To get the most out of the Plug and Play support in Windows 95, here are three policies to observe:

- Whenever possible, buy Plug and Play peripherals in preference to legacy peripherals.

- When buying a new computer, look for one that uses a Plug and Play BIOS.

- Do not use the Windows 95 Device Manager to adjust IRQ, DMA, I/O, or memory assignments for Plug and Play devices.

   If you manually set a resource assignment for a Plug and Play device, Windows can no longer adjust those settings dynamically, and you'll be giving up one of the principal benefits of Plug and Play technology.

Installing a Plug and Play Peripheral

After attaching a Plug and Play peripheral, you might see a message indicating that Windows has recognized the new device. (If you have installed the device while your computer was turned off, this message appears at the start of your next Windows session. If your computer was on at the time you connected the device, the message simply pops up on your desktop.) If Windows needs a driver that it doesn't currently have, you may be prompted to insert a disk or the Windows CD-ROM.

   If you don't see a message and your new device is working fine, assume that all is well. If you don't see a message and your device does not seem to be working, use the Add New Hardware wizard to let Windows know you've installed something new.

Installing a Legacy Peripheral

After you install a new legacy peripheral (one that is not Plug and Play–compatible), use the Add New Hardware wizard to let Windows know what you've done. Choose Settings from the Start menu and Control Panel from the Settings submenu. Then double-click the Add New Hardware icon in Control Panel. After reading the wizard's introductory screen and clicking Next, you'll come to a screen similar to the one shown in Figure 13-5.

FIGURE 13-5.

The Add New Hardware wizard lets you tell Windows what's new on your system.

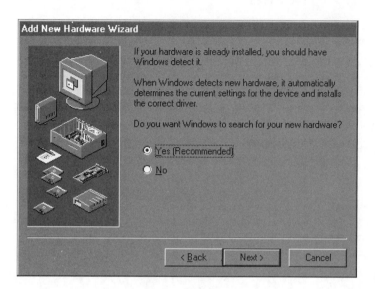

The wizard can detect many types of devices, even if they don't support Plug and Play. If you want the wizard to try to determine what you've added, select the Yes (Recommended) option button and click Next. You'll see a warning that the detection process may take several minutes and may cause your system to lock up. If you still want to go ahead, close all your applications (for safety's sake) and click Next again. If Windows succeeds in identifying one or more new devices, it presents you with a list of all devices found. Select the first member of the list and click Next. You'll then receive instructions about what to do next. (For example, you may be asked to insert a disk or the Windows CD-ROM so that Windows can get one or more driver files.) If the wizard is unable to detect the new device, click Next after the wizard informs you of this result. You'll then see a screen similar to the one shown in Figure 13-6, where you can identify the device yourself.

If you prefer to skip Windows' automatic-detection services, select the No option button in the screen shown in Figure 13-5. In the screen shown in Figure 13-6, select the type of hardware you're installing and

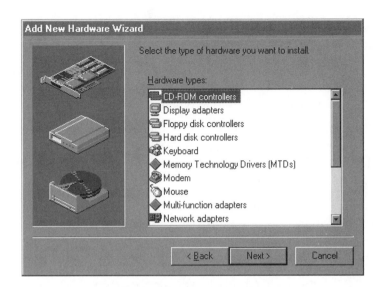

FIGURE 13-6.

If you decide not to let the wizard detect your new hardware (or it's unable to), you must tell it what type of hardware you want to install.

click the Next button. Make-and-model options appear in the next screen. (See Figure 13-7.) Select the vendor of your new hardware on the left side of this dialog box and the specific model on the right. Then click Next once more and follow the ensuing instructions.

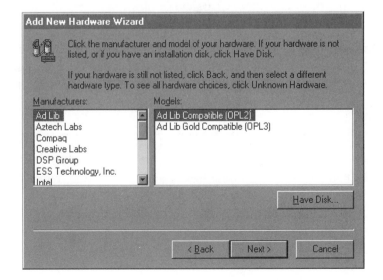

FIGURE 13-7.

After telling the wizard what kind of hardware you're installing, you'll be asked to identify the hardware's make and model.

Alternative Ways to Install Certain Legacy Devices

You can use the Add Hardware wizard to install any type of new device. For a new display, modem, mouse, keyboard, or printer, however, you can also use other Control Panel items to let Windows know what you've done.

- To install a new monitor, double-click the Display icon in Control Panel or right-click the desktop and choose Properties. Click the Settings tab in the Display property sheet, and then click the Change Display Type button.

- To install a new modem, double-click the Modems icon in Control Panel, and then click the Add button in the Modems property sheet.

- To install a new mouse, double-click the Mouse icon in Control Panel. Click the General tab in the Mouse property sheet, and then click the Change button. Select the Show All Devices option button to see the mouse make-and-model list.

- To install a new keyboard, double-click the Keyboard icon in Control Panel. Click the General tab in the Keyboard property sheet, and then click the Change button. Select the Show All Devices option button to see the keyboard make-and-model list.

- To install a new printer, double-click the Printers icon in Control Panel. (Or double-click the Printers icon in your My Computer folder.) Then, in the Printers folder, double-click the Add Printer icon.

See Also: For more information about *setting up a modem*, see "Changing Modem Settings and Dialing Locations," page 287.

For more information about *setting up a printer*, see "Installing a New Printer," page 237.

Uninstalling a Legacy Peripheral

After permanently removing a legacy peripheral from your system, you should let Windows know the device is gone so that the resources it used can be reassigned as needed. To inform Windows that a device is no longer present, follow these steps:

1. Right-click your My Computer icon, and then choose Properties from the object menu.

   Alternatively, you can double-click the System icon in Control Panel.

2. Click the Device Manager tab.

3. Select the View Devices By Type option button.

   The Device Manager presents a list of your hardware devices organized by type, as shown in Figure 13-8. Like the left pane in a Windows Explorer window, this list is organized as an outline.

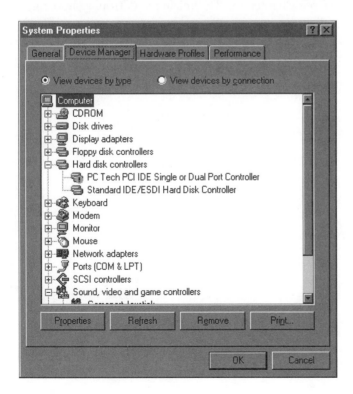

FIGURE 13-8.

To remove a device, click the plus sign to expand the device's category display. Then select the device and click Remove.

Plus signs indicate outline headings that can be expanded. Minus signs indicate entries that can be collapsed back into their headings.

4. Click the plus sign beside the category heading that describes the hardware you have removed.

5. Select the name of the item you have removed.

6. Click the Remove button.

NOTE: The Device Manager is not the place to carry out casual experimentation. If you're at all unsure which entry to remove, get help from your company's support staff, your vendor's technical support service, or a knowledgeable colleague!

See Also: For more information about *using the System item in Control Panel*, see Chapter 15, "Optimizing and Troubleshooting," page 375.

14

Windows to Go: Special Features for Mobile Computing

f your work requires you to travel, you know that computing on the road presents a number of challenges. You need to work in a physically scaled-down environment, you need to be able to get your electronic mail via modem, and you need to be able to access information stored on your home computer or on servers at the home office. In addition, there is the headache of synchronizing files that you carry with you on your laptop with versions of the same files stored at home.

Windows 95 can help reduce the trials and complexity of mobile computing. With Dial-Up Networking (and a suitably equipped server at your home location), you can stay current with vital data stored at the office. Dial-Up Networking also makes it easy to send and receive electronic mail while you're away; you simply use the same procedures you would use at home, and the operating system makes the physical connections via modem. The new Briefcase feature makes it easy to synchronize your traveling files with the files on your home system. You simply pack your briefcase when you're ready to travel and unpack it when you return.

For both home and road use, Windows 95 includes a smart Phone Dialer. You can store frequently used phone numbers and have Windows dial and log your calls. And whether or not you use Phone Dialer, the Modems section of Control Panel lets you record your dialing requirements—information such as area codes, calling-card numbers, and dial-tone access numbers—for multiple calling locations. While you're traveling, any dialing or communications application that's written for Windows 95 can use your setup information to dial appropriately from any of your regular locations.

 For information about *Phone Dialer*, see "Using Phone Dialer," page 533.

Setting Up Windows for Use on a Portable Computer

To help you conserve disk space on a laptop computer, the Setup program for Windows 95 includes a Portable option. If you choose Portable when installing Windows, the Setup program refrains from setting up the following items:

- WordPad
- Image Color Matching support
- Microsoft Exchange
- Microsoft Fax
- The Microsoft Network
- Multimedia drivers and applications (unless Setup detects that you have a multimedia device)

Setup does install the following optional components:

- Dial-Up Networking
- Direct Cable Connection
- Briefcase
- HyperTerminal

Depending on how you use your laptop, you might want to make some adjustments after setting up with the Portable option. For example, if you use Microsoft Mail (or another Exchange-supported mail system), you'll want to install Microsoft Exchange. If you don't happen to need a rudimentary communications program, you can dispense with Hyper-Terminal—and so on.

 If disk space is scarce, consider using DriveSpace, the on-the-fly file-compression utility included with Windows 95. For information about DriveSpace, see "Doubling Your Disk with DriveSpace," page 390.

To add or delete components of Windows 95, you can use the Add/ Remove Programs item in Control Panel.

See Also: For information about *the Add/Remove Programs item in Control Panel,* see "Adding or Removing Parts of Windows," page 339.

Monitoring and Conserving Battery Power

Windows 95 supports the Advanced Power Management (APM) standard for monitoring and conserving battery power on portable computers. If your laptop or notebook is one that can take advantage of APM, you may see a power-meter icon in the notification area of your taskbar, right beside your clock. If you're running your computer on battery power, this icon looks like a battery; if you're running on AC power, you'll see a different icon—one that looks like an electrical cord with a plug on the end.

If your computer supports APM and you don't see a power symbol in the notification area, double-click the Power item in Control Panel. In the Power property sheet, select the Enable Battery Meter On Taskbar check box.

In addition to reminding you about what form of power you're using, the taskbar's power-meter icon can provide useful status information:

- If you double-click the power-meter icon while running on battery power, a dialog box tells you what percentage of the battery's power is still available.

- If you double-click the power-meter icon while running on AC power, a dialog box tells you what percentage of the battery's power has been recharged.

■ If the remaining battery life falls below about 20 percent while you're running on battery power, a red exclamation point appears beside the power-meter icon.

 You can also find out what percentage of your battery's power is still available by resting your mouse on the power-meter icon for a few seconds and reading the tool tip that pops up.

 For information about *automatically shutting off your display after a period of inactivity*, see "Taking Advantage of Your Monitor's Energy-Saving Features," page 111.

Transferring Files with Direct Cable Connection

If your laptop can be connected to your network, you can easily copy files to it from your desktop computer. Simply share the folders that contain the files you want to copy, open Network Neighborhood on your laptop, open the folders containing the files you need, and then copy those files to folders on your laptop. (Or copy the files to a Briefcase on your laptop, if you want to keep the copies synchronized with the originals on your desktop. For information about Briefcase, see "Synchronizing Files with Briefcase," page 363.)

If your laptop cannot connect to your network, you can move files to and from it with the help of floppy disks. Or you can use a cable to connect your desktop and portable computers and then transfer files with the help of the Direct Cable Connection utility. Using Direct Cable Connection may be quicker than using floppy disks if you need to move a large number of files. Direct Cable Connection also has the advantage of letting you copy files that might be too large to fit on a floppy disk.

NOTE: If you set up Windows to include Direct Cable Connection, you'll probably find an entry for it in the Accessories section of your Start menu. If Direct Cable Connection has not been installed on your computer, double-click the Add/Remove Programs item in Control Panel, click the Windows Setup tab, select Communications, and click the Details button. Select Direct Cable Connection and click OK.

What Kind of Cable to Use

Direct Cable Connection supports the following kinds of cables:

- Null-modem serial cables

- Basic four-bit parallel cables, including LapLink and InterLnk cables available before 1992

- Extended Capabilities Port (ECP) cables

- Universal Cable Module (UCM) cables

ECP cables provide faster performance than any of the other alternatives, but they require an ECP-enabled parallel port on both computers. A UCM cable can be used with different types of parallel ports.

Setting Up Direct Cable Connection

When two machines are hooked together via Direct Cable Connection, one acts as host and the other acts as guest. The host computer has the privilege of assigning a password to the connection (as well as separate passwords for any folders it chooses to share with the guest). The guest computer can access any folders shared by the host, but the host cannot access shared folders on the guest.

You need to set up Direct Cable Connection first on the host computer, and then on the guest computer. Begin by choosing Direct Cable Connection from the Accessories section of your Start menu. The Direct Cable Connection wizard, shown in Figure 14-1 on the next page, appears.

In the wizard's first dialog box, identify the current computer as host or guest. Then click Next. In the second dialog box, shown in Figure 14-2 on the next page, you'll see a list of available ports. Choose the port you plan to use, connect your cable if it isn't already connected, and click Next again.

FIGURE 14-1.

The first step in setting up Direct Cable Connection is to tell the wizard whether the current computer will act as host or guest.

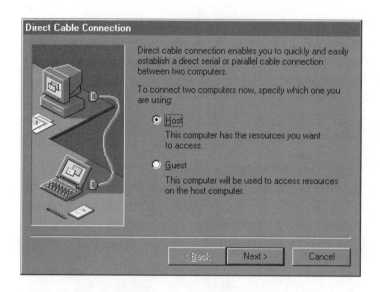

FIGURE 14-2.

The wizard's second dialog box presents a list of available ports.

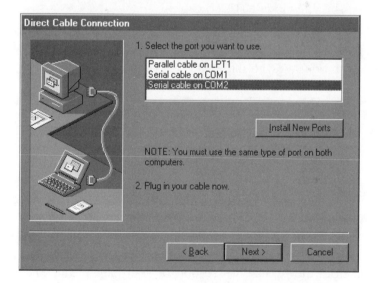

If you're setting up a host computer, the wizard's third dialog box gives you the opportunity to specify a password. After you've done this (or declined to do it) and clicked Next once more, your host will be ready. If you're setting up a guest computer, the password step is omitted.

Once you've set up both computers, you can begin transferring files right away. Or you can click Close to leave the wizard for the time being. When you're ready to transfer files, simply run Direct Cable Connection again on both computers.

NOTE: When you first establish a connection, your guest computer may be asked to enter the name of the host computer. Type that computer's name without any backslash characters. (That is, do not enter the host computer's UNC path; simply enter the name.)

 Be sure to share any host computer folders that contain files you want to copy to the guest computer. For information about sharing folders, see "Sharing Folders with Other Users," page 190.

Synchronizing Files with Briefcase

When you travel, you might need to take copies of documents stored on your desktop computer or network server. On return, you'll want to recopy any of those files that you've changed back to the desktop or server folders from which they originated. Sometimes synchronizing mobile and home-base document versions is a simple matter, but sometimes it's not. If you copy a great many files to your traveling machine, for example, it can be a nuisance to figure out which ones you really need to copy back to the desktop computer and which ones you don't. The matter becomes even more complex if you have one computer for home use and one for the office. If you regularly work at both computers, you probably have parallel copies of important documents on each, and you need to be careful not to overwrite a later version of a file with an earlier version.

The Briefcase utility takes care of these details for you. When you put a copy of a file in a Briefcase, Windows keeps track of where the file came from and always knows which version of the file—the one in the Briefcase or the one outside the Briefcase—is the more current. An Update command, available from Briefcase's menu bar or object menu, automatically updates the older version with the newer.

NOTE: If you set up Windows 95 to include Briefcase, you may find an icon labeled My Briefcase on your desktop. If you do not see this icon, right-click the desktop (or within any folder), and choose New from the object menu. If Briefcase is installed on your system, you'll see a Briefcase item on the list of object types that can be created with the New command. If you don't find Briefcase on this list, you need to install the feature. Double-click the Add/Remove Programs item in Control Panel, click the Windows Setup tab, choose Accessories, and click Details. Then select Briefcase and click OK.

 You can also use Briefcase to synchronize versions of documents stored on your desktop computer and a network server.

The basic procedure for using Briefcase is as follows:

1. Open an existing or new Briefcase on your portable computer.

2. Copy into this Briefcase all documents that you need to travel with.

3. While traveling, work with your documents in the Briefcase.

 Do not move a Briefcase file out of the Briefcase. If you do, Windows can no longer keep track of which version of the file—the one you copied out of the Briefcase or the version that you copied into the Briefcase—is the current version.

4. On return, open the Briefcase and use either the Update All or the Update Selection command.

The details vary, however, depending on whether or not your portable computer can be connected (via network or Direct Cable Connection) to your desktop computer.

If you right-drag a file into a Briefcase, the default option on the object menu is Make Sync Copy. This is the option you want. When you make a sync copy, Windows duplicates the file and at the same time records (in a hidden Briefcase file) information about the file's properties. It uses this information later to determine which version of the file is current.

When you right-drag a folder into a Briefcase, the object menu includes the Make Sync Copy command as well as a Make Sync Copy Of Type command. Make Sync Copy copies the entire folder (including all files and subfolders) into the Briefcase. Make Sync Copy Of Type lets you make sync copies of particular file types only—for example, all Microsoft Excel spreadsheets.

Using Briefcase with a Network or Direct Cable Connection

You'll find it easiest to use Briefcase if you can first connect your laptop and desktop computers via the network or Direct Cable Connection. Then you can simply copy as many files as you need from your desktop computer to the Briefcase on your portable computer. When it comes time to synchronize, reconnect the two machines. Then you can use the Update All or Update Selection command from the Briefcase on the portable computer.

Using Briefcase with Floppy Disks

If your portable and desktop computers cannot be connected, you need to use floppy disks as intermediaries between the two machines. In this case, you need to be aware of one limitation: a Briefcase cannot span multiple diskettes. This doesn't mean you can take only one diskette's worth of files on the road. Rather, it means you might need to take along multiple Briefcase folders. Here's the procedure:

1. Put a diskette (preferably a freshly formatted one) in a floppy drive.

2. Open My Computer and double-click the icon for your floppy drive.

3. In the floppy disk's folder, right-click, choose New, and then choose Briefcase.

    The first time you open a new Briefcase, a Briefcase wizard appears. Simply click Finish to dismiss the wizard. When you do this, the wizard sets up your new Briefcase, creating the hidden files that Windows will use to track the status of your files.

4. Copy files into this new Briefcase until the floppy disk is somewhat less than full. Do not fill the disk, because you need to leave room for your files to grow as you work with them.

5. Insert the floppy disk in your portable computer and move or copy the Briefcase to your portable's hard disk.

6. Repeat steps 1 through 5 for as many floppy disks as you need, but give each Briefcase a unique name before moving it to your portable computer.

7. On return, copy each Briefcase to a floppy disk, transfer the disk to your desktop computer, and use the Update All or Update Selection command.

 You can nearly double the capacity of your floppy disks by compressing them with DriveSpace. For details, see "Doubling Your Disk with DriveSpace," page 390.

Getting Status Information About Briefcase Files

In icon view, the inside of a Briefcase looks pretty much like the inside of any other folder window, except for the presence of a Briefcase menu. But if you switch to details view, Briefcase provides useful information about the provenance and status of your documents. As Figure 14-3 shows, the Status column in details view shows you which files are current and which need updating (in other words, which files have changed since you copied them into the Briefcase). The Sync Copy In column tells you where the original copy of each of your files is stored.

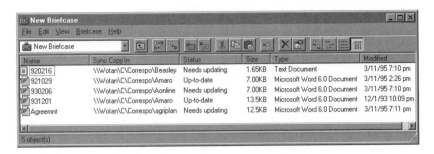

FIGURE 14-3.

By choosing details view in a Briefcase, you can see which of your files have changed since you copied them into the Briefcase.

When your Briefcase is on line with the computer on which it was created (for example, when your portable is connected to your desktop via direct cable or network, or when the Briefcase is on a floppy disk in the desktop computer's diskette drive), you can also get status information about a particular file by right-clicking it and viewing the Update Status tab of its property sheet. Figure 14-4 shows the Update Status tab for a file that has been changed in the Briefcase.

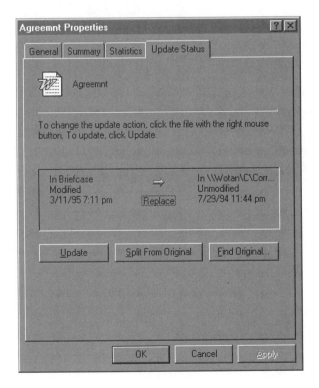

FIGURE 14-4.

The property sheet for a Briefcase file can tell you where the file's sync copy resides and which version of the file is more current.

Updating Files

When you're ready to synchronize your Briefcase files with their sync copies, you can either work one file at a time or update the whole Briefcase at once. To update a single file, select it, and then choose Update Selection from the Briefcase menu. (You can also update a group of selected files this way. Hold down the Ctrl key while you click each file you want to update. Then choose Update Selection.)

To update the entire Briefcase, choose Update All. You'll see a dialog box similar to the one shown in Figure 14-5.

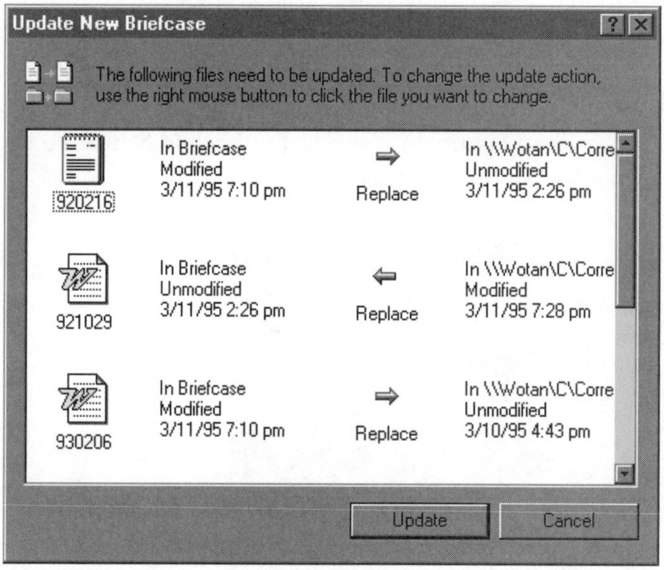

FIGURE 14-5.

When you choose
Update All, Windows
uses left-pointing
and right-pointing
arrows to show
which copy of each
changed file is
newer.

Notice that the Replace arrows in the center of the dialog box can point either direction, depending on which version of a file is most current. When you click the Update button, Windows copies the newer version of each file, wherever it may reside, over the older version.

If the update action that Briefcase proposes for an item is not the action you want, right-click its entry in the Update New Briefcase dialog box. Then, from the object menu, choose the action you prefer. For example, in Figure 14-5, if you want to copy the "sync" version of the file 920216 over the "in Briefcase" version, right-click the 920216 icon and choose the Replace command with the left-pointing arrow from the object menu. To prevent changes to either file, choose Skip.

Divorcing a Briefcase File from Its Sync Copy

If you move a file from a Briefcase to any other folder, the link between that file and its sync copy is broken. The result is an ordinary copy. You can also sever the link between a file and its sync copy without removing it from the Briefcase. To do this, select the file and choose Split From Original from the Briefcase menu. In Briefcase's Status field, your file will then be listed as an *orphan*. You can carry as many orphans as you please in your Briefcase.

Creating New Files While Traveling

While you're on the road, you'll probably create new files as well as modify existing ones. Any such files that you store in your Briefcase will also enjoy orphan status. Briefcase's Update commands will not copy these files to your desktop machine for you (because Briefcase would not know where they should go), but you can do that manually by using the same techniques you would use to copy files between any two ordinary folders.

Using Deferred Printing While You're Away from the Office

If you've set up your portable computer to use one or more printers at the office, you can continue to print documents while you're away. With its normal printer(s) off line, Windows simply stores any print jobs you create on your portable's hard disk. When you return to the office, you can send all pending jobs to their printers. If your printers and portable computer support Plug and Play, Windows recognizes that the printers are back on line and begins printing the pending jobs automatically. Otherwise, you can use a simple menu command to let Windows know the printers are back on line:

1. Choose Settings from the Start menu.

2. Choose Printers from the Settings submenu.

3. In the Printers folder, select each offline printer in turn (the offline printers stand out because their icon is dimmed) and choose the File menu's Work Offline command again to remove its check mark.

 Use the same procedure to resume printing on a network printer that has become available again after being unavailable. (This can happen, for example, if the server to which the network printer is attached gets turned off.)

Setting Up Your Modem for Multiple Calling Locations

If you travel regularly to particular locations and use your modem to initiate calls from those locations, you can simplify your life considerably by letting Windows know exactly how it should place a call in each location. When you arrive at one of your regular destinations, you can use a simple command to tell Windows where you are. Any Windows application that uses the Windows 95 telephony interface (formally known as *TAPI*, which stands for telephony application programming interface) will then use the dialing information you've supplied.

To specify dialing information for a location, follow these steps:

1. Choose Settings from the Start menu.

2. Choose Control Panel from the Settings submenu.

3. In Control Panel, double-click the Modems icon.

4. On the General tab of the Modems property sheet, click the Dialing Properties button.

Begin by filling out the Dialing property sheet for your "default" location—the location from which you make the majority of your calls. Then click the New button, type the name of the next location you use, click OK, and fill out the property sheet for that location. You can repeat this process for as many locations as you need.

Figure 14-6 shows how the Dialing property sheet would be filled out for a user whose default location has the following characteristics:

■ The area code is 503. (Windows-based applications that use TAPI know that the area code should be omitted when dialing another number with the same area code and should be included when dialing a number outside that area code.)

■ Getting an outside dial tone, for both local and long-distance calls, requires 9 followed by a pause. (A comma in the dial string causes the modem to pause briefly.)

■ Calls are not billed to a calling card.

■ The line has call-waiting service; the code to disable call waiting is *70.

■ The line uses tone dialing.

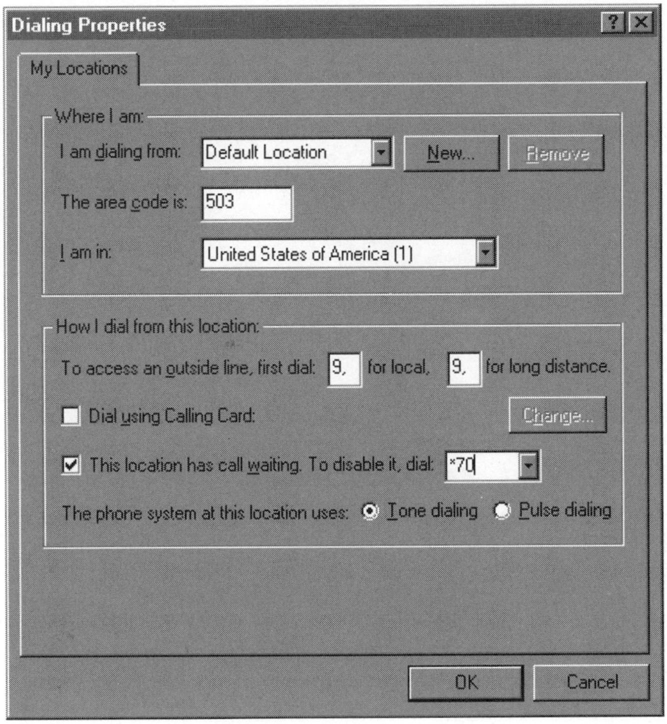

FIGURE 14-6.

The Dialing property sheet lets you specify dialing requirements for as many locations as you need.

Using Dial-Up Networking

Dial-Up Networking allows you to connect to a remote computer by means of your modem and then access shared resources on the remote computer—as well as other network resources available to the remote computer. The computer to which you connect is known as a *remote-access server (RAS)*. The computer initiating the call is the *Dial-Up Networking (or remote-access) client*. The remote-access server typically acts as a gateway to additional network servers.

Once you've connected to the remote-access server, you can browse the remote network using Network Neighborhood. You can also access remote folders and files using UNC path specifications and map remote folders to drive letters on your own computer. In other words, all the techniques you use to work with local-area network resources function the same way with a remote, or wide-area, network.

For Dial-Up Networking to work, the computer you connect to must be configured to act as a remote-access server. Windows 95 does not include RAS support, but RAS support for a server running Windows 95 is included in Microsoft Plus! A Windows 95 server equipped with Microsoft Plus! can handle one remote client at a time. A Windows NT system acting as a remote-access server can handle 256 remote sessions at once. RAS software and hardware from other vendors can also handle multiple remote sessions.

NOTE: Configuring a remote-access server is a topic beyond the scope of this book. For detailed information, consult the *Windows 95 Resource Kit*, available from Microsoft Press.

See Also: For information about *Network Neighborhood, using remote folders and files, and mapping folders to drive letters*, see Chapter 6, "Using and Sharing Files on the Network," page 179.

For information about *Microsoft Plus!*, see Appendix A, "Using the Power of Your 486 or Pentium with Microsoft Plus!," page 727.

Setting Up a Dial-Up Networking Connection

If you set up Windows to include Dial-Up Networking, you'll find a system folder called Dial-Up Networking in your My Computer folder. If Dial-Up Networking has not been installed on your computer, double-click the Add/Remove Programs item in Control Panel, click the Windows Setup tab, choose Communications, and click the Details button. Select Dial-Up Networking and click OK.

Before you can connect to a remote-access server the first time, you need to set up the connection. You do that as follows:

1. Choose Dial-Up Networking from the Accessories section of your Start menu. Alternatively, open My Computer and double-click the Dial-Up Networking folder.

2. If you've never before set up a remote connection, step 1 takes you directly to the Make New Connection wizard. Otherwise, double-click the Make New Connection item in your Dial-Up Networking folder.

3. In the wizard's first dialog box, type a descriptive name for your new connection and tell the wizard which modem you plan to use (if you have more than one). Click Next to continue.

4. In the wizard's second dialog box, supply the dialing information required to connect to your remote-access server. Click Next to continue.

5. In the wizard's third dialog box, click Finish to store the new connection as an icon in your Dial-Up Networking folder.

Connecting to a Remote-Access Server

Once you've set up a Dial-Up Networking connection, you can access the remote server by simply double-clicking the connection icon in your Dial-Up Networking folder. The first time you do this, you'll be asked to identify yourself, following whatever security methods are used by the remote-access server. If the dialog box in which you do this includes a Save Password check box, you can select this check box to save yourself the trouble of retyping your password each time you connect. If you're concerned about the possibility that another user will try to connect to your remote-access account without your permission, do not select this check box. To connect, click the Connect button.

After you've connected to the remote server, and after the server has authenticated your logon information, a small "Connected To" dialog box confirms your connection and displays the length of time you've been connected. You can minimize this dialog box or leave it on screen. To see what resources are available while you're connected, double-click your Network Neighborhood icon. To terminate the session, return to the Connected To dialog box and click Disconnect.

 If a modem icon appears in the taskbar's notification area, you can double-click it to see additional information about your current session.

Reconnecting to a Remote Folder or File

To simplify reconnection to a particular remote folder or file, create a shortcut for it *while you're connected to the dial-up network*. Then, after you disconnect, you can reconnect by double-clicking the shortcut. Alternatively, you can map a dial-up folder to a drive letter on your own system. Then you can reopen that "drive" just as you would reopen an ordinary local drive. If Windows determines that the mapped drive is not part of your local-area network, it presents a dialog box asking if you want to use a dial-up connection.

 You can also reconnect to a remote-access server by choosing the Start menu's Run command and typing the server's name.

 For information about *creating a shortcut*, see "Using Shortcuts to Run Programs and Open Documents," page 71.

For information about *mapping a folder to a drive letter*, see "Mapping a Network Folder to a Drive Letter," page 187.

15

Optimizing and Troubleshooting

f you've upgraded from an earlier version of Windows to Windows 95, you've already taken the most important step toward enhancing the efficiency of your system and the performance of your Windows-based applications. Windows 95 includes major architectural changes designed to give you a faster-running and more robust operating environment. These changes include the following:

- Most of the operating system is now written in 32-bit, protected-mode code. Windows 95 also provides 32-bit device drivers for better performance and resource management.

- Windows now incorporates MS-DOS, rather than being an extension to MS-DOS. Thus, a problem at the MS-DOS level cannot bring Windows down.

- Windows 95 offers preemptive multitasking, a more efficient way of scheduling the concurrent execution of multiple applications.

- Windows 95 makes smaller demands on the "system resource" areas of memory, allowing you to run more large applications simultaneously without reducing your free system resources to dangerously low levels.

- Windows 95 uses 32-bit, protected-mode mechanisms for accessing your hard disk and file system, bypassing the real-mode BIOS calls that were used for some hardware by earlier versions of Windows.

In addition, Windows 95 includes three important new "self-tuning" features:

- The operating system configures the size of its hard-disk cache dynamically, increasing or decreasing the cache size in accordance with conditions on your system.

- Windows 95 can automatically choose an optimal amount of disk space to use for virtual memory. Like the cache, the virtual-memory "swap file" can shrink or grow dynamically, depending on the needs of your system and the amount of disk space available.

- Windows 95 automatically makes certain adjustments at setup to provide optimal performance on systems with a small amount of memory. These include turning off background print rendering.

Windows 95 users, therefore, should have less need to tinker with their systems in order to achieve satisfactory performance. Barring device conflicts, inadequate memory, or an overfull hard disk, you should be able to set up Windows 95 and run it—without losing sleep over inscrutable lines in your SYSTEM.INI file or wondering whether you've chosen the right size and type of swap file. Nevertheless, there are some things you should know about how to keep Windows 95 and your applications humming along in good cheer.

 In Windows 95 you will probably *not* be troubled by dwindling system resources, as you may have been under Windows 3.x. If you're in the habit of checking the percentage of free resources, however, you can still do it. Right-click My Computer, choose Properties, and then click the Performance Tab. The Performance property sheet tells you the free system-resource percentage.

This chapter presents basic strategy and tips for maximizing performance under Windows 95. We'll look first at ways to ensure that you're getting the most out of the system you currently have. Later, we'll look at options for enhancing your hardware.

NOTE: This chapter does not address network performance issues, a topic beyond the scope of this book. For technical information about networking under Windows 95, consult the *Windows 95 Resource Kit*, available from Microsoft Press.

Maximize Your Current Hardware Resources

Before the hardware reviews in your latest computer magazine persuade you to buy a faster video adapter, a bigger hard disk, or a whole new computer, be sure you're using the system you have as effectively as possible.

A basic strategy for optimizing your current resources includes the following steps:

- Let Windows manage your virtual memory (swap file).

- Keep your hard disk in good order, and be sure you leave ample space on it for virtual memory. Run ScanDisk and Disk Defragmenter regularly, don't let the Recycle Bin eat up too much disk space, and consider using DriveSpace if you're habitually short of room.

- If your system is using any real-mode (MS-DOS compatibility) drivers, try to eliminate them.

- Check for and eliminate any device conflicts or other device problems.

- Don't ask for background processing of MS-DOS–based applications unless you need it.

- Watch out for MS-DOS–based applications that grab all available extended memory.

- Evaluate printing performance tradeoffs.

- Evaluate video performance tradeoffs.

Let Windows Manage Your Virtual Memory

Like earlier versions of Windows, Windows 95 uses your hard disk as an extension of internal memory, moving data to a swap file on disk when memory becomes full and restoring it from disk to memory as needed. This use of the hard disk is known as *virtual* memory.

In earlier versions of Windows, you had the opportunity to choose between two types of swap files—a permanent swap file or a temporary swap file. The permanent file used faster disk-access methods but required you to commit a portion of your hard disk to the swap file at all times, even when you were running MS-DOS instead of Windows.

Windows 95 has eliminated the need to choose between a temporary and a permanent swap file. The type of swap file it uses combines the virtues of both the earlier types: it employs 32-bit, protected-mode access (bypassing your computer's real-mode BIOS routines) but adjusts the swap file's size in accordance with system demand. Thus, you get the fastest performance possible without overcommitting your hard disk.

Windows' ability to configure the swap file dynamically also means that you don't need to decide how big your swap file should be. You *can* specify a minimum and a maximum size for the swap file, but there's not likely to be a good reason for doing this. You should assume that you will get the best possible performance by letting Windows manage the swap file size.

Changing the Swap File Disk

By default, Windows creates the swap file on the hard disk that contains your Windows system files. If you have another hard disk that's faster or has more available space, you might achieve some performance gain by having Windows put the swap file on that disk. To do so, follow these steps:

1. Right-click your My Computer icon and choose Properties from the object menu. (Or double-click the System item in Control Panel.)

2. Click the Performance tab of the System property sheet.

3. Click the Virtual Memory button.
   You see the Virtual Memory dialog box, shown in Figure 15-1.

4. Choose the option button labeled "Let me specify my own virtual memory settings."

5. Choose a hard disk from the drop-down list.

6. Click OK and answer the confirmation prompt.

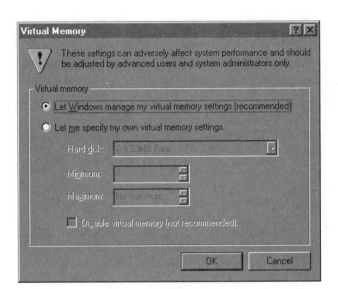

FIGURE 15-1.

The Virtual Memory dialog box, accessible from the System property sheet, lets you control swap file settings.

 It's okay to put your swap file on a disk compressed with DoubleSpace or DriveSpace. There's no particular advantage to doing so, but no disadvantage, either.

Keep Your Hard Disk in Good Order

Because Windows 95 uses your hard disk for virtual memory, and because many Windows-based applications write temporary files to disk while you work, keeping your disk in good working order is vital. Windows provides two important tools to help you maintain a healthy hard disk. ScanDisk is a diagnostic tool that reads all of the vital signs of your disk and either fixes or warns you of any problems. Disk Defragmenter rearranges the physical locations of your disk files, so that all files are stored in contiguous blocks. It's a good idea to make regular use of both programs.

What Happened to SMARTDrive?

Like previous versions of Windows, Windows 95 uses a disk cache to improve performance. The cache is an area of memory that holds a copy of data recently read from disk. When Windows needs to read the disk, it checks first to see if the information it needs is in the cache. If possible, the system gets what it needs from the cache. Because data transfers between memory locations are far faster than operations involving the disk, these *cache hits* provide a gigantic boost to the performance of the operating system and your applications.

Earlier versions of Windows use a cache utility called SMART-Drive and require you to make choices about the size of the SMARTDrive cache. SMARTDrive is invoked and configured by means of a command in your AUTOEXEC.BAT file. Windows 95 uses a dynamically adjustable cache called VCACHE, which is fully integrated with the operating system. The cache used by VCACHE grows and shrinks in accordance with system demands. Because Windows manages the cache size for you, and because VCACHE is integral to Windows, you no longer have to concern yourself with command-line parameters and AUTOEXEC.BAT statements.

Like SMARTDrive, VCACHE performs write-caching as well as read-caching. That means that when you save a file, some of your data may be held for a few seconds in the cache before being committed to disk. Write-caching entails very little risk, despite the fact that information you've saved may not be written to disk instantly. But if your system is particularly prone to power interruptions, you might want to disable this feature. To do so, right-click My Computer, choose Properties, click the Performance tab, click the File System button, click the Troubleshooting tab, and then select the check box labeled "Disable write-behind caching for all drives."

Finding and Repairing Disk Errors with ScanDisk

ScanDisk can be used with any hard disk or floppy disk, including disks compressed with DriveSpace or DoubleSpace. ScanDisk cannot be used

A "standard" ScanDisk test (one that checks the logical structure of your disk without testing the media for bad sectors) takes only a few minutes. Consider adding Scan-Disk to the StartUp group of your Start menu. That way, if any problems arise, you'll know about them almost immediately.

with CD-ROM disks. The program finds and fixes the following kinds of logical errors (errors involving the organization of files and other data structures):

- Problems with the file allocation table (FAT)

- Problems involving long filenames

- Lost clusters

- Cross-linked files

- Problems involving the directory structure

- On disks compressed with DriveSpace or DoubleSpace, problems involving the volume header, volume file structure, compression structure, or volume signature

(The *file allocation table* is a data structure that keeps track of the physical location and file ownership of each cluster on a disk. A *cluster,* also known as an *allocation unit,* is the smallest group of sectors that the operating system can allocate to a file. A *lost cluster* is one that's not used by any file but that the FAT hasn't marked as available for new data. A *cross-linked file* is a file containing clusters that have been erroneously allocated to more than one file.)

ScanDisk can also be used to find physical disk errors (bad sectors). The program doesn't physically repair your media, but it moves data away from any bad sectors it finds.

A simple way to run ScanDisk is as follows:

1. Open My Computer and right-click the icon for the disk you want to check.

2. Choose Properties from the object menu.

3. Click the Tools tab.

4. Click Check Now.

You will probably also find a command for ScanDisk on your Start menu. Look under System Tools, in the Accessories section.

In the ScanDisk dialog box (see Figure 15-2), select the disk you want to check. (You can select more than one disk for checking by holding down the Ctrl key as you click each disk name.) To perform only a logical test, choose the Standard option button. To check the media as well as the logical structure, choose Thorough. If you want errors fixed automatically, select the Automatically Fix Errors check box. (After it finishes, ScanDisk can display a message indicating whether it found any errors. It can also create a log file on disk, detailing the errors it found and the steps it took to correct them.) If you want to decide, case-by-case, whether ScanDisk should fix errors, deselect this check box. ScanDisk will then stop and display a dialog box each time it finds an error. (See Figure 15-3.) Click Start when you're ready to begin the test.

FIGURE 15-2.

Choose Standard if you want ScanDisk to check logical structures only. Choose Thorough if you also want to check for bad sectors.

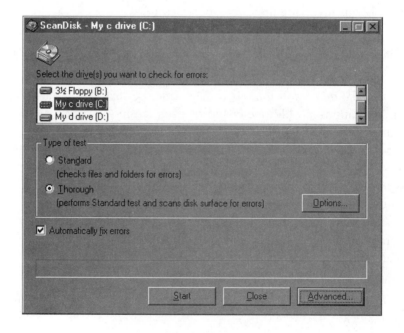

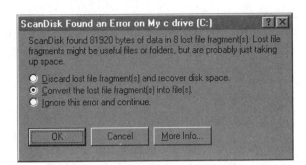

FIGURE 15-3.

When ScanDisk finds an error, it displays a dialog box that explains the error and, in some cases, offers choices about correcting the problem.

Testing the physical integrity of every disk cluster takes time, particularly with large disks. While ScanDisk is testing, you can continue to work, but you may find your system rather sluggish, and if any data is written to the disk that's being tested, ScanDisk will have to start over. You can simplify the thorough test somewhat by clicking the Options button in the dialog box shown in Figure 15-2. As Figure 15-4 shows, your options include restricting the test to the system or data area and eliminating write-testing. (When testing thoroughly, ScanDisk normally reads each disk sector and then writes the same data back into the sector. If you skip the write-testing, ScanDisk still finds sectors whose data cannot be read, but it won't find any problems that might arise only during the writing process.)

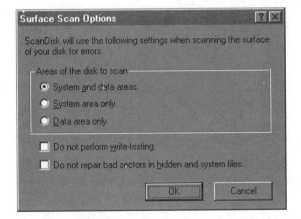

FIGURE 15-4.

The thorough test takes awhile. You can make it quicker—if somewhat less thorough—by eliminating write-testing.

You can also use the Options dialog box (see Figure 15-4) to restrict ScanDisk's test to the system area of your hard disk. This makes the test go much more quickly because the system data structures occupy a relatively small portion of any disk. A system-only test also turns up the most disastrous kinds of media errors—those that involve the boot sector, the partition table, or the file allocation table.

> **WARNING:** If you use copy-protected software, don't let ScanDisk repair bad sectors in hidden and system files. ScanDisk "repairs" bad sectors by relocating data to good sectors. Some copy-protected programs record the absolute physical location of particular hidden or system files. If they find such files in new locations, they assume your program has been illegally copied. To prevent this from happening, select the check box labeled "Do not repair bad sectors in hidden and system files," in the dialog box shown in Figure 15-4.

Other ScanDisk Options

The Advanced button in ScanDisk's dialog box provides additional options, as shown in Figure 15-5.

FIGURE 15-5.

Among other things, ScanDisk's "advanced" options let you tell it what to do with lost clusters and cross-linked files.

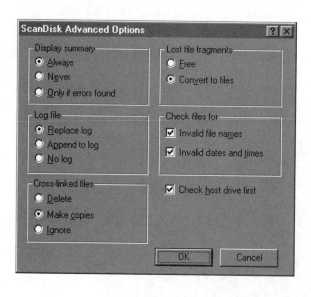

By default, ScanDisk finishes its work by displaying its findings on screen and recording them in a log file called SCANDISK.LOG. The log file is stored in the top-level folder (root directory) of the tested disk and, by default, replaces the log file from any previous test. You can override all these defaults by using the Display Summary and Log File option-button groups.

If ScanDisk finds any cross-linked clusters, its default procedure is to create a new copy of the cross-linked data in each affected file and, in the process, eliminate the cross-links from your file allocation table. In most cases, the cross-linked data belongs to only one of the affected files. After ScanDisk has done its work, you may be able to use ordinary editing procedures to eliminate the data from the file to which it does not belong. Thus, the Make Copies option button in the Advanced Options dialog box is usually the appropriate setting. But if you'd rather, you can have Scan-Disk simply delete or ignore cross-linked data.

By default, ScanDisk organizes any chains of lost clusters it finds into new disk files, storing the files in the top-level folder (root directory) of the disk on which the lost clusters were located and giving them names such as FILE0000. If ScanDisk's summary report indicates that lost clusters were found, you can then open the top-level folder and read the lost-cluster files with Notepad or another editor. If you find anything you want to keep, you can copy and save it. Otherwise, you'll probably want to send the whole file to the Recycle Bin. If you'd rather skip this process and have ScanDisk simply free up any lost clusters it finds, choose the Free option button in the Advanced Options dialog box.

By default, ScanDisk ensures that files have valid filenames, but it doesn't bother checking for valid dates and times. That's because an invalid filename is a serious error and may prevent an application from opening the affected file. An invalid date or time may affect file-sorting operations or the operation of backup programs, but it does not prevent you from using the file. To override either default setting, use the check boxes in the Check Files For section of the Advanced Options dialog box.

Finally, when testing disks compressed via DoubleSpace or Drive-Space, ScanDisk normally checks the host drive first. That's because apparent errors in a compressed volume can result from errors in the host drive. There's probably no good reason to change this default, but ScanDisk will let you change it if you want. (Deselect the Check Host Drive First check box.)

See Also: For information about *DriveSpace*, see "Doubling Your Disk with DriveSpace," page 390.

Optimizing Disk Performance with Disk Defragmenter

When you store files on a freshly formatted disk, Windows writes each file's data in a set of adjacent disk clusters. One file might use clusters 3 through 24, for example, the next 25 through 31, a third 32 through 34, and so on. As soon as you begin deleting files, however, this neat pattern is likely to be broken.

For example, if you delete the file that occupies clusters 25 through 31, and then create a new file 20 clusters in length, Windows stores the new file's first 7 clusters in 25 through 31 and the remaining 13 somewhere else. This new file, in other words, would be *fragmented*; it would occupy at least two noncontiguous blocks of clusters. As time went on and you added and deleted more files, the odds are good that more and more of your files would become fragmented.

Fragmentation does not affect data integrity, but it does reduce the efficiency of your hard disk. Fragmented files take longer to read and write than contiguous ones.

You can eliminate disk fragmentation and enhance Windows' performance with regular use of a disk defragmentation utility, such as the Disk Defragmenter program that's included with Windows 95. This program rearranges files, storing each file in a block of contiguous sectors. You can use Disk Defragmenter with any uncompressed local hard disk or floppy disk, or with any local disk that has been compressed with DoubleSpace or DriveSpace. You cannot use Disk Defragmenter with network drives, disks that have been compressed with programs other than DriveSpace and DoubleSpace, read-only disks, or locked drives.

A simple way to run Disk Defragmenter is as follows:

1. Open My Computer and right-click the icon for the disk you want to defragment.

2. Choose Properties from the object menu.

3. Click the Tools tab.

4. Click Defragment Now.

You will probably also find a command for Disk Defragmenter on your Start menu. Look under System Tools, in the Accessories section.

After you click Defragment Now, Disk Defragmenter looks at your disk and tells you what percentage of its space is currently fragmented. If the percentage is low, the program lets you know that you don't need to bother defragmenting at this time. Of course, you can go ahead and defragment it anyway if you want to.

Disk Defragmenter normally checks out the logical structure of your disk before it starts repositioning files. This part of the program's work simply duplicates work that can also be done by ScanDisk. If you use ScanDisk regularly, you might want to speed up the defragmentation process by skipping the checkup. To do this, click the Advanced button in the dialog box that reports the disk's current degree of fragmentation. Then, in the Advanced Options dialog box, deselect the Check Drive For Errors check box.

The Advanced Options dialog box also gives you the opportunity to limit Disk Defragmenter's work to either the portion of your disk that's currently in use for files or only the portion that's currently not in use. Unless you're in a great hurry, however, there's no compelling reason to choose either of these options.

 While Disk Defragmenter is working, you can click a Show Details button to see a real-time diagram of the program's progress. It's a pretty display, but it slows down the defragmentation process. To get the fastest performance from Disk Defragmenter, skip the details display and don't use the disk that's being defragmented.

Conserving Disk Space

For virtual memory to be effective, there must be ample (and preferably unfragmented) space available on the hard disk that contains the swap file. If the amount of free space falls below about 20 MB, you run the risk of seriously impairing your system's performance. To keep this from happening, here are some steps you can take:

- Delete applications or Windows components that you no longer need.

- Reduce the maximum size of your Recycle Bin.

- Consider using DriveSpace to compress your disk files.

See Also: For information about *deleting applications*, see "Uninstalling Applications," page 344.

For information about *deleting Windows components*, see "Adding or Removing Parts of Windows," page 339.

For information about *reducing the Recycle Bin size*, see "Setting Your Recycle Bin's Capacity," page 152.

Doubling Your Disk with DriveSpace

DriveSpace is a program that increases the effective capacity of hard and floppy disks. It does this by creating a "compressed volume file" (CVF) on a disk. When you save a file to a CVF, DriveSpace compresses the file "on the fly" (that is, without requiring any special action by you). When you read a file from a compressed disk, the file is automatically expanded. The net result is that, while you continue to work with your files the way you always have, your disk has much more room than it ever had before.

How much extra room you get depends on what kind of data your files hold. DriveSpace achieves its compression by identifying patterns in your data. Files that are highly structured—for example, a bitmap graphics file, in which certain pixel patterns appear over and over—can be compressed more than files whose contents are relatively random. Executable files and DLLs are usually less compressible than documents. In the typical case in which both executables and documents are involved, you can expect the effective size of your disk to nearly double.

What about performance? Your computer's processor has to do extra work when reading files from or saving files to a CVF. On the other hand, your system has to spend less time interacting with your hard disk because the files occupy fewer clusters. Because the hard disk is a relatively slow component of your system, you may experience no performance penalty at all when using DriveSpace. And if your encompassed disk doesn't have room for an adequate swap file, you'll undoubtedly get *better* performance by using DriveSpace.

The important tradeoff for using DriveSpace is not performance but data security. When DriveSpace compresses a disk, it combines *all* the compressed files on that disk into a single file. Under ordinary circumstances you never see that file, because DriveSpace gives it hidden and system attributes. What you see instead is a "virtualized" disk that looks exactly the same as your disk looked before you ran DriveSpace—except that it's much larger.

For example, suppose your C drive has a capacity of 200 MB and you currently have files filling all but 10 MB of that space. After running DriveSpace on this disk, you'll still have a C drive, and your files will have the same size properties that they had before. That is, Windows will still report that drive C contains 190 MB of data. But drive C will now appear to be a 400-MB drive (or something close to 400 MB).

To achieve the illusion that your files are the same size as before but your disk has ingested a packet of growth hormone, DriveSpace creates a new (uncompressed) "host" drive on your disk. It assigns this drive an unused drive letter, such as H. Then it compresses all your files and combines them into a single file on the host drive. That single file is your CVF. When you read or save a document, you're actually interacting with some piece of the CVF, but DriveSpace deploys its smoke and mirrors to make it look as if you're working with ordinary files on the original drive.

The only hazard in all of this is that corruption or accidental deletion of the CVF can wipe out a whole disk's worth of data. Because the CVF does not ordinarily show up in folder or Windows Explorer windows, or in directory listings generated at the MS-DOS prompt, it's unlikely that you would ever delete it accidentally. But the consequences would be severe if you did. Therefore, *if you use DriveSpace, it's more important than ever that you back up your data regularly!*

DriveSpace or DoubleSpace?

DriveSpace replaces an earlier Microsoft product called Double-Space. Windows 95 can be installed on disks compressed with either DriveSpace or DoubleSpace, and it can read from and write to either kind of CVF. If you're already using DoubleSpace, you don't need to change anything. But if you're going to create new CVFs, you'll use DriveSpace instead of DoubleSpace.

 Microsoft Plus! includes DriveSpace 3, a compression tool that is significantly more powerful than the version of DriveSpace shipped with Windows 95. For details, see Appendix A, "Using the Power of Your 486 or Pentium with Microsoft Plus!," page 727.

 See Also: For information about *backup strategies and a description of the Backup program shipped with Windows*, see Chapter 16, "Protecting Your Data with Backup," page 405.

Compressing a Disk

To compress a disk with DriveSpace, open the Start menu, choose Programs, then Accessories, then System Tools. On the System Tools menu, choose DriveSpace.

 As a quicker alternative for compressing a particular drive, you can right-click the drive's icon in a folder or Windows Explorer window. Choose Properties from the object menu and then click the Compression tab.

NOTE: If DriveSpace has not been installed on your computer, double-click the Add/Remove Programs item in Control Panel, click the Windows Setup tab, select Disk Tools, and click the Details button. Select Disk Compression Tools and click OK.

To compress a disk, simply select it in DriveSpace's initial dialog box (see Figure 15-6), and then choose Compress from the Drive menu. As Figure 15-7 on the next page shows, DriveSpace presents before and after diagrams of your disk, illustrating the estimated effect of the step you're about to take. To proceed, click the Start button.

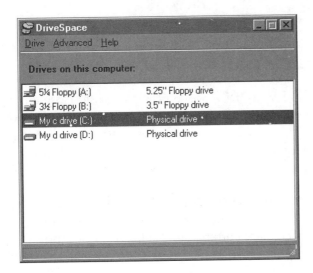

FIGURE 15-6.

DriveSpace lets you nearly double the effective capacity of any local hard or floppy disk.

By default, DriveSpace uses the drive letter H (or the next available letter after H) for the host drive, makes the host drive just large enough to hold the CVF, and then hides the host drive (so that it doesn't ordinarily appear in folder or Windows Explorer windows). These are good defaults, but you can change any of them by clicking the Options button.

After you click Start to begin the compression process, DriveSpace prompts you to back up your files. This is a prudent but optional step. If you want, you can run the Microsoft Backup program directly from within the DriveSpace dialog box.

The compression process itself may take an hour or more on a large hard disk. During this time, you will not be able to use any files stored on

FIGURE 15-7.

These diagrams
illustrate the
estimated effect of
running DriveSpace
on a 230-MB hard
disk.

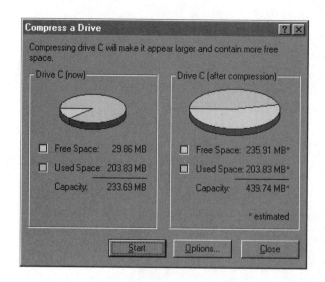

the disk you're compressing. (DriveSpace prompts you to close any open files before it goes to work.) If the disk contains files that cannot be closed (such as your swap file), DriveSpace restarts your computer and runs a limited version of Windows. After DriveSpace has finished, your system restarts again with the full Windows 95.

Compressing Only the Free Space on a Disk

As an alternative to compressing an entire disk, you can ask DriveSpace to compress only the space that's currently unused. DriveSpace turns this free space into a new compressed drive and assigns that drive an unused drive letter.

To compress the free space only, select the drive whose free space you want to compress, and then choose Create Empty from the Advanced menu. You'll see a dialog box similar to the one shown in Figure 15-8.

This dialog box reports the drive letter that DriveSpace plans to use, the amount of space that will be compressed, the estimated capacity of the new compressed volume, and the amount of free space that will remain on your uncompressed volume. (The program leaves a small amount so that your uncompressed files have room to grow.) You can change any of these settings before beginning the compression process.

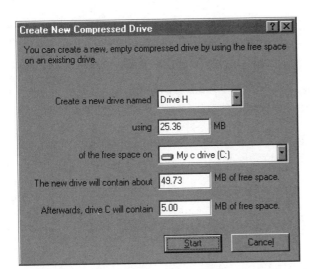

FIGURE 15-8.

As an alternative to compressing an entire disk, you can compress just the free space that remains on the disk.

Compressing Large Hard Disks

The version of DriveSpace that ships with the standard version of Windows 95 cannot create CVFs larger than 512 MB. If you want to compress a hard disk that's larger than about 256 MB, you may need to do it in two or more separate steps. (Alternatively, if you have Microsoft Plus!, you can use DriveSpace 3.)

Compressing Floppy Disks

You can use the Compress command to compress an entire floppy disk. You cannot, however, compress only the free space on a floppy.

Compressed floppy disks are "mounted" by default. That simply means they're made available to the system as soon as you've finished compressing them or whenever you insert such a disk in the drive. DriveSpace includes an Unmount command (on the Advanced menu) that lets you make a floppy's CVF unavailable, but there's no particular reason to use this command.

Formatting a Compressed Floppy Disk

To format a compressed floppy disk, select the disk in DriveSpace's main dialog box. Then choose Format from the Drive menu. Note that the disk must be compressed before you can use this command and that you cannot use the standard Format command with a compressed diskette. (To turn a compressed diskette back into an uncompressed one, use the Uncompress command, discussed next.)

Decompressing a Compressed Volume

If you no longer want a drive to use DriveSpace's compression services, you can "uncompress" it—provided enough room remains to accommodate all the files in their uncompressed state. If the drive does not have enough room, you'll first need to move some of its files from the compressed volume to another drive.

To restore a compressed drive to its normal state, select the drive in DriveSpace's main dialog box. Then choose Uncompress from the Drive menu.

Eliminate Real-Mode (MS-DOS Compatibility) Drivers

Windows 95 supplies 32-bit drivers that run in your computer's protected mode. These drivers provide better performance and security than the 16-bit, real-mode drivers that were used by earlier versions of Windows and MS-DOS. If you have installed Windows 95 on a system that previously used an earlier operating system, however, it is possible that Windows is continuing to use some of your earlier drivers. You can find out whether this is the case by doing the following:

1. Right-click My Computer and choose Properties from the object menu. (Alternatively, double-click the System item in Control Panel.)

2. Click the Performance tab.

If your system is using any real-mode drivers, you will see some indication of that fact on the Performance property sheet. Figure 15-9, for example, depicts a system whose performance is impaired by the presence of a real-mode fax driver.

If you see the words "compatibility mode" anywhere on this property sheet, your system is not giving you optimal performance. You can

Chapter 15: Optimizing and Troubleshooting

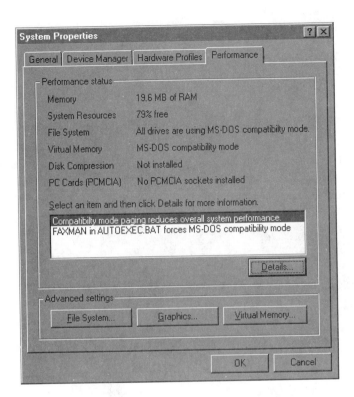

FIGURE 15-9.

Check the Performance tab of the System property sheet to see if your system is using any real-mode drivers.

learn more about what's going on by selecting each item in the property sheet's list box in turn and then clicking the Details button. If your system *requires* a real-mode driver for some reason, you might need to live with less than ideal performance. In many cases, however, real-mode drivers can easily be eliminated. In the system shown in Figure 15-8, for example, a single statement in the AUTOEXEC.BAT file was slowing down all activity of the hard disk. Removing that statement restored the system to optimal performance.

 To inspect or edit your AUTOEXEC.BAT or CONFIG.SYS file, use the Start menu's Run command and run SysEdit.

Eliminate Device Conflicts and Other Device Problems

Conflicts or problems involving devices can adversely affect your system's performance or behavior, possibly without you knowing it. To see if you have any problems of this kind, right-click My Computer and choose Properties from the object menu. (Alternatively, double-click the System item in Control Panel.) Then click the Device Manager tab. Conflicts or other device problems are flagged with exclamation points on the Device Manager tab, as shown in Figure 15-10.

FIGURE 15-10.

The Device Manager flags problem devices with exclamation points.

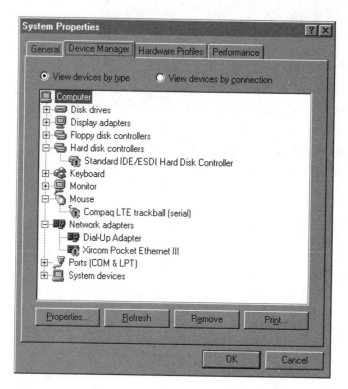

To learn more about a device problem, select its entry in the Device Manager list, and then click the Properties button. The Device Status box in your device's property sheet might tell you everything you need to know. (See Figure 15-11.) If the problem involves a resource conflict, click the Resources tab in the device's property sheet to see what resources—interrupt request (IRQ) lines or direct memory access (DMA) channels, for example—your device is using.

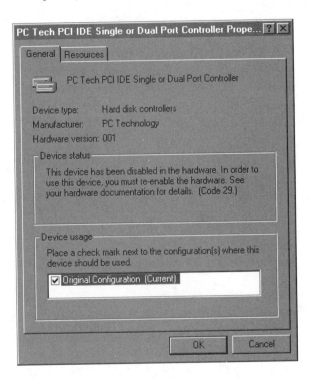

FIGURE 15-11.

To learn more about a device problem, select the device name, click the Properties button, and read the device's property sheet.

For a complete summary of the devices in your system and the resources they use, right-click My Computer, choose Properties, click the Device Manager tab, click the Print button, and then choose the All Devices And System Summary option. The resulting report summarizes IRQ and DMA commitments; shows what I/O addresses are in use and what devices are using them; lists drivers by filename, size, and version number; and more.

Unless you're an expert at working with hardware resource conflicts, it's best to use the Device Manager as a diagnostic tool. Leave the conflict resolution to someone in your company who gets paid for doing that sort of thing, or call your hardware vendor to get instructions on how to proceed. Be aware that careless changes in the Device Manager have the potential to bring your whole system down.

Disable Background Processing of MS-DOS–Based Applications

When you run an MS-DOS–based application and then switch away to a different application, Windows continues to allocate some of your computer's processing time to that MS-DOS–based program, even though it's no longer running in the foreground. Letting an MS-DOS–based program run in the background may degrade your system's overall performance unnecessarily. Unless you really need background processing, it's a good idea to turn it off. You can do that as follows:

1. Right-click the icon for the MS-DOS–based program, and then choose Properties from the object menu.

2. Click the Misc tab.

3. Select the Always Suspend check box.

Certain MS-DOS–based programs—for example, communications programs—might not function reliably without background processing. And with some programs (language compilers, for example), background processing provides a benefit that compensates for any performance degradation it may cause. You'll need to decide on a case-by-case basis whether it makes sense to leave background processing on. But, as a rule, if you don't need it, don't use it.

Watch Out for MS-DOS–Based Programs That Hog Extended Memory

The default extended-memory setting for an MS-DOS–based program is "Auto," which means that Windows imposes no limit on the amount of extended memory the program can have. Generally, that works out fine. Windows allocates as much extended memory to the MS-DOS–based program as it thinks it needs, subject to overall system constraints. But a few ill-behaved programs, when offered a large helping of extended memory, take every byte and hoard it, whether they need a large amount or none at all. If you find your system slowing down markedly whenever a particular MS-DOS–based program is running, try limiting the amount of extended memory that program may use. You can do this as follows:

1. Right-click the icon for the MS-DOS–based program, and then choose Properties from the object menu.

2. Click the Memory tab.

3. Open the Extended (XMS) Memory drop-down and choose an amount other than "Auto."

See Also: For more information about *memory settings for MS-DOS–based applications*, see "Options on the Memory Tab," page 325.

Evaluate Printing Performance Tradeoffs

When you send a document to a non-PostScript printer, Windows first creates an intermediate disk file, called a *spool file* or *enhanced metafile* (EMF). While the EMF is being created, you cannot work in the application that's printing the document. (During this time, the application normally displays a dialog box that monitors the progress of the printing process.) As soon as Windows has finished creating the EMF, you can go on working in your application. At that point, if the print job is at the head of its print queue, Windows *despools* the EMF. That is, it converts the EMF to language specific for your printer and sends the printer-specific commands to the printer.

Exactly where each of the steps takes place depends on whether the printer is attached to your computer, to a server running Windows 95, or to a server running another operating system (such as Novell NetWare or Windows NT).

If the printer is attached to a server running Windows 95, the conversion of the EMF to your printer's language takes place on the server. If the printer is attached locally or to a server running another operating system, the EMF-to-printer-language conversion occurs on your own computer. This process takes place in the background but still has some temporary effect on the overall performance on your system. Therefore, all other things being equal, you might want to give preference to printers attached to servers that are running Windows 95.

Assuming a print job does not have to wait behind other jobs in a print queue, Windows normally begins despooling it as soon as the first page has been rendered into EMF form. Windows continues despooling pages as they become EMF-ready. This overlapping of the EMF-building and despooling processes gives you the shortest possible time from when you click OK until the last page drops into the tray. It also minimizes the size of the temporary disk files that Windows has to use. But it makes you wait a little longer until you can resume working in your application.

If you want to be able to get to work more quickly, you can tell Windows *not* to despool until the entire EMF has been created. To do this:

1. Open the Start menu, choose Settings, and then choose Printers.

2. Right-click the printer you're going to use, and then choose Properties from the object menu.

3. Click the Details tab.

4. Click Spool Settings.

5. Select the option button labeled "Start printing after last page is spooled."

Note that this option requires Windows to create a larger temporary disk file and produces a somewhat later finish time for the entire print job.

Evaluate Video Performance Tradeoffs

High screen resolutions and high color depths make your processor work harder than low screen resolutions and low color depths. If you work primarily with text, or if your video system is less snappy than you'd like, consider switching to a lower resolution or color depth. (Of the two factors, color depth has the greater impact on performance.)

See Also: For information about *changing the resolution*, see "Changing Display Resolution," page 94.

For information about *changing color depth*, see "Changing the Color Depth of Your Display," page 97.

Priorities for Upgrading Your System

Here are some guidelines to consider if you're planning to upgrade your hardware:

- Officially speaking, Windows 95 runs on a system with 4 MB of memory (RAM), but "runs" is a relative term. Other things being equal, if you're now working with less than 8 MB, your first priority should be to add memory.

- Windows 95 is (mostly) a 32-bit operating system. The 386 microprocessor does not make nearly as effective use of 32-bit code as do the 486 and the Pentium. If you're now using a 386-based machine, you'll get dramatic improvement by moving to a 486 of any clock speed. You'll get relatively less improvement by moving from a 486 to a Pentium.

- Windows 95 runs significantly better in 16 MB of memory than in 8 MB. If you're now using an 8-MB 486 or Pentium, spend upgrade money first on memory. Moving from 16 MB to 24 MB provides relatively less gain, unless you're working with very large-scale applications, such as computer-aided design (CAD) programs.

- Think of your hard disk as an extension of internal memory. If your hard disk is frequently filled to within 20 MB of capacity and you're not comfortable using DriveSpace, get another (or a larger) hard disk.

- If you're running on a 486, be sure your processor's cache (not to be confused with the disk cache supplied by Windows) is at least 64 KB. If possible, boost it to 256 KB. Increasing it beyond 256 KB provides relatively little gain, however.

- A faster video board will pay performance dividends, particularly when you work at a high resolution and color depth. But speedy video won't make up for a slow processor or inadequate memory.

- You may get some performance gain by upgrading your Windows applications to versions written specifically for Windows 95. It's difficult to generalize about this, however.

If you're serious about getting maximal performance from Windows, it's a good idea to read one or two of the Windows-specific magazines regularly. There you'll find plenty of reviews of the latest, hottest hardware, as well as new tips for squeezing more power out of what you already have.

Protecting Your Data with Backup

You don't have to use computers for long to know the frustration of losing data. It happens to everyone. Although Windows 95 can't prevent mistakes and accidents from occurring, Microsoft Backup, the backup program included with Windows 95, provides a form of insurance to help you deal with such misfortunes.

With Backup, you can back your files up to QIC (quarter-inch cartridge) tape drives, to local or remote hard disks, or to floppy disks. You can create named "file sets" to describe the files you want to back up, and then repeat your backup procedures by simply dragging the file sets onto Backup's icon. You can tell Backup to back up all files in a file set, only those files that have changed since your most recent backup, or only those files that have been modified since a particular date (whether or not they've changed since your last backup).

Backup also includes an easy-to-use restore command with which you can copy particular files or all files from your backup medium to your original disks (or to some other disks). Options associated with the restore command let you specify whether the restore operation should copy all files from the backup medium or only those files that are not newer than like-named files on your original disks.

Backup Types: Full and Incremental

Two common types of backup operations are called *full* and *incremental*. When you do a full backup, Backup copies *all* specified files to the backup medium, regardless of when they were last changed. When you do an incremental backup, the program copies only the files that have changed since your most recent backup. The first incremental backup after a full backup copies all files that have changed since the full backup. Your second incremental backup copies only those files that have changed since the first incremental backup, and so on. A common strategy is to combine the two types of backup operations as follows:

- At some regular interval, such as once a week, perform a full backup.

- At regular intervals between full backups—for example, at the end of each work day—perform an incremental backup.

What's in a Name?

Here are some important definitions to keep in mind as you work with Microsoft Backup:

Back up. To copy files from a disk to some backup medium—a tape, another disk, or one or more floppy disks.

Restore. To copy files from a backup medium to their original locations or to some other location.

Full backup. A backup operation that copies all files in a file set, whether or not they have changed since your most recent full backup. Note that a full backup does not have to include all files on a disk or computer.

Full system backup. A full backup of everything on your system, including the Windows registry and other system files. Microsoft Backup automatically creates a file set called Full System Backup, which you can use to perform a full system backup.

Incremental backup. A backup operation that copies only those files in a file set that have changed since your most recent backup.

File set. A collection of files that meet some specification—such as "all files on Drive C except for .EXE and .DLL files." A file set's definition is stored in a file with the extension .SET, so that you can easily reuse the file set.

Backup set. The collection of files that were backed up in a single operation. When you perform a backup, Microsoft Backup asks you to name the resulting backup set. When you need to restore one or more files, you must tell Backup which backup set it should copy the file or files from.

Tape name. A name that you assign to a tape cartridge. A tape name is comparable to the volume name that you can assign to a hard disk or diskette. Do not confuse the tape name with the name of your backup sets. A particular tape can contain many backup sets.

If you follow this strategy, it's a good idea not to collect more than a half-dozen or so incremental backups between full backups. Otherwise, you might have to search through a lot of backup sets to find particular files in the event that you need to restore from the backup medium.

For extra security, it's a good idea to rotate backup media. For example, if you do a full backup once a week and incremental backups on the intervening days, you might want to keep one week's worth of backups on one tape cartridge and then use a different cartridge the following week. If disaster strikes twice—your original storage medium *and* your backup medium are both damaged— you'll still be able to restore files from the previous time period's backup medium. The files you restore probably won't be the most current versions, but you'll be better off than if you had to re-create everything from scratch.

If possible, store your backup media away from your computers. Otherwise, if you experience a fire or theft you may lose both your backups and your originals.

For information about *selecting a backup type*, see "Choosing Backup Options," page 416.

Deciding What Files to Back Up

Exactly what you need to back up depends on your circumstances, of course, but here's a general principle worth observing: don't make your backup routine so onerous and time-consuming that you lose the motivation to adhere to it.

In practice, what this means for many users is the following:

- If you have a backup medium large enough to accommodate all files on a disk, it's a good idea to do a complete backup of that disk at *infrequent* intervals. Microsoft Backup automatically creates a file set called Full System Backup that you can use for this purpose.

- Exclude from your regular full backup/incremental backup routine program files and DLLs that you have installed from diskettes. Instead, back these files up *before* you install the programs in the first place.

- Also exclude CD-ROM–based program files and DLLs from full and incremental backups if you have created a full backup of the entire hard disk on which those programs are installed.

- Include all data files (documents) in your full and incremental backups. These are the files that change the most and that would be most difficult to replace.

- If you don't have a regular full and incremental backup routine, learn at least to perform ad hoc backups of the files you're currently working with. If you don't have a tape drive, back these files up to another hard disk. If you don't have another hard disk, back them up to floppies. It doesn't take *that* long.

 See Also: For information about *specifying the files to back up*, see "Creating a File Set," page 411.

Formatting a Backup Tape

Before you can back up files to magnetic tape, you have to format the tape. This is easy but time-consuming. Proceed as follows:

1. Insert the tape in your tape drive.

2. Run Microsoft Backup. (From the Start menu, choose Programs, then Accessories, and then System Tools. Then choose Backup.)

3. Choose Format Tape from the Tools menu.

   NOTE: If Backup does not appear on the System Tools submenu, you can also get the program running by the following method: Double-click My Computer, right-click any disk-drive icon, choose Properties, click the Tools tab, and then click Backup Now. If Backup has not been installed on your computer, double-click the Add/Remove Programs item in Control Panel, click the Windows Setup tab, select Disk Tools, and click the Details button. Select Backup and click OK.

   If the Format Tape command is not available but you hear your tape drive working, wait a moment or two. Sometimes it takes a few seconds for Backup to recognize that there's a tape ready to use. If the Format Tape command is not available and you don't hear your tape drive working, choose Redetect Tape from the Tools menu. In a few moments, the Format command should become available.

   While you're formatting, you can make modest use of the computer to which the tape is attached. But heavy use may abort the formatting process. Because it may take Backup more than an hour to format a sizable tape, you might want to begin your formatting at the end of a work day.

 You can have Backup format the tape at the same time it performs your first backup to that tape. To do this, choose the Format When Needed On Tape Backups check box, on the Backup tab of the Options dialog box.

Creating a File Set

Figure 16-1 on the next page shows the initial Backup screen for a typical computer that has one floppy disk drive, two hard disks, and a CD-ROM drive. The window is divided vertically into two panes. The left pane displays an outline of the computer's disk resources, and the right pane shows the contents of whatever is selected in the left pane.

FIGURE 16-1.

The left pane of
Backup's window
displays an outline of
your disks, and the
right pane displays
particulars for the
selected left-pane
item.

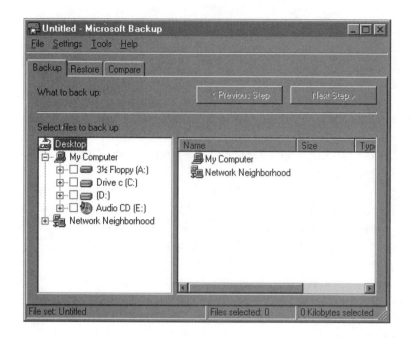

To create a file set, do the following:

1. Use the left and right panes to select all the folders and files you want to back up.

2. If you want to exclude any files from selected folders, choose File Filtering from the Settings menu and fill out the File Filtering dialog box. (See "Applying a File Filter," page 414.)

3. Choose Options from the Settings menu, and specify any backup options you want. These option settings will be saved with your file set. (See "Choosing Backup Options," page 416.)

4. Click Next Step.

5. Specify a destination for your backup by clicking in the left pane.

   Figure 16-2 shows the display you'll use to specify your backup medium. If you're using a tape drive, you should see the name of the tape in the drive at the bottom of the destination list. If instead you see "Microsoft Backup did not detect a tape drive," choose Redetect Tape from the Tools menu.

6. Choose Save As from the File menu and supply a filename.

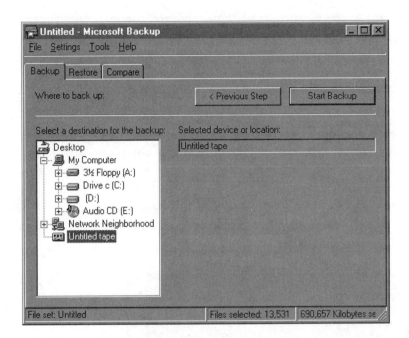

FIGURE 16-2.

After you specify the files you want to back up, clicking Next Step brings you to this screen, where you choose your backup medium.

As you work with the Backup window, keep in mind the following:

- As in Windows Explorer, plus signs in the left pane denote outline items that can be expanded, and minus signs signify items that can be collapsed.

- To make the right pane display the contents of a disk or folder, click the *name* of that disk or folder (not the plus sign) in the left pane.

- To select all files in a folder, click the check box beside the folder name, in either the left pane or the right pane. (Alternatively, select a folder name with cursor keys, and then press Spacebar to select the associated check box.)

- If you want to select all files except those of certain classes (for example, all but .EXE and .DLL files), go ahead and select all. Then apply a filter to remove the files you don't want.

- To select only particular files in a folder, click the name of the folder in the left pane. Then, in the right pane, click the check box beside each file you want to select.

As you select files, the number of files you've selected and the total (uncompressed) space they occupy are reported in the status bar at the bottom of Backup's window.

Applying a File Filter

You can use a file filter to exclude from the backup process particular types of files as well as to exclude files whose last-modification date falls within a particular date range. Files that you exclude will not be backed up, even if you explicitly select their names when you create a file set. To apply either kind of filter, choose File Filtering from the Settings menu. Figure 16-3 shows the File Filtering dialog box.

FIGURE 16-3.

You can use filters to exclude particular types of files or files whose last-modification date falls within a particular date range.

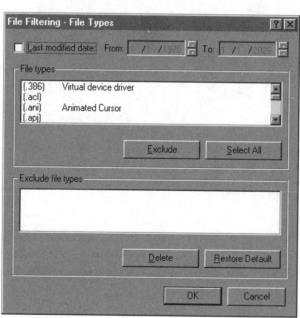

In the File Types section of this dialog box, select the types you want to exclude. Then click the Exclude button.

If you want to include only one or two types of files and exclude everything else, first click the Select All button, and then scroll through the File Types list and click the types of files you want to include. Then click the Exclude button. Be aware, however, that you can exclude only registered file types. Therefore, if you use this technique to back up particular file types, your backup may also include numerous unregistered file types.

To exclude files whose last-modified date falls within a particular range of dates, select the check box at the top of the dialog box. Then fill out the From and To boxes appropriately. Note that the dates in these boxes specify files to be *excluded.* Therefore, if you just want to back up those files that have been modified during the past 24 hours, you would leave the From box alone and enter yesterday's date in the To box.

Backing Up the Files Named in a File Set

To back up the files identified in a file set, proceed as follows:

1. Start Backup if it's not already running.

2. Choose Open File Set from the File menu. Select a file set and click Open.

3. Use the check boxes in the left and right panes, as well as the File Filtering dialog box, to make any appropriate adjustments to the set of files identified by the file set.

4. Choose Options from the Settings menu, and then click the Backup tab to choose options that affect your backup. (See "Choosing Backup Options," page 416.)

5. Click Next Step.

6. Specify a destination for your backup by clicking in the left pane.

   To back up to a particular folder on another hard disk, use the plus signs in the destination list to navigate, and then select the name of the folder.

7. Click Start Backup.

8. Supply a name for the backup set you're about to create.

9. If you want to protect your backup set with a password, choose Password Protect.

10. Click OK.

 Unlike files in a folder, backup sets on a tape can have identical names. If you do two incremental backups on Monday and want to call them both Monday Incremental, for example, that's not a problem to the Backup program. If you need to restore files from a tape with identically named backup sets, you'll be able to distinguish the sets by their creation times.

 While the backup is taking place, you can still work with your computer.

Choosing Backup Options

Figure 16-4 shows the Backup tab of the Options dialog box. (To display the Options dialog box, choose Options from the Settings menu.) In the top of this dialog box, be sure to let Backup know whether you want a full backup or an incremental backup.

The remaining options, including those in the Advanced section, are neither particularly advanced nor difficult to understand. Be aware, though, that the Verify option adds considerably to the backup time, and the Use

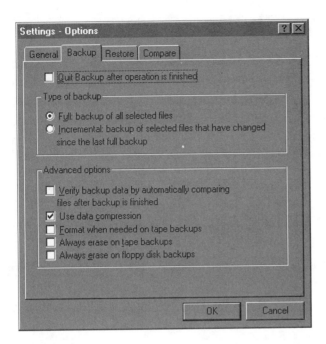

FIGURE 16-4.

Among other choices, the Options dialog box lets you indicate whether you want a full or an incremental backup. Settings in this dialog box are preserved when you save a file set.

Data Compression option requires that your system have a compression technology (such as DriveSpace) installed. You do not need to use DriveSpace on the source or backup media to compress your backup files, but the technology must be available to the Backup program.

If you choose the "Verify backup data . . ." option, Backup carries out the entire backup, and then compares each file in the backup set with its original counterpart. If you use your computer during the backup and you change any of the files that were backed up, the verify operation reports errors. Be sure to read the error report to see if the errors merely reflect changes that have taken place while the backup was in progress.

 For information about *DriveSpace*, see "Doubling Your Disk with DriveSpace," page 390.

Backing Up with the Full System Backup File Set

The first time you run Microsoft Backup, the program creates a file set called Full System Backup. This file set includes everything on your local hard disks. More important, it also includes all current registry information. When you open the Full System Backup file set, you'll be asked to wait a moment or two while Windows 95 collects and prepares to save the registry information.

Performing an Ad Hoc Backup

Although file sets offer convenience and support good backup habits, you're by no means required to use them. If all you want to do is copy a set of files to a backup medium on an ad-hoc basis, you can simply start Backup, select the files you want to copy (following the same procedures you would use to create a file set), click Next Step, select your backup medium, and click Start Backup.

Backing Up to Multiple Tapes or Floppy Disks

You can back up more files than will fit on the chosen backup medium. If you fill a tape, Backup prompts for another tape. If you fill a floppy disk (as you almost certainly will when you do any sizable backup to floppy media), Backup tells you to put in another disk. Backup also can split files across backup media, so you don't need to worry about backing up a file that's larger than the capacity of your floppy disks.

When Backup has finished copying all files in your file set or file selection, it records the location of each backed-up file on the last tape or disk. Be sure to number your tapes or disks! That way, if you need to restore one or more files from the set, you'll be able to find the right medium quickly and easily.

Backing Up with Drag and Drop

As an alternative to opening the Backup program and interacting with dialog boxes, you can back up a file set by simply dragging its icon and dropping it on the icon for Microsoft Backup. Your file sets have the extension .SET, and they are identified in details view as "File Set for Microsoft Backup." By default, file sets are stored in the same folder as Backup itself—\Program Files\Accessories.

NOTE: You must drag the actual file-set icon, not a shortcut to the file set.

When you drag a file set to the Backup program, Backup uses the options set via the dialog box shown in Figure 16-5.

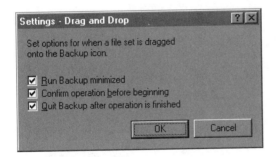

FIGURE 16-5.

By setting these options and dragging a file set to the Backup icon, you can do your backups without opening the Backup program.

To view or change these options, choose Drag And Drop from Backup's Settings menu.

When you do a backup with drag and drop, Backup does not prompt you to supply a name for the backup set. Instead, it uses the name of the file set with a number appended to it. Thus, if you do this repeatedly and add successive backups to the same backup medium, you'll have a number of similarly named backup sets. If you need to restore from any of these sets, you can simply use the creation dates to distinguish the sets.

Restoring

To restore files from a backup set, start by launching the Backup program and clicking the Restore tab. You'll see a two-paned display, similar to the one you used when specifying files to back up. In the left pane, Backup lists potential backup media—including your system's hard disks and floppy disk drives, as well as the name of the tape in your tape drive, if you have one.

If the backup set you're planning to restore from spans multiple tapes or disks, insert the last tape or disk in the drive. Then select the name of the backup medium in the left pane. When you do this, the names of all backup sets on that medium appear in the right pane.

To see what files are included in a backup set, double-click the name of the backup set in the right pane or click Next Step. When you do this, Backup fills the left and right panes with a folder outline and filenames, respectively. (See Figure 16-6.) You can select files and folders in this display using exactly the same techniques you use to select files for backing up.

FIGURE 16-6.

To restore files, click the Restore tab, choose your backup medium and backup set, and then select files and folders.

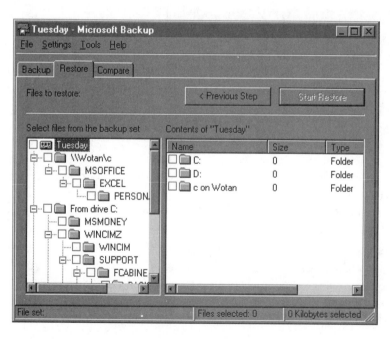

Options for Restoring

Figure 16-7 shows the options available for restoring. To get to this dialog box, choose Options from the Settings menu and click the Restore tab.

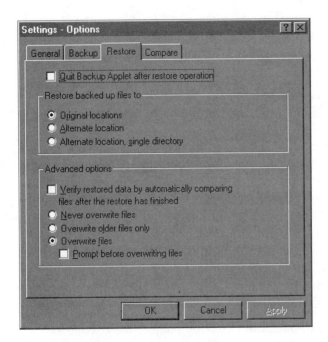

FIGURE 16-7.

Option buttons in the top half of this dialog box let you tell Backup where to put the restored files.

As the figure shows, you can use option buttons in the top half of this dialog box to restore your files to a location other than the one from which they were backed up. You'll find these choices particularly handy if you're restoring files in the aftermath of a disk crash.

If you choose Alternate Location, Backup restores files to the location you specify and re-creates your original folder structure. If you choose the Alternate Location, Single Directory option button, Backup puts all the restored files in a single folder, ignoring the original folder structure. In either case, the program prompts you for your desired location before it goes to work.

The remaining options on the Restore tab of the Options dialog box are probably self-explanatory. If you're restoring files to the disk from which you backed them up, pay particular attention to the three Overwrite option buttons. For example, if you've made changes to some of the files since you backed them up, you might want to choose the Overwrite Older Files Only option. That way, Backup will restore only those files that have not changed.

421

Once you've made all your file and option selections, simply click the Start Restore button. If you're restoring files from multiple tapes or floppy disks, Backup prompts you for the tapes or disks it needs.

Comparing a Backup Set to the Original Files

As Figure 16-4 on page 417 shows, Backup provides an option to verify backup data when it creates a backup set. If you choose this option, Backup performs a detailed comparison of each file in the backup set with its corresponding original file, after all files have been copied to the backup medium. This step adds considerably to the time required to perform the backup.

If you want, you can skip the verify step and compare files yourself whenever it's convenient. Simply click the Compare tab in Backup's program window, and then proceed as follows:

1. Select a backup medium in the left pane.

2. Select a backup set in the right pane.

3. Click Next Step.

4. Use the left and right panes to select the folders and files you want to verify.

5. Click Start Compare.

Printing the Names of Files in a Selection

Any time you select files in Backup—whether for backing up, restoring, or comparing—you can use the File menu's Print command to print the names of everything in your selection. Be aware that Backup prints the names of all files in the selection when you do this, even if what you're about to do is an incremental backup. Also note that the printout puts each filename on a separate line, so a large-scale file selection may easily generate a report of 100 pages or more.

17

Using the Accessibility Features

Windows 95 offers a wide range of features to make computer use more accessible for people with disabilities. Whether the issue is impaired vision or hearing or an inability to use both hands for typing, Windows has a solution.

And you'll find that these features are not only for the "disabled." If you work in a noisy environment or it's not convenient to use the mouse, for example, the accessibility features can help. Following are some of the available options. You can:

- Use visual cues instead of sounds to alert you to system events

- Use a special high-contrast color scheme throughout your Windows applications

- Use the keyboard instead of the mouse to click, double-click, and drag

- Attach an alternate input device to your serial port if you are unable to use a standard mouse or keyboard

- Turn on "StickyKeys," which enables you to use Ctrl, Alt, and Shift key combinations without having to hold down more than one key at a time

This chapter covers these and other accessibility features. You'll learn how to use each option, in what situations it might be appropriate, and tips for effective use. In addition, at the end of this chapter you'll find a list of resources that allow you to get more help and information about computer use and disabilities.

 If more than one person uses your computer, but not all users require the accessibility features, set up a different profile for each user. For information about user profiles, see "Taking Advantage of User Profiles," page 87.

Getting to the Accessibility Features

Most of the accessibility features are grouped in one place. To get to them, do the following:

1. Choose Settings from the Start menu, and then choose Control Panel from the menu that unfolds.

2. Double-click the Accessibility Options icon.

   This opens the Accessibility Properties dialog box, as shown in Figure 17-1.

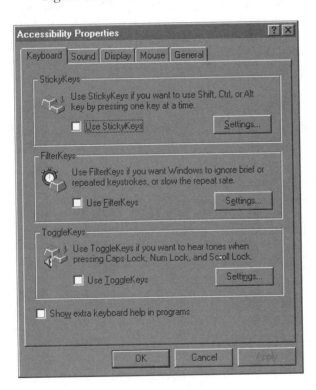

FIGURE 17-1.

The Accessibility Properties dialog box displays the Keyboard tab when you first open it.

As you can see, this dialog box includes five tabs. Simply click the tab for the areas whose settings you want to adjust.

NOTE: If your Control Panel does not include an Accessibility Options icon, double-click the Add/Remove Programs icon. Then click the Windows Setup tab and select Accessibility Options in the Components list. Click OK to begin installation. You'll then need to close and reopen Control Panel for the Accessibility Options icon to appear.

Emergency Shortcuts

Because most of the accessibility features are designed for users who have difficulty with certain standard Windows functions, the operating system includes "emergency shortcuts" that temporarily turn a specific feature on or off. These are especially useful in cases in which a particular accessibility feature must be activated to enable a user to access the computer. In a case like this, the user wouldn't be able to open Control Panel to activate the feature, so the shortcut can provide initial access. In addition, the emergency shortcuts are a great way to turn the accessibility features on or off when several people use the same computer. We point out the shortcuts throughout this chapter.

If no one who uses the computer has any use for a particular accessibility option, consider disabling its shortcut. That way, a user can't accidentally activate the feature. If you later develop a need for the feature, simply go back to the Accessibility Properties dialog box and make any necessary changes.

Adjusting Keyboard Input Options

The options on the Keyboard tab allow you to control how Windows handles keyboard input.

- StickyKeys allows you to type keystroke combinations without the need to hold down one key while you press another.

- FilterKeys can be set to ignore accidentally repeated keystrokes or brief keystrokes that are made by touching a key in error.

- ToggleKeys provides an audible notification whenever you press the Num Lock, Caps Lock, or Scroll Lock key.

Facilitating Entry of Keyboard Shortcuts with StickyKeys

Windows makes extensive use of keyboard shortcuts, which generally require you to press more than one key at a time. For example, to use the keystroke combination Ctrl-Alt-Del, a user would have to hold down the Ctrl and Alt keys while pressing the Del key. In cases where a user is limited to one hand or a mouthstick, pressing multiple keys at the same time might not be possible.

StickyKeys enables users to input key combinations by pressing the applicable keys in sequence rather than simultaneously. This option causes the Ctrl, Alt, and Shift keys to become *sticky*—when a user presses one of these *modifier keys*, the key is locked down until any other key (except for Ctrl, Alt, or Shift) or a mouse button is pressed and released. Pressing the modifier key twice locks it "permanently"—until you press that modifier key a third time.

While a key is locked, that key's space in the notification area of the taskbar is shaded.

To turn StickyKeys on, simply select the Use StickyKeys check box on the Keyboard tab of the Accessibility Properties dialog box.

 The keyboard shortcut for activating or deactivating StickyKeys is to press either Shift key five times.

You can also adjust several StickyKey options. To do so, click the Settings button to open the dialog box shown in Figure 17-2 on the next page. The following list describes the available options:

- By default, pressing the Shift key five times activates or deactivates StickyKeys. To disable the shortcut, deselect the Use Shortcut check box.

- As mentioned, the StickyKeys feature allows users to lock a modifier key (Ctrl, Alt, or Shift) by pressing a modifier key twice. The

FIGURE 17-2.

The Settings For
StickyKeys dialog
box lets you
customize
StickyKeys behavior.

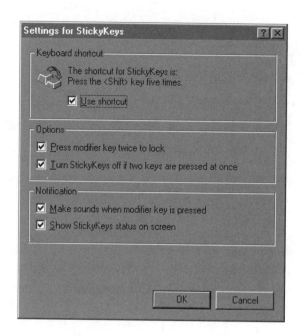

key remains locked until you press it a third time. As a general rule, if you have a need for the StickyKeys feature at all, you should leave this option enabled. You can, however, disable it by deselecting Press Modifier Key Twice To Lock.

■ If several people use the same computer, keep Turn StickyKeys Off If Two Keys Are Pressed At Once enabled (as it is by default). With this option checked, users who don't require StickyKeys can turn off the feature simply by pressing a modifier key and any other key at the same time. This option is great for multiple users—the Sticky-Keys feature can be kept on for those who need it, and users who don't need it can use standard key combinations.

■ Make Sounds When Modifier Key Is Pressed can provide useful auditory feedback each time a Ctrl, Alt, or Shift key is pressed. It's a handy reminder that StickyKeys is active. If, however, you're the only user and have no need to be reminded, deselect this option.

■ You shouldn't need to change the default option for Show Sticky-Keys Status On Screen, which displays an icon in the taskbar's notification area. In addition to alerting you that the feature is active (and which modifier keys are currently locked), you can right-click the icon for quick access to StickyKeys settings. Right-clicking the taskbar icon also offers a command that displays an enlarged StickyKeys icon in a movable window.

Controlling the Keyboard Repeat Rate with FilterKeys

The FilterKeys options provide precise control over the keyboard repeat rate. These options are particularly useful if involuntary hand movements cause accidental key presses. To activate this feature, select the Use Filter-Keys check box on the Keyboard tab of the Accessibility property sheet.

You can also adjust several FilterKeys options. To do so, click the Settings button to open the Settings For FilterKeys dialog box shown in Figure 17-3.

Use the Ignore Repeated Keystrokes option button to instruct Windows to ignore all but the first keystroke when a key press is rapidly repeated. The dialog box shown in Figure 17-4 on the next page allows you

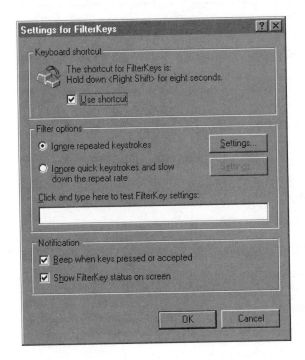

FIGURE 17-3.

The Settings For FilterKeys dialog box lets you ignore repeated keystrokes or brief keystrokes.

to set the minimum time before which repeated keystrokes are ignored. Test your settings in the test area provided before you accept them.

FIGURE 17-4.

With FilterKeys enabled, key presses repeated more rapidly than the time shown in the Advanced Settings For FilterKeys dialog box are ignored.

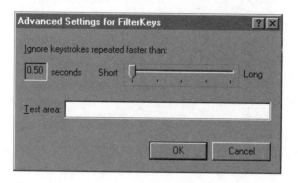

The keyboard shortcut for activating or deactivating FilterKeys is to hold down the right Shift key for eight seconds.

The Ignore Quick Keystrokes And Slow Down The Repeat Rate option causes the computer to ignore keys that are pressed only briefly. When FilterKeys is active, these settings override Control Panel's Keyboard repeat settings. Figure 17-5 shows the Advanced Settings dialog box for this option.

Select No Keyboard Repeat to turn off the keyboard repeat feature altogether. With this option selected, it doesn't matter how long you hold down a key; it won't repeat under any circumstances.

Select Slow Down Keyboard Repeat Rates and adjust the Repeat Delay and Repeat Rate settings if you want to retain the ability to repeat keystrokes.

For more information about *setting the keyboard repeat rate,* see "Adjusting the Keyboard Repeat and Cursor Blink Rates," page 113.

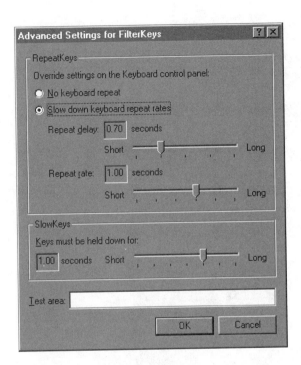

FIGURE 17-5.

Adjust keyboard
speed and repeat
rates here.

Using ToggleKeys to Indicate Keyboard Status Changes

The ToggleKeys option causes Windows to sound a tone each time the Caps Lock, Num Lock, or Scroll Lock key is pressed. The only change you can make in the Settings dialog box is to disable the keyboard shortcut.

 The keyboard shortcut for activating or deactivating ToggleKeys is to hold down Num Lock for five seconds.

Adjusting Sound Options

The options in the Sound tab (shown in Figure 17-6 on the next page) are designed for users who are hearing-impaired.

FIGURE 17-6.

These adjustments
facilitate use for the
hearing-impaired.

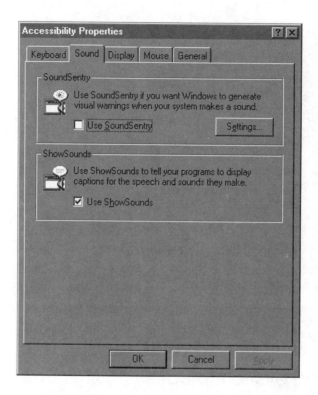

SoundSentry causes Windows to display a visual cue whenever your computer beeps. As you can see in Figure 17-7, the Settings For Sound-Sentry dialog box allows you to customize the visual cues for windowed and full-screen programs.

NOTE: The SoundSentry actions take place only when your system plays a sound through its internal speaker. (Most programs that beep through the internal speaker are MS-DOS–based programs.) Sounds played through external speakers via a sound card do not invoke SoundSentry.

ShowSounds is the Windows 95 equivalent of closed-captioned television. In applications that use digitized speech or other audible cues, ShowSounds instructs the application to provide visible feedback, such as text captions. Not all programs have this capability.

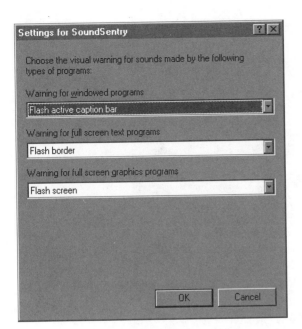

FIGURE 17-7.

The Settings For SoundSentry dialog box lets you specify a different action for different types of programs.

 The accessibility features designed for hearing-impaired users can also be used effectively in situations in which the computer's speakers must be turned off or in extremely noisy workplaces.

Adjusting Display Settings

The High Contrast option on the Display tab, shown in Figure 17-8 on the next page, allows users with impaired vision to select among several color schemes designed to provide sharp contrast, which makes it easier to distinguish foreground and background colors.

 The keyboard shortcut for activating or deactivating High Contrast is to press the left Alt, left Shift, and Print Scrn keys simultaneously.

FIGURE 17-8.

Use the Display tab
to select a high-
contrast color
scheme.

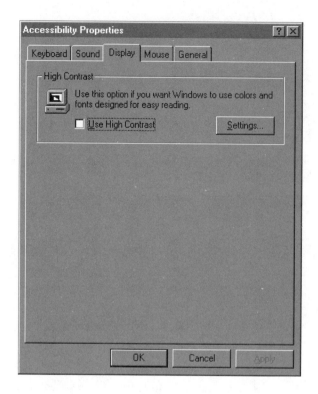

Click the Settings button to display the Settings For High Contrast
dialog box, in which you can select a white-on-black or black-on-white
scheme. In addition, you can select any of the color schemes that appear
in the Appearance tab of the Display property sheet, which is accessible
from Control Panel.

 Because you can have one color scheme set in the Display
property sheet and another one in the Settings For High
Contrast dialog box, you can easily toggle between two
color schemes by pressing the shortcut for High Contrast.

See Also: For information about *color schemes*, see "Changing the Colors, Fonts, and Sizes of the Windows User Interface," page 98.

Using the Keyboard
Instead of the Mouse

Yes, it is possible to use Windows 95 without a mouse. Although most mouse actions in Windows have a keyboard equivalent, some tasks can be performed only by moving the mouse pointer, clicking, and dragging. The MouseKeys feature, whose settings dialog box is shown in Figure 17-9, allows you to use the keys on the numeric keypad to simulate mouse actions.

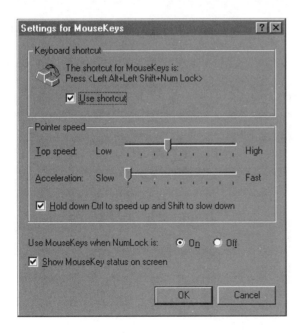

FIGURE 17-9.

You can use the keyboard to replace mouse actions.

With MouseKeys, you can use the numeric keypad to do the following:

- To move the mouse pointer, press any number key except 5. Figure 17-10 shows the direction in which each key moves the pointer.

- To perform a single mouse click, press the 5 key.

- To double-click, press the Plus (+) key.

- To drag, position the mouse pointer on the object and press the Ins key. Then use the directional number keys to move the mouse pointer. Press Del to "release" the mouse button, which completes the drag operation.

- To move the mouse pointer in larger increments, hold down the Ctrl key while you use the direction keys.

- To move the mouse pointer a single pixel at a time, hold down the Shift key while you use the direction keys.

NOTE: If you hold down a direction key, the mouse pointer begins moving slowly and then accelerates to its maximum speed. If you hold down Shift while you hold down a direction key, the mouse pointer moves at a slow, steady rate. (The check box labeled "Hold down Ctrl to speed up and Shift to slow down" in the Settings For MouseKeys dialog box must be selected to enable this "throttle control.")

FIGURE 17-10.

Use the numeric keypad to imitate mouse actions.

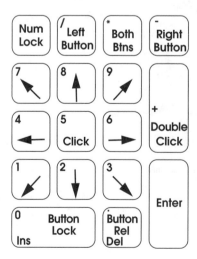

The keyboard shortcut for activating or deactivating MouseKeys is to press the left Alt, left Shift, and Num Lock keys simultaneously.

General Accessibility Settings

The options on the General tab, shown in Figure 17-11, apply to all of the accessibility features.

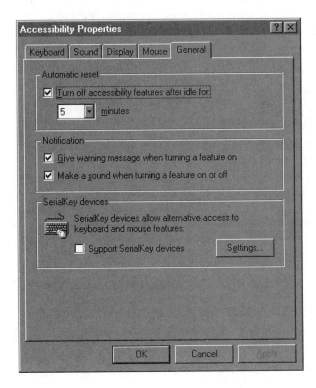

FIGURE 17-11.

Options on the General tab determine how Windows controls all the accessibility features.

The following options determine whether Windows automatically turns off accessibility features and how Windows notifies you when a feature is turned on or off:

■ You can instruct Windows to deactivate accessibility features that haven't been used for a specified time period, from 5 minutes through 30 minutes. Select the Turn Off Accessibility Features After Idle For check box, and then select a time in the Minutes drop-down.

■ The Notification options instruct Windows to display a visual message or to play a sound when any accessibility feature is turned on or off.

Additional Accessibility Resources

In addition to the accessibility features in Windows 95, Microsoft and many other organizations provide services to make computer use even more accessible for people with disabilities.

■ Recording for the Blind

Recording for the Blind offers more than 80,000 titles, including Microsoft product documentation, on audio cassettes and floppy disks. For more information or to order products, contact:

Recording for the Blind, Inc.
20 Roszel Road
Princeton, NJ 08540
Phone: (800) 221-4792 or (609) 452-0606
Fax: (609) 987-8116

■ Special keyboard layouts

Microsoft distributes two Dvorak keyboard layouts designed for single-handed users. There's one for people who use only their right hand, and one for those who use only their left. These layouts also work for users who type with a single finger or a mouthstick. No additional equipment is required to use these layouts.

To obtain these layouts, download the file GA0650.ZIP (available on most online services) or GA0650.EXE on the Microsoft Download service.

■ Text Telephone service (TT/TDD)

To contact Microsoft Sales and Service on a text telephone, call (800) 892-5234 between 6:30 A.M. and 5:30 P.M. Pacific time. To contact Microsoft Product Support Services on a text telephone, call (206) 635-4948 between 6:00 A.M. and 6:00 P.M. Pacific time.

■ Trace Resource Book and CO-NET CD

The Trace Resource Book provides descriptions and photographs of over 2,000 products that help people with disabilities use computers. The CO-NET CD is a searchable database of over 17,000 products, services, and other information. These resource guides are issued semi-annually by the Trace R&D Center at the University of Wisconsin–Madison. For more information, contact:

Trace R&D Center
S-151 Waisman Center
1500 Highland Avenue
Madison, WI 53705-2280
Voice telephone: (608) 263-2309
Text telephone: (608) 263-5408
Fax: (608) 262-8848

■ Center for Developmental Disabilities

Assistive technology programs throughout the country can provide you with customized assistance for specific needs. To find a program in your area, contact:

National Information System
Center for Developmental Disabilities
Benson Building
University of South Carolina
Columbia, SC 29208
Voice/text outside South Carolina: (800) 922-9234, ext. 301
Voice/text inside South Carolina: (800) 922-1107
Voice/text outside the U.S.: (803) 777-6222
Fax: (803) 777-6058

Using the
Windows
Accessories

18

Writing with WordPad

This chapter introduces WordPad, the word processor that comes with Windows 95. Is it a full-featured word processor that will take care of all your writing needs? No. But does it give you a lot to play with as you explore the power of Windows word processing? Definitely. Your WordPad documents can include basic text and paragraph formatting—font changes, indents, tabs, and so on. WordPad also supports OLE so you can add graphical images and even sound and video clips to your documents.

WordPad replaces Write, the entry-level word processor that was bundled with earlier versions of Windows. WordPad can read .WRI files—documents that were created in Write. In the past, many Windows-based applications, particularly shareware programs, have used Write documents for documentation, for licensing information, and as last-minute "read me" files. You can still read those files in Windows 95, even though Write itself is no more. Simply double-click a Write document to open it in WordPad. WordPad can also read (and save) documents in any of three file formats: Word for Windows 6.0, Rich Text Format, and text only.

Notepad, the plain-text editor of earlier Windows days, is also included in the Windows 95 package. Notepad differs from WordPad in that it offers no formatting capability whatever and is limited to files of about 40 KB or smaller. Its virtue is speed. It's fast to load and supremely easy to use (because it doesn't do much). Text files (files with the extension .TXT) are Notepad's registered document type. If you double-click one of these, you'll be transported to Notepad—provided the file isn't too large for Notepad to handle. If the file is too large, Notepad diplomatically offers to hand the document off to WordPad.

Starting WordPad

To get WordPad running , click its icon, which can be found in the Accessories folder within the Start menu's Programs folder.

NOTE: If WordPad has not been set up on your computer, double-click the Add/Remove Programs item in Control Panel, click the Windows Setup tab, select Accessories, and click the Details button. Select WordPad and click OK.

WordPad's opening screen looks like the one shown in Figure 18-1.

FIGURE 18-1.
WordPad opens with a blank editing area.

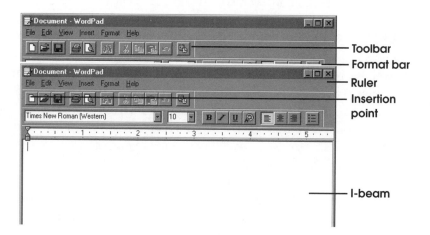

The following elements make up the WordPad window:

Toolbar. WordPad's toolbar, like the toolbar in most other Windows-based programs, contains buttons for gaining access to commonly used commands. To see what a particular button does, simply move your mouse pointer over the button. A short description appears just below the mouse pointer, and a somewhat more detailed description appears on the status bar. Table 18-1 describes the buttons on the toolbar.

Format bar. Like the toolbar, the format bar provides one-click access to commands. Most of WordPad's formatting options are available on the format bar. Table 18-2 on page 448 describes the buttons on the format bar.

Table 18-1. WordPad Toolbar

Toolbar Icon	Description
	Creates a new, blank document
	Opens an existing document
	Saves the current document to disk
	Prints the current document
	Displays a preview of the printed page—without committing it to paper
	Finds text that you specify
	Cuts (deletes) the selection and places it on the Clipboard
	Copies the selection to the Clipboard
	Pastes the Clipboard's contents at the insertion point
	Undoes your last editing or formatting action
	Inserts the date and time in your document

Ruler. The ruler provides an easy way to change tab and margin settings.

Insertion point. The flashing vertical line is the insertion point. When you type, text appears to the left of the insertion point. To change the position of the insertion point, move the mouse pointer where you want it and click. If you don't have a mouse, you can use the arrow keys to move the insertion point.

I-beam. When you're working in the editing window, the mouse pointer takes the shape of an I-beam.

Table 18-2. WordPad Format Bar

Format Bar Icon	Description
Times New Roman (Western)	Changes the font (typeface) of the selection
10	Changes the font size of the selection
B	Changes the selection to boldface (or, if the selection is already boldface, changes it back to normal)
I	Changes the selection to italic (or, if the selection is already italic, changes it back to normal)
<u>U</u>	Underlines the selection (or, if the selection is already underlined, removes the underline)
	Changes the color of the selection
	Left aligns the selected paragraphs
	Center aligns the selected paragraphs
	Right aligns the selected paragraphs
	Changes the selected paragraphs to an indented, bulleted list (or, if the selection is already bulleted, removes the bullets and indents)

Creating a WordPad Document

The process of creating a basic WordPad document couldn't be easier. There are only two essential steps:

1. Type.

   When you start WordPad, all you have to do is type the text you want, pressing Enter twice when you want a blank line between paragraphs.

2. Save.

To save a document for the first time, click the Save button on the toolbar (or choose Save from the File menu). Give the document a name, and choose a document type (Word for Windows 6.0, Rich Text Format, Text Document, or Text Document–MS-DOS Format).

That's all you need to know to create a WordPad document. The rest of this chapter simply goes into more detail on typing and saving and covers embellishments and related topics (such as embedding objects from other applications into WordPad documents).

 See Also: For information about *document types*, see "Choosing a File Type," page 472.

Inserting the Date or Time

You can easily add the date or time to a WordPad document. Just click the Date/Time toolbar button, select a format from the Date And Time dialog box shown in Figure 18-2, and choose OK. The current date or time appears at your insertion point location in the format you selected.

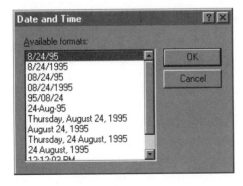

FIGURE 18-2.

WordPad allows you to choose from several date and time formats.

Starting a New Document

When you click the New button on the toolbar or choose New from the File menu, WordPad opens the New dialog box shown in Figure 18-3 on the next page.

FIGURE 18-3.

The New dialog box lets you specify a document type.

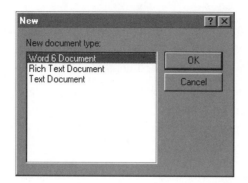

When you select a document type and choose OK, WordPad closes the current document (prompting you to save if necessary) and presents you with a blank document window. The document window uses the view options for the document type you select.

For information about *document types*, see "Choosing a File Type," page 472.

For information about *view options,* see "Changing View Options," page 473.

Editing Text

As you'll recall from Chapter 1, the insertion point in Windows documents always lies *between* characters. To insert text into an existing document, simply position the insertion point where you want the new material to go. Whatever you type will be inserted to the left of the insertion point, and the existing text moves to the right to accommodate the new text.

To replace existing text with new text, start by selecting the text you want to replace. (The next section reviews the procedures for selecting text.) When a block of text is selected, whatever you type replaces the text in the selection.

To erase a small amount of text, position the insertion point either before or after the text you want to erase. Then press Backspace or Del. Backspace erases the character to the left of the insertion point; Del erases text to the right of the insertion point. Careful! The Backspace and Del keys both repeat—if you hold down either key it continues to erase text until you release the key.

To erase a large amount of text, start by selecting the text. Then press Del. If you want to delete a block of text but preserve it on the Clipboard, select the text and choose Cut from the Edit menu (or press Ctrl-X). Keeping the deleted text on the Clipboard gives you the option of putting it right back in the place you removed it from (if you should change your mind) or of reusing it in another location or even in another document. Keep in mind, though, that the Clipboard stores only the last item you cut or copied to it. So any text you place on the Clipboard can be reused only before you cut or copy something else to the Clipboard.

 See Also: For more information about *editing text*, see "Entering and Editing Text in Documents," page 38.

For more information about *using the Clipboard*, see "What the Cut, Copy, Paste, and Paste Special Commands Do," page 257.

Selecting Text

WordPad uses the same methods for selecting text that were described in Chapter 1. (See "Selecting Text," page 42.) You can do any of the following:

- Position the mouse pointer at one end of the area you want to select, press and hold down the left mouse button, drag the mouse to the other end of the area to be selected, and then release the mouse button.

- Place the insertion point at one end of the area you want to select, move the mouse pointer to the other end of the area to be selected (without clicking), and then hold down the Shift key while you click.

- Hold down the Shift key while you press any of the arrow keys or other navigation keys. You can also select text with the keyboard by using the Shift key with any of the navigation keystroke combinations described in Table 18-3. For example, to select text and spaces to the beginning of the next word, hold down the Shift key while you press Ctrl-Right arrow.

Table 18-3. Navigation Keystrokes in WordPad

Keystroke	Moves the Insertion Point
Right arrow	To the next character
Left arrow	To the previous character
Down arrow	To the next line
Up arrow	To the previous line
Ctrl-Right arrow	To the beginning of the next word
Ctrl-Left arrow	To the beginning of the previous word if the insertion point is between words or to the beginning of the current word if the insertion point is in a word
Ctrl-Down arrow	To the beginning of the next paragraph
Ctrl-Up arrow	To the beginning of the current paragraph or to the beginning of the previous paragraph if the insertion point is at the beginning of a paragraph
PgDn	Down one windowful
PgUp	Up one windowful
Ctrl-PgDn	To the end of the last line in the current window
Ctrl-PgUp	To the beginning of the first line in the current window
Home	To the first character in the current line
End	To the last character in the current line
Ctrl-Home	To the beginning of the document
Ctrl-End	To the end of the document

NOTE: If you extend the selection so that it includes more than one word, WordPad selects whole words automatically, so you needn't be so precise in cursor positioning. If you prefer to make selections character by character, choose Options from the View menu, click the Options tab, and deselect Automatic Word Selection.

Additional techniques, specific to WordPad, allow mouse users to quickly select the current word, the current line, the current paragraph, or the entire document.

- Double-click to select the current word

- Triple-click to select the current paragraph

To use the following techniques, start by positioning the mouse pointer in the margin area to the left of your text. You can tell you're in the correct place when the mouse pointer changes from an I-beam to a "northeast"-pointing arrow.

Now you can do any of the following:

- Click once to select the current line

- Double-click to select the current paragraph

- Triple-click or hold down the Ctrl key and click once to select the entire document

Press Ctrl-A to quickly select the entire document. For this shortcut, it makes no difference where the insertion point or mouse pointer is located.

Navigation Techniques

You can use the mouse or the keyboard to move around in WordPad documents. The keystrokes you use in WordPad for moving the insertion point are listed in Table 18-3.

Don't use Tab, Spacebar, or Backspace when all you want to do is move the insertion point. The Tab key and Spacebar add blank space to your document, and the Backspace key erases the character to the left of the insertion point.

Undoing Mistakes

WordPad's Edit menu includes a valuable Undo command that enables you to recover from many mishaps—unwanted deletions, formatting changes that don't produce the desired effect, and even search-and-replace operations of which you immediately repent.

As a keyboard shortcut for the Undo command, press Ctrl-Z.

WARNING: Undo undoes only your last action. If you do something you didn't mean to do, be sure to use Undo before you do anything else. For example, if you delete a word and then immediately choose Undo, the deleted word reappears in your document. But if you press Spacebar after you delete the word, choosing Undo only deletes the space you just added.

Copying and Moving Text

You can use the standard Clipboard procedures to copy or move text from one place to another within a WordPad document, from one WordPad document to another WordPad document, or from a WordPad document to a document created in a different application.

See Also: For information about *copying and moving text*, see Chapter 10, "Exchanging Information: The Clipboard and OLE," page 251.

Finding Text

WordPad's Find command helps you locate a particular combination of text (letters, numbers, or words and spaces).

To open the Find dialog box shown in Figure 18-4, choose Find from the Edit menu or click the Find button on the toolbar. (That's the button that looks like a pair of binoculars.) As a keyboard shortcut for the Find command, press Ctrl-F. You type the text you're looking for in the Find What text box.

Select Match Whole Word Only if you want WordPad to find the search text only if it's a whole word. With this option checked, a search for

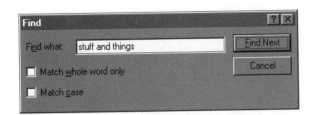

FIGURE 18-4.

Enter the text you want to search for in this box.

and would find only the word *and*, but not *band*, *android*, or *sandal*. Select Match Case if you want WordPad to find instances of the search text only if the case is an exact match. With this option checked, a search for *Microsoft* would find *Microsoft*, but not *microsoft* or *MICROSOFT*.

Starting a Search

After you have filled out the Find What text box and chosen your search options, you can start the search by clicking the Find Next button or pressing Enter. WordPad searches from the insertion point forward; if it reaches the end of your document without finding your search text, it continues the search starting at the top of the document.

As soon as WordPad finds an occurrence of your search text, it selects the text and stops searching, but the dialog box remains on screen. At this point, you have several options:

- If you have found what you're looking for and don't want to do any more searching, close the dialog box by pressing Esc or by clicking Cancel or the dialog box's Close button.

- If you want to search for the next occurrence of the same search text, click Find Next again.

- If you want to search for different text, replace the text that's currently in the Find What text box with the new text, and then click Find Next.

Repeating a Search

If you want to resume working on your document but you think you might need to search for the same text again, you can do either of the following:

- Move the Find dialog box to a position on your screen where it won't be in your way. Then click outside the dialog box (or press

Alt-F6) to return to the document. When you're ready to repeat the search, simply click the Find Next button again, or press Alt-F6 to return to the Find dialog box and then press Alt-F to choose the Find Next command.

■ Close the dialog box. When you want to repeat the search, press F3 (or choose Find Next from the Edit menu).

Replacing Text

The Edit menu's Replace command lets you replace one set of characters or words with another. As a keyboard alternative for Replace, press Ctrl-H. You can confirm each change, or you can have WordPad change every occurrence of the search text automatically.

FIGURE 18-5.

When you choose the Replace command, this dialog box opens.

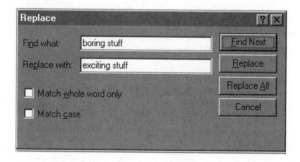

Telling WordPad What to Change

To specify the text you want to change, fill out the Find What text box. (This box works exactly the same way as the Find What text box in the Find dialog box.) Enter the new text in the Replace With text box.

Replacing What You Want to Replace

When you've filled out the Replace dialog box, you can start the Replace operation in either of two ways:

■ To replace all occurrences of the search text automatically, click Replace All.

■ To have WordPad pause for confirmation before making each change, click Find Next.

If you click the Find Next button, WordPad stops as soon as it finds an occurrence of your search text. At that point, you can do any of the following:

❑ If you do *not* want WordPad to change this occurrence of the search text, click Find Next.

❑ If you want WordPad to change this occurrence and continue searching for further occurrences, click Replace.

❑ If you want WordPad to change all occurrences of the search text, click Replace All.

❑ To stop the Replace operation without making any further changes, press Esc or Alt-F4, click the dialog box's Close button, press Alt-F6, or click anywhere outside the dialog box.

If you press Alt-F6 or click outside the dialog box, the dialog box remains on screen. You can use it at any time by pressing Alt-F6 again or clicking within the dialog box.

Changing Your Document's Appearance

WordPad provides several options for formatting documents. These include options that can be applied to characters, to paragraphs, or to the entire document.

The following options can be applied either to a selection of existing text or to new text that you're about to enter. If you select a character or group of characters before choosing one of these options, the option is applied to the selection only. If you do not select text before choosing the option, the option is applied to everything new that you type ahead of the current insertion point position, but not to existing text. You can:

■ Choose fonts and point sizes

■ Apply boldface, italics, strikeout, or underlining

■ Change text color

The following options apply to individual paragraphs or selections of consecutive paragraphs. You can:

- Create bulleted lists (such as the one you're looking at right now)
- Apply indents
- Set a paragraph alignment style (flush left, flush right, or centered)
- Define tab stops

The File menu's Page Setup command contains several more formatting options that apply to the entire document. You can:

- Specify paper size
- Specify left, right, top, and bottom margins

  NOTE: You can use the ruler to apply left and right margin settings to selected paragraphs (or to all paragraphs from the insertion point onward, if the insertion point is at the end of the document).

- Select a page orientation: portrait (vertical, like a portrait painting) or landscape (sideways, like a landscape painting)

Changing Fonts

The easiest way to assign a typeface or point size is by making selections from the format bar. Simply pull down the Font list to select a new typeface, or pull down the Font Size list to select a new size.

Adding Font Attributes

WordPad's attribute options include Bold, Italic, Underline, Text Color, and Strikeout. Buttons for all of these except Strikeout are located on the format bar. (Strikeout must be accessed through the Font dialog box.) All of these options can be used singly or in conjunction with one another.

 You can press Ctrl-B, Ctrl-I, or Ctrl-U as keyboard shortcuts for bold, italic, and underlining, respectively.

Changing Text Color

To change the color of your text, click the Color button on the format bar and pick the color you want. (See Figure 18-6.) Keep in mind that the color will appear only on your screen (unless, of course, you have a color printer).

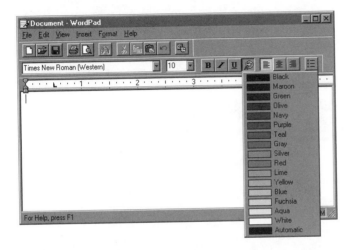

FIGURE 18-6.

You can open the Text Color drop-down list by clicking its format bar button.

You might have noticed the color named Automatic at the bottom of Figure 18-6. "Automatic" applies no color attribute at all. Instead, text formatted as Automatic is displayed in the Window font color defined in the Display Properties dialog box. For most color schemes, the Window font color (and, therefore, the Automatic color in WordPad) is black. If you select any color other than Automatic, WordPad uses that color regardless of the settings in the Display property sheet.

For information about *setting the Window font color in the Display property sheet*, see "Changing the Colors, Fonts, and Sizes of the Windows User Interface," page 98.

Using the Font Dialog Box

All of the character formatting options just covered can be accessed from the Font dialog box shown in Figure 18-7 on the next page. (Choose Font from the Format menu.) If you plan to make several changes at once, it can be easier to use the Font dialog box than to click several buttons on the format bar.

 The object menu that appears when you right-click a selection provides a handy set of formatting commands that might save you a trip to the menu bar at the top of the window.

FIGURE 18-7.

The Font dialog box presents all the character formatting options in one place.

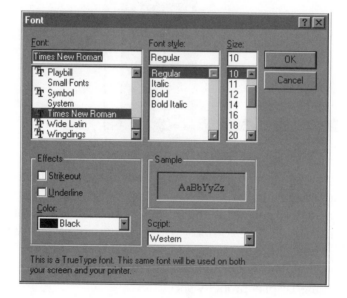

 For more information about *character formatting*, see Chapter 8, "Installing and Using Fonts," page 205.

Adding Bullets

With WordPad, it's easy to add a bullet in front of a paragraph. With your insertion point anywhere in the paragraph, simply click the Bullets button on the format bar (or choose Bullet Style from the Format menu). To add bullets to several consecutive paragraphs, select the paragraphs before choosing the bullet style.

Indenting Text

You can use three kinds of indents in WordPad paragraphs:

- An indent from the left margin that applies to all lines in a paragraph

- An indent from the right margin that applies to all lines in a paragraph

- An indent from the left margin that applies only to the first line in a paragraph

The last of these options can be used to set up automatic paragraph indenting or to create a paragraph with hanging indention. (For details, see "Using Hanging Indents," page 462.)

Choose Paragraph from the Format menu to open the dialog box shown in Figure 18-8.

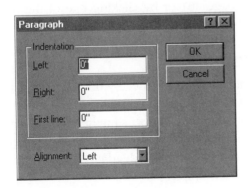

FIGURE 18-8.

The Paragraph dialog box sets indents and alignment.

Left and right indents are measured from the left and right margins, respectively. The first-line indent is measured from the left indent. Simply fill out the appropriate boxes and click OK.

You can also set indents by dragging the ruler's indent markers. For details, see "Using the Ruler," page 463.

Using Hanging Indents

A paragraph is said to have *hanging indention* when all of its lines *except* the first are indented. This style is useful for such things as bibliographies and bulleted or numbered lists. To set up a hanging indent, simply specify a positive left indent and a negative first-line indent.

With a left indent of 2 inches and a first-line indent of –2 inches, for example, all lines except the first will appear two inches from the left margin. The first line will start at the left margin.

Aligning Text

WordPad offers three paragraph-alignment styles:

- Flush left (left margin straight, right margin ragged)
- Centered (both margins ragged, each line centered between the margins)
- Flush right (left margin ragged, right margin straight)

You can apply any of these options either from the Paragraph dialog box shown in Figure 18-8 on page 461 or by clicking one of the format bar's paragraph-alignment buttons.

Setting and Using Tab Stops

By default, WordPad documents have tab stops every 0.5 inch. You can replace those default stops with tab stops of your own wherever you like. You can do this by filling out a dialog box or by using the ruler. When you set your own tab stops by either method, WordPad removes its 0.5-inch tab stops to the left of your tab stops. All of the WordPad tab stops to the right of your rightmost tab stop remain in place.

Tab stops apply to the entire paragraph in which the insertion point is positioned when you set them. You can set different tab stops in each paragraph if you like.

To set tab stops with a dialog box, choose Tabs from the Format menu. In the text box, type the distance from the left margin to where you want a tab stop to be, and then click Set to add the setting to the Tab Stop Position list. Repeat this procedure for each tab stop you want to add. When you're finished adding tab stops, click OK.

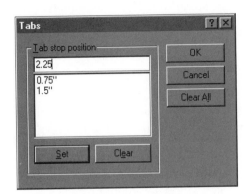

FIGURE 18-9.

Use the Tabs dialog box to set tab stops.

To remove a tab stop from the Tabs dialog box, select the tab stop you want to remove and click Clear. To remove all tab stops at once, click Clear All.

Setting Margins

WordPad's default top and bottom margins are 1 inch. The default left and right margins are 1.25 inches. To override any of these settings, choose Page Setup from the File menu and make changes in the appropriate margin text boxes.

Note that the margin settings in the Page Setup dialog box apply to the entire document. If you want to change left or right margins for particular paragraphs, set indents. (See "Indenting Text," page 461.)

Using the Ruler

As mentioned earlier, the ruler (shown in Figure 18-10 on the next page) provides an easy way to set tabs and indents. If the ruler isn't displayed, choose Ruler from the View menu to display it.

FIGURE 18-10.

WordPad's ruler
shows the space
between a
document's margins,
as well as the
indents and tab
stops for a
paragraph.

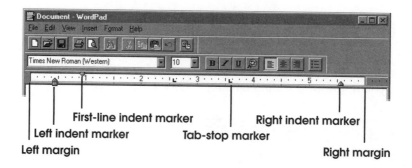

First-line indent marker

Left indent marker

Right indent marker

Tab-stop marker

Left margin

Right margin

The white area of the ruler indicates the space between the left and right margins of the page. Markers on the ruler indicate the indent and tab-stop settings for the paragraph that contains the insertion point.

NOTE: You can change the units used by the ruler. To do so, choose Options from the View menu, and then click the Options tab. In the Measurement Units section, select Inches, Centimeters, Points, or Picas.

Setting Indents with the Ruler

To set left or right indents with the ruler, simply drag the left or right indent marker to a new location. Note that if you drag the triangular left indent marker, only the left indent changes. If you instead drag the rectangular box below the left indent marker, the left indent and the first-line indent markers move in unison.

To set the first-line indent for a paragraph or selected paragraphs, drag the first-line indent marker to a new location.

Setting Tab Stops with the Ruler

To set tab stops with the ruler, just position the mouse pointer where you want the tab stop and then click.

To adjust the position of any tab stop, drag the tab-stop marker along the ruler.

To remove a tab stop by using the ruler, simply drag the tab-stop marker off the ruler and release the mouse button.

Putting Pictures in WordPad Documents

WordPad documents can include pictures as well as text. You can use ready-made clip art or create your own images in Paint or other programs. Images (as well as other objects such as documents and sound or video clips) can be copied, embedded, or linked into WordPad documents.

To incorporate a graphical image in a WordPad document, do the following:

1. Create the image in a Windows-based graphics program, such as Paint (or load an image from disk into a program such as Paint).

2. Select the image (or portion of it) that you want to use in your WordPad document.

3. Use the program's Copy or Cut command to put the image on the Windows Clipboard.

4. Open (or switch to) WordPad and place your insertion point where you want the picture to appear.

5. Use the Paste command (choose Paste from the Edit menu or click the Paste button) to insert the picture.

If your source program has put the graphic on the Clipboard in more than one format, the Paste Special command (on WordPad's Edit menu) will also be available. You can use this command to choose among the available formats. (See "Controlling a Pasted Object's Format," page 466.)

See Also: For more information about *copying, linking, and embedding, the differences among them, and the advantages and disadvantages of each*, see "To Link, to Embed, or Merely to Paste?" on page 262.

Sizing or Moving a Picture

To change the size of a picture, simply select the picture and then drag one of its handles. (To select a picture or other object, simply click it.) Release the mouse button when the picture is the size you want.

To move a picture, start by selecting the picture. Then, with your mouse pointer anywhere inside the picture, drag the picture to a new location.

Using Data from Other Applications

WordPad is capable of acting as an OLE destination and source application. This means that you can embed or store links to the following kinds of data, among others, in your WordPad documents:

- Graphical images copied to the Clipboard from OLE source programs, such as Paint or Microsoft Word

- Charts or worksheet "pictures" copied from Microsoft Excel

- Sound annotations copied from Sound Recorder

To embed data from the Clipboard, simply use WordPad's Paste command. If the data's source application is an OLE source, the data will automatically be embedded. To link the data instead of embedding it, choose Paste Special instead of Paste from the Edit menu.

Alternatively, you can embed or link data by choosing the Paste Special command. (See "Controlling a Pasted Object's Format," below.) If the data on the Clipboard came from an OLE source, the Paste Special dialog box indicates what type of data it is and which program it came from, as you can see in Figure 18-11.

To edit a linked or embedded object, double-click anywhere within the object.

Controlling a Pasted Object's Format

Sometimes when you copy a graphical image to the Clipboard, the source program puts the image on the Clipboard in more than one format. It might, for example, store the image on the Clipboard in both *picture* format

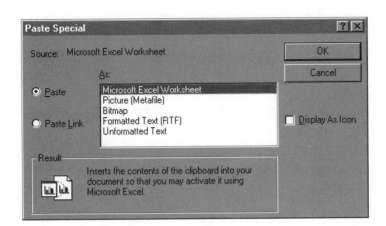

FIGURE 18-11.

Here's the Paste Special dialog box with more than one format available.

and *bitmap* format. Whenever the data to be pasted is available in more than one format, WordPad's Paste command uses the most information-rich format. But in these cases WordPad also enables the Paste Special command (also on the Edit menu), allowing you to make your own choice about which format to use. Simply select the format you prefer, and then click the Paste button.

Usually, WordPad's Paste command makes the best choice for you automatically. For example, when the available formats are picture and bitmap, it chooses picture—and, generally speaking, the picture format gives you more satisfactory results. (In particular, because the picture format is not tied to the resolution of a specific output device, it usually gives you a much better printed image than the bitmap format.) However, the Paste Special command is there, just in case you want to override the default choice.

When the source application happens to be an OLE source, WordPad's Paste command normally embeds the data stored on the Clipboard. If you want to control whether WordPad copies the Clipboard data to your document as a static object rather than embedding it, you need to use the Paste Special command instead of Paste.

Embedding an image doesn't add any more bulk to your file than pasting the image in as a picture, and it allows you to edit the image quickly and easily.

To maintain a link to OLE source data, you must save that data in a disk file. Therefore, if you are creating a link to data in a new document, you must save the source document before you create a link to it.

 See Also: For more information about *data formats and the Clipboard*, see "Controlling the Outcome with Paste Special," page 259.

Moving and Sizing Embedded or Linked Objects

For display purposes, WordPad handles embedded and linked objects the same way it handles static graphical images. You can move and size such objects using the same procedures you would use with static objects. For more information, see "Sizing or Moving a Picture," page 466.

 If you edit an embedded image after changing its size in WordPad, don't worry when the image appears at its original size in the source application. When you update the WordPad document after making your edits, the image will reappear at the modified size.

Activating, Playing, and Editing Embedded or Linked Objects

When you select an object in a WordPad document that was embedded or linked from an OLE source, the Object command at the bottom of WordPad's Edit menu becomes available. It also changes to reflect the kind of object you select. Figure 18-12 shows how the Object command appears if you select a chart embedded from Microsoft Excel.

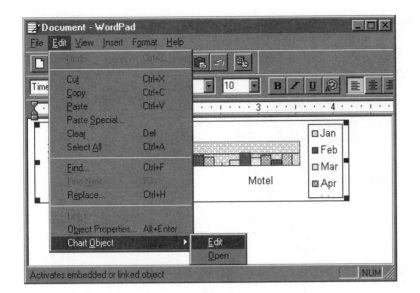

FIGURE 18-12.
The Edit Object command tells you what kind of object is selected.

The cascading menu for most object types offers two choices, Edit and Open. Choosing the Edit command activates the object's source application—Microsoft Excel in this example—and allows you to edit the object in place. The Open command opens the object in a separate window.

 The simplest way to edit a graphical object, such as a picture or chart, is to double-click it.

If the embedded or linked object is an iconic representation of a nongraphical data type, such as a sound annotation, the Object command presents a small cascading submenu like the one shown in Figure 18-13 on the next page.

Choosing Play "renders" the object (lets you hear the sound annotation, for example), whereas choosing Edit invokes the object's source application so you can make changes. Double-clicking a nongraphical object is a shortcut for the Play command. If you want to edit the object, you have to choose the command from the menu.

FIGURE 18-13.

You can choose to Play or Edit a sound object.

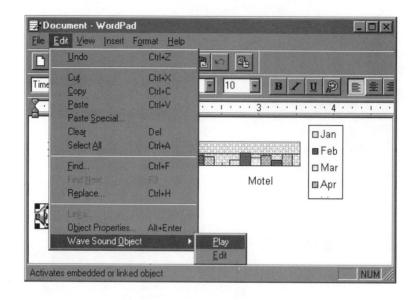

Embedding with the Insert Object Command

The Object command on the Insert menu lets you initiate the embedding or linking process from within your WordPad document, instead of from within an object's source application. When you choose this command, WordPad displays a dialog box that lists the linkable and embeddable object types available to Windows on your system. (See Figure 18-14.)

FIGURE 18-14.

The Insert Object dialog box lets you create an object from within WordPad.

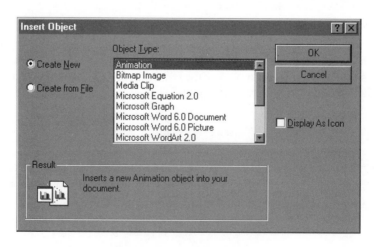

Choose the kind of object you want to link or embed, and then click OK. WordPad activates the object type's source application, allowing you to create an object (if you select the Create New option button) or load one from a disk file (if you select Create From File).

Modifying Links with the Links Command

When you link an object, as opposed to embedding it, WordPad does not store the object in your file. Instead, it stores a "pointer" to the object's source, such as the name of the source application and the file in which the object is stored. If you subsequently rename or move the object's source file, the stored link will no longer be valid. In that case, you can repair the link with the help of WordPad's Links command.

The Links command, on WordPad's Edit menu, lists all objects linked to the current WordPad document.

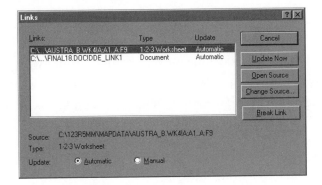

FIGURE 18-15.

Use the Links dialog box to change or update links.

To change the source file for a link, select the link you want to modify, and then click the Change Source button. WordPad presents a file-browser dialog box, allowing you to pick the file you need.

The Links command also allows you to change a link from automatic to manual, or vice versa. Links are always automatic by default, which means that any changes in the source data are reflected as soon as possible in your WordPad document. If you prefer to have them updated only on demand, choose the Links command, select the link you want to change, and then click the Manual option button. After you do this, your links will be updated only when you choose Update Now from the Links dialog box.

The Link tab in a linked object's property sheet contains, for that object, all the commands that appear in the Links dialog box. You can view an object's property sheet by right-clicking the object and choosing Object Properties.

Saving and Retrieving Documents

WordPad uses the same procedures for saving and retrieving documents as most other Windows-based applications. Use the following File menu commands (all of them except Save As have toolbar counterparts):

- Save, to save the current document

- Save As, to save the current document under a new name or to choose different file-saving options

- New, to remove the current document from memory and begin creating a new one

- Open, to load an existing document from disk into memory

By default, WordPad is set up to save new documents in Word for Windows 6.0 format with an extension of .DOC. To save a file as a different type, choose Save As, open the Save As Type drop-down list, and choose the type you want. If you don't specify an extension, WordPad automatically uses .DOC for Word for Windows 6.0 files, .TXT for text files, and .RTF for Rich Text Format files.

Choosing a File Type

When you save a document with Save As or begin a new document, WordPad gives you the opportunity to choose a different file format. The following file format descriptions will help you make an informed choice:

- **Word for Windows 6.0:** This is the same file format used in Microsoft Word for Windows 6.0. If you use a document saved in this format with any version of Word, or with another word processor that accepts Word for Windows 6.0 documents, all of your formatting will remain intact.

- **Rich Text Format (RTF):** RTF is a compromise between the Word for Windows 6.0 and Text Document formats. It's a format that was designed for transferring formatted text between diverse applications. Most word processors have an option for saving documents in RTF format. If you want to use a document created in another word processor in WordPad, saving it in the original program in RTF format is the best solution (unless the word processor contains an option for saving in Word for Windows 6.0 format).

- **Text Document:** This option saves documents as plain (unformatted) text. WordPad saves the words in your document but removes all character, paragraph, and document formatting. Your document also loses any embedded or linked data and any pictures pasted in as static objects. The main reason to use the Text Document format is if you need to transmit the document over a modem to a system that cannot accept a binary file transfer. (For information about binary and text file transfers, see "Transferring Files," page 528.) This format can also be used to create or edit MS-DOS batch files and Windows configuration files.

- **Text Document–MS-DOS Format:** This option is like Text Document in every respect except one: it saves documents using the extended ASCII character set instead of the Windows-standard ANSI character set. (For more information about character sets, see "Fonts and Character Sets," page 219.) Use this format if you plan to reopen the document in an MS-DOS–based application.

Changing View Options

Each document type has its own default options that determine whether the ruler, toolbars, and status bar are displayed and how word wrap behaves when you open or start a new document in that format. You can choose separate settings for regular and embedded text.

To look at or change the view options, choose Options from the View menu. The Options dialog box appears, as shown in Figure 18-16 on the next page.

Click the tab for the document format you want and make the changes you desire.

FIGURE 18-16.

Change text viewing
options here.

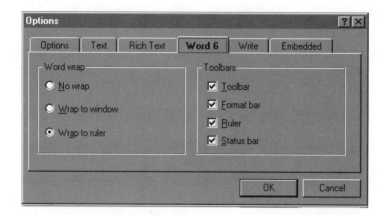

Word wrap, which is the default action in most word processors, means that when the text you type reaches the right margin, the rest of the text automatically moves to the next line. Here's what the different options mean:

■ The No Wrap option disables word wrap altogether. By default, word wrap is turned off (No Wrap is selected) for text files. That's because text format is often used for entering program codes, for which you don't want text to move around on you.

■ If you select Wrap To Window, when the text you type reaches the right edge of the document window, the text wraps to the next line. This is the default setting for Rich Text.

■ If you select Wrap To Ruler, when the text you type reaches the right margin as defined on the ruler, the text wraps to the next line.

In the Toolbars section of the Options dialog box, you can select which options you want displayed; uncheck the ones you don't. You can always override these selections by choosing View menu commands.

Putting It on Paper

To print your document, choose Print from the File menu. As a keyboard alternative, press Ctrl-P. The Print dialog box appears, as shown in Figure 18-17.

■ To switch to a different printer, open the Name drop-down list and make a selection.

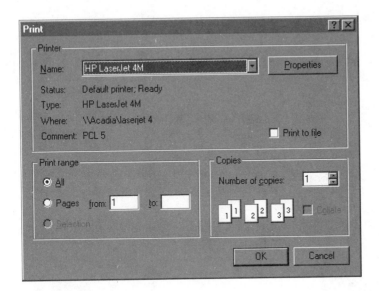

FIGURE 18-17.

The Print dialog box allows you to choose printing options and send your document to the printer.

■ To change the settings for your selected printer, click Properties.

■ To print more than one copy, change the number in the Number Of Copies box.

■ To print a range of pages instead of the entire document, fill in the page numbers you want in the From and To boxes.

When you've made all your selections in the Print dialog box, choose OK to send your document to the printer.

If you want to print your document and don't plan to change any options in the Print dialog box, simply click the Print toolbar button. This sends the document directly to the printer, bypassing the Print dialog box. If you choose Print from the File menu or press Ctrl-P, the dialog box opens.

Saving Paper with Print Preview

If you want to see what your document looks like before you print it, click the Print Preview button (or choose Print Preview from the File menu).

Print Preview, shown in Figure 18-18, allows you to do the following things:

■ Move from page to page to see where WordPad has placed page breaks. To do this, click Next Page or Prev Page.

■ View two pages of your document at once by clicking Two Page.

■ Zoom in to get a closer look at the document, or zoom out to get back to the default full-page view. Click Zoom In or Zoom Out.

■ Open the Print dialog box by clicking Print. You can easily preview a document and then print it in one procedure.

FIGURE 18-18.

Use the Print Preview window to preview your printed output.

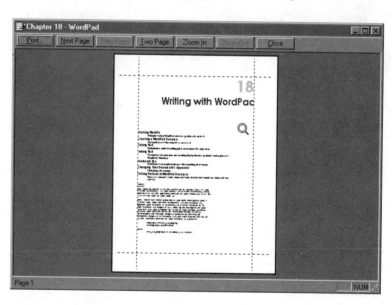

In Figure 18-18, notice that the mouse pointer has changed to a magnifying glass. When the magnifying glass is visible, click anywhere in the document to zoom in one level, and then click again to zoom in to the second level. When the mouse pointer turns back to an arrow, clicking zooms you back out to full-page view.

19

Drawing with Paint

his chapter introduces Paint, the painting program included with Windows 95 that lets you create and edit graphics images. You can use Paint to produce anything from simple text-oriented flyers and line diagrams to complex works of art. You can start from scratch on a blank canvas, or you can modify existing images. Any graphics information that can be copied to the Clipboard can be pasted into Paint and modified—everything from clip art images to images created in other Windows-based programs (like Microsoft Excel charts) to scanned images.

Paint replaces Paintbrush, the painting program that was included in Windows 3.x. If you used Paintbrush, you'll appreciate Paint's similarities, and you won't have any difficulty adapting to the changes, which include more "zoom" levels, more precise stretching and skewing, and the ability to save an image as wallpaper for your desktop.

Starting Paint

To get Paint running, click its icon, which you can find on the Accessories menu within the Start menu's Programs submenu. Paint's opening screen looks like the one shown in Figure 19-1.

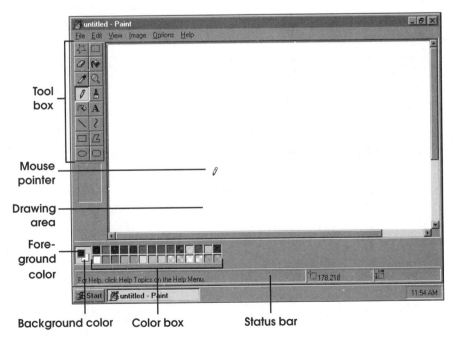

FIGURE 19-1.

When you start Paint, you get a blank drawing area.

Tool box

Mouse pointer

Drawing area

Foreground color

Background color   Color box   Status bar

479

NOTE: If Paint has not been installed on your computer, double-click the Add/Remove Programs item in Control Panel, click the Windows Setup tab, select Accessories, and click the Details button. Select Paint and click OK.

The blank area that makes up most of Paint's window is the *drawing area*. The icons to the left of the drawing area make up the *tool box*. These icons represent the drawing and editing tools that you use to draw and edit images in the drawing area.

At the left side of the *color box*, Paint displays the current foreground and background color selections. When you start Paint, the foreground color is black and the background color is white.

In Figure 19-1, notice that the Pencil tool in the tool box appears pushed in and the mouse pointer in the drawing area is in the shape of a pencil. The pointer changes shape depending on which tool is active. Like the insertion point in a word processing program, the pointer indicates where your next drawing action will take place.

Painting 101

When you use Paint to create a picture, you use tools to apply various elements to the drawing area—your canvas in Paint. This works much like painting in real life. If you were creating a real painting on a real canvas, you might use a variety of paintbrushes. If you were painting a house, you might use rollers, spray cans, and so on. The Paint program provides the tools to make it easy to create exactly what you have in mind.

The general steps for creating a picture are:

1. Select a drawing tool.

   To select a tool, just click it.

   Each drawing tool is specialized for a particular kind of object. For straight lines, for example, you choose the Line tool; to create a rectangle, select the Rectangle tool—and so on.

   It's easy to figure out what many of the tools do just by looking at their icons. If that doesn't give you enough of a clue, remember that you can position the mouse pointer over a tool to display a tool tip that tells you what the tool is. For information about each of the tools and its properties, see "Exploring the Tool Box," page 492.

2. Choose a line width, brush shape, or rectangle type from the group of choices below the tool box. (Notice that the choices change depending on which tool you have selected.)

   You can draw lines from one pixel to five pixels wide, and you can choose from several different brush shapes and rectangle types.

3. Choose a foreground color.

   To choose a foreground color, click a color or pattern in the color box.

   If you don't find the color or pattern you want in the color box, you can create it with the Edit Colors command on the Options menu. For more information, see "Editing Colors," page 509.

4. Choose a background color.

   Some tools, such as Rectangle and Ellipse, can use the current background color to fill the shape they draw in the foreground color. Other tools, such as Line, use the foreground color if you use the left mouse button and the background color if you use the right button. You need to concern yourself with this step only if you're using a tool that uses the background color.

   To choose a background color, point to the color or pattern you want to use and click the right mouse button.

5. Draw.

   After drawing the new object on the canvas, it's not too late to change your mind, thanks to the Undo command. For more information, see "Using the Undo Command," page 484.

Saving and Opening Paint Documents

To save a Paint document for the first time, choose Save or Save As from the File menu. The Save As dialog box appears.

You can choose from several bitmap formats. To pick one, open the Save As Type drop-down list, as shown in Figure 19-2 on the next page. Click the format of your choice and then click the Save button.

- Choose Monochrome Bitmap to store the picture as a black-and-white image.

FIGURE 19-2.

The Save As dialog box lets you specify the name, format, and location of the file.

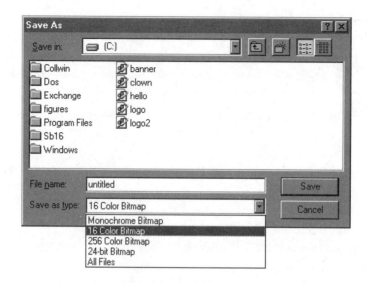

- Choose 16 Color Bitmap to store the picture in color but without the full spectrum of colors. This is an efficient way to store images in which you haven't used more than 16 colors because it uses less disk space than the 256-color and 24-bit color options.

- Choose 256 Color Bitmap to include more of the color spectrum. This takes more disk space and is usually a good compromise format.

- Choose 24-bit Bitmap to save the picture with the full spectrum of colors. You'll generally want to use this option for photographic quality images, such as scanned images or those imported from a high quality clip art collection. The 24-bit format takes the largest amount of disk space, but it retains the highest degree of picture accuracy.

NOTE: There's usually no reason to save an image using more colors than your system can display (unless you're going to use the image on a system that can display more colors or print it on a color printer). If you use a 16-color display driver, for example, you'll never see the additional colors stored by a 256-color or 24-bit color image. By default, Paint proposes to save the image using the maximum number of colors your system can display. To find out how many colors are in your system's palette, or for information about changing this setting, see "Changing the Color Depth of Your Display," page 97.

To open a saved Paint document when the Paint application is already running, choose Open from the File menu and double-click the name of the file you want.

 Paint lists the last four documents you used at the bottom of the File menu. To open one of these recent documents, just select the name of the file you want to open from the File menu.

You can also open a Paint document by double-clicking its icon in a folder window, a Find window, or a Windows Explorer window.

To create a new Paint document, right-click on the desktop or in a folder window, and then choose New. Choose Bitmap Image from the cascading menu. Double-click the resulting icon to open the new document.

 For more information about *using the common dialog boxes*, see "Navigating in the File Open and File Save Dialogs," page 126.

For information about *other ways to open Paint documents*, see Chapter 2, "Running Programs and Opening Documents," page 55.

For information about *folder windows*, see Chapter 4, "Working with Folders," page 115.

For information about *Find windows*, see "Finding Files and Folders," page 195.

For information about *Windows Explorer*, see Chapter 5, "Managing Folders and Files with Windows Explorer," page 163.

Quick Fixes: The Undo and Repeat Commands

Mistakes happen. When you draw something you didn't mean to or change your mind after an editing procedure, Paint lets you gracefully take one, two, or even three steps back.

Using the Undo Command

To undo your last Paint action, choose Undo from the Edit menu. To undo your second-to-last action, choose Undo again. Choose Undo a third time to undo your third-to-last action.

Using the Repeat Command

Paint is so forgiving, it even lets you change your mind after you use Undo. You can restore any actions you changed with Undo by choosing Repeat from the Edit menu.

Just as with Undo, you can repeat up to three actions.

 The keyboard shortcut for Undo is Ctrl-Z. Just like choosing Undo from the Edit menu, you can press Ctrl-Z up to three times to undo up to three actions.
The keyboard shortcut for Repeat is F4.

Setting Up for a New Picture

Although you can start a new picture without any planning, taking a few minutes to prepare your "canvas" can save time later. You should consider these items when setting up for a new picture:

- The background color or pattern that will be used for your picture

- The dimensions of the picture

- Whether you want to work in color or black and white

Choosing a Background Color or Pattern

Paint uses one color (or black-and-white pattern) as its default background color. You might think of this as the color of the canvas before you start to paint. You can override the background color any place you choose, with any color you choose. But after you've started a picture, you can't change the color of the canvas as a whole.

To choose a background color or pattern, right-click the color of your choice in the color box. Then choose New from the File menu to use the background color on the new canvas.

Establishing the Size and Shape of Your Picture

Just as a word processing document can extend beyond a single screen, the actual size of your picture may be larger or smaller than what you see in Paint's drawing area.

To specify the dimensions of your picture, choose Attributes from the Image menu. You'll see a dialog box like the one shown in Figure 19-3.

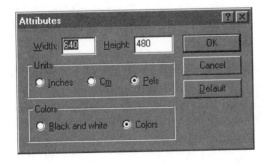

FIGURE 19-3.

The Attributes dialog box sets the size and colors for your picture.

Specify the width and height you want for your picture, in whatever units you find most convenient to work with. You can use inches, centimeters, or pels. The term *pel* is a synonym for *pixel*, which is a single "dot" on your display.

To revert to the default size for your screen's resolution, click the Default button.

NOTE: Unlike the Paintbrush program included with Windows 3.x, Paint allows you to change the image size at any time—even after you've begun painting. However, if you reduce the picture size so that part of the image gets cropped, that part of the image won't be restored if you later enlarge the picture. (You can recover it by using the Undo command. See "Using the Undo Command," page 484.)

Choosing Color or Black and White

The Attributes dialog box is also the place where you decide whether your image will be in black and white or color. (If you're working on a mono-chrome display, the Colors option is grayed out.)

NOTE: If your Windows system is set up for a monochrome (black-and-white) display, you can't create color pictures. You can load a color picture into Paint, but it will be converted to black and white.

When making this choice, it's a good idea to consider the medium in which you're most likely to output your new image. Color is unquestion-ably more interesting to work with than black and white, but if you're going to print your image on a black-and-white printer, you'll get better control of the final product by working in black and white.

NOTE: You can change the setting of the Colors section of the Attributes dialog at any time—even after you've begun painting. (Paintbrush, the program included with Windows 3.x, does not offer this ability.) If you switch from Colors to Black And White, all colors in your image change to black or white. Be sure this is what you want before you proceed, for the Undo command does *not* restore colors that have been converted this way.

Seeing the Larger Picture

Figure 19-4 shows a picture that's considerably larger than the drawing area of Paint's window. Paint offers three ways to see more of a large picture. You can:

- Use the View Bitmap command

- Remove the tool box, color box, and status bar

- Use the scroll bars to bring other parts of the picture into view

FIGURE 19-4.

Paint can create and edit a picture that's larger than the drawing area.

Using the View Bitmap Command

The View Bitmap command, on the View menu, temporarily removes all elements from the screen except your picture, giving it the maximum possible space, as you can see in Figure 19-5 on the next page. If your picture is smaller than your screen, Paint centers the picture on the screen. If your picture is larger than the screen, Paint places the upper left corner of the image from the drawing area in the upper left corner of the screen.

After you use this command, your very next keystroke or mouse click returns the display to its previous state, so you can't do any work

487

FIGURE 19-5.

The View Bitmap command removes all extraneous screen clutter.

with your picture in this mode. It's a useful command, though, when you want to see those parts of your picture that lie just off screen.

 The keyboard shortcut to the View Bitmap command is Ctrl-F. After pressing Ctrl-F, press any key to return to the normal display.

Removing the Tool Box, Color Box, and Status Bar

To give your picture as much breathing room as possible and still be able to work with the picture, use the Tool Box, Color Box, and Status Bar commands on the View menu. Removing the tool box extends the drawing area to the left edge of Paint's application window. Removing the color box extends the drawing area to just above the status bar. Removing the status bar extends the drawing area to the bottom of Paint's application window.

All three commands are toggles. Choose Tool Box once, for example, to make the tool box go away. Choose it again to make it reappear.

The keyboard shortcut for toggling the tool box on or off is Ctrl-T. To toggle the color box on or off, press Ctrl-A.

Navigating on a Large Canvas

Paint displays scroll bars whenever the entire picture won't fit in the drawing area. Use the scroll bars to move to a different part of a large picture. For example, the right side of a large picture comes into view with just a couple of clicks on the horizontal scroll bar, as you can see in Figure 19-6.

FIGURE 19-6.

By scrolling to the right, you can see that this picture has more people than first appeared.

Precise Pointer Positioning

For certain kinds of work in Paint, it's helpful to know precisely where the mouse pointer is or how large an object is as you're drawing it. This information could be useful if, for example, you're trying to draw two vertical lines of exactly the same length. The numbers that are displayed toward the right side of Paint's status bar whenever the mouse pointer is in the drawing area give you pointer position information, which you can use for that purpose.

In Figure 19-7, the numbers on the far right end of the status bar indicate the size of the object being drawn. The first of the two size numbers shows how much horizontal space the object occupies. The second number shows the vertical space.

While you're drawing an object, the numbers just to the left of the size numbers (the pointer position numbers) indicate the mouse pointer position where you began. After you release the mouse button, those numbers show the location of the pointer.

FIGURE 19-7.

The size and position of the rectangle are shown on the right side of the status bar.

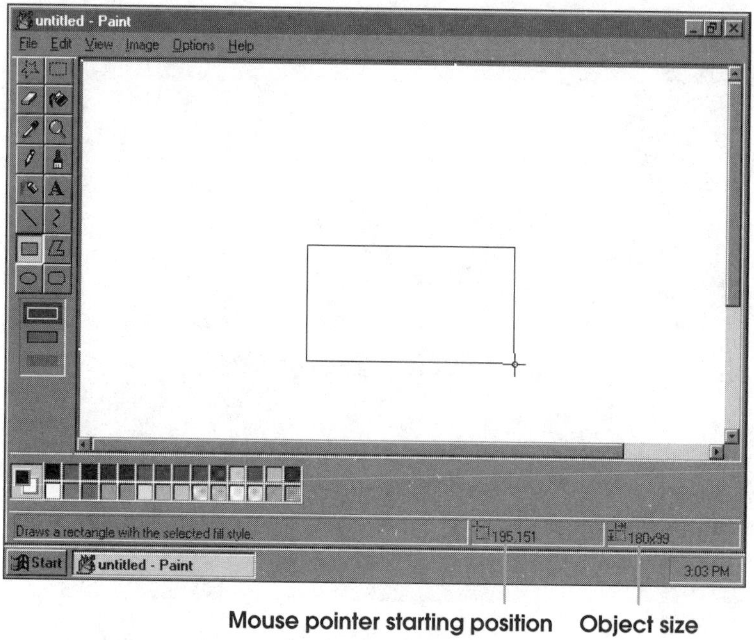

Mouse pointer starting position   Object size

These numbers are expressed in *pixels*. A pixel is the smallest dot your screen can display and the smallest increment by which you can move the mouse pointer. So if the size numbers are, for example, 2×40, the object occupies 2 horizontal pixels and 40 vertical pixels.

The pointer position numbers to the left of the size numbers represent the offset from the upper left edge of the picture. For example,

200,100 means 200 pixels from the left and 100 pixels from the top edge of the picture.

 The position numbers are always visible on the status bar as you move the mouse pointer over the drawing area. The size numbers, however, are visible only while you're drawing an object.

What the Pointer Shapes Mean

The drawing or editing tool you use determines the mouse pointer's shape. Paint's default tool is the Pencil, and the pointer shape corresponding to that tool is the pencil shape. At other times during your work in Paint, it won't be quite so clear from the pointer shape what tool you've selected. Table 19-1 shows the variety of pointer shapes Paint uses.

Pointer	Used with These Tools
+	Free-Form Select, Select, Text, Line, Curve, Rectangle, Polygon, Ellipse, Rounded Rectangle
▢	Eraser
	Fill With Color
	Pick Color
○	Magnifier
	Pencil
	Brush
	Airbrush

TABLE 19-1.

Mouse pointer shapes used in Paint.

When you work with text in Paint, the mouse pointer is replaced by an insertion point and an I-beam. These look and function exactly like the insertion point and I-beam you've seen in WordPad and other text-processing applications. (For information about the insertion point and the I-beam, see "Entering and Editing Text in Documents," page 38.)

Exploring the Tool Box

To use a tool in Paint, you simply click its icon in the tool box. Paint's tool box includes the following sixteen tools:

The Free-Form Select tool selects an irregularly shaped cutout. (A cutout is a selection that can be cut, copied, moved, and manipulated in a variety of other ways. See "Working with Cutouts," page 502.)

The Select tool selects a rectangular cutout.

The Eraser tool erases portions of an object from a picture.

The Fill With Color tool fills enclosed shapes with the foreground or background color.

The Pick Color tool changes the foreground or background color to match the color in another part of the picture.

The Magnifier tool zooms in on portions of the picture.

The Pencil tool draws free-form lines.

The Brush tool draws free-form lines using a variety of brush shapes.

The Airbrush tool creates "spray-paint" effects.

The Text tool adds text to a picture.

The Line tool draws straight lines.

The Curve tool draws smooth curves.

The Rectangle tool draws rectangles and squares.

The Polygon tool draws irregular closed shapes.

The Ellipse tool draws ellipses and circles.

The Rounded Rectangle tool draws rectangles and squares with rounded corners.

You might think of the Free-Form Select, Select, Eraser, Pick Color, and Magnifier tools as editing tools and the rest as drawing tools. We'll look at the drawing tools first, and then examine the editing tools.

Using Paint's Drawing Tools

Paint provides 11 drawing tools that let you apply paint to your canvas.

Free-Form Drawing with the Pencil Tool

The Pencil tool is the default drawing tool when you start Paint. To draw in the foreground color with the Pencil, move the mouse pointer into the drawing area, press the left mouse button, and drag. (To draw in the background color, use the right mouse button.)

 If you want to draw perfectly straight vertical, horizontal, or diagonal lines with the Pencil tool, hold down the Shift key while you draw.

 For more information about *drawing straight lines*, see "Drawing Straight Lines with the Line Tool," page 494.

For information about *drawing curved lines*, see "Drawing Curved Lines with the Curve Tool," page 495.

Free-Form Drawing with the Brush Tool

The Brush tool works like the Pencil tool except that you can choose from a variety of brush shapes.

To use the Brush tool, click the Brush icon in the tool box. The available brush shapes appear in the box just below the tool box, as shown in Figure 19-8 on the next page. Click the brush shape you want to select it. The mouse pointer shape changes to reflect the brush shape you choose.

If you're adept at calligraphy, try one of the diagonal shapes. They allow you to paint with thick and thin brush strokes.

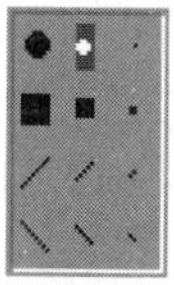

FIGURE 19-8.

The palette of brush shapes appears when you select the Brush tool.

To draw with the Brush, hold down the left mouse button (to draw in the foreground color) or the right mouse button (to draw in the background color) and drag.

The Brush tool is primarily intended for free-form drawing. If you want to draw straight lines, it's best to use the Line or Pencil tool.

Drawing with Spray Paint: The Airbrush Tool

The Airbrush tool deposits a circular pattern of dots. To draw with the Airbrush tool, click the Airbrush icon in the tool box, and then click one of the three spray sizes that appear below the tool box. Finally, move the mouse pointer to the drawing area, hold down the left mouse button (to draw in the foreground color) or the right mouse button (to draw in the background color) and drag.

Like a real can of spray paint, the slower you drag the mouse, the denser the spray; the faster you drag, the lighter the spray.

Drawing Straight Lines with the Line Tool

The Line tool creates straight lines. To draw a line, click the Line tool, and then choose the line width from the choices that appear below the tool box. Move the mouse pointer to the drawing area and hold down the left mouse button (to draw in the foreground color) or the right mouse button (to draw in the background color) and drag.

 To draw perfectly straight vertical, horizontal, or diagonal lines, hold down the Shift key while you drag. Using the Shift key to create lines will eliminate—or at least reduce—the jagged edges that lines at other angles sometimes have.

Drawing Curved Lines with the Curve Tool

The Curve tool lets you create a line with two curves in it. To use the Curve tool, follow these steps:

1. Click the Curve tool in the tool box.

2. Click one of the line width choices that appear below the tool box.

3. Position the mouse pointer in the drawing area at the place where you want the curve to begin, and then hold down either mouse button and drag to where you want the curved line to end.

    At this point you have a straight line.

4. Move the mouse pointer near the part of the line you want to bend. Hold down either mouse button and drag in the direction you want the line to curve.

    Now you have a line with one curve.

5. To add a second bend, repeat step 4. Use the left mouse button if you want the curve to appear in the foreground color, or the right mouse button to use the background color.

It might take some practice to get used to the behavior of the Curve tool. If your curve isn't shaping up the way you want it, click both buttons any time before finishing the second bend to delete the line, and then start over.

Drawing Rectangles and Squares with the Rectangle Tool

To create rectangles and squares, use the Rectangle tool. Click the Rectangle tool, and then choose the rectangle type from the three choices below the tool box.

The first rectangle type lets you draw the outline of the rectangle using the foreground or background color. The second type lets you draw the outline in either the foreground or background color with the interior filled in with the other color. The third type lets you draw a rectangle filled with the background or foreground color, but without a border.

After choosing the rectangle type, move to the drawing area, and then hold down the left mouse button (to use the foreground color for the rectangle's outline) or the right button (to use the background color) and drag diagonally to create the rectangle.

You can create a perfect square by holding down the Shift key while you drag.

Drawing Rectangles with Rounded Corners

To draw rectangles with rounded corners, use the Rounded Rectangle tool. The Rounded Rectangle tool works exactly the same as the regular Rectangle tool except that it produces rounded corners.

Drawing Ovals and Circles with the Ellipse Tool

To create ellipses or circles, use the Ellipse tool. The Ellipse tool works much like the Rectangle tool described above. After selecting the tool, you choose a type—unfilled border, filled with border, or filled without border, just as with the rectangles. Then put the mouse pointer where you want the corner of an imaginary rectangle that will contain your figure. Hold down the left mouse button (to use the foreground color for the ellipse's outline) or the right mouse button (to use the background color) and drag to expand the figure. When the figure reaches the desired size, release the mouse button.

 To create a perfect circle, hold down the Shift key while dragging.

Drawing Irregular Closed Shapes with the Polygon Tool

To create any kind of closed shape other than a rectangle, square, ellipse, or circle, use the Polygon tool. With this tool you can draw as many straight line segments as you want. Each segment begins where the last one ended. When you double-click, Paint closes the polygon by connecting the end of your last line segment with the beginning of your first.

You can create anything from simple triangles to complex shapes with overlapping lines. To create a polygon, follow these steps:

1. Click the Polygon tool.

2. Choose the polygon type from the three choices below the tool box: unfilled, filled with border, or filled without border.

3. Move the mouse pointer to the beginning of the first line segment. Hold down the left mouse button (to use the foreground color for the polygon's outline) or the right mouse button (to use the background color) and drag to the end of the first line segment.

4. Move the mouse pointer to the place where you want the next line segment to end and click using the same mouse button.

   Paint draws a new line segment from the end of the first line.

5. Repeat step 4 until you reach the end of the next-to-last line segment you want, and then double-click.

 To create perfect vertical, horizontal, or diagonal line segments, hold down the Shift key while creating each segment.

Using the Fill With Color Tool to Fill an Enclosed Shape

The Fill With Color tool allows you to fill any enclosed portion of your picture with the current foreground or background color.

To use the Fill With Color tool, click it in the tool box, and then position the mouse pointer over the area in the picture you want to fill. Click the left mouse button to fill the area with the foreground color, or click the right mouse button to fill the area with the background color.

Note that if the area you want to fill has any gaps—even a gap of a single pixel—the color will leak through the gap. If that happens, use the Undo command, and then patch the leak and try again. To patch a very small leak, you might want to use the Zoom command. (For information about the Zoom command, see "Fine Tuning Your Image with Zoom," page 508.)

Adding Text with the Text Tool

Paint's Text tool is a special kind of implement. You don't really *draw* with this tool; instead you choose a typeface, style, and point size, and then type characters from the keyboard (or paste them from the Clipboard). Nevertheless, after you've completed your text entry, the text behaves just like any other part of your picture.

By default, text frames are "transparent"—which means that text appears in the foreground color and the frame's background is "clear," allowing the image underneath to show through. This can be a problem if you're adding text on top of a colored background. Black text on a black background, for example, isn't legible. To use the color box's background color for your text frame's background color, click the icon for the opaque option just below the tool box. The text frame is filled with the selected background color. Remember, you change the background color by right-clicking the color that you want to use in the color box.

The general procedure for adding text is as follows:

1. Select the Text tool.

2. Drag diagonally to create a rectangular text frame about the size you want for your text.

   An insertion point—like the one in a word processing program—appears inside the rectangle to let you know where your text will appear.

3. Type your text or choose Paste from the Edit menu.

4. Change text attributes using Paint's Fonts toolbar, shown below, which automatically appears when you create a text rectangle. (If the Fonts toolbar isn't visible, choose Text Toolbar from the View menu.) You can select a typeface, size, and style (bold, italic, underlined, or a combination).

5. Click outside the text rectangle or select another tool from the tool box to confirm the text entry.

NOTE: Until you confirm the text entry by clicking outside the rectangle or by choosing another tool, you can edit the text or change the typeface, size, or style of the text. However, once the text entry is confirmed, no further text editing can be performed other than erasing or using the Undo command and starting over.

Before you confirm the text entry, you can move the text frame. To do so, move the mouse pointer to any edge of the frame; the pointer changes to a standard pointer arrow. Then drag the frame where you want it. You can also resize the frame. Point to one of the resizing handles (the solid boxes along each side of the frame) and drag.

For more information about *formatting text*, see Chapter 8, "Installing and Using Fonts," page 205.

Using Paint's Editing Tools

The editing tools in Paint's tool box let you clean up your drawing as well as select or view part of it for further manipulation.

Using the Eraser Tool to Clean Up Mistakes

The Eraser tool lets you "erase" anything in the drawing area by simply dragging the mouse over the portion of the object you want to remove. What the eraser is really doing, however, is painting with the current background color. So, if you have a black object—text, rectangle, whatever—on a white background, dragging the Eraser tool over any of the black portions of the object appears to erase them, but it's really just "whitewashing" them to match the white background.

To use the Eraser tool, click the Eraser icon in the tool box, and then select from one of the four eraser sizes that appear below the tool box. Finally, position the mouse pointer where you want to start erasing, hold down the left mouse button, and drag.

Dragging the Eraser tool while holding down the right mouse button erases (applies the current background color) only portions of the drawing area that are in the current foreground color. Set the foreground color to match the color of the object you want to erase and nothing else in the drawing will be disturbed. This works just like the color eraser tool in the old Paintbrush program.

 For information about *erasing a large area of your drawing*, see "Erasing a Cutout," page 507.

Selecting a Color with the Pick Color Tool

The Pick Color tool lets you change the foreground or background in the color box to the color of any object in your drawing. To change the foreground color, click the Pick Color tool, and then click the object or area in your drawing with the color you want to use as your new foreground color. To change the background color, click the Pick Color tool, and then right-click the object or area in your drawing with the color you want to use as your new background color.

Using the Magnifier Tool

Using the Magnifier tool, you can zoom in to a specific portion of your drawing or magnify the entire image. To magnify a particular area of the drawing, click the Magnifier tool. Move the pointer—which assumes the shape of a large rectangle—over the portion of the drawing you want to enlarge, and then click. Paint magnifies the drawing and places the portion of the drawing area that the enlargement rectangle was over at the center of the drawing area. To return to normal, unmagnified view, click the Magnifier tool again, and then click anywhere in the drawing area.

If you want to enlarge the image by a factor of 2, 6, or 8, click the Magnifier tool, and then click 2×, 6×, or 8× just below the tool box. You can return the drawing area to normal size by clicking the Magnifier tool, and then clicking the 1× choice just below the tool box.

Paint remembers the last magnification you used and uses that factor as its default the next time you use the Magnifier tool to select an area to be enlarged.

See Also: For more information about *magnified views*, see "Fine Tuning Your Image with Zoom," page 508.

Defining Cutouts with the Free-Form Select Tool and the Select Tool

The Free-Form Select and Select tools at the top of the tool box are used for specifying *cutouts*—selected areas of the drawing that can be manipulated in various ways. (See "Working with Cutouts," page 502.)

With the Select tool, you can define a rectangular-shaped cutout. With the Free-Form Select tool, you can define any portion of any shape of the drawing area as a cutout. The Free-Form Select tool is particularly useful when you want to select an irregularly shaped object and don't want to include any of the surrounding canvas.

To use the Free-Form Select tool, start by clicking the Free-Form Select tool icon. Then position the mouse pointer somewhere along the edge of the object you want to select. Hold down the left mouse button and then drag around the object. A solid line is drawn as the mouse is dragged. When you have the object completely surrounded, release the mouse button. (You don't actually have to close the selection. When you release the mouse button, Paint connects the current pointer position to the place where you started.) When you release the mouse button, Paint displays a dotted rectangular line around the object you've selected.

When the object you want to select is rectangular, or when it doesn't matter if you select a bit of background canvas along with the object, the Select tool is the best way to go.

To use the Select tool, position the mouse pointer at one corner of the object you want to select, and then drag to the opposite corner.

Working with Cutouts

After you've defined a cutout, you can do any of the following with it:

- Cut it to the Clipboard
- Copy it to the Clipboard
- Copy it to a separate disk file
- Move it to another place within the current picture
- Copy it to another place within the current picture
- "Sweep" it across your picture, leaving a trail of copies in its wake
- Change its size or shape
- Stretch (distort) or skew (slant) it
- Flip or rotate it
- Reverse its colors
- Erase it

 The easiest way to perform most cutout operations is to select a command from the cutout's object menu. After you define a cutout, right-click it to display its object menu.

 For information about *defining a cutout*, see "Defining Cutouts with the Free-Form Select Tool and the Select Tool," page 501.

Cutting or Copying a Cutout to the Clipboard

To put your cutout on the Clipboard, choose Cut or Copy from the Edit menu (or from the object menu that appears when you right-click the selection). If you choose Cut, Paint removes it from the current picture and transfers it to the Clipboard. If you choose Copy, Paint puts a copy of the cutout on the Clipboard and leaves the current picture unchanged.

Linking and Embedding Cutouts

Paint is an OLE server application. That means that pictures created or edited in Paint can be linked or embedded in documents created by OLE client applications, such as WordPad, Microsoft Excel, or Microsoft Word. For information about OLE, see Chapter 10, "Exchanging Information: The Clipboard and OLE," page 251.

When you use the Cut command to put the cutout on the Clipboard, the area of the picture that was occupied by the cutout assumes the current background color. If you want the area to look like the blank canvas after the cutout is removed, be sure the current background matches your initial background color.

Copying a Cutout to a Disk File

You can copy a cutout to a separate disk file, thereby creating a new Paint document. It's a good idea to do this if you want to use the cutout in different pictures.

To save the cutout to a new document, choose Copy To from the Edit menu or the cutout's object menu and fill out the Save As dialog box that appears.

See Also: For information about *the Save As dialog box*, see "Saving and Opening Paint Documents," page 481.

Pasting a Cutout from the Clipboard

To paste a cutout from the Clipboard, choose Paste from the Edit menu. Your cutout appears in the upper left corner of the drawing area surrounded by a dotted line. At this point you can drag it to any part of the drawing area. Or you can manipulate it in any of the other ways described in the following sections.

Note that pasting in Paint is a bit different from pasting in other applications. In a word processor, for example, you first position the insertion point where you want the contents of the Clipboard pasted, and then choose Paste. In Paint, you paste first, and then you position the pasted object.

NOTE: Paint handles Clipboard text differently from graphics. When you paste text from the Clipboard, you must position the insertion point first, and then choose the Paste command.

Pasting from a Disk File

To paste a cutout that was saved as a separate disk file, choose Paste From from the Edit menu, and then choose the file you want from the Open dialog box that appears. This is the same dialog box as the one that appears when you choose Open from the File menu.

When you choose Paste From, the cutout appears in the upper left corner of the drawing area, just as when you paste from the Clipboard.

 If you want to place the contents of a saved cutout some-where other than the drawing area's upper left corner, you can drag it after you choose Paste From. But there's an easier way: use the Select tool to define a cutout *before* you choose Paste From, and the saved cutout is then pasted into the upper left corner of the selected cutout.

Moving a Cutout

To move a cutout from one place to another, position the mouse pointer anywhere within the dotted line (the pointer changes to a four-headed arrow), and then drag. When you move a cutout, the portion of the picture you move the cutout onto is obscured by the cutout object.

Copying a Cutout Within a Picture

To make a duplicate of a cutout, position the cursor within the dotted area surrounding the cutout and hold down the Ctrl key while dragging the mouse. The original cutout remains where it was and a duplicate appears where you release the mouse button.

Sweeping a Cutout

To "sweep" a cutout means to create a trail of copies with it as you pass the mouse across the canvas. Figure 19-9 shows an object that has been swept across the canvas.

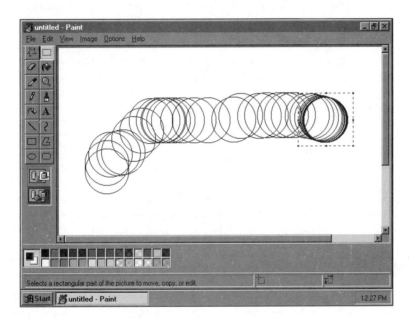

FIGURE 19-9.

Sweeping can be useful, or it can just make a mess.

To sweep a cutout, first move the cutout where you want to begin the sweep. Then position the cursor within the dotted area and hold down the Shift key while dragging.

The speed at which you drag the mouse determines the number of copies that result from the sweep.

Resizing a Cutout

You can change the size of a cutout horizontally, vertically, or both. To change the size of a cutout, position the mouse pointer over one of the handles in the dotted rectangle surrounding the cutout. There are eight handles—one in each corner and one in the middle of each side.

> ### This Ought to Clear Things Up
>
> Cutouts can be moved, copied, or swept either opaquely or transparently. When you move, copy, or sweep a cutout opaquely (the default), any background portions of the cutout are moved, copied, or swept along with the foreground material and can obscure another object that the cutout lands on. If you move, copy, or sweep a cutout transparently, any parts of the cutout that are in the current background color disappear, allowing the underlying image to show through. To select transparent operations so the background won't obscure other parts of the drawing, choose Draw Opaque from the Options menu to remove the check mark, or click the draw transparent icon below the tool box.
>
> The opaque and transparent options also control the background of a text box when you use the Text tool.

When the mouse pointer is correctly positioned, it assumes the shape of a double-headed arrow. If it's on a corner handle, the arrow is diagonal and you can size vertically and horizontally at the same time.

Stretching and Skewing a Cutout

To adjust a cutout with absolute precision, choose Stretch/Skew from the Image menu to display the Stretch And Skew dialog box, as shown in Figure 19-10. Using this dialog box you can alter the size of the cutout either horizontally or vertically by specifying a percentage greater or smaller than its original 100 percent. You can skew the cutout horizontally or vertically by specifying the number of degrees to skew.

To change the size of a cutout, click the Horizontal or Vertical option button in the Stretch portion of the dialog box, and then enter the percentage in the text box next to the option button. For example, to double the vertical size of a cutout, click the Vertical option button, and enter 200 in the text box.

To skew the cutout, click the Horizontal or Vertical option button in the Skew portion of the dialog box, and then enter the number of degrees to skew. Use a positive number to skew the cutout in the direction of the

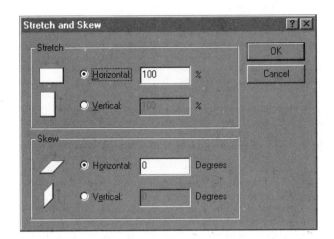

FIGURE 19-10.

With the Stretch And Skew dialog box, you can precisely control the image's size and shape.

arrows in the dialog box, or a negative number to skew the cutout in the opposite direction.

Flipping or Rotating a Cutout

With the Image menu's Flip/Rotate command, you can flip any image vertically or horizontally, or rotate it 90, 180, or 270 degrees. To flip or rotate a cutout, choose Flip/Rotate from the Image menu; the Flip And Rotate dialog box appears. Click the Flip Horizontal, Flip Vertical, or Rotate By Angle option button. If you choose Rotate By Angle, you must also select one of the angle option buttons. Finally, click OK.

Reversing the Colors of a Cutout

The Image menu's Invert Colors command "reverses" the colors of your cutout. Black becomes white, white becomes black, and colors switch to their complementary color on the red-green-blue color wheel.

Inverting color can give unexpected, and sometimes unwanted, results. Just remember that you can use the Undo command if the new colors aren't what you had in mind.

Erasing a Cutout

You can erase a large area by defining it as a cutout and then choosing the Clear Selection command from the Edit menu or the cutout's object menu. Like the Cut command (see "Cutting or Copying a Cutout to the Clipboard," page 502), this command removes the cutout and replaces it with the current background color. However, it does not move the cutout to the Clipboard, so if you want to leave the Clipboard contents unchanged, use the Clear Selection command.

Fine Tuning Your Image with Zoom

Paint stores images you create as *bitmaps*, which record the position and color of each dot in the picture. The individual dots on the screen are known as *pixels*.

You might not normally be aware of separate pixels as you create and modify your Paint images. But, when you want to see and edit the image pixel by pixel, Paint can accommodate you.

Simply choose Zoom from the View menu, and then choose Large Size from the Zoom submenu. The image appears enlarged with a small section of the picture shown in "real size" in a small window in the upper left corner of the drawing area, as shown in Figure 19-11. The small window is called a *thumbnail*. (If the thumbnail doesn't appear, choose Show Thumbnail from the Zoom submenu.)

FIGURE 19-11.

In Zoom view, every pixel is visible.

To make it easier to edit in the zoomed-in view, choose Show Grid from the Zoom submenu. This shows each pixel in its own square, as you can see in Figure 19-11.

To specify a zoom percentage, choose Zoom from the View menu, and then choose Custom to display the Custom Zoom dialog box. The dialog box lets you choose zoom percentages of 100%, 200%, 400%, 600%, or 800%. Click the option button next to the desired zoom percentage, and then click the OK button.

You can also specify a zoom percentage using the Magnifier tool. Click the Magnifier tool in the tool box, and then click 1×, 2×, 6×, or 8× just below the tool box.

You can perform any of the normal picture creation and editing maneuvers while you're zoomed in. One of the more useful tools is the Pencil because you can manipulate one pixel at a time. You can click to paint a single pixel, or drag to draw in the usual way.

 For information about *Paint's drawing and editing tools*, see "Exploring the Tool Box," page 492.

Editing Colors

For most of your day-to-day painting needs, the standard set of 28 colors or patterns that appear in the default color box are more than adequate. However, when the creative need arises, Paint lets you replace any of the standard colors by choosing from a group of 48 predefined colors or by creating almost any custom colors you can imagine.

Choosing Predefined Colors

To replace one of the colors in the color box with any of the 48 predefined colors, click the color you want to replace, and then choose Edit Colors from the Options menu to display the Edit Colors dialog box shown in Figure 19-12 on the next page.

FIGURE 19-12.

The Edit Colors
dialog box gives you
additional colors to
splash on your
palette.

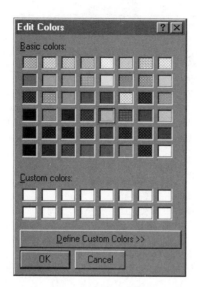

In the Basic Colors group, click the color you want to use as the selected color's replacement, and then click the OK button. The color you originally selected is replaced in the color box with the new color.

Repeat the process to replace as many of the default colors as you want. If you want to use the replacement colors only for the current Paint session, just use them as you would use the default colors. The default color set will reappear the next time you start Paint.

If you want to be able to use the group of colors you selected in future Paint sessions, save the color palette by choosing Save Colors from the Options menu, and then entering a name for the palette and clicking the Save button. When you want to use the saved palette, choose Get Colors from the Options menu and select the name of the palette you want to retrieve.

Adding Custom Colors

When none of the 48 predefined colors will do, you can create virtually any color in the rainbow and add it to your color palette. To create a custom color, click the color in the color box that you want to replace with the custom color, and then choose Edit Colors from the Options menu. When the Edit Colors dialog box appears, click the Define Custom Colors button to expand the dialog box, as shown in Figure 19-13.

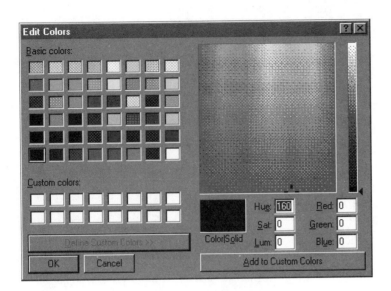

FIGURE 19-13.

The expanded Edit Colors dialog box lets you create custom colors.

Drag the cross-hair pointer and the luminosity pointer until the color you want to use as a new color appears in the Color|Solid box. (Or you can enter numeric values in the Hue, Sat, and Lum or Red, Green, and Blue text boxes.) Then click the Add To Custom Colors button. The new color is added to the first empty square in the Custom Colors portion of the dialog box. The new color replaces the original color you selected in the color box when you click the OK button.

NOTE: Before leaving the Edit Colors dialog box, you can create as many as 16 custom colors, which you can use to replace colors in the color box, as described in the previous section.

After creating all the custom colors you want to use and replacing the colors in the color box, be sure to save your palette as discussed in the previous section or you won't be able to use the custom colors in future Paint sessions. The next time you start Paint and want to use the color palette with your custom colors, choose Get Colors from the Options menu, and select the name of the palette you want to use.

NOTE: Any custom colors you define appear in the color box when you retrieve a palette using Get Colors. However, the custom colors don't appear in the Custom Colors portion of the Edit Colors dialog box in future Paint sessions.

See Also: For more information about *using the Edit Colors dialog box,* see "Defining Custom Colors," page 100.

Printing Your Paint Image

To print your Paint image, choose Print from the File menu.

Specify which pages to print in the Print Range portion of the dialog box, and the number of copies to print in the Copies box. When all the settings are as desired, click the OK button.

Changing Page Settings

If you want to change paper size, orientation (direction), or margins, choose Page Setup from the File menu before you choose the Print command. In the Page Setup dialog box, choose the paper size from the Size

Printing Color Images to Black-and-White Printers

You don't have to make any special accommodations to print color Paint images to your black-and-white printer. However, the results might not be what you expect—or want. When color images are sent to a black-and-white printer, the colors are converted to black-and-white dot patterns (called dithering) to simulate gray shades.

You can adjust the way colors are dithered by clicking Properties in the Print dialog box. Then click the Graphics tab of your printer's property sheet, and experiment with different dithering options.

drop-down list, and, if the option is available for your printer, the source from the Source drop-down list. To change the print orientation, click the appropriate option button in the Orientation portion of the dialog box.

To change the margins—the white space surrounding your picture—select the entry in the text box for the margin you want to change (Left, Right, Top, or Bottom) and enter the new values.

When the settings are correct, click the OK button and then print the document.

 You can use Print Preview to see what your printout will look like before sending it to the printer. Choose Print Preview from the File menu. If you like what you see, click the Print button in the Print Preview window. If you don't, click Close to return to the main Paint window for further editing.

Making Wallpaper

Printing your pictures on paper isn't the only way to use your Paint creations. You can also use them as Windows wallpaper—the background for your desktop. If you already have a Paint image saved on your computer's hard disk, you can use the Display property sheet to choose it as your wallpaper. However, there's an easier way to use the current Paint image as wallpaper without using the Display property sheet at all.

Before you can use a Paint image as wallpaper, you must save it. Once the image is saved, choose Set As Wallpaper (Tiled) or Set As Wallpaper (Centered) from the File menu. The Tiled option displays as many copies of the picture as required to fill the screen. Centered uses one copy of the image—centered on the screen.

As soon as you choose one of the Set As Wallpaper commands, the image immediately becomes your wallpaper, although you won't be able to see it if Paint is maximized or if your desktop is covered with other applications.

Before you use a Set As Wallpaper command, you might want to move the wallpaper file to the directory in which your other wallpaper files are stored. This makes the file easier to find in case you ever change to another wallpaper file and then want to switch back. The default folder for wallpaper files is C:\Windows.

 For information about *using the Display property sheet to apply wallpaper*, see "Adding Wallpaper," page 108.

20

Connecting with HyperTerminal and Phone Dialer

f your computer has a modem—a device for connecting your computer to a telephone line—HyperTerminal and Phone Dialer provide the means for your computer to communicate with the world.

HyperTerminal lets your computer talk to other computers. The Phone Dialer allows you to store a list of frequently used phone numbers and use your computer to dial them for plain old voice conversations.

NOTE: To use either HyperTerminal or Phone Dialer, a modem must be properly installed in your computer and configured in Windows 95. If you haven't done so already, install the modem, and then double-click the Modems item in Control Panel. Click the Add button to start the Install New Modem wizard, which leads you through the configuration process.

Why HyperTerminal?

If you read Chapter 25, "Using The Microsoft Network," you'll find that you don't have to get involved with HyperTerminal to have your computer cruising the information superhighway. In fact, many of the popular online services, such as The Microsoft Network, PRODIGY, and America Online, require their own specialized software to make the connection.

Terminal communications programs like HyperTerminal are designed to let you connect with the vast array of bulletin board systems (BBS's) and other online services, such as CompuServe and Delphi Internet, that don't need proprietary software.

 Even when connecting to services that don't need special software, you're often better off using special software. For example, although you can connect to CompuServe with HyperTerminal, you'll be more efficient with communications software designed specifically for use with CompuServe, such as WinCIM (the Windows version of CompuServe Information Manager).

See Also: For information about *using a modem to connect to a network*, see "Using Dial-Up Networking," page 372.

For information about *The Microsoft Network*, see Chapter 25, "Using The Microsoft Network," page 675.

A Typical HyperTerminal Session

A typical communications session using HyperTerminal goes something like this:

1. Start HyperTerminal. For details, see "Starting HyperTerminal," page 519.

2. Open or create a connection file.

    Before establishing a communications link, you have to supply HyperTerminal with the phone number and some additional information about how to communicate with the service you're calling. For details, see "Making New Connections," page 520.

3. Choose Connect from the Call menu or click the Connect toolbar button, and then click the Dial button in the Dial dialog box. (Table 20-1 on the next page describes the toolbar buttons.)

    HyperTerminal uses your modem's built-in dialing capabilities to establish a telephone connection with the remote computer, which is often called the *host computer* (or simply *host*). After a connection has been established, whatever you type in HyperTerminal's window is sent across the phone line to the host computer. If the person or computer at the other end of the line sends information back, it appears in HyperTerminal's window as though someone behind the screen were typing.

4. Log on to the host computer or service.

    If you're communicating with a mainframe or information service, you'll probably be required to enter your name and password as soon as the connection is established. This process is called *logging on*.

Table 20-1. HyperTerminal Toolbar

Toolbar Icon	Description
	Creates a new connection file
	Opens an existing connection file
	Connects to a remote system (dials the modem)
	Disconnects from a remote system (hangs up the modem)
	Sends a file to the remote system
	Receives a file from the remote system
	Displays the property sheet for the current connection file

5. Interact with the party you're connected to.

Your conversation might consist of nothing more than messages typed at the keyboard. Or you might transmit a great deal of information stored on the Clipboard by choosing Paste To Host from HyperTerminal's Edit menu. You can also exchange files with the host computer. For details, see "Transferring Files," page 528.

6. Log off the host computer or service.

The procedure for logging off depends on the service you use. Typically, you type *quit, exit, bye,* or a similar command at the service's command prompt or main menu.

7. Choose the Disconnect command from HyperTerminal's Call menu.

When you log off, the host computer might end the telephone connection itself. HyperTerminal might not recognize that, however, so it's best to use the Disconnect command regardless of what the other party does.

8. Close HyperTerminal.

If the telephone connection is still open (or if HyperTerminal thinks it is), HyperTerminal prompts you to disconnect from the host computer before quitting.

Starting HyperTerminal

To start HyperTerminal, click the Start button, and then choose Programs, Accessories, HyperTerminal. This opens a folder that contains an icon for the HyperTerminal program and for each HyperTerminal connection you have created and saved. To open an existing connection, double-click its icon. Otherwise, double-click the HyperTerminal icon. HyperTerminal's opening screen appears, followed by the Connection Description dialog box, as shown in Figure 20-1.

FIGURE 20-1.

The Connection Description dialog box is the place to enter specifications for a new terminal connection.

NOTE: If HyperTerminal has not been set up on your computer, double-click the Add/Remove Programs item in Control Panel, click the Windows Setup tab, select Communications, and click the Details button. Select HyperTerminal and click OK. Click OK again in the Add/Remove Programs Properties dialog box.

If connection settings have already been specified—perhaps to dial up a company's support bulletin board or the local university's online research service—click the Cancel button to close the Connection Description dialog box.

Making New Connections

The first time you use HyperTerminal, or when you want to connect to a new computer service, HyperTerminal doesn't have a clue about what you want to connect to, so you'll have to supply the details it needs to get hooked up.

To create a new connection, follow these steps:

1. Type a descriptive name for the connection in the Name text box.

   The name doesn't have to be the actual name of the service you're connecting to, just something that will be descriptive enough for you. For example, you might call your connection to the local bicycle club BBS "Bike BBS" instead of using its official name, "UWBIKECLUB."

2. Select an icon to represent the new connection.

   You can use the horizontal scroll bar to view the available connection icons.

3. Click OK.

   HyperTerminal displays the Phone Number dialog box, as shown in Figure 20-2.

FIGURE 20-2.

Use the Phone Number dialog box to enter the number for the new connection.

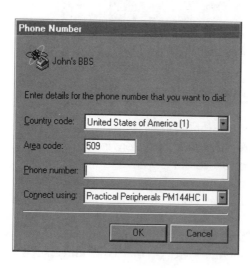

520

4. Fill in the phone number and area code.

   If you have more than one modem connected to your computer, use the Connect Using drop-down list to select the modem you want to use for this connection.

5. Click the OK button.

   The Connect dialog box appears, as shown in Figure 20-3.

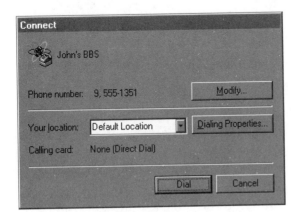

FIGURE 20-3.

The Connect dialog box shows the current primary settings for the new connection.

6. Click Dial to connect to the service now or Cancel if you want to go on line with the service later.

7. After you log off or after choosing Cancel without logging on, choose Save from the File menu to retain the connection settings you just created.

Opening Existing Connections

To open a connection that has already been defined, double-click its icon in the HyperTerminal folder. If HyperTerminal is already running, choose Open from the File menu, or click the Open toolbar button. The Open dialog box appears, as shown in Figure 20-4 on the next page.

Click the name of the file you want to use in the list box, and then click Open. Like other applications for Windows, the HyperTerminal title bar displays the name of the connection you've chosen.

After you have opened the connection file, choose Connect from the Call menu or click the Connect button. Then click the Dial button to proceed with the connection.

FIGURE 20-4.

The Open dialog box lets you choose the predefined connection you want to use.

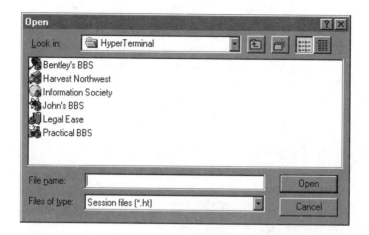

Modifying Connection Settings

In most cases, the basic connection information you enter in the Connection Description (see Figure 20-1 on page 519) and Phone Number (Figure 20-2 on page 520) dialog boxes is sufficient. You can, however, customize the settings in a number of ways to suit your needs. This can be done as you create a new connection or after the connection has been defined.

To modify a connection's properties after it has been defined, open the connection as described in the previous section. Then choose Properties from the File menu. The Properties dialog box for the open connection appears, as shown in Figure 20-5.

The Phone Number tab of the Properties dialog box includes the following controls for changing options:

■ The Change Icon button lets you pick a different icon from the same group of icons that was presented when you created the connection. You can also change the connection name via the Change Icon button.

■ The Country Code lists the part of the world where the host computer is located.

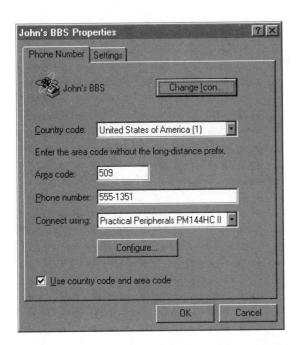

FIGURE 20-5.

The Phone Number tab of the Properties dialog box provides access to several basic settings.

■ The entries in the Area Code and Phone Number text boxes need to be changed only if the number for your connection changes or you made a mistake when you entered them initially.

■ Use the Connect Using drop-down list to specify a different modem if your computer has more than one modem attached.

 Some computer services use separate phone numbers for different modem speeds and charge on the basis of your current access speed. For this reason, you may want to have multiple connection settings for the same service so you can log on at the slower (cheaper) speed, perhaps to check your e-mail messages, or the faster speed to download large files.

NOTE: The Connect Using drop-down list also provides for direct connection to each of your computer's serial (Com) ports. Although you can use this method to connect two nearby computers with HyperTerminal (and no modems), a better solution in that case is to use Direct Cable Connection. For details, see "Transferring Files with Direct Cable Connection," page 360.

- To change the modem settings for this connection, click the Configure button. HyperTerminal displays the Properties dialog box for your modem. The modem properties dialog box lets you select a port, baud rate (modem speed), and other communications parameters and dialing settings. For details, see "Changing Modem Settings and Dialing Locations," page 287.

 If you're connecting to a service that charges by the minute—or it's a long distance call—you can set up your modem to disconnect automatically if you don't use it for a period of time. In the Properties dialog for the connection, click Configure to display the modem Properties dialog box. Click the Connection tab, and then check the Disconnect A Call If Idle For More Than check box. Enter a reasonably short time (perhaps 10 or 15 minutes) so you won't be paying for a lot of connect time while you're not using the system. (Unfortunately, this check box is not available in the Properties dialog for all brands and types of modems.)

The Settings tab in the Properties dialog box for the connection includes the following additional options, as shown in Figure 20-6.

- Choose Terminal Keys (the default) or Windows Keys to specify how function keys, arrow keys, and Ctrl-key combinations are used during connections. If you choose Terminal Keys, these keystrokes are sent to the host computer; if you choose Windows Keys, Windows processes these keystrokes as it does in other applications.

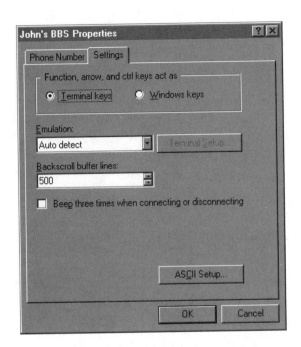

FIGURE 20-6.

The Settings tab of the connection's Properties dialog box controls the appearance of transmitted data, among other functions.

For example, with some services, pressing Ctrl-C stops the transmission of a file. If you have selected Windows Keys, however, pressing Ctrl-C copies the current selection (if any) to the Clipboard. It's usually best to leave this option set to Terminal Keys so these keystrokes will be passed to the host computer.

■ The Emulation drop-down list is set to Auto Detect. Unless you have trouble with your connection, keep this at the default setting. If you do have trouble, contact the host computer's support staff to find out what type of terminal the remote system needs to see at your end. (A *terminal* is a simple device—consisting of a monitor, a keyboard, and a physical connection—for communicating with a host computer. HyperTerminal can act like any of several different terminal models.)

■ The Backscroll Buffer Lines text box lets you specify how many lines of a communication session you can view by pressing the PgUp key. (A *buffer* is an area of memory used to store something temporarily.) While you're connected to another computer, everything you send and receive is stored in a buffer and displayed in

HyperTerminal's window. The buffer gives you a way to review what you send and receive without capturing the "conversation" in a disk file or generating a printed transcript. As long as the buffer's capacity has not been exceeded, you can scroll up and down in the HyperTerminal window to reread everything that has passed back and forth over the telephone line. (There is one exception: Binary files that you send or receive are not recorded in the buffer.)

When the buffer reaches its capacity, each new line replaces the oldest line in the buffer. For example, if the buffer size is set at 500 lines, when the 501st line arrives, the first line is discarded.

You can set the buffer size at anywhere from 25 to 500 lines. If you have plenty of memory, reserve a full 500 lines; if memory is scarce, choose a smaller size. If you don't have enough memory for the buffer size you request, HyperTerminal gives you as much as it can.

 The buffer is convenient because it lets you reread material that has scrolled off your screen. But if you want a complete record of your communications session, consider sending a copy of it to your printer or recording it in a text file. For information about printing or recording to a text file, see "Creating a Transcript of Your Communications Session," page 532.

- If the check box labeled "Beep three times when connecting or disconnecting" is selected, HyperTerminal beeps to let you know whenever a connection to a remote system is made or broken, or if the remote system sends a "bell" character (Ctrl-G). Unless you object to the sound, it's probably best to leave this option selected.

- The ASCII Setup button displays a dialog box, shown in Figure 20-7, that lets you control how text is transferred between your computer and the remote computer. You might need to adjust one of these options if your display is unreadable while you're

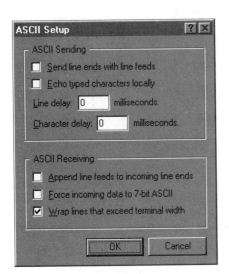

FIGURE 20-7.

The ASCII Setup dialog box sets options that control the display of transmitted text in your HyperTerminal window.

connected, for example. The ASCII Setup dialog box offers the following options:

❑ The check box labeled "Send line ends with line feeds," when selected, causes HyperTerminal to add a line feed character each time you press Enter. You won't need to change this setting when communicating with most online services, but if you're communicating with a live person who complains that everything on his or her screen is displayed on one line, put a check in this box.

❑ If, after you've established connection with a remote computer, the characters you type are not displayed on your screen, select the Echo Typed Characters Locally check box. On the other hand, if every character you type appears twice on your screen, remove the check from this check box.

❑ The check box labeled "Append line feeds to incoming line ends" provides a function similar to that of the "Send line ends with line feeds" check box—except that it affects *your* display, not the remote system's. If everything sent by the host computer appears on a single line on your screen, select this check box. Conversely, if everything you receive is double spaced, deselect this option.

❑ The check box labeled "Force incoming data to 7-bit ASCII," when selected, ensures that you receive only standard letters, numbers, and punctuation—the original 128-character ASCII character set.

❑ The check box labeled "Wrap lines that exceed terminal width," when selected, causes HyperTerminal to start a new line when text you receive from the host computer reaches the right edge of the HyperTerminal window.

 See Also: For information about *configuring modem properties*, see "Changing Modem Settings and Dialing Locations," page 287.

Transferring Files

Two common HyperTerminal tasks are sending *(uploading)* and receiving *(downloading)* files. For example, you might download new video drivers for your computer from the manufacturer's BBS, or you might need to upload an error log to a software publisher's support forum.

You can transfer two distinct types of files: text files and binary files.

Text files, sometimes called ASCII files, are human-readable, unformatted files that contain only letters, numbers, punctuation symbols, and basic control codes, such as line-ending codes. Text files don't require any special transfer protocols on the part of either the sending or receiving computer.

A binary file is any file that is not a text file. Formatted documents created in word processing, spreadsheet, or graphics programs, for example, are binary files. Programs, such as the ones to create word processing, spreadsheet, and graphics documents, are also binary files. When transferring binary files, you should use a file transfer protocol to ensure accurate transmission. (A *protocol* is a method for transferring files that provides error checking and, sometimes, data compression for faster transmissions.)

NOTE: You can also use a protocol to send or receive text files. To do so, follow the procedure for sending or receiving binary files.

Sending a Text File

To send a text file, follow these steps:

1. Open the connection you'll use for the transfer.

2. Log on to the host computer.

   Prior to sending a text file, you may need to alert the host computer to get ready for an incoming message. You can obtain the details you need from the help screens or the support staff at the remote service.

3. Choose Send Text File from the Transfer menu.

   The Select File To Send dialog box appears for you to enter the name and location of the text file you want to send.

4. Enter the name of the file to send, and then click the Open button.

   The text file appears in the HyperTerminal window. If it's a large file, the beginning of the file scrolls off the screen and you'll see the end of the file.

5. Press Enter to send the file.

When you use the method described above to send a text file, the host computer receives the file as a message incorporated in the other text of the communications session. If the text needs to be stored as a separate file, the users at the host computer will have to capture the session to a file, and then edit out the unwanted portions of the session.

To avoid causing the folks at the remote site these inconveniences, you can send the text file as a binary file—covered in the next section—so that it will be received as a separate file that's ready to use with no further fuss.

Sending a Binary File

To send a binary file, follow these steps:

1. Open the connection you'll use for the transfer.

2. Log on to the host computer.

   As with sending text files, you might need to alert the operators of the host computer that you're about to send a file so they can prepare their system to receive the file. If you try to send the file before the remote system is ready, HyperTerminal waits for a ready signal from the host computer.

3. Choose Send File from the Transfer menu.

4. In the Send File dialog box, enter the name of the file you want to send in the Filename text box. (Click the Browse button for point-and-click selection if you don't want to type the file's name and location.) Then select a file transfer protocol from the Protocol drop-down list.

   The Protocol drop-down list, shown in Figure 20-8, offers a list of the available file transfer protocols.

FIGURE 20-8.

The Send File dialog box displays the file transfer protocol options.

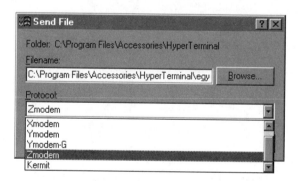

The default protocol is Zmodem, which is a commonly used, fast, and very reliable protocol. If the host computer can use Zmodem, this is a good choice. Xmodem is even more widely used than Zmodem but is a slower protocol, so it should be a second choice. If the host computer doesn't like either of these protocols, check with its help screens or support staff to help you choose one of the other protocols.

The host computer often displays a list of available protocols when you initiate the transfer process. Just remember, the file transfer protocol on your computer and the host computer must match.

5. Click the Send button.

During the transfer, a dialog box keeps you informed about the progress of the transfer, as shown in Figure 20-9. The cps/bps button lets you change the displayed throughput—how fast data is being transferred—between characters per second (cps) and bits per second (bps). If you're sending multiple files, you can click the Skip File button to skip the current file. Use the Cancel button if you want to abort the transfer.

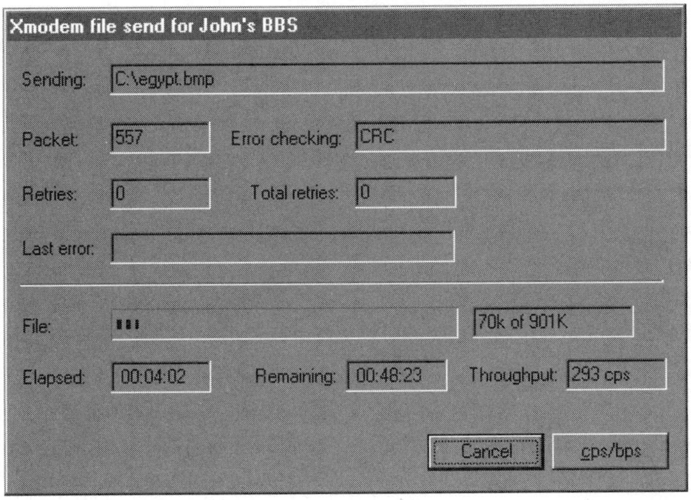

FIGURE 20-9.

You can monitor the progress of your file transfer with this dialog box.

Xmodem file send for John's BBS		
Sending:	C:\egypt.bmp	
Packet:	557	Error checking: CRC
Retries:	0	Total retries: 0
Last error:		
File:	▪▪▪	70k of 901K
Elapsed:	00:04:02	Remaining: 00:48:23 Throughput: 293 cps
		Cancel cps/bps

When the transfer is completed, the dialog box disappears.

Receiving a Binary File

To receive a binary file, follow these steps:

1. Open the connection you'll use for the transfer.

2. Log on to the host computer.

3. Use the appropriate procedures to request the file you want to receive from the host computer.

In most remote systems, you'll need to navigate to a special download or file library area before requesting a file to download. You'll also usually need to specify a transfer protocol before receiving the file. HyperTerminal's default protocol, Zmodem, is a good choice if it's available on the host computer.

4. Choose Receive File from the Transfer menu.

The Receive File dialog box appears, as shown in Figure 20-10. If you want the downloaded file to be stored in a folder other than the default \Program Files\Accessories\HyperTerminal folder, change the entry in the Place Received File In The Following Folder box. Change the transfer protocol in the Protocol drop-down list to match the host computer's protocol if it doesn't support the default Zmodem protocol.

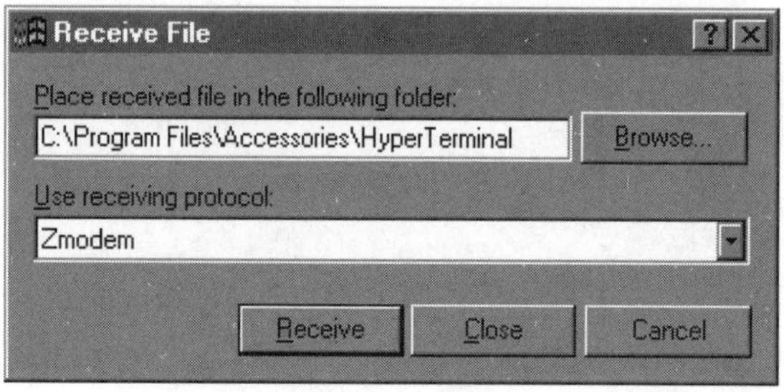

FIGURE 20-10.

The Receive File dialog box specifies where the received file is stored.

5. Click Receive and follow the on-screen directions to begin the transfer. With some protocols, such as Zmodem, the transfer begins automatically. Other protocols require you to specify a filename or otherwise signal your readiness to receive the file.

During the transfer, a dialog box similar to the one for sending files keeps you informed about the progress of the transfer. When the transfer is completed, the dialog box disappears.

Creating a Transcript of Your Communications Session

You can create a transcript of any communications session in either of two ways. You can capture (save) the session information to a text file on disk, or you can send it directly to the printer. With either method you can stop and restart the process to capture only the portion of the communications session you want.

To record your session in a text file, choose Capture Text from the Transfer menu. Enter a name for your file in the File text box of the Capture Text dialog box, and then click the Start button. Notice that the word *Capture* in the status bar is now black, indicating that capture mode is on.

You can temporarily pause capturing by choosing Pause from the Capture Text submenu. To resume capturing text, choose Resume from the Capture Text submenu. When you finish capturing, choose Stop from the Capture Text submenu.

To create a printed transcript, choose Capture To Printer from the Transfer menu. A check mark will appear in front of the Capture To Printer command and all the session information you send or receive will be spooled to a print file in preparation for printing.

You can stop capturing to the printer—or start again—by choosing the Capture To Printer command again to toggle the check mark off and on. When you stop capturing, HyperTerminal prints the information.

As an alternative to capturing to the printer, you can print the contents of the backscroll buffer by choosing Print from the File menu. You can also print a selection of information from your online session by following this procedure:

1. In the HyperTerminal window, scroll to the information you want to print.

2. Select the information, using the standard Windows text-selection methods.

3. Choose Print from the File menu.

4. Select the Selection option button and click OK.

Using Phone Dialer

Phone Dialer is a handy little program that does just what its name implies—dials your telephone. You can set up eight speed-dial numbers that can be dialed with the click of a button.

Unlike HyperTerminal, which is used for computer-to-computer communications, Phone Dialer's sole purpose is to dial phone numbers for voice communications.

To start Phone Dialer, click the Start button, and then choose Programs, Accessories, Phone Dialer. Phone Dialer appears, as shown in Figure 20-11.

FIGURE 20-11.

Phone Dialer includes eight speed-dial buttons.

NOTE: If Phone Dialer has not been set up on your computer, double-click the Add/Remove Programs item in Control Panel, click the Windows Setup tab, select Communications, and click the Details button. Select Phone Dialer and click OK.

For information about *dialing phone numbers stored in your Exchange personal address book*, see "Using an Addressee's Property Sheet as a Phone Dialer," page 627.

Setting Up the Speed-Dial Numbers

You can enter the eight speed-dial numbers in two ways. If you want to enter them all at once, or edit existing numbers as a group, choose Speed

Dial from the Edit menu. The Edit Speed Dial dialog box appears, as shown in Figure 20-12.

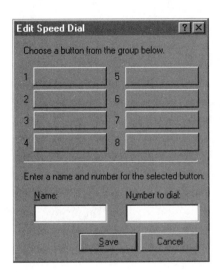

FIGURE 20-12.

The Edit Speed Dial dialog box is for entering a group of speed-dial numbers at once.

Click the button for the first speed-dial button you want to set up or edit, and then enter or edit the text you want to appear on the button in the Name text box. Then enter the phone number (or edit the existing number) in the Number To Dial text box. After completing all the entries, click the Save button.

To set up numbers one at a time, click one of the blank speed-dial buttons in the main Phone Dialer window. The Program Speed Dial dialog box for that button appears, as shown in Figure 20-13.

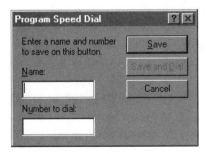

FIGURE 20-13.

The Program Speed Dial dialog box lets you program a single speed-dial button.

After entering the name and number in the appropriate text boxes, you can click the Save button to save the entry, or click the Save And Dial button to save the entry and dial it immediately.

Making a Call

To use Phone Dialer to place a call, you must have a modem installed in your computer. You must also have a telephone connected to the modem. If you try to make a call without a modem installed, Phone Dialer prompts you to install one. (If you try to make a call without a telephone connected to the modem, you'll have no way to talk with the person who answers!)

To make a call, click the speed-dial button for the number you want to call. The Dialing dialog box appears while the connection is being made, and then the Dialing Status dialog box appears. Pick up your telephone's handset and click the Talk button to start the conversation, or click the Cancel button to disconnect.

After the call is completed, you simply hang up the handset to terminate the call.

> **NOTE:** Although you can use Phone Dialer to dial phone numbers by typing them into the Number To Dial text box or clicking the numbers on Phone Dialer's number pad, it's usually more efficient to just dial your telephone without using Phone Dialer. However, if you must precede each phone number with a lengthy calling card code or long distance access code, you might find Phone Dialer to be convenient. Another possible advantage to using Phone Dialer even for manually dialed calls is to have them included in Phone Dialer's history log. See the next section for details.

Viewing a Log of Your Calls

To see a list of the calls you've made using Phone Dialer, choose Show Log from the Tools menu. The Call Log window appears, as shown in Figure 20-14.

To delete an entry in the call log, click the entry and choose Delete from the Edit menu.

To call one of the numbers in the call log, click the entry and choose Dial from the Log menu, or double-click the entry.

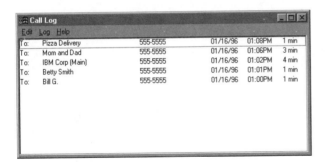

FIGURE 20-14.
The Call Log window shows your call activity.

To hide the log, choose Hide Log from the Tools menu.

Changing the Dialing Properties

You can change several dialing properties to make Phone Dialer more useful. To change the dialing properties, choose Dialing Properties from the Tools menu.

See Also: For information about *dialing properties*, see "Setting Up Your Modem for Multiple Calling Locations," page 370.

21

Using the Multimedia Accessories

Using sound and video (which fall under the *multimedia* umbrella) can greatly enhance your computing experience. Some programs use multimedia to demonstrate concepts that aren't easily explained by words alone. Others use multimedia to provide realistic simulations of faraway places. And multimedia has more mundane uses too, such as chirping to let you know that a new e-mail message has arrived.

Most recent computers include at least the basic equipment necessary to take advantage of the multimedia capabilities in Windows 95. With the cost of multimedia hardware—primarily sound cards and CD-ROM drives—plummeting, it makes sense for most people to explore what multimedia can do for them.

See Also: For information about *sounds that Windows plays*, see "Assigning Sounds to Events," page 103.

What Windows 95 Does for Multimedia

Multimedia may seem like an overwhelmingly complicated topic to cover in one chapter. It is. However, Windows 95 makes working with multimedia faster, better, and almost automatic.

If you've ever tried to install multimedia equipment in a pre–Windows 95 system, you'll be thrilled with the Plug and Play capabilities of Windows, which make setting up sound cards and CD-ROM drives a snap. Unless you have particularly esoteric equipment, Windows can usually figure out what you have and set it up for you.

In addition to making the installation of multimedia hardware easier, Windows includes a number of new technologies and features for multimedia with higher performance and fewer problems. The following are some of the new multimedia goodies included in Windows:

- A 32-bit CD file system speeds CD-ROM disk access on CD-ROM drives that are directly supported by Windows. (A CD-ROM drive is "directly supported" if it doesn't require any device drivers to be loaded by CONFIG.SYS or AUTOEXEC.BAT.)

- AutoPlay CD launching makes playing audio CDs and CD-ROM programs a snap. When you put an audio CD in your CD-ROM drive, Windows 95 launches the CD Player application and starts playing the CD. Put a CD-ROM in the drive (assuming the CD-ROM has the startup information Windows needs to launch it) and the CD-ROM's program installs itself and then starts running. (If the program was previously installed, it just starts running.) Microsoft refers to AutoPlay as "Spin and Grin."

- Improved digital audio and video compression offers both better performance and smoother operation.

- Bigger and better full-motion video makes it realistic to have full-screen video instead of the 320×240 pixel video image that was typical in Windows 3.1—and that some wags called "dancing credit cards."

- Multimedia games perform much better.

 See Also: For more information about *setting up your computer's hardware*, see Chapter 13, "Installing and Uninstalling Software and Hardware," page 337.

For information about *games*, see Chapter 22, "Playing Games with Windows," page 563.

Multimedia Basics

If you haven't explored computer multimedia, or you associate the term with grade-school slide shows featuring musical accompaniment, you may find the scope of multimedia possibilities mind boggling. "Multimedia" encompasses everything from simple little beeps and dings that occur during the course of normal Windows operations to full-motion video (movies) with CD-quality sound that any Hollywood movie studio would be proud of.

Here are some of the things you can do with the multimedia tools provided by Windows 95:

- Add sounds to documents. For example, you can record spoken instructions for the users of a spreadsheet or a word processing document.

- Play audio CDs on your computer. You can certainly be more productive while listening to Beethoven or Pearl Jam.

- Attach custom sounds to various Windows events. For example, instead of the traditional "ta da" when you start Windows, you could have Windows say "Good morning" or "Time to get to work."

- See an electronic encyclopedia come to life with movies of Neil Armstrong stepping onto the moon or Martin Luther King giving his "I Have a Dream" speech. Or watch an animation of the workings of a CD player.

- Play interactive multimedia games with lifelike sound, video, and animation. Games can be a productivity tool if they help relieve stress—in case you needed an excuse.

Equipment Requirements

If your computer is up to the task of running Windows 95, you already have much of what you need for multimedia. You have, at least, a 386-based computer with 4 MB of RAM and a color monitor. Add a sound card, speakers, and a CD-ROM drive, and you're all set.

However, to get the most out of Windows' multimedia capabilities, your computer needs to meet—or better yet, exceed—the Multimedia PC Marketing Council's specifications. Unfortunately, computers that barely meet the original Multimedia PC standard (MPC Level 1 Specification) aren't exactly dazzling multimedia performers. MPC calls for nothing more than a 386SX CPU, 2 MB of RAM, a 30-MB hard drive, 16-color VGA video, a single-speed CD-ROM drive, and an 8-bit monaural sound card. That configuration doesn't even provide enough power to run Windows 95— let alone complex multimedia—in a sprightly fashion.

Fortunately, the more recent MPC Level 2 Specification (also known as MPC2) is much more realistic. The new specification calls for at least a

The Sound of Music

When it comes to multimedia sound, there are two main varieties: wave (.WAV) and MIDI (.MID) files. The primary advantage of wave files is that they can be faithfully reproduced on any multimedia computer system. Like an audio CD, a wave file is a recording of the sound. Of course the quality of the playback is affected by the quality of the equipment, but a voice sounds pretty much like a voice and a piano like a piano, regardless of the equipment.

MIDI files are more like sheet music. Sheet music describes how the music should be played and which instruments should play which parts. If you give a piece of sheet music to two bands or orchestras, you'll get two different renditions. Because MIDI files only describe the music, they can be stored in a small fraction of the size of wave files. For this reason, many multimedia programs provide sounds in the MIDI format.

Fortunately, Windows 95 supports the General MIDI standard that at least ensures that the correct instruments are used for playback of each part of the sound file. However, there is no guarantee that a voice or a piano will sound anything like a voice or a piano. That is determined by the MIDI capabilities on your computer's sound card.

MIDI files can be translated into real sounds by simulating the sounds with a process called FM (Frequency Modulation) synthesis, or by using samples of actual instruments. FM synthesis produces sounds that are, at best, low-quality facsimiles of what the creators of the sounds intended.

The route to realistic MIDI sounds is a sound card (or an add-on card) with wave-table sampling, which uses samples of actual musical instruments to play sounds. The results are much closer to recordings of real music and can greatly enhance the listening experience.

486SX computer running at 25 MHz, 4 MB of RAM, a 160-MB hard drive, a double-speed CD-ROM drive, a 16-bit stereo sound card, and 640×480 video resolution with 16-bit color, which is capable of displaying over 64,000 colors.

If all you want to do with multimedia is make an occasional voice annotation to a document or add some cute sounds to Windows system events, the original MPC spec will suffice, with the addition of some extra RAM and a larger hard drive. Consider 8 MB of RAM as a good starting point for Windows 95—even without multimedia. However, because more complex multimedia—especially full-motion video—eats up so much of your system's resources, consider all the MPC2 specifications as bare minimums.

Some of today's larger programs require dozens of disks for installation. The time you can save by installing huge programs from one CD rather than a stack of disks can make a CD-ROM drive almost essential.

These handy little devices, therefore, aren't just for multimedia. Even if you have no desire to delve into the exciting world of computer sound and video, a CD-ROM drive is still one of the best additions you can make to your computer system—if for no other reason than the extra convenience CDs bring to installing new software programs.

Playing Audio CDs with CD Player

It's so simple to play audio CDs in Windows 95 that it hardly requires explanation. Insert any audio CD in your computer's CD-ROM drive. That's all there is to it. The CD Player applet launches and starts playing the CD. A CD Player button appears on the taskbar, and all you have to do is listen and maybe adjust the volume.

There are a few features you can use to determine how the CD plays. Let's take a look at CD Player and its options. To open CD Player if it's already running, simply click the CD Player button on the taskbar. If CD Player isn't running, start it by clicking the Start button, and then choosing Programs, Accessories, Multimedia, CD Player. The CD Player window appears, as shown in Figure 21-1.

FIGURE 21-1.

The CD Player window looks much like the front panel of a full-size CD player.

NOTE: If CD Player has not been set up on your computer, double-click the Add/Remove Programs item in Control Panel, click the Windows Setup tab, select Multimedia, and click the Details button. Select CD Player and click OK. Click OK again in the Add/Remove Programs Properties dialog box, and have your original Windows disks or CD-ROM handy.

Just like the CD player in your stereo system, CD Player has buttons to jump from track to track, skip forward or backward, pause, stop, start, and eject, as shown in Table 21-1.

Table 21-1. CD Player Buttons

Button	Description
►	Plays the CD, beginning at the location shown in the track and time window
❚❚	Pauses CD playback; you can resume play by clicking the Play button or the Pause button
■	Stops playback and resets the track and time window to the beginning of the CD
◄◄ ►►❘	Moves to the beginning of the current track (subsequent clicks move to the previous track) or next track
◄◄ ►►	Skips backward (fast reverse) or forward (fast forward)
▲	Ejects the CD from the drive

> You can jump directly to a track by clicking the Track drop-down arrow and then selecting the track you want to jump to.

NOTE: The eject feature works only with CD-ROM drives that can respond to an eject command.

The upper left portion of the CD Player window displays track and time information. You can choose to display the track time elapsed, the track time remaining, or the time remaining for the entire disk by choosing the appropriate option from the View menu. You can also switch among these three display views by clicking in the time portion of the window.

To display a toolbar with shortcut buttons for some of the more common features, choose Toolbar from the View menu. Table 21-2 describes the functions of the toolbar buttons. You can remove the default Disk/Track Info or Status Bar by choosing those commands from the View menu to remove their check marks.

Table 21-2. CD Player Toolbar

Toolbar Icon	Description
	Allows you to edit information about the current CD, including the names of the artist, album, and tracks; also lets you select the tracks you want to hear and the order in which they play
	Changes the time and track window to display the elapsed time for the current track, the remaining time for the track, or the remaining time for the disc
	Plays tracks from the play list in random order
	Continuous play; restarts the play list after the last track is played
	Intro play; plays only the beginning of each track

You can choose to play the tracks of the audio CD in random order (this is called "shuffle play" on some players), continuously (repeating the entire CD over and over), or just play a few seconds (the default is 10) of each track by choosing the option you want from the Options menu.

To change some of CD Player's default settings, choose Preferences from the Options menu. The Preferences dialog box appears, as shown in Figure 21-2.

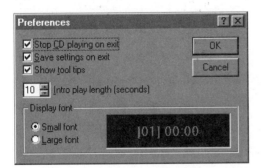

FIGURE 21-2.

Choose Preferences from the Options menu to open CD Player's Preferences dialog box.

By default, CD Player stops playing the current CD when you close the CD Player program. If you want CDs to continue playing after CD Player is closed, uncheck the Stop CD Playing On Exit check box. The CD continues to play until the end. The other useful option in the Preferences dialog box is Intro Play Length (Seconds). By changing this number, you can change the amount of each track that is played when the Intro Play option is chosen.

The one other item you may want to change is the volume level. To change the volume, choose Volume Control from the View menu. This command opens the Volume Control application.

See Also: For information about *the Volume Control application*, see "Controlling Sound Volume," page 554.

Creating a Play List for an Audio CD

One of the really nice options available in the CD Player application is the capability to create a play list for each of your CDs. You can enter the title of the CD as well as the track titles. Once this information is added, CD Player recognizes the CD when you insert it, and, instead of displaying New Artist, New Title, and Track 1 or Track 2, CD Player displays the name of the disk, artist, and track.

To create a play list for the CD that's currently in the drive, follow these steps:

1. Choose Edit Play List from the Disc menu, or click the Edit Play List button if the toolbar is visible.

   The Disc Settings dialog box appears with New Artist in the Artist text box selected, as shown in Figure 21-3.

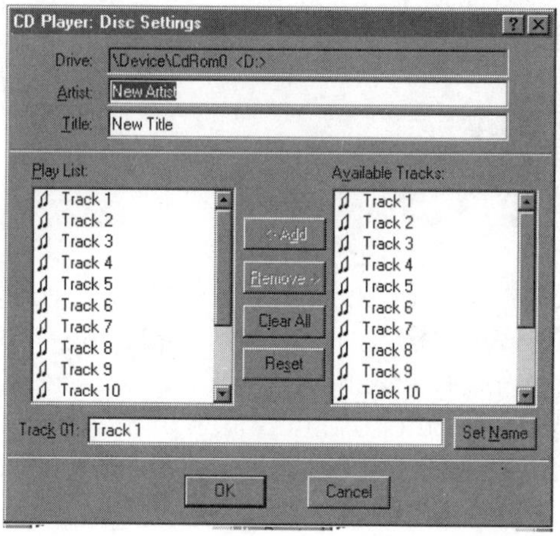

FIGURE 21-3.

The Disc Settings dialog box lets you edit the names of titles and tracks, as well as select which tracks you want to play and their order.

2. Type the artist's name in the Artist text box, and then press the Tab key to select New Title in the Title text box.

3. Type the name of the CD in the Title text box.

4. Click the first track you want to name in the Available Tracks list, and then type the name of the track in the Track box at the bottom of the dialog box. Press Enter or click the Set Name button to confirm the name change.

5. Repeat step 4 for all the tracks you want to name, and then click OK to close the Disc Settings dialog box.

After entering the titles, CD Player automatically recognizes the CD the next time you insert it. You'll also be able to choose tracks from the

Track drop-down list by name instead of by track number, as shown in Figure 21-4.

FIGURE 21-4.

Once you enter information about a CD, CD Player thereafter recognizes the disk and displays the track names in the Track drop-down list.

You can also use the Disc Settings dialog box to choose which tracks to play and in which order to play them. To remove a track, click the track you want to remove in the Play List, and then click the Remove button. To add a track, click the track in the Available Tracks list, and then click the Add button.

The easiest way to change the play order is to select the track (or tracks) you want to move in the Play List box, and then drag the selection up or down to the desired position.

If you want to restore the play list to the default setting, which is to play all tracks in order from first to last, click the Reset button.

Playing Sounds, Video, and Animation with Media Player

What CD Player does for audio CDs, Media Player does for other sound and video sources. If you want to play any multimedia sound or video file, start Media Player, open the file, and click the Play button.

NOTE: You can play audio CDs from Media Player, but CD Player lets you play CDs using controls that are more like a standard CD player, and CD Player gives you more control over the way tracks are played. For information about CD Player, see "Playing Audio CDs with CD Player," page 544.

In most instances, multimedia files are part of a program, such as an encyclopedia or a game. Normally you'll access these files automatically as you explore the encyclopedia or play the game. However, Media Player is often useful when you want to copy a multimedia file as a linked or embedded object into another document or for playing files that aren't played as part of another program.

 You can learn about a media file by right-clicking that file's icon in a folder window or in Windows Explorer. Then choose Properties from the object menu. In addition to the usual file information available on the property sheet's General tab, the Details tab often provides copyright, format, and length information. The Preview tab lets you play a sound or video file without involving Media Player.

To play a multimedia file using Media Player, follow these steps:

1. Start Media Player by clicking the Start button, and then choosing Programs, Accessories, Multimedia, Media Player. Media Player appears, as shown in Figure 21-5.

FIGURE 21-5.

Media Player's controls are similar to those of CD Player.

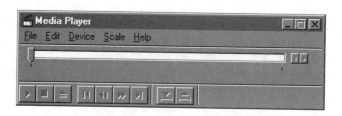

NOTE: If Media Player has not been set up on your computer, double-click the Add/Remove Programs item in Control Panel, click the Windows Setup tab, select Multimedia, and click the Details button. Select Media Player and click OK. Click OK again in the Add/Remove Programs Properties dialog box, and have your original Windows disks or CD-ROM handy.

2. Choose Open from the File menu and use the Open dialog box to open the file you want to play.

    If the file you open is a video clip, a window displaying the first frame of the video appears, as shown in Figure 21-6.

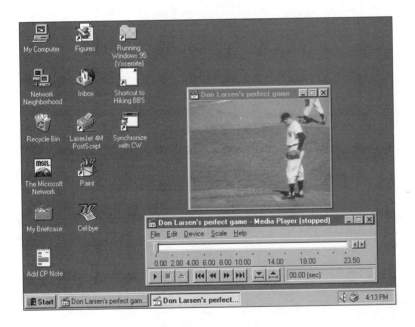

FIGURE 21-6.

Media Player opens a separate window to display .AVI (video clip) files.

 You can also open Media Player and open a media file by right-clicking that file's icon in a folder window and choosing Open.

3. Click the Start button to begin playing the media file.

The Play button becomes a Pause button while the file is playing. You can use the other buttons to navigate through the file in much the same way as the buttons for CD Player are used. You can also use the slider and the scroll forward and scroll backward buttons to move to different positions in the file. Table 21-3 describes each button.

Table 21-3. Media Player Buttons

Button	Description
▶	Plays the current media file
‖	Pauses playback
■	Stops playback
▲	Ejects the CD or video disc from the drive
◀◀ ▶▶	"Rewind" or "fast forward"; scrolls backward or forward through the media file
◀◀ ▶▶	Moves to the beginning of the previous or next track (if any), to the previous or next mark (if any), or to the beginning or end of the file
▼ ▲	Places a mark at the beginning and end of a selection; you can quickly jump to these marks

Media Player usually figures out which device to use to play your chosen media file. But, if it doesn't choose correctly, you can select a device from the Device menu.

The scale below the slider can be changed to Time, Frames, or Tracks, although not all of these options are available for all types of media. For example, video clip (.AVI) files allow only the Time and Frames scale options; video clips do not have "tracks." To change the scale, choose the command you want from the Scale menu.

By default, when you open a video clip with Media Player, the clip is displayed in a separate window, as shown in Figure 21-6. You can combine the two windows into one with a simplified set of controls by double-clicking Media Player's title bar. Double-click the title bar again to restore the dual-window arrangement.

Changing Media Options

You can change several of the options for the media clip by making choices in the Options dialog box. To open the Options dialog box, choose Options from the Edit menu. The Options dialog box appears, as shown in Figure 21-7.

FIGURE 21-7.

Media Player's Options dialog box lets you set playback and OLE options.

You can choose to have a media file automatically rewind or repeat by clicking the appropriate check boxes. The Options dialog box also lets you choose which OLE options to use for the file if you choose to link the file to or embed the file as an icon in a document you create with another application. You can, for example, choose a caption for the linked or embedded object, whether to place a border around the object, and whether to play the object in the destination document.

NOTE: The OLE options are relevant only if you intend to place the object (the media file or a portion of it) in another application. Otherwise, you don't need to bother with these items.

Linking and Embedding Media Files

One of the primary uses for Media Player is to copy media files so they can be linked to or embedded in documents created in other applications. The procedures for linking and embedding media files are similar to linking and embedding any other files.

The first step to linking or embedding a media file is to open it with Media Player as described above. With the file open, choose Copy Object from the Edit menu. Then, open the application and document you want to link or embed the object in.

To embed the object, choose Paste (on the Edit menu) in the destination document. To link the object, choose Paste Special. Then select Paste Link in the Paste Special dialog box.

See Also: For more information about *linking and embedding*, see Chapter 10, "Exchanging Information: The Clipboard and OLE," page 251.

Controlling Sound Volume

The Volume Control application allows you to control the loudness of your computer's various sound sources. You can open the Volume Control program by itself or from either the CD Player or the Media Player program. To open Volume Control from CD Player, choose Volume Control from the View menu. To open it from Media Player, choose Volume Control from Media Player's Device menu.

> **NOTE:** If Volume Control has not been set up on your computer, double-click the Add/Remove Programs item in Control Panel, click the Windows Setup tab, select Multimedia, and click the Details button. Select Volume Control and click OK. Click OK again in the Add/Remove Programs Properties dialog box.

To open Volume Control by itself, click the Start button, and then choose Programs, Accessories, Multimedia, Volume Control. The Volume Control window appears, as shown in Figure 21-8.

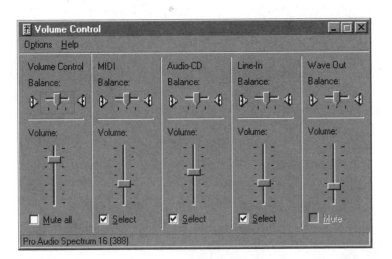

FIGURE 21-8.

The Volume Control application window displays sliders for each sound source.

 You can also open Volume Control by double-clicking the volume icon in the taskbar's notification area.

NOTE: The sound sources available on your computer depend on what type of sound card you have. Your Volume Control window might have controls for sources different from the ones shown in Figure 21-8.

Use the sliders to adjust the balance and volume for each audio source. For example, use the Internal balance and volume sliders to change the balance and volume of your internal CD output.

The balance and volume controls marked "Volume Control" let you adjust the overall balance and volume. If the master volume is at its lowest level, it won't matter what the other levels are, you won't hear anything.

 A single click on the taskbar's volume icon brings up a slider that serves the same function as the Volume Control section of the Volume Control window—without opening the Volume Control application.

The Mute and Select check boxes let you turn off the volume for any of the audio sources. As with the master volume sliders, be careful with the Mute All check box. If Mute All is checked, all sound is turned off.

The Wave Out sliders control the wave (.WAV) files that are used in a number of multimedia applications. The Line-In sliders control the balance and volume of a device you might have connected to the line input of your sound card.

You can choose to display sliders for only the devices you want to control by choosing Properties from the Options menu. Uncheck the boxes for the devices you don't want to control in the Properties dialog box, shown in Figure 21-9.

FIGURE 21-9.

The Properties dialog box lets you select which sound sources you want to control.

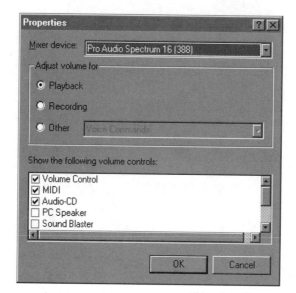

For more information about *controlling sound volume,* see "Setting Volume Levels," page 291.

Recording Sounds with Sound Recorder

If you have a microphone attached to your sound card, you can use Sound Recorder to make your own voice recordings, which can then be added to other documents. And if your sound card has a Line In connector, you can connect a stereo receiver or other sound source to it and use Sound Recorder to make recordings from that source.

You can use voice recordings to annotate documents. For example, suppose you want to provide explicit instructions about how to interpret a particular portion of a spreadsheet—how you arrived at your assumptions, and so on. You could add those instructions to the spreadsheet so the person using it could hear the instructions in your own words—and in your own voice.

> **NOTE:** If Sound Recorder has not been set up on your computer, double-click the Add/Remove Programs item in Control Panel, click the Windows Setup tab, select Multimedia, and click the Details button. Select Sound Recorder and click OK. Click OK again in the Add/Remove Programs Properties dialog box, and have your original Windows disks or CD-ROM handy.

To make a sound recording, follow these steps:

1. Open Sound Recorder by clicking Start, and then choosing Programs, Accessories, Multimedia, Sound Recorder.

   The Sound Recorder window appears, as shown in Figure 21-10.

FIGURE 21-10.

Sound Recorder lets you record your voice.

2. Choose Audio Properties from the Edit menu. In the Recording section of the dialog box (see Figure 21-12 on page 560), make sure the Volume, Preferred Device, and Preferred Quality settings are the way you want them.

3. If you want to change the Preferred Quality setting, click the Customize button to open the Customize dialog box, shown in Figure 21-11.

FIGURE 21-11.

The Customize dialog box lets you select recording attributes and indicates the amount of disk space required for each combination of attributes.

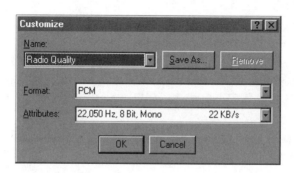

Choose the file format and attributes you want. Higher sampling rates require more disk space but provide better quality. (Expressed in hertz, the sampling rate measures the number of times that a sound is recorded in each second.) If you find the sound quality unacceptably low, use the Attributes drop-down to choose a higher sampling rate or 16-bit sound.

4. Turn on the microphone, if it has an on/off switch, and then click the Record button and start talking. (See Table 21-4 for a description of the buttons.)

As you record, the green line expands and contracts like an oscilloscope to indicate sound levels. You can see how much time has elapsed. The maximum recording length is 60 seconds.

5. When you finish the recording, click the Stop button.

6. Choose Save from the File menu, and then name the file if you haven't already.

Sound Recorder saves its documents as wave files and gives them the filename extension .WAV.

Table 21-4. Sound Recorder Buttons

Button	Description
◄◄	Moves to the beginning of the sound document
►►	Moves to the end of the sound document
►	Plays the sound
■	Stops playing or recording
■	Begins recording

You can embed a sound file in any application that supports OLE linking and embedding. To do so, follow these steps:

1. Open or record the file you want to embed.

2. Use Sound Recorder's Copy command to put the sound data on the Clipboard.

3. Activate the application into which you want to embed the sound (the destination application).

4. Put the cursor where you want the sound file to be embedded. Then use the destination program's Paste command.

In the destination document, the embedded sound file is displayed as a small microphone icon. To play the sound, double-click the icon.

Controlling Input Levels for Recording

You can control the input volume level for the sounds that you record. To make volume adjustments, choose Audio Properties from the Edit menu. The Audio Properties dialog box appears, as shown in Figure 21-12 on the next page.

Move the slider in the Recording portion of the dialog box to the left to reduce the volume or to the right to increase it.

You can also adjust the recording volume using the Volume Control program. With the Volume Control program running, choose Properties

FIGURE 21-12.

The Audio
Properties dialog
box lets you adjust
the recording input
level.

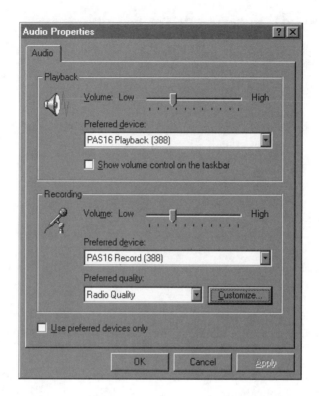

from the Options menu to display the Properties dialog box. Click the
Recording option button and click OK. Balance and volume sliders let you
adjust the recording volume level for each sound source.

 For more information about *the Volume Control program,*
see "Controlling Sound Volume," page 554.

Editing Sound Files

Sound Recorder's Edit menu has six editing commands, in addition to the
Copy command.

The Insert File and Mix With File commands allow you to combine
two or more sound files. To use either command, first position the slider
at the point in the current file where you want the incoming file to appear.

The Position indicator to the left of the oscilloscope display will help you find the appropriate spot.

The Insert File command adds a sound file at the current location and moves the remainder of the file forward. The Mix With File command superimposes the incoming sound file on whatever sound data is already at the current location.

The Paste Insert and Paste Mix commands combine sounds in a similar manner, except that they use the Clipboard as their source instead of a sound file.

The two Delete commands on the Edit menu simply delete data from the current location to the beginning or the end of the file.

You can also edit a sound file with commands on the Effects menu, shown in Figure 21-13.

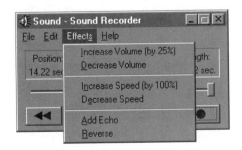

FIGURE 21-13.

The Effects menu commands let you distort sounds.

These commands actually change the sound data that makes up your file, not merely the playback mode. For example, if you increase the speed of a file and then use the Save command, the file plays at the increased speed each time you open it.

22

Playing Games with Windows

If you love the Solitaire computer game, try FreeCell. It puts a new spin on Solitaire-type games.

I f you use only the business and productivity applications in Windows, you're missing a lot. Windows 95 is a terrific gaming environment, and playing games can be a great way to get some entertainment value from your computer investment.

What Windows 95 Brings to the Gaming Table

When it comes to playing games, Windows has finally come of age. If you are a computer-game enthusiast, you already know that the previous versions of Windows were not the best gaming platforms. For the most part, those versions were too slow for many non-Windows-based action games, and offered only limited multimedia capabilities.

Windows 95 changes everything. Almost all the multimedia advances that Windows 95 provides are as beneficial to complex multimedia games as they are to other multimedia applications. In fact, because games can be more demanding and resource intensive than any other software category, Windows 95 is truly a blessing for avid gamers.

Until now, Windows-based games made up only a tiny fraction of the total game market. The vast majority of games were MS-DOS–based programs. The reason for this situation is that the layers of software that Windows added between the game and your computer exacted a tremendous performance penalty. Games that employ incredibly complex sound and video, such as the wildly popular DOOM from id Software, were originally written as MS-DOS–based games so they could have the maximum direct control of your computer's hardware.

It's a shame that the limitations of Windows caused many game programmers to avoid creating Windows-based games. After all, one of the primary advantages of Windows has always been its device independence, which makes it easier to write programs that take advantage of all Windows-supported hardware devices. Now WinG (pronounced "Win-Gee"), a group of programming libraries designed to make it easier for programmers to write high-performance games for Windows, is available. Although WinG is not specifically a Windows 95 feature (the WinG libraries are also available for use with previous versions of Windows), WinG is bound to attract more game programmers to Windows 95. You can expect that, with the performance and compatibility improvements in Windows 95, most new games will be Windows-based games.

Here's what Windows 95 brings to the gaming table:

- Built-in joystick support lets you just plug in a joystick, follow Windows through the calibration routine, and play. (Your computer must have a game port, which typically is included on a sound card or a multifunction I/O card.)

- Plug and Play makes the installation and setup of the requisite gaming hardware—sound cards, joysticks, CD-ROM drives, and so on—nearly painless.

- Multiplayer support means more—and better—multiplayer games. The popularity of multiplayer games is evidenced by the number of network and modem DOOM players. To show off the multiplayer capabilities built into Windows, a multiplayer version of Hearts is included. With all the built-in modem and networking capabilities in Windows 95, more games are likely to appear that support playing against other people rather than only the computer.

See Also: For information about *multimedia*, see Chapter 21, "Using the Multimedia Accessories," page 539.

For information about *Plug and Play*, see "Plug and Play: The End of the Hardware Blues?," page 346.

For information about *the Hearts game*, see "Playing Hearts," page 572.

Running MS-DOS–Based Games Under Windows 95

Along with making Windows a friendlier environment for Windows-based games, Windows 95 also goes a long way toward accommodating MS-DOS–based games that need most of the computer's resources.

Windows 95 gives MS-DOS–based programs more memory and better access to the computer's hardware than previous versions of Windows. You'll probably find that MS-DOS–based programs that simply refused to run under previous versions of Windows run flawlessly under Windows 95 because of its improved management of memory and other resources.

Most MS-DOS–based games work with Windows 95 and require no modification. However, if you do encounter difficulties running an MS-DOS–based game, here are some steps you can take to overcome the problems:

- Windows 95 automatically runs most graphics-oriented MS-DOS–based games in a full-screen display. However, if a particular game isn't running in full-screen display mode, you can press Alt-Enter to enlarge the window to full screen. This generally yields better and more stable performance.

- You might need to increase the amount of memory available to the game. Open the program's property sheet by opening the folder that contains the program, right-clicking the program's icon, and choosing Properties from the object menu. When the Properties dialog box appears, click the Memory tab and modify the memory settings as necessary.

- If all else fails, run the game in MS-DOS mode. To do this, right-click the program's icon and choose Properties from the object menu. When the Properties dialog box appears, click the Program tab, and then click the Advanced button to display the Advanced Program Settings dialog box. In the Advanced Program Settings dialog box, click the MS-DOS Mode check box. MS-DOS mode should be used as a last resort because all other programs must be closed before starting the game.

 If you try everything you can think of and a game still refuses to run, try calling the manufacturer of the program. Perhaps they have a solution—or a later version—that allows the game to run under Windows 95.

See Also: For more information about *using MS-DOS–based programs in Windows 95*, see Chapter 12, "Running MS-DOS–Based Programs," page 301.

For more information about *full-screen display mode*, see "Windowed Versus Full-Screen Display," page 307.

For more information about *memory settings*, see "Options on the Memory Tab," page 325.

For more information about *MS-DOS mode*, see "Running a Program in MS-DOS Mode," page 323.

Playing the Games That Come with Windows 95

You don't have to rush right out and buy games to test your gaming ability. Windows includes several games that provide a nice diversion from the more business-oriented computing that you probably have to spend the bulk of your time on.

The remainder of the chapter covers the basic concepts, rules, and strategies for playing the games that come with Windows. All the games are in the Games folder, so the procedure for starting any of them is the same. Click the Start button, choose Programs, Accessories, Games, and then choose the game you want to play.

NOTE: If the games included with Windows have not been installed on your computer, double-click the Add/Remove Programs item in Control Panel, click the Windows Setup tab, select Accessories, and click the Details button. Select Games and click OK.

 Most of the games included with Windows have a "boss key." Simply press Esc to quickly reduce the game window to a taskbar icon—and not let onlookers know what you're *really* doing.

For information about *3-D Pinball*, see Appendix A, "Using the Power of Your 486 or Pentium with Microsoft Plus!," page 727.

Playing Minesweeper

Minesweeper is a game of logic and deduction. The objective is to uncover all the squares in a minefield (presented as a grid of squares) that don't contain mines, and mark the squares that do, as quickly as possible—all without "stepping on" a mine.

When you start Minesweeper, a gridlike minefield appears, as shown in Figure 22-1.

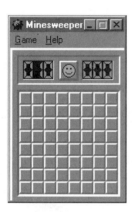

FIGURE 22-1.

Minesweeper depicts a "minefield," where each square in the grid could be concealing a mine.

The game starts when you make your first move by clicking a square to uncover it. Each square contains a number or a mine, or it is blank. If the square contains a number, the number indicates how many mines are in the surrounding squares. If the square you reveal is blank, there are no mines in the adjacent squares, so the surrounding squares are uncovered automatically. If you click a square that contains a mine, you lose and all the mines are displayed.

If you win a game (no small feat), the smiley face between the counters appears with sunglasses. If you lose, the smiley face starts frowning. Figure 22-2 shows a winning game and a losing game.

FIGURE 22-2.

A winner (left) and a loser. Notice that all the mines are displayed in the losing game.

 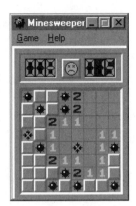

To start a new game, choose New from the Game menu, or click the smiley face.

The counter in the upper left portion of the Minesweeper window indicates the number of unmarked mines in the minefield. The counter in the upper right portion of the Minesweeper window displays the elapsed game time from the instant you uncover the first square. The clock stops when you finish the game—or when it finishes you.

You can mark squares that you think contain mines by right-clicking them. When you mark a square, the number in the counter displaying the total number of mines is decreased even if the square doesn't actually contain a mine. This can be misleading.

If you're not certain that a square contains a mine, right-click twice to mark it with a question mark. If you mark a square with a question mark, you can clear the question mark by right-clicking. You can then uncover the square by clicking the square or mark it as a mine square by right-clicking again. You can disable the feature that lets you mark squares with question marks by choosing Marks (?) from the Game menu to clear its check mark.

Customizing Minesweeper's Levels of Play

Minesweeper offers three levels of difficulty—Beginner, Intermediate, and Expert. You can also specify custom levels. To specify the degree of difficulty, choose the level from the Game menu.

The Beginner level is the default and presents a grid of 8 rows by 8 columns with 10 mines. Intermediate uses a 16 by 16 grid with 40 mines. Expert uses a 16 by 30 grid with 99 mines.

You can set a custom level by choosing Custom from the Game menu. The Custom Field dialog box appears, as shown in Figure 22-3.

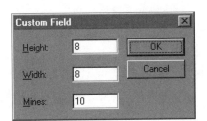

FIGURE 22-3.

The Custom Field dialog box lets you control the difficulty.

Enter the number of rows you want (up to a maximum of 24) in the Height box, the number of columns (up to 30) in the Width box, and the number of mines (from 10 to 667, depending on grid size). Then click the OK button.

NOTE: Whichever level you choose becomes the new default.

Keeping Score

You're playing against the clock, so you improve your score by winning as quickly as possible. As soon as you win (or lose), the timing counter stops so you can see how long the game lasted.

Minesweeper keeps track of the best winning times for each of the three predefined levels but not for custom levels. To display your best times, choose Best Times from the Game menu.

Strategies for Successful Minesweeping

Your first click in a new game is a "safe" one. You won't blow up with this first move, no matter where you make it. Your second click is another matter, however.

Once you've uncovered a few squares, you can start to deduce which squares are the most likely to be concealing mines. The following tips might help:

■ Remember that the number that is revealed in a square you click indicates the number of mines in the surrounding squares.

■ If you uncover a square labeled 1, and there is only one covered square next to it, it must contain a mine. Mark the uncovered square by right-clicking it.

■ If you're not sure about the contents of a square, mark it with a question mark (two right-clicks), and then clear it or mark it as a mine square later.

■ If you point at an uncovered square that contains a number and press both mouse buttons, Minesweeper flashes the surrounding squares. If you have already marked the requisite number, Minesweeper uncovers the remaining surrounding squares, saving you the time and effort of clicking each one individually.

Playing Hearts

Yes, this is the same traditional card game you played with grandma. The only difference is that the other players can be anywhere in the world, connected only by a modem or a network. (To play Hearts via modem, players must connect to the network using Dial-Up Networking.) And if you can't rustle up anyone to play with, you can play against the computer.

When you start Hearts, the dialog box shown in Figure 22-4 is displayed. (Hearts bypasses this dialog box if your computer is not connected to a network.)

■ To join an existing game and play with others on a network, select the I Want To Connect To Another Game option button. If you select this option and click OK, Hearts then asks for the name of the dealer's computer. (Note that it's not looking for the dealer's name, but the name of the dealer's *computer.*)

■ To play a stand-alone game against the computer or to initiate a game with others, select I Want To Be Dealer.

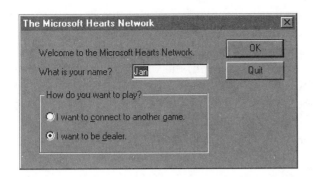

FIGURE 22-4.

When you start Hearts, you have a choice of joining someone else's game or starting your own.

To begin a new game, press F2 or choose New Game from the Game menu. (Only the dealer can start a new game, so if you chose the first option, you must wait for the dealer.)

Rules of the Game

The goal of Hearts is to end up with the lowest score. When you begin a new game, each player is dealt a hand of 13 cards. As shown in Figure 22-5, your cards are face up while the other players' cards are face down.

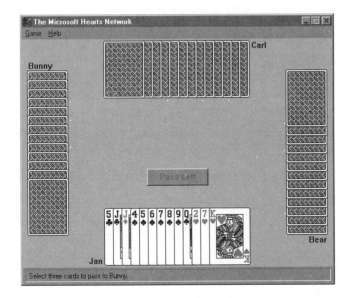

FIGURE 22-5.

An opening Hearts hand.

The game begins with each player selecting three cards to pass to another player. To pass cards, click each card you want to pass, and when you have selected three cards, click the Pass button.

After the cards have been passed, the player with the two of clubs begins play. Play moves in a clockwise direction—players must play a club if they have one; otherwise, they may play any card except a game card. To play a card, you simply click the card when it's your turn.

Each round of play is called a *trick*, and the player with the highest card in the lead suit (the suit that begins the trick) takes the trick. The player who takes the trick gets points for each heart or for the queen of spades; the same player then leads the next trick. The first trick is the only one that must begin with a specific suit.

Play continues until all cards are played. This is considered a *hand*. At the end of each hand, Hearts displays the scores and then begins the next hand. The game ends when one player accumulates 100 points or more. The player with the lowest score at that point is the winner.

You can check out the score of the current game by choosing Score from the Game menu. A Score Sheet dialog box appears with the scores for all the players.

The rules of hearts are pretty simple:

- The queen of spades counts as 13 points.

- Each heart counts as 1 point.

- No points are awarded for other cards.

- Aces are considered high cards.

- In order to end up with a low score, you want to avoid taking tricks that include the queen of spades or any hearts.

- You can't play a game card (the queen of spades or any heart) on the first trick.

- You can't lead with a heart until hearts have been "broken" (unless you have no other suits). Hearts are broken when a player uses a heart during a trick.

Shooting the Moon

This technique can be the fast track to winning at Hearts. If you can win all of the hearts and the queen of spades in one hand, you get 0 points and the other players each get 26 points. If you are dealt a hand with lots of high-value hearts and spades, consider trying this strategy. Be careful though! If any other player gets even one heart or the queen of spades, the strategy fails and you can end up with unwanted points.

Hearts Options

After you've played a few games of Hearts, you might want to customize certain options. Hearts provides a variety of options to suit you:

- By default, sounds are turned off. If you turn on sounds, Hearts uses sounds to proclaim when hearts are broken, when the queen of spades is played, and so on. You can turn on sounds, or turn them off again, by choosing Sounds from the Game menu.

- To change the animation speed, choose Options from the Game menu and click the Slow, Normal, or Fast option button.

- To change the names of the computer players—when you don't have four live players—choose Options from the Game menu and then enter the names you want to use in the Computer Player Names text boxes.

Strategies for Successful Hearts Play

The most obvious strategy is simply to try to get rid of your hearts, the queen of spades, and other high cards as quickly as possible. But there's more to it—if there weren't, where would the challenge be? The following tips and guidelines will help in your quest for that winning hand:

- If the cards you're dealt include the queen of spades, don't give away the ace or king of spades if you have them. You can often use these cards to take a trick when otherwise you would have to play the queen of spades.

- Unless you're trying to shoot the moon (or trying to prevent someone else from doing so), try not to take any tricks that include hearts or the queen of spades.

- Try to get rid of the queen of spades as quickly as possible. Until you get rid of it, don't worry too much about your hearts.

- Notice which player takes the queen of spades and try to determine whether that player may be trying to shoot the moon by taking all the hearts as well. If you see that happening, it's in your interest to win at least one heart, if possible, to thwart the attempt.

- Try to get rid of all the cards in one or more suits. When you have no more cards in any one suit, you can then play any card you like when another player leads with that suit.

Playing Solitaire

The Solitaire game that comes with Windows 95 is a computerized version of the addictive card game known as Klondike. If you've played solitaire with a deck of cards, you'll have no trouble adjusting to the program.

When the game is started, the deck appears in the upper left corner of the playing area with all the cards face down, and placeholders for four suit stacks appear in the upper right corner. Below the deck and the suit stack placeholders are seven row stacks, as shown in Figure 22-6.

The seven row stacks below the deck and suit stacks have one face-up card each. The row stack on the left end has only one card. The number of cards in each row stack increases by one, so the row stack on the right has seven cards.

The objective of the game—just like the card game—is to build four complete suit stacks, each containing all the cards of one suit from ace through king.

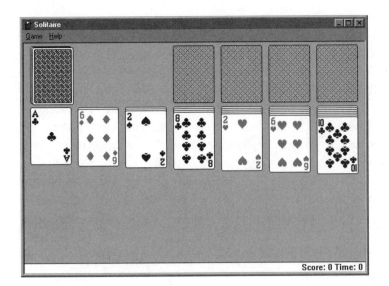

FIGURE 22-6.

The opening
Solitaire window.

Rules of the Game

You can add cards to the row stacks from the deck or from other row stacks
in decreasing order and alternating color. For example, you could move a
black three onto a red four.

You can add cards to the suit stacks only in consecutive, ascending
order. You can move cards to the suit stack from the top of the deck or
from the last card in a row stack.

To move cards from one place to another, drag them. As a shortcut
for moving a card to the suit stacks, you can double-click the card. For
example, if you double click an ace, it automatically jumps to an empty
suit stack.

If you create an empty row stack by moving some cards, you must
use a king to start that row stack.

When you move cards in the row stacks, you'll eventually uncover a
face-down card. You can turn over a face-down card by clicking it.

After exhausting all the available moves, you can deal more cards from the deck by clicking the deck. By default, three cards are dealt when you click the deck, but you must use the top card first. If the top card is an ace, double-click it to move it to an empty suit stack. It the card is not an ace, but it can be used in a row stack or an existing suit stack, drag it there. If you can't move the card anywhere, click the deck again to deal another three cards. If you run through all the cards in the deck, you can turn over the dealt cards by clicking the circle that appears when the last card has been dealt.

Figure 22-7 shows a Solitaire game in progress with all four suit stacks under construction. Notice the circle to the left of the cards that have been dealt.

FIGURE 22-7.

Click the circle to turn over the dealt cards so you can go through the deck again.

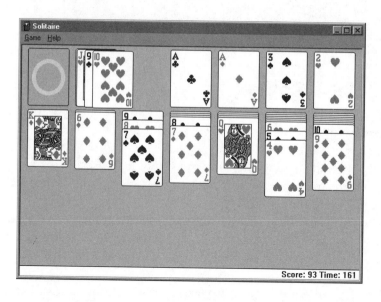

NOTE: When you get to the point that you can run through all the cards in the deck without being able to make any additional moves, the game is over.

Changing Game Options

To change the game's options, choose Options from the Game menu. The Options dialog box appears, as shown in Figure 22-8.

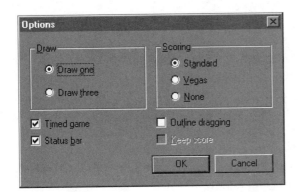

FIGURE 22-8.

The Options dialog box lets you select dealing and scoring options.

The Draw Three option specifies that three cards are dealt when you click the deck. You can choose the Draw One option to have only one card presented each time you click the deck, which makes the game less challenging—purists might even call it cheating. (If you select Draw One while using Vegas-style scoring, however, you're allowed only one pass through the deck.)

The Timed Game option lets you choose whether to time the game or not. If you uncheck the Status Bar check box, you won't be able to see your score or time.

If you're using a slower computer and you find that cards move in a jerky fashion when you drag them, choose the Outline Dragging option. With this check box selected, you'll drag only an outline of the card, which puts less stress on your computer's processing power.

The scoring options, Standard, Vegas, and None, are described in the next section.

In addition to making functional changes to the game with the Options dialog box, you can change the design that appears on your face-down cards by choosing Deck from the Game menu to display the Select Card Back dialog box. Just click the design that strikes your fancy, and then click the OK button.

Scoring

Solitaire lets you choose one of two methods for scoring your games. Or you can choose not to keep score. You select scoring options in the Options dialog box, shown in Figure 22-8. Choose Options from the Game menu to display this dialog box. By default, Solitaire uses Standard scoring and game timing, which awards points for various moves and deducts points for other moves and for playing too slowly.

When using Standard scoring, you receive 10 points for every card you move to a suit stack, 5 points for every card you move to a row stack, and 5 points if you turn over a card in a row stack. You lose 15 points if you move a card from a suit stack to a row stack, 20 points each time you turn the deck after the third pass through the deck (if you're using the default Draw Three option), and you lose 100 points each time you turn over the deck (if you're using the Draw One option).

When the Timed Game option is on, you lose 2 points for every ten seconds of play, but you'll receive bonus points at the end of a fast game. The faster your game, the more bonus points you'll receive.

If you choose Vegas scoring, you start the game by betting $52 and are awarded $5 for every card you move to a suit stack. The objective of the game when playing with Vegas scoring is to win back your $52 and more. Solitaire tracks your cumulative winnings if you also select the Keep Score check box.

With Vegas scoring, you're limited to three passes through the deck if you choose the Draw Three option, or only one pass if you choose Draw One.

Strategy Tips

Even though the objective of the game is to build up your suit stacks, you might find it useful to move a card from a suit stack to a row stack to make additional moves possible.

You can move a group of cards from one row stack to another by dragging the highest number card that you want to move and dropping it on the other row stack.

Pay attention to all the possible moves as you play. It's easy to be lulled into ignoring some possible moves as you focus on the most obvious. For example, after using one of the cards you were dealt, you might find that additional moves become possible between row stacks, or from row stacks to suit stacks.

 Tip You can undo any card move by choosing Undo from the Game menu.

Playing FreeCell

FreeCell is in some ways similar to Solitaire. The objective is to stack all of the cards in their respective suits, beginning with the ace. What's different about this game is that all of the cards are dealt face up—there's nothing hidden. Figure 22-9 shows a FreeCell game in progress.

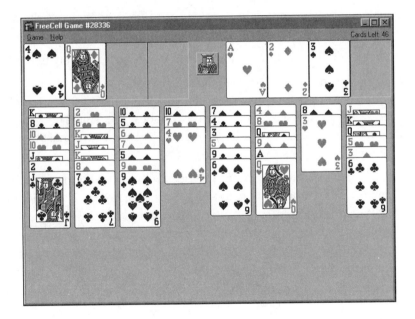

FIGURE 22-9.

The objective of FreeCell is to move cards to the home cells in the upper right corner.

The four rectangles in the upper left are the free cells. During play, you move cards to the free cells to get them out of the way temporarily. Each free cell can hold only one card; you cannot stack cards in a cell. In Figure 22-9, several low-numbered cards were uncovered by moving the four of spades and the queen of diamonds from the deck to free cells.

The four rectangles in the upper right are the home cells. That's where you build stacks for each suit, beginning with the ace. In Figure 22-9, notice that the ace of hearts has been moved to a home cell, but the two of hearts is tucked away at the top of the second column. The trick is to somehow move the rest of the cards in the column out of the way in order to get the two of hearts stacked on its home cell.

To move a card, click to select it, and then click where you want the card moved. You can cancel a move by clicking the card again. As a short-cut, you can double-click a card in the columns to move it directly to an open free cell.

Rules of the Game

You win FreeCell by moving all the cards to the home cells. Following are the legal moves in FreeCell:

- Only the bottom card in each column and cards in the free cells can be moved.

- The bottom card in any column can be moved to any empty free cell.

- Cards can be moved to a home cell from the bottom of any column or from a free cell. You can move a card to a home cell, however, only if the card is the next highest in a suit. The bottom card on each home cell must be an ace. The next card must be the two of that same suit, and so on.

- Cards can be stacked within the deck as in a traditional solitaire game (cards of opposite colors in descending order). Using Figure 22-9 as an example, you could move the jack of clubs in the first column onto the queen of hearts in the sixth column. This would free the two of clubs. You can move cards back and forth between the deck and the free cells.

- Any card can be moved to an empty column.

Sometimes you can't tell the suit of a card that's partially covered by other cards. To see the covered card entirely, right-click it.

Strategy Tips

FreeCell can be extremely frustrating at first—don't expect to jump right in and win every game. Relax and scope out the situation—FreeCell becomes more interesting as you become more familiar with it. Here are some tips:

- Study the deck. Know where your aces and other low cards are and get a sense of what you have to do to get at them.

- Try to keep at least one free cell open. Don't move a card to a free cell just because you can—if you do, you won't have an empty free cell when you really need it.

- Empty columns can be even more useful than empty free cells, because you can stack more than one card in them.

Changing Game Options

You can play 32,000 different hands of FreeCell. When you press F2 or choose New Game from the Game menu, FreeCell selects a game at random. To select a specific game, press F3 or choose Select Game from the Game menu, and enter the number of the game you want to play. If you want to play the same hand over, choose Restart Game.

Sharing and Communicating Information

Using Microsoft
Exchange

f you're like many computer users, you probably rely on a variety of forms of electronic communication to stay in touch with your business contacts and friends. Perhaps you use a network-based electronic mail system for exchanging memos and files with office mates, one or more public information services for sending messages to associates outside the office, and fax for communicating with people and businesses that aren't accessible via "e-mail."

Electronic communication is indispensable, but managing it can be a headache, particularly when you need to use several different programs and services to stay in touch with everyone. To relieve that headache, Windows 95 includes the Microsoft Exchange Inbox, a program that handles mail and fax communication from a single "information store." Exchange offers a rich-text message editor, a central set of address books, and a single set of folders that you can use to organize incoming mail and faxes, regardless of where they originated.

The Exchange editor, like a miniature word processor, includes a spelling checker and offers many formatting options. You can use a variety of fonts, styles, point sizes, and colors in your messages. Because the editor supports OLE, your messages can also include linked or embedded data objects. Attaching a spreadsheet to an e-mail note, for example, is as simple as dragging an icon from a folder window and dropping it into the editor window.

Exchange can work with any mail or fax service for which you have a suitable driver. Windows 95 includes drivers for the workgroup edition of Microsoft Mail, for Microsoft Fax, and for The Microsoft Network online service. The Microsoft Plus! add-on adds a driver for Internet mail. Drivers for other mail systems may be available from third parties.

The workgroup edition of Microsoft Mail allows you to exchange messages within a single workgroup on a local-area network. If you have installed Dial-Up Networking, you can also use the workgroup edition of Microsoft Mail to post and receive messages over telephone lines.

The Microsoft Exchange program included with Windows 95 can be expanded to provide connectivity with Microsoft Exchange Server, an advanced mail system that was not yet shipping at the time of Windows 95's debut. Exchange Server provides many additional capabilities, such as shared public folders, replication of shared folders across wide-area networks, and rules-based options for organizing folders and displaying messages. Upgrading to Microsoft Exchange Server requires a dedicated computer running Windows NT to host the server software, as well as an upgrade to the Microsoft Exchange program on each client computer.

This chapter covers the configuration and use of the standard Exchange Inbox, which we refer to from here on simply as Microsoft Exchange. (If you have upgraded to the Microsoft Exchange Server, your Inbox menus and dialog boxes will probably include additional options not described here.) The chapter assumes that you have already established accounts for whatever mail services you are planning to use. Issues involving the setup and administration of a Microsoft Mail post office, for example, lie beyond the scope of this chapter (and this book).

> **NOTE:** Because Exchange is an extensible platform, application software from Microsoft or third parties may also add functionality to the version of Exchange shipped with Windows 95. For example, if you have installed Microsoft Office 95, you might discover a WordMail Options command on Exchange's Compose menu, and when you compose a new message you might find yourself working in Microsoft Word 7.0 instead of in Exchange's own message editor! Be that as it may, this chapter should still serve as a reliable road map to the basic Exchange feature set.

See Also: For information about *Microsoft Fax*, see Chapter 24, "Using Microsoft Fax," page 641.

For information about *The Microsoft Network*, see Chapter 25, "Using The Microsoft Network," page 675.

For information about *Microsoft Plus!,* see Appendix A, "Using the Power of Your 486 or Pentium with Microsoft Plus!," page 727.

Installing and Running Exchange

If you've installed Microsoft Exchange, you probably have a desktop icon named Inbox and an item named Microsoft Exchange in the Programs section of your Start menu. If you haven't yet installed Exchange, you can do so as follows:

1. Choose Settings from the Start menu, and then choose Control Panel.

2. In Control Panel, double-click Add/Remove Programs, and then click the Windows Setup tab.

3. Select Microsoft Exchange, and then click the Details button.

4. Select the check box for Microsoft Exchange, as well as the check boxes for any mail services that you plan to use. Then click OK.

5. If you're also going to use Microsoft Fax, select its check box.

6. If you're going to use The Microsoft Network, select its check box.

7. Click OK to begin the installation.

Once you have installed Exchange, you can run it by double-clicking the Inbox icon on your desktop or by choosing Microsoft Exchange from the Programs section of your Start menu.

 If you use a LAN-based e-mail system, such as Microsoft Mail, you might want to consider putting Exchange in the Startup section of your Start menu. The program name you need in the shortcut's Command Line text box is Exchng32; this file is normally located in the \Program Files\Microsoft Exchange folder. For information about adding an item to the Start menu, see "Customizing the Start Menu," page 81.

Working with Profiles

Before you can use Exchange, you have to have something called a *profile*. A profile is a named collection of settings, encompassing the following details:

- The name and location of at least one *personal folder file*
- The name and location of a *personal address book*
- Configuration details for each mail service you plan to use

Immediately after you install Exchange, a wizard guides you through the creation of a profile. If you have already installed Exchange, therefore, your profile is probably already set up and your mail system is probably ready for use. If, for any reason, you do not have a working profile or you need to create a new one, you can do that by double-clicking the Mail And Fax item in Control Panel.

Although most users will find that one profile is enough, you can set up as many as you want. If you do have multiple profiles, those profiles can use the same personal address book and personal folder file.

See Also: For information about *creating a profile*, see "Creating a New Profile," page 594.

The Personal Folder File

Your personal folder file is a repository for incoming and outbound messages. Within the file, messages are kept in folders. Messages that you're about to send, for example, are stored in a folder called Outbox. Incoming messages arrive in a folder called Inbox. Messages that you have sent are (optionally) stored in a folder called Sent Items. You can create additional folders, including folders within folders, to help you organize your mail.

All messages in a personal folder file are kept in a single disk file with the extension .PST. This file is comparable to the .MMF file used by earlier versions of Microsoft Mail, except that the messages in a .PST file may have been sent to or originated in a variety of different mail systems, not just Microsoft Mail.

 If you're upgrading from a previous installation of Microsoft Mail or another LAN-based mail system, you may be able to import messages you sent and received under the previous system. To do this, choose Import from Exchange's File menu.

Your profile can include more than one personal folder file, although most users will find that one is enough.

 To protect your privacy, you can assign a password to your personal folder file. See "Assigning or Changing Your Personal Folder File's Password," page 597.

 You might want to keep separate personal folder files for current and archived messages.

 For information about *creating a personal folder file*, see "Adding or Removing a Mail Service," page 595.

The Personal Address Book

Your personal address book is a place where you can list the names, e-mail addresses, and other details about the people you contact most often. You will probably also have separate address books specific to particular mail services. For example, if you use Microsoft Mail, your mail administrator can maintain a global address book of Mail users on your network. You can add names to your personal address book at any time by copying them from service-specific address books.

 Your profile can have only one active personal address book, but you can create multiple personal address books and switch between them at any time. For details, see "Changing Your Personal Address Book," page 597.

Creating a New Profile

To create a profile, follow these steps:

1. Choose Settings from the Start menu, and then choose Control Panel.

2. Double-click the Mail And Fax item in Control Panel.

   This takes you to the Microsoft Exchange Settings property sheet.

3. Click the Show Profiles button.

4. Click the Add button.

   The Inbox Setup wizard, shown in Figure 23-1, appears.

5. Select the check box for each mail service you plan to use. Then click Next and fill out the rest of the wizard's dialog boxes.

FIGURE 23-1.

The Inbox Setup wizard guides you through the steps of creating a profile.

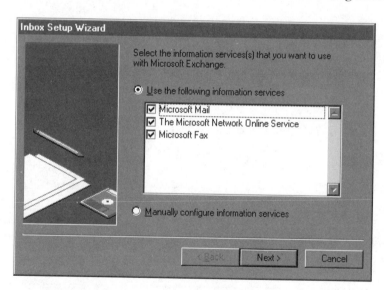

Modifying an Existing Profile

To modify an existing profile, follow these steps:

1. Choose Settings from the Start menu, and then choose Control Panel.

2. Double-click the Mail And Fax item in Control Panel.

3. Click the Show Profiles button.

4. Select the name of the profile you want to modify, and then click the Properties button.

Figure 23-2 shows the property sheet for a profile named MS Exchange Settings. The sheet includes three tabs, named Services, Delivery, and Addressing. The Services tab lists three mail services (Microsoft Fax, Microsoft Mail, and The Microsoft Network Online Service), a personal address book (Personal Address Book), and two personal folder files (My Current Messages and My Archived Messages). Note that while a personal folder file, an address book, and a mail service may seem like distinct fauna to you, Exchange regards them all as installable "services" and therefore lumps them together in this dialog box.

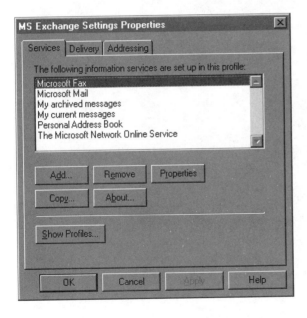

FIGURE 23-2.

In a profile's property sheet, you can add or remove mail services, change the order in which Exchange polls your mail services, and tailor the display of your address books.

Adding or Removing a Mail Service

To add a new mail service, simply click the Add button in the Services tab of your profile's property sheet, and then choose the service you want in the ensuing list. After you've done this, Exchange prompts you for whatever information it needs to set up the new service.

To remove a mail service, simply select its name in the Services tab of your profile's property sheet, and then click the Remove button.

Modifying a Mail Service's Properties

If you need to change any details about the way you interact with a mail service—such as your logon name, account number, password, or the number you use to connect to the service—you can do so by displaying the service's property sheet. First display the property sheet for your profile, following the instructions presented earlier in this section. Then, in the Services tab of the profile's property sheet, select the service you're interested in. Finally, click the Properties button. The choices available to you depend on the service in question. Figure 23-3 shows the property sheet for the Microsoft Mail service.

FIGURE 23-3.

You can change your logon name, account number, and other details associated with a mail service by displaying the service's property sheet.

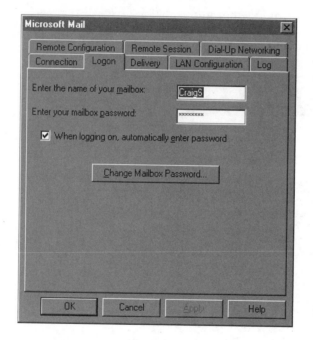

 You can also change service-specific properties from within Exchange. Choose Services from the Tools menu, select a service's name, and then click Properties to get to that service's property sheet.

Assigning or Changing Your Personal Folder File's Password

To password-protect your personal folder file, or to change the password associated with your personal folder file, display the property sheet for your profile, following the instructions presented earlier in this section. Then select the name of your personal folder file and click the Properties button. In the property sheet that appears, click the Change Password button, and then fill out the ensuing dialog box.

 To change the password you use for a specific mail system, visit the property sheet for that mail system. You can do that by choosing Services from Exchange's Tools menu, or by double-clicking the Mail And Fax item in Control Panel, selecting the mail service, and clicking the Properties button.

Changing Your Personal Address Book

A profile can have only one personal address book. But you can create several personal address books—for example, one for business contacts and one for personal contacts—and then switch between them.

To change personal address books, first display the property sheet for your profile, following the instructions presented earlier in this section. Then, in the Services tab of your profile's property sheet, select Personal Address Book. Finally, click the Properties button. Figure 23-4 on the next page shows the property sheet for a personal address book.

To switch to a different personal address book, enter a new filename on the Path line (or click the Browse button and point to a new filename). If you specify a file that doesn't exist, Exchange creates a new, empty personal address book. You can then populate this new book with entries stored in your other address books. If you specify an existing personal address book, Exchange makes that the active personal address book.

FIGURE 23-4.

You can maintain separate personal address books and switch between them. To switch, display this property sheet and enter a new filename on the Path line.

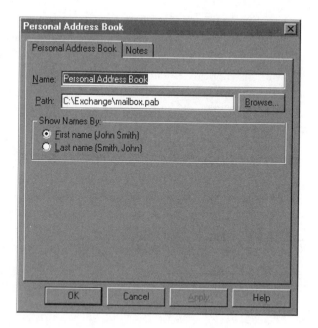

 For more information about *address books*, see "Working with Addresses and Address Books," page 622.

Sending and Receiving Mail

Most electronic messaging systems are based on the store-and-forward principle. The mail you send goes to a "post office" on some other computer—a server on your network, for example, or a computer maintained by The Microsoft Network—and waits there until your recipients come to collect it. When Exchange delivers your outbound mail to a mail service's post office, it retrieves any messages waiting for you at that post office and deposits them in the inbox of your personal folder file. This process is sometimes called *polling.*

Exactly when polling occurs depends on the mail service. You may be able to schedule regular delivery/pickup times by visiting the property sheet for each service you use.

For example, if you're using Microsoft Mail, your system polls, by default, every 10 minutes. You can change this interval by going to the Delivery tab of the Microsoft Mail property sheet. (To get to the property sheet, double-click the Mail And Fax item in Control Panel, select Microsoft Mail, and click the Properties button. Or, from within Exchange, choose Services from the Tools menu, select Microsoft Mail, and then click Properties.)

 When Exchange retrieves new mail for you, a letter icon appears in your notification area. You can double-click this icon to display your inbox. Once you have opened all new messages, the letter icon disappears.

Sending and Receiving on Demand

If your mail service doesn't offer scheduled polling times, or if you want to transfer mail immediately, choose the Deliver Now Using command on Exchange's Tools menu. A submenu appears, listing each of your mail services. Choose the one you want to poll.

The submenu also includes an All Services command. If you choose this, Exchange polls each service in turn, following an order specified in your profile's property sheet. To change this order, double-click the Mail And Fax item in Control Panel. Then click the Show Profiles button, select the name of your profile, and click Properties. In the property sheet, click the Delivery tab.

As Figure 23-5 shows, the Delivery tab of your profile's property sheet lists all your information services and shows the order in which the system polls in response to a Deliver Now Using All Services command. To move a service up or down in this polling order, select it in the list, and then click either the upward or downward pointing arrow.

 Ctrl-M is the keyboard shortcut for the Deliver Now Using All Services command.

FIGURE 23-5.

When you choose the Deliver Now Using All Services command on Exchange's Tools menu, the system polls your mail services in the order listed on this property sheet.

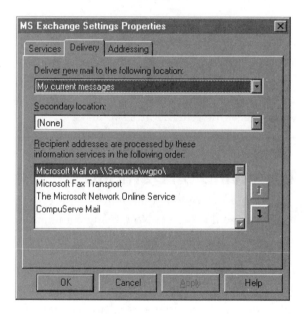

Creating Mail

To create a new message, start by pressing Ctrl-N, clicking the New Message tool (the third tool from the left in Exchange's default toolbar, shown

in Table 23-1), or choosing New Message from the Compose menu.
Exchange presents a new message window, as shown in Figure 23-6 on the
next page.

Table 23-1. Exchange Toolbar

Toolbar Icon	Description
	Moves up one level to parent of currently displayed folder
	Displays (or hides) the folder-list pane
	Creates a new message to another user
	Prints the selected message
	Moves the selected message
	Deletes the selected message
	Replies to the sender of the selected message
	Replies to the sender and all recipients of the selected message
	Forwards the selected message
	Opens the address book
	Opens the Inbox folder
	Displays the help pointer, which causes Exchange to display help about the next item you click

In the top portion of the new message window, you enter the names
of your addressees, the names of those to whom you want a courtesy
copy (Cc) sent, and a subject heading for your message. The large space
at the bottom of the window is where you type your message.

FIGURE 23-6.

To create a message, press Ctrl-N and fill in the blanks. You can enter addresses by clicking the To or Cc button and then selecting names from your address books.

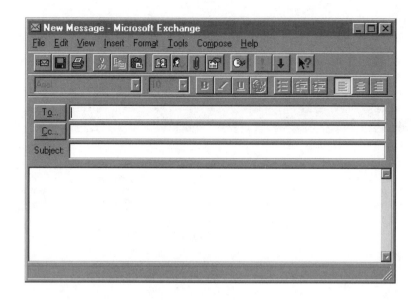

Addressing a Message

You can include as many names as you please on both the To and Cc lines. The easiest way to supply this information is by picking names from one or more of your address books. And the easiest way to get to your address books is by simply clicking the To or Cc button. Clicking either button gets you an Address Book window similar to the one shown in Figure 23-7.

To address your message, select names in the left side of this window, and then click the To or Cc button.

If the names you need are in a different address book, start by selecting that address book from the drop-down list in the upper right corner of the window.

The address book that appears first in the window shown in Figure 23-7 is determined by the property sheet for your profile. You can change this by going to the Addressing tab of your profile's property sheet.

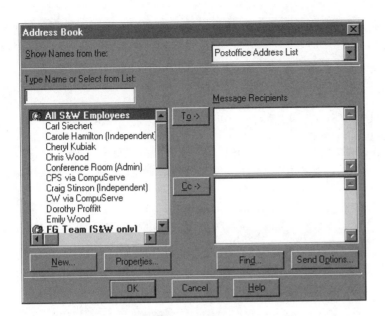

FIGURE 23-7.

To address your message, select an address book from the drop-down list at the upper right corner of this window. Then select names and click the To or Cc button.

 To speed up the selection of an addressee's name, simply begin typing the name in the Type Name text box, near the upper left corner of the Address Book window. Exchange scrolls the list to the entry that most closely matches what you've typed.

 As an alternative way to address a message, start by displaying your address book. (Click the Address Book tool, press Ctrl-Shift-B, or choose Address Book from the Tools menu.) In the address book, select one or more names (hold down Ctrl while clicking to select multiple names), and then click the New Message tool (or press Ctrl-N) to get to the message form—with your selected names on the To line.

Using and Customizing Exchange's Toolbar

All of Exchange's toolbars include tool tips. If you're not sure what a tool does, rest your mouse on it for a half-second or so and read the description that emerges.

Two of Exchange's toolbars—the ones directly below the menu bar in the Exchange window and the message window—are customizable. You can tailor either toolbar to your preference by choosing Customize Toolbar from the Tools menu. You'll see a display like the following:

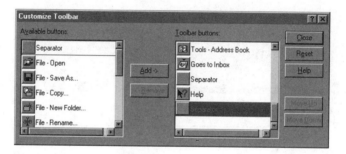

The window on the right shows the toolbar's current layout, including the separators between groups of tools. The window on the left shows tools that you can add to the toolbar.

To add a tool, select it in the left window and click the Add button. To remove a tool, select it in the right window and click the Remove button. To move a tool to the left in the current toolbar layout, select it in the right window and click the Move Up button. To move a tool to the right, select it and click Move Down. To restore the default toolbar arrangement, click Reset.

Sending a Message to a Distribution List

If you find yourself regularly sending messages to the same group of recipients, you might want to assemble those recipients in a distribution list. You can then simply specify the name of the list on your To or Cc line.

See Also: For information about *creating distribution lists*, see "Creating Personal Distribution Lists," page 625.

Entering Recipients' Names "by Hand"

You can also address a message by typing the names of your recipients on the To and Cc lines, using semicolons to separate multiple recipients. If you're not sure how an addressee's name is spelled, simply type a portion of the name. When you send your message, Exchange checks your address lines against all available address books. If what you've typed is sufficient to identify your addressees uniquely, Exchange finishes the typing for you. If not, Exchange presents a list of candidates and lets you choose the recipient you want. For example, if all you type on the To line is the letter *C*, Exchange presents a list of everyone in all your address books whose name starts with *C.*

Sending Blind Courtesy Copies

In addition to the To and Cc lines, the message window can include an optional Bcc (blind courtesy copy) line. Each recipient you specify on the Bcc line receives a copy of your message, but other recipients (those on the To and Cc lines) do not see the names of the Bcc recipients.

To display the Bcc line in your message window, choose Bcc Box from the message window's View menu.

Composing a Message

To compose your message, simply type in the big box at the bottom of the message window. As mentioned, this part of the window acts like a reasonably sophisticated word processor, with plenty of formatting options.

Using the Formatting Toolbar

While you type your message, you can take advantage of the tools on the message window's formatting toolbar, shown in Table 23-2 on the next page.

You can also apply these options by choosing commands on the Format menu. The Format menu's Font command also includes a strikeout option, which does not have a toolbar equivalent.

Table 23-2. Exchange Formatting Toolbar

Toolbar Icon	Description
MS Sans Serif (Western)	Changes the font (typeface) of the selection
10	Changes the font size of the selection
B	Changes the selection to boldface (or, if the selection is already boldface, changes it back to normal)
I	Changes the selection to italic (or, if the selection is already italic, changes it back to normal)
U	Underlines the selection (or, if the selection is already underlined, removes the underline)
	Changes the color of the selection
	Changes the selected paragraphs to an indented, bulleted list (or, if the selection is already bulleted, removes the bullets and indents)
	Decreases left indent
	Increases left indent
	Left aligns the selected paragraphs
	Center aligns the selected paragraphs
	Right aligns the selected paragraphs

Exchange's default font for original messages is 10-point Arial regular, in black. To choose a different font, color, or style, choose Options from Exchange's Tools menu. Click the Send tab in the Options dialog, and then click the Font button.

 Keyboard shortcuts for boldface, italic, and underline are Ctrl-B, Ctrl-I, and Ctrl-U, respectively.

Rearranging Text with Drag and Drop

You can rearrange text in a message by using the traditional cut and paste procedures. Alternatively, if a block of text is out of place, you can simply select it and drag it to wherever it's supposed to go.

To copy a block of text instead of moving it, hold down the Ctrl key while you drag.

Using Find and Replace to Edit Text

Exchange's message editor includes Find and Replace commands comparable to those found in most word processing programs. You'll find these commands on the Edit menu. The shortcuts are Ctrl-Shift-F for Find and Ctrl-H for Replace.

Inserting Text from a File

If you plan to mail a body of text that already exists in another application, you can copy it to the Clipboard and paste it into your message. If the text is stored on disk, however, you'll find it easier to choose the File command from the message window's Insert menu. This brings up a variant of the File Open common dialog box. In the top part of this dialog box, choose the name of the file you want to insert. In the bottom part of the dialog box, choose the Text Only option button. Click OK, and your text will appear in the message window.

Attaching a Document

An *attachment* is a document or other file embedded in or linked to an e-mail message. Attachments allow you to send nontextual data via electronic mail or fax. Your recipient sees the attachment as an icon and can render the attached data by double-clicking the icon. Other file-processing options appear when the recipient right-clicks the icon.

If the attachment is embedded, your recipient must have an application capable of rendering the embedded data. Typically, that application is the program that created the original document, but it doesn't have to be. If you attach a Microsoft Excel worksheet, for example, your recipient may be able to read it in another spreadsheet program as well as in Excel. Alternatively, your recipient can use the Windows 95 Quick View feature to make the data visible (assuming Quick View capability is available for the type of data you're attaching).

If the attachment is linked to your message, your recipient must have access to the original data. Typically you would link, rather than embed, when your recipient is another user on your own local-area network and has no need for a separate copy of the file. Linking may also be preferable to embedding when you're sending the same data to a large number of recipients. Embedding a copy of the attachment for each recipient would consume a lot of disk space on whatever machine was acting as the post office for your network mail system.

To attach a file to a message, do the following:

1. In the message window, choose File from the Insert menu.

2. In the top part of the dialog box that appears, choose the file you want to attach.

3. In the bottom part of the dialog box, select the An Attachment option button.

4. If you want to link the attached file, select the check box labeled "Link attachment to original file." If you want to embed the attachment, be sure this check box is not selected.

5. Click OK to return to your message window.

 To attach more than one file, hold down the Ctrl key while you select the files.

 You can also embed an attached file by dragging the file from a folder or Windows Explorer window and dropping it into your message window.

 For information about *Quick View*, see "Inspecting Documents and Programs with Quick View," page 67.

For information about *saving attachments*, see "Saving Attachments," page 620.

Attaching Another Message

Exchange includes a Forward command that allows you to forward copies of messages you've received, with optional comments from you, to other recipients.

Another way to forward a message is to create a new message, and then embed or link the message you want to forward. To do that, choose the Message command from the message window's Insert menu. In the dialog box that appears, point to the message you want to attach.

See Also: For information about *forwarding a message*, see "Forwarding Messages," page 620.

Embedding or Linking an Object

Attachments embed or link entire files. You can also embed or link a portion of a file (an *object*) provided the file originates in a program that supports OLE. To embed or link an object, copy it from its source application to the Clipboard. Then choose the Paste Special command from the message window's Edit menu.

See Also: For more information about *embedding and linking*, see Chapter 10, "Exchanging Information: The Clipboard and OLE," page 251.

Printing an Outbound Message

To create a printed copy of a message you're about to send, choose Print from the message window's File menu or click the Print tool.

Checking the Spelling of Your Messages

To check the spelling of a particular message, press F7 while that message is displayed. (Alternatively, choose Spelling from the message window's

Tools menu.) To have Exchange check the spelling of all messages before they're posted, do the following:

1. Choose Options from the Tools menu.

2. Click the Spelling tab.

3. On the Spelling tab (see Figure 23-8), select the check box labeled "Always check spelling before sending."

4. Select any of the other options shown in Figure 23-8, and then click OK.

FIGURE 23-8.

You can spell-check particular messages or, by filling out this dialog box, have Exchange automatically spell-check every message you compose.

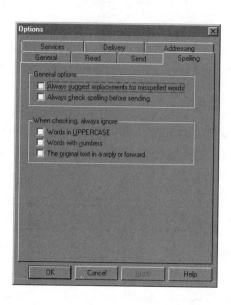

Posting a Message

When you've finished composing your message, you can post it by doing any of the following:

- Clicking the Send tool, the first tool on the left on the message window's default toolbar, which is shown in Table 23-3

- Choosing the Send command from the message window's File menu

- Pressing Ctrl-Enter, the keyboard shortcut for the Send command

Table 23-3. New Message Toolbar

Toolbar Icon	Description
	Sends message
	Saves message in a disk file
	Prints message
	Standard Clipboard operations: cut, copy, and paste
	Opens address book
	Checks names against address book
	Inserts a file in the message
	Displays the message's property sheet
	Requests a read receipt
	Sets importance to high
	Sets importance to low

When you post a message, Exchange stores it temporarily in your Outbox folder. It stays in that folder until Exchange has polled the mail systems through which each of the message's recipients is addressed. At that point, the message moves to your Sent Items folder—unless you have asked Exchange not to retain copies of your sent mail.

For information about *polling*, see "Sending and Receiving Mail," page 598.

For information about *the Sent Items folder*, see "Retaining Copies of Your Posted Messages," page 616.

If Your Message Cannot Be Delivered

Occasionally, one of your outbound messages may prove undeliverable. This can happen, for example, if a recipient is no longer at the e-mail address you've used, if some component of the delivery sequence—such as a gateway between two e-mail systems—is not working, or if you abort the transmission of a long message yourself.

If one of your messages cannot be delivered, you will be notified in a message from the "System Administrator"—which is actually Exchange itself, not a person in your organization. Figure 23-9 shows an example of such a message. As you can see, the message provides some information about what went wrong and also includes a Send Again button that you can use when you're ready to make another try. You can use this button at any time. If you don't want to resend right away, simply leave the System Administrator message in your inbox and return to it when you think the telecommunications gods are more favorably disposed to transmitting your mail.

FIGURE 23-9.

If a message cannot be delivered, the "System Administrator" lets you know—in a special form that includes a handy Send Again button.

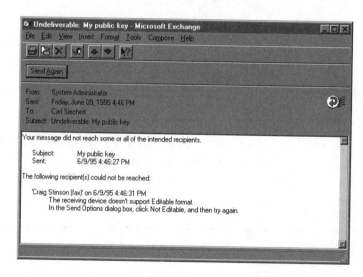

Importance Options

Exchange can send mail at three levels of importance—high, normal, and low. Messages that you send with the high importance option will be flagged with a red exclamation point in your recipients' inboxes. Messages that you send with the low importance option will be flagged with a downward-pointing black arrow. Messages of normal importance are not flagged with either symbol.

You'll find tools for changing the level of importance to high or low on the default message window toolbar. You can mark an outbound message as a high-importance or low-importance item by clicking the exclamation point or downward arrow before you send it. Alternatively, you can choose Properties from the message window's File menu. In the property sheet (see Figure 23-10), choose one of the buttons in the Importance option-button group.

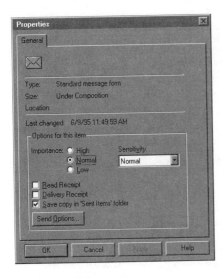

FIGURE 23-10.

The property sheet for a message lets you set importance and sensitivity options for that message.

The default importance level is normal, and it's unlikely that you'll want to change it to high or low for all your messages. If you do, however, Exchange will accommodate you. Choose Options from Exchange's Tools menu and click the Send tab. In the Send dialog box (see Figure 23-11 on the next page), choose one of the buttons in the Set Importance option-button group.

NOTE: Particular mail systems may offer their own importance or priority options. If the options provided by the service you're using differ from those of Exchange (for example, if your service provides four or more importance levels), you should ignore

FIGURE 23-11.

By choosing Options from Exchange's Tools menu and clicking the Send tab, you can set defaults for all your outgoing messages.

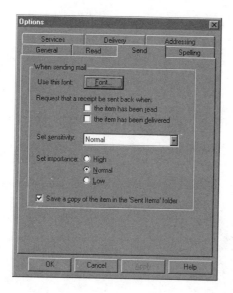

Exchange's options. Instead, before posting a message, choose Send Options from the message window's File menu. Click the tab for your mail service, and then choose options from that dialog box. To set a new default for a particular service, choose Options from Exchange's Tools menu, click the Services tab, select the name of the service, and then click Properties.

Sensitivity Options

In addition to the three importance options, Exchange offers four mutually exclusive sensitivity options: Normal, Personal, Private, and Confidential. Messages marked Personal, Private, or Confidential will be flagged as such in the Sensitivity column of your recipients' personal folder files—provided your recipients choose to display the Sensitivity column. (For information about displaying particular columns, see "Customizing the Column Layout," page 632.) Your recipients will also see a description of each message as personal, private, or confidential in the status bar of their message windows—assuming they have chosen to display the status bar.

In addition, messages sent with the Private sensitivity option arrive in read-only mode. That is, your recipients will not be able to edit these messages, even when they reply to them or forward them.

The default sensitivity setting is Normal. To send a message with a different setting, choose Properties from the message window's File menu (or click the Properties tool). Then, in your message's property sheet (see Figure 23-10), choose one of the options in the Sensitivity drop-down list. To change the default sensitivity setting from Normal to Personal, Private, or Confidential, choose Options from Exchange's Tools menu and then click the Send tab. In the Send dialog box (see Figure 23-11), choose an option from the Set Sensitivity drop-down list.

Receipt Options

You may request two types of receipts for messages that you send: delivery receipts and read receipts. A delivery receipt is returned to your inbox as soon as your message has been delivered to your recipient's inbox. A read receipt is returned when your recipient has opened your message. You can request either or both of these receipts for particular messages or for all messages.

To request either type of receipt for a particular message, choose the Properties command from the message window's File menu. Then select either or both of the receipt check boxes near the bottom of the property sheet. (See Figure 23-10 on page 613.)

To request receipts of either type for all your messages, choose Options from Exchange's Tools menu, click the Send tab, and then select either or both of the receipt check boxes in the ensuing dialog box. (See Figure 23-11.)

Exchange does not display any kind of obvious flag to alert you that a sender has requested a read or delivery receipt for a message you've received. To see whether a receipt has been requested, check the message's properties. You can do that by pressing Alt-Enter in the message window or by selecting the item in Exchange and clicking the Properties tool.

Retaining Copies of Your Posted Messages

By default, copies of your outbound messages are retained in your Sent Items folder after the messages are delivered. Thus, you have a record of everything you send, and you can copy or move posted messages from the Sent Items folder to any other folders that you set up for organizing your correspondence.

If you prefer not to retain copies of your posted messages, you can turn this default off. Choose Options from Exchange's Tools menu and click the Send tab in the ensuing dialog box. (See Figure 23-11 on page 614.) Then deselect the check box labeled "Save a copy of the item in the 'Sent Items' folder."

If you decide not to retain copies of sent messages by default, you can still retain copies of particular messages. Before you post a message that you want to retain, choose Properties from the message window's File menu (or click its toolbar equivalent). At the bottom of the property sheet (see Figure 23-10 on page 613), select the check box labeled "Save copy in 'Sent Items' folder."

Reading and Replying to Your Mail

By default, Exchange signals the arrival of new mail by displaying an envelope in the notification area of your taskbar. Double-clicking the envelope opens your inbox, where you'll find new messages listed in boldface type. To read a message, double-click its entry in your inbox (or in any other folder), or select it and press Enter. To close a message, press Esc or click the message window's close button.

Notification Options

Having an icon appear in your notification area might not be an adequate way to herald the arrival of important mail, particularly if you don't keep your taskbar visible at all times. If you want to be sure you know about new messages the moment they arrive, you can have Exchange beep or play a tune, change the mouse pointer momentarily, or display a message in the center of your screen. To amplify the notification in any or all of these ways, choose Options from Exchange's Tools menu. In the top section of the dialog box that appears (see Figure 23-12), choose the methods by which you want to be notified.

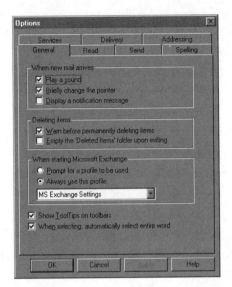

FIGURE 23-12.

If you want to be aware of new mail the instant it arrives, choose any or all of the three options in the top section of this dialog box.

If you choose the Play A Sound option, Exchange will play whatever wave file you've assigned to the New Mail Notification event in the Sounds section of Control Panel. If you don't have a sound board in your computer, you'll hear a simple beep when new mail arrives.

If you choose the Briefly Change The Pointer option, Exchange will turn your customary mouse pointer into an envelope for a second or so. This is a subtle form of notification, to say the least.

For an announcement that you can scarcely miss, choose Display A Notification Message. When new mail arrives, you'll be informed by means of a dialog box, and by clicking Yes in that dialog box you'll be able to go directly to the first new message. This option may be useful at times when responding to new mail is your top priority. At other times, you may find it an irritant. (And because the dialog box is "application-modal," you'll have to respond to it before you'll be allowed to do anything else in Exchange.)

While you're reading messages, you can move to the next message in the current folder by pressing Ctrl-> or clicking the Next tool on the message window's toolbar. To move to the previous message, press Ctrl-< or click the Previous tool.

Replying to Mail

To reply to a message, simply click the Reply To Sender or Reply To All tool on the message window's toolbar. (Or, if you prefer, choose these commands from the Compose menu.) Exchange opens a new message window with the address lines already filled out.

 If you choose Reply To All, your reply will go not just to the sender but also to all direct and Cc recipients—including yourself. If you'd rather not have your own outbound mail coming back at you, select your name on the To line of the reply and press the Del key.

Including the Original Message with Your Reply

By default, Exchange includes the text of the original message at the end of your reply. A line separates your reply from the original message, and the original text is indented. Including the original message with your reply can help both you and those with whom you're corresponding follow the thread of a discussion, but it does make for verbose communication. If you prefer not to include the original, choose Options from Exchange's Tools menu, click the Read tab to get to the dialog box shown in Figure 23-13, and de-select the check box labeled "Include the original text when replying."

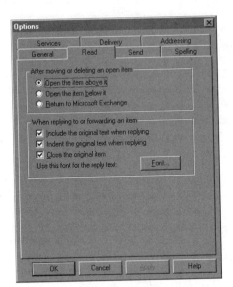

FIGURE 23-13.

Exchange normally includes the original message text when you use the Reply To Sender or Reply To All command.

If you sometimes maintain long chains of replies and counter-replies in your messages, you might want to turn off the automatic indenting of original text. Otherwise, the earliest entries in the chain may be crammed into a very narrow space at the right side of your message window. To turn off indenting, deselect the Indent The Original Text When Replying check box in the dialog box shown in Figure 23-13.

Choosing a Default Reply Font

The dialog box shown in Figure 23-13 also lets you choose a default font for your replies. Exchange normally gives you a bright blue font to help your reply stand out from the original message. With this sharply contrasting font, you can also easily interpolate comments into original text when you send back a reply.

You might want to choose a default reply font that's different in color, face, or size from fonts used by others in your workgroup. That way, if you create messages with lengthy chains of replies to replies, readers will more easily recognize which comments are yours. To specify a default reply font, click the Font button in the dialog box shown in Figure 23-13. (Be aware, though, that if you choose a font that recipients don't have on their systems, they will see a substituted font. For example, if you send OddBallSerif, your recipient will probably see Times New Roman.)

Forwarding Messages

To forward a message, do any of the following:

- Click the Forward tool on either the message window's or the Exchange window's toolbar.

- Choose Forward from the Compose menu.

- Press Ctrl-F.

Exchange opens a new message window with the text of the original message displayed below a separator line. Fill out the address portion of the window, add your comments (if any) above the separator line, and click the Send tool (or press Ctrl-Enter).

Editing Messages

Unless a message has been sent with the Private sensitivity option, you're free to edit it. When you close the message window, Exchange will ask whether you want to preserve or discard your changes.

Saving Attachments

If a message has an embedded file ("attachment"), you can view the embedded file by double-clicking its icon. You might find it convenient, however, to save the attachment as a separate file—to "detach" it from your message. You can do that as follows:

1. Choose Save As from the File menu.

2. Select the Save These Attachments Only option button, near the bottom of the Save As dialog box.

3. If your message has more than one attachment, select the one(s) you want to save in the list that appears below the Save These Attachments Only option button.

Printing Messages

To print a message, press Ctrl-P, choose Print from the File menu, or click the Print tool on the toolbar. You can do this either from within a message window or from any Exchange folder. From an Exchange folder, you can select multiple messages (hold down the Ctrl key while you select) before issuing the Print command.

Moving or Copying Messages to Other Folders

After you have finished reading a message, you might want to move or copy the message from your Inbox folder to another folder. You can do this without leaving the message window by choosing the Move or Copy command from the File menu. (The keyboard shortcuts for these commands are Ctrl-Shift-M and Ctrl-Shift-C, respectively.) Exchange displays an outline diagram of your folder structure, allowing you to point to the folder to which you want your message moved or copied.

You can also use drag and drop to move and copy messages between folders.

For more information about *moving and copying messages*, see "Using Folders to Manage Your Personal Folder File," page 628.

Deleting Messages

If after reading a message, you never want to see it again, click the Delete tool on the toolbar, press Ctrl-D, or choose Delete from the File menu. Your message will be relocated to the Deleted Items folder. When the deleted message departs for good is up to you. If you want to purge the Deleted Items folder each time you quit Exchange, choose Options from the Tools menu. In the General tab of the Options dialog box (see Figure 23-12 on page 617), select the check box labeled "Empty the 'Deleted Items' folder upon exiting." If you do not select this check box, your deleted mail remains in the Deleted Items folder until you purge that folder yourself—by selecting items there and deleting them once more.

Working with Addresses and Address Books

Exactly what address books you have available to you in Exchange depends on what mail services you're using and how you're connected to those services. If you use Microsoft Mail and are on line with your network's post office, for example, you will normally have access to the Post-office Address List. This is an address book, maintained by your Mail administrator, containing entries for everyone with an account at your Microsoft Mail post office. If you use Microsoft Mail but work off line, that address book will not be available to you.

On the other hand, The Microsoft Network online service does not provide you with a locally stored address book. To send mail to an MSN user, you can connect to MSN and use the online service's member-search facility. But because there's no locally stored MSN address book, you'll want to be sure to add the names of your regular MSN correspondents to your personal address book in Exchange.

Displaying Your Address Books

To display any available address book, click the Address Book tool on Exchange's toolbar, press Ctrl-Shift-B, or choose Address Book from the Tools menu. You'll see a window similar to that shown in Figure 23-14.

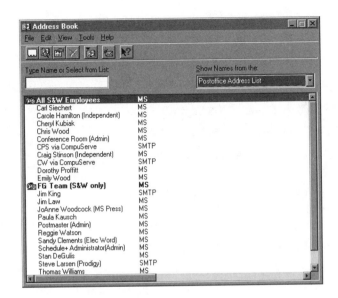

FIGURE 23-14.

The Address Book window displays all the names in a particular address book. Some address books show additional information in columns to the right of the names.

The drop-down list at the upper right corner of this display tells you which address book you're looking at and lets you switch to a different one. The text box in the upper left corner provides "speed search" capability.

Using Speed Search and Find to Locate Addresses

To move quickly to a particular name in the current address book, begin typing that name in the text box in the upper left corner of the Address Book window. As you type, Exchange's speed-search feature scrolls the list to the item that most closely matches what you've typed so far.

Exchange's speed-search feature works fine when you know the beginning characters of the entry you're looking for. To search for entries based on characters *within* a name, or to look for groups of entries that have certain letters in common, use the Find command. You can initiate a Find by clicking the Find tool on the Address Book's toolbar, by choosing Find from the Edit menu, or by pressing Ctrl-Shift-F.

In the Find dialog box, type any character or group of characters. Like the Find command on your Start menu, this Find command locates all entries that contain the specified character string.

NOTE: The Find command searches only the currently displayed address book. If you're not sure which address book contains the party you're looking for, you may need to search each one in turn.

Addressing a New Message from Within the Address Book

You can begin a new message from within an address book. Simply select the names of one or more recipients, and then click the New Message tool or press Ctrl-N. Exchange opens a new message window and includes the selected names on the To line.

Using the Personal Address Book

The Personal Address Book is designed to give you quick and dependable access to people to whom you send mail regularly. It's quick because the list is (presumably) a subset of your company's complete address book as well as a compilation of the most important names in your other mail services' address books. It's dependable because it's stored on your own hard disk instead of on a local or remote server, so you have access to it even when you're working off line.

To copy an entry to your Personal Address Book from any other address book, first select the name you want to copy. Then click the Add To Personal Address Book tool or choose Add To Personal Address Book from the File menu.

 Don't worry about creating duplicate entries in your Personal Address Book. If you copy a name that already exists in the Personal Address Book, Exchange simply disregards your action.

You can also copy an address to your Personal Address Book from the addressee's property sheet or by "capturing" the address from the To or Cc line of a message you receive.

For information about *addressee property sheets*, see "Using the Property Sheets of Address Book Entries," page 627.

For information about *capturing an address*, see "Capturing Addresses from Messages You Receive," page 626.

Creating New Addresses

To create a new entry in an address book, first display any address book. Then click the New Entry tool or choose New Entry from the File menu. In the New Entry dialog box, choose the type of address you want to create and the address book in which you want to create it. Exchange then displays a property sheet for your new addressee, allowing you to enter the new address as well as other pertinent details.

Creating Personal Distribution Lists

A distribution list is a named collection of addressees. Entering the name of a distribution list on the To or Cc line of a message is equivalent to entering the name of each member of the list separately. To create a new personal distribution list, follow these steps:

1. Display any address book.

2. Choose New Entry from the File menu or click the New Entry tool.

3. In the drop-down list at the bottom of the dialog box, select Personal Address Book. In the top part of the New Entry dialog box, select Personal Distribution List.

   Click OK, and Exchange then displays a property sheet for your new distribution list.

4. Type a name for your new list, and then click the Add/Remove Members button.

5. In the next dialog box that appears (see Figure 23-15 on the next page), choose the names you want to include from the list on the left. Then click the Add button to move those names to the list on the right. To select names from a different address book, choose

FIGURE 23-15.

To add names to a distribution list, select them from the list on the left and then click the Members button. You can then select a different address book and repeat the process.

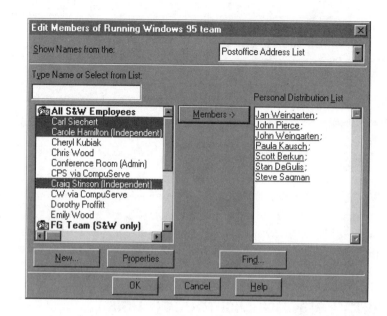

the book you want from the drop-down list at the upper right corner of the dialog box. Your list can include names drawn from several different address books.

6. When your list is complete, click OK to return to the property sheet, and then click OK again to return to your address book.

The name of your new distribution list will appear in boldface type in the address book. Its type will be identified as MAPIPDL, which stands for "mail applications programming interface personal distribution list."

Capturing Addresses from Messages You Receive

After receiving a message from someone you've never corresponded with before, you might want to add the sender's address to your Personal Address Book.

1. Select a name from the From, To, or Cc lines of your message.

2. Right-click and choose Add To Personal Address Book. Or choose Recipient Object from the Edit menu, and then choose Add To Personal Address Book from the submenu that appears.

Using the Property Sheets of Address Book Entries

Like almost everything else in Windows 95, address book entries have properties and property sheets. The property sheet for an address book entry includes information vital to Exchange, such as the addressee's name, e-mail address, and mail service. But it also includes places where you can enter information that Exchange cares nothing about—for example, the addressee's physical (Postal Service) address, his or her home and business telephone numbers, and any miscellaneous annotations you care to supply.

The details available in an addressee's property sheet vary somewhat depending on the mail service involved. Entries for The Microsoft Network, for example, may include personal and professional details that the addressee supplied when opening his or her MSN account. Moreover, certain fields in an addressee's property sheet are read-only, while others are read/write. Read-only fields are displayed in gray.

 You can't alter the contents of a read-only property-sheet field, but you can select all or some of it and copy it to the Clipboard. To copy what you've selected, press Ctrl-C. To paste it into another (editable) field in the same or a different property sheet, press Ctrl-V.

To display an addressee's property sheet, select the addressee's name in an address book or on the From, To, or Cc line of a message. Then click the Properties tool, press Alt-Enter, or choose Properties from the File menu. (Alternatively, right-click the addressee's name and choose Properties from the object menu.)

Using an Addressee's Property Sheet as a Phone Dialer

If your addressee's property sheet includes fields for telephone numbers, you can use that property sheet as a phone dialer. Simply click the Dial button beside any telephone number.

For information about *dialing with the Phone Dialer applet,* see "Using Phone Dialer," page 533.

Checking Properties of Address Books

Address books also have property sheets, though they are generally less elaborate than the property sheets of address-book entries. To display the property sheet for an address book, first display that address book. Then right-click the entry in the drop-down list at the upper right corner of the Address Book window and choose Properties from the object menu that appears.

Using Folders to Manage Your Personal Folder File

Whenever you create a new personal folder file (or when you first install Exchange), Exchange supplies you with four standard folders, named Inbox, Outbox, Sent Items, and Deleted Items. New mail arrives in the Inbox folder, outbound mail lives in the Outbox folder until it's delivered to the appropriate mail systems, copies of messages you send are (optionally) retained in the Sent Items folder, and items you delete move to the Deleted Items folder. You will undoubtedly want to expand this default folder structure.

You can create as many folders as you need, and you can nest folders within folders to any level of complexity. You can organize your folders by correspondent, by topic, by date range, or by any other way you please. Figure 23-16 shows an example of a personal folder file that has been organized by a combination of message topic and correspondent.

 While the right pane has the focus, the folder you're working in is marked by an open-folder icon in the left pane. You can also tell what folder is open by looking at the Exchange title bar.

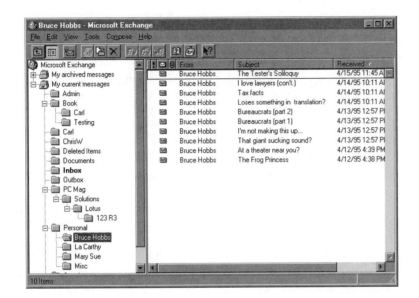

FIGURE 23-16.

To organize your messages, you can create as many folders as you need and nest them to any level of complexity.

If you've spent any time working with Windows Explorer, you will probably feel comfortable right away with Exchange's folder system. The basic things you need to know are as follows:

- The Exchange window can be divided into two panes. The left pane displays an outline of your folder structure. The contents of the folder that's selected in the left pane are displayed in the right pane. (If your Exchange window does not have a left pane displayed, click the Show/Hide Folder List tool or choose Folders from the View menu.)

- Folders containing unread messages are identified in the left pane by boldface type.

- You can adjust how space is distributed between the two panes by dragging the vertical bar (the "split" bar) that divides the window.

- To adjust the width of any right-pane column, drag the vertical bar at the right side of the column heading. (To adjust a column's width with the keyboard, choose the Columns command from the View menu. In the right side of the dialog box, select the column you want to adjust. Then type a number in the Width box.)

You can customize the right pane so that only particular columns appear, and you can change their order. For details, see "Customizing the Column Layout," page 632.

- You can change the sort order of the messages in the right pane. For details, see "Sorting Messages," page 632.

- A plus sign in the folder-list pane indicates an entry that can be expanded. To see the subentries, click the plus sign.

    A minus sign in the folder-list pane indicates an entry that can be collapsed. Click the minus sign to collapse the entry.

    To expand an entry with the keyboard, select it and press the Right arrow key. To collapse an entry, select it and press the Left arrow key.

- To create a new folder, select the new folder's parent folder, and then choose New Folder from the File menu. For example, to create a folder within your Inbox folder, start by selecting Inbox in the left pane. Then choose the New Folder command.

- To move an item to a different folder, drag the item from the right pane and drop it on the destination folder in the left pane. To copy an item to a new folder, hold down the Ctrl key while you drag the item to its destination.

    To move or copy an item without using drag and drop, select the item and then choose Move or Copy from the File menu. (Or right-click the item and choose Move or Copy from the object menu.) Exchange displays your folder hierarchy in a new dialog box (see Figure 23-17), allowing you to point (or navigate with the keyboard) to your destination folder.

    To move or copy multiple messages in the same folder, hold down the Ctrl key while you select each message. Then drag and drop, or choose commands from the File or object menu.

- You can move or copy a folder by dragging it from either pane and dropping it on its new parent folder. For example, in Figure 23-16, you could move the ChrisW folder from its current location to the Book folder by dragging it in the left pane and dropping it on Book. (If you copy a folder to a new destination within the

FIGURE 23-17.

You can move or copy a message by dragging with your mouse or by choosing commands from the File menu. If you take the latter route, Exchange uses this window to let you specify a destination folder.

same folder, Exchange supplies a new name based on the original name.)

■ To delete a message, a group of messages, or an entire folder, select what you want to delete. Then click the Delete tool, press the Del key, or right-click and choose Delete from the object menu.

 Exchange neither prompts for confirmation when you delete messages or folders nor provides an Undo command. But all deleted items (including entire folders) go to the Deleted Items folder. You can restore a deleted item by moving or copying it out of the Deleted Items folder.

■ To rename a folder, right-click it and choose Rename from the object menu. Or select it and choose Rename from the File menu.

Note that the Exchange window displays all personal folder files in your profile. The left pane in Figure 23-16, for example, shows two personal folder files: My archived messages and My current messages. You can use the same techniques to move or copy items between personal folder files that you would use to copy or move them between folders in the same personal folder file.

Sorting Messages

To sort the items in a folder on the basis of the contents of any column, click the column heading. For example, to sort by subject, click the Subject heading. Alternatively, choose Sort from the View menu. In the dialog box that appears, select a column name from the drop-down list and choose either the Ascending or Descending option button.

When you sort by clicking a column heading, Exchange uses the default sorting order—ascending or descending—for that column. When you sort by the Received column, for example, Exchange sorts in descending order, putting the most recently received messages at the top. When you click Subject or From, Exchange sorts in ascending order—that is, in "normal" alphabetical order. To reverse the sort on any heading, hold down the Ctrl key while you click.

Right-click a column heading to display a two-command object menu—Sort Ascending and Sort Descending—that lets you select a sort field (the column you click) and sort order.

Fortunately, you don't need to memorize the default sort orders for each column. Exchange displays a gray triangle next to the heading on which you last sorted. An upward-pointing triangle denotes an ascending-order sort. A downward arrow means the column has been sorted in descending order.

When you sort by Subject, Exchange ignores the REs and FWs that appear in the Subject field of replies and forwarded messages.

Customizing the Column Layout

New folders, by default, are organized in seven columns. From left to right, those columns are Importance, Item Type, Attachment, From, Subject,

Received, and Size. You can change the column order, delete columns, or add new columns by choosing the Columns command from the View menu. Figure 23-18 shows the Columns dialog box.

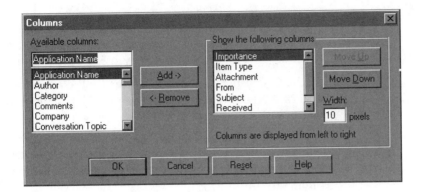

FIGURE 23-18.

The Columns command lets you reorganize the information displayed in Exchange's right pane.

By selecting items in the Show The Following Columns section of this dialog box and then clicking Move Up or Move Down, you can change the order in which columns are displayed. In Figure 23-18, for example, you could move the Item Type column to the left (making it appear before the Importance column) by selecting it and clicking the Move Up button.

To remove a column, select it in the right side of the dialog box and click the Remove button. To add a new column, select that column in the left side of the dialog box and click the Add button. To restore the default column layout, click Reset.

Using the Find Command

Exchange includes a handy Find command that works much like the Find command on your Start menu except that it searches Exchange folders instead of disk folders. Once Find has located a message or group of messages, you can work with those items directly from the Find window. You can read messages, reply to or forward messages, move messages into folders, and so on. You can also customize the display of items in the Find window, using the same techniques you use to customize any "normal" Exchange folder.

You can open as many Find windows as you need. If you ask Find to look for items from a particular sender, the sender's name will appear on Find's title bar as well as on your taskbar.

If you leave a Find window open, Find will add any new qualifying messages to the window as they arrive, identifying the new arrivals by means of boldface type. If you select the Only Unread Items check box (in the Advanced section of the Find dialog box), Find removes items from its window as soon as you read them. Thus, Find is convenient for trapping particular types of new messages—high priority items, for example, or items from a particular sender—allowing you to postpone the reading of non-qualifying items.

To use the Find command, choose Find from the Tools menu, press Ctrl-Shift-F, or right-click a folder and choose Find from the object menu. Figure 23-19 shows the dialog box that appears. Click the Folder button, near the top of the dialog box, and tell Find where you want it to look. Supply your search criteria in the remainder of the dialog box (using the Advanced section if appropriate), and then click the Find Now button.

FIGURE 23-19.

You can use the Find command to locate existing messages that meet search criteria, as well as to capture newly arriving messages that meet those criteria.

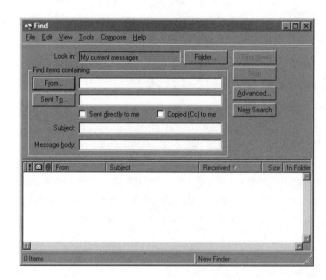

When you click the Folder button in the Find dialog box, Exchange presents an outline diagram of your entire Exchange window, including all personal folder files and all folders within each personal folder file. By choosing a personal folder file and selecting the Include All Subfolders check box, you can gather together messages from many different folders that have some property in common. So, for example, even if you don't take the trouble to move messages in your Sent Items folder to more particular folders, you can still use Find to collect sent and received mail on a common topic in a single window.

If you leave one or more Find windows open when you close Exchange, Exchange automatically closes the Find windows as well. The next time you start Exchange, Exchange reopens the Find windows.

Once you set up your criteria for a Find window and click Find Now, drag the window's split bar (right above the column headings) to the top of the window. This not only provides more room for message headers, but prevents you from inadvertantly changing your search criteria.

Archiving Items in Your Personal Folder File

Although Exchange does not include an Archive command per se, you can winnow aging messages from your personal folder file as follows:

1. Create a separate personal folder file for your archive. For details, see "Adding or Removing a Mail Service," page 595.

2. Use the Find command to display items of a certain age.
   To find items that you have received prior to a specified date, click the Advanced button in the Find dialog box.

3. In the Find window, choose the Select All command from the Edit menu.

4. Choose the Move command from the File menu, and then point to your archival personal folder file.

 For information about *the Find command*, see "Using the Find Command," page 633.

Using a LAN-Based Mail System with Dial-Up Networking

If you use a local-area-network-based mail system, and you sometimes need to get your mail from outside the office, check your system's property sheet to see how it handles offline work and dial-up connections. Choose Services from Exchange's Tools menu, select the name of the mail system you're using, and then click Properties. If you're working with Microsoft Mail, you'll find dial-up options on the Connection tab. (See Figure 23-20.)

Note that there are three ways to use Microsoft Mail from outside the local-area network. If you select the option button labeled "Remote using a modem and Dial-Up Networking," Exchange always invokes Dial-Up Networking to establish connection with Mail. If you select Automatically Sense LAN Or Remote, Exchange calls on Dial-Up Networking any time the network is unavailable. If you select Offline, Exchange lets you post messages to your Outbox, but it won't try to send those messages until you revisit the property sheet and choose one of the other connection options.

To use a dial-up connection to your LAN-based mail system, you need to have Dial-Up Networking installed, and you must have access to a remote access server. On the property sheet for your mail system, you will find a place to specify the name of your Dial-Up Networking connection. You may also find scheduling options, options for using remote preview, and such other details as redial and timeout settings. For Microsoft Mail, these matters are all handled by the Remote Configuration, Remote Session, and Dial-Up Networking tabs of the property sheet.

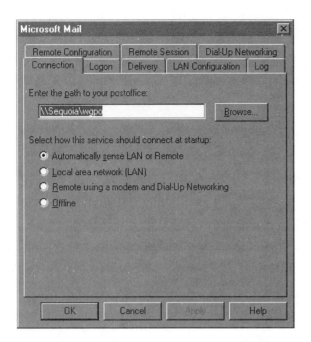

FIGURE 23-20.

You can set up Microsoft Mail so that it always connects via Dial-Up Networking, connects via Dial-Up Networking whenever the network is unavailable, or always works in offline mode.

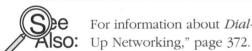

For information about *Dial-Up Networking*, see "Using Dial-Up Networking," page 372.

Using Remote Mail with Local and Dial-Up Connections

With any kind of dial-up connection, whether it be to your LAN-based mail system via Dial-Up Networking or to CompuServe or The Microsoft Network online service, downloading messages can be time-consuming. Some services provide a "remote preview" option that lets you download only the message headers (the messages' senders, subjects, dates, and sizes). You can peruse the headers, either on line or off line, mark the ones you're interested in, and then fetch the messages you want to read.

Depending on the mail system, you might also be able to use remote preview to screen your network-based mail. With Microsoft Mail, for example, remote preview is turned on by default when you're working with a dial-up connection. But you can also turn it on when you're working on line. You might find this option handy if you're working on a slow network or you just want to be able to screen messages before you receive them.

 To turn remote preview on for online connections to Microsoft Mail, choose Services from the Tools menu, select Microsoft Mail, click Properties, and click the LAN Configuration tab. Then select the Use Remote Mail check box. You will need to quit and restart Exchange for your change to take effect.

To use remote preview with any service for which it's available, choose Remote Mail from the Tools menu. Then choose from the menu of mail services that appears. Exchange opens a Remote Mail window for the selected service. (See Figure 23-21.)

FIGURE 23-21.

If you choose Remote Mail, headers for your messages appear in a window like this. You can mark the ones you want to download and ignore or delete the rest.

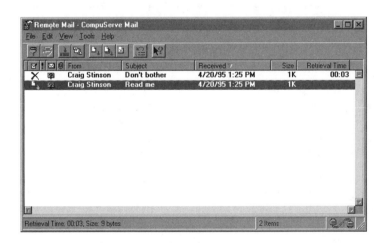

To connect to the service and retrieve headers, choose Connect And Update Headers from the Tools menu, or click the third tool from the left on the toolbar. (See Table 23-4.) After the system has retrieved your headers, you will probably remain on line. (Some systems may disconnect you,

Table 23-4. Remote Mail Toolbar

Toolbar Icon	Description
	Connects to remote mail service
	Disconnects from remote mail service
	Updates the list of message headers, connecting to the service if necessary
	Retrieves marked messages from the remote service and sends outgoing messages
	Marks selected messages for retrieval
	Marks selected messages for retrieval of copies, leaving the original messages on the remote service
	Marks selected messages for deletion
	Unmarks all messages

however.) You can disconnect at this point by choosing Disconnect from the Tools menu or by clicking the second tool from the left on the toolbar. Or you can stay on line and read the headers.

For each header, you can choose one of three marking options from the Edit menu: Mark To Retrieve, Mark To Retrieve A Copy, and Mark To Delete. To transfer a message from your mail service to your Exchange inbox, choose Mark To Retrieve. To transfer a message to your inbox but leave a copy with your mail service, choose Mark To Retrieve A Copy. To remove a message from your mail service without reading it, choose Mark To Delete. You'll find tools for these three marking options in the middle of the toolbar and commands for them on the Tools menu.

After you mark the message headers appropriately, choose Connect And Transfer Mail from the Tools menu, or click the Transfer Mail tool. This step carries out your marking instructions and sends any messages waiting in your Outbox folder.

In the Retrieval Time column of the Remote Mail window, Exchange presents an estimate of the length of time it will take you to download the message. This information might help you decide whether or not to mark a header for retrieval.

 You can sort messages and reorganize column headings for the Remote Mail window by using commands on the View menu.

Working with Mail-Enabled Applications

A mail-enabled application is one that lets you send messages directly to other users on your LAN-based mail system without requiring you to activate Exchange and use Exchange's New Message command. Most of the major desktop productivity applications these days fall into this category. If your program has a Send, Send File, Routing Slip, or other comparable command, it's mail-enabled. Any program that's enabled for MAPI mail systems (*MAPI* is Microsoft's mail application programming interface) should work fine with Exchange.

Typically, when you use the Send or a comparable command in a mail-enabled program, the program creates a new mail message (possibly using a custom form instead of the default Exchange message form) with the current file as an attachment. In some programs you may be able to mail a selection of the current file this way, as an alternative to mailing the entire file. In some programs, you also have the option of sending the current file sequentially to a distribution list.

Note that you do not have to have Exchange running to use an application's mail features. The application will open those components of Exchange that it needs when you choose Send or another mail command.

24

Using Microsoft Fax

Microsoft Fax provides a rich set of features to support fax communications. Provided your computer has a fax-modem or has access to a shared network faxmodem, Microsoft Fax lets you send and receive messages and documents as though your computer were a fax machine.

You can send faxes in a variety of ways. For example, you can choose Compose New Fax from your Start menu and let the Compose New Fax wizard guide you through the steps of addressing and formulating your message. Or you can choose any application's Print command and print a document to the fax "printer" installed by Microsoft Fax. If your application is mail-enabled, you can choose its Send (or equivalent) command and specify a fax addressee. And because Microsoft Fax is integrated with Microsoft Exchange, you can also send faxes by composing messages in Exchange's message window and choosing fax addressees from your personal address book. Faxes that you receive appear as messages in your Exchange inbox.

Microsoft Fax supports Binary File Transfer (BFT). That means that if you're sending to someone whose system also supports BFT, Microsoft Fax can transmit your fax as an editable e-mail message. Of course, if you're sending a fax to someone using a standard (Group 3) fax machine, Microsoft Fax delivers a "rendered" (uneditable) image of your message or document. By default, the system sends your fax in "best available" format—which means it sends editable documents if the recipient can accept them and rendered documents if not.

Other important features in Microsoft Fax include support for RSA encryption, support for connection to fax-on-demand systems, a fax viewer that lets you look at received faxes in full-screen or thumbnail views, and a program that you can use to design personalized cover pages.

Setting Up Microsoft Fax

To use Microsoft Fax, you must install both Microsoft Exchange and Microsoft Fax. If you've installed Microsoft Fax, you probably have a Fax submenu in your Start menu. (The default position for this submenu is under the Accessories menu. To get there, click Start, choose Programs, and then choose Accessories.)

In addition to installing both Exchange and Fax, you need to add the fax service to your Exchange profile. For details about how to do this, see "Adding or Removing a Mail Service," page 595.

When you install Fax, the system creates an item called Microsoft Fax in your Printers folder. This is simply a special kind of logical printer—a driver that takes output from your applications and sends it, properly formatted, to the faxmodem. You can configure the driver by displaying your Printers folder (choose Settings from the Start menu, then Printers from the submenu that appears), right-clicking the Microsoft Fax item, and choosing Properties from the object menu.

Figure 24-1 shows how the Details tab of the Microsoft Fax printer driver property sheet should be filled out, assuming your faxmodem is connected locally. Note that the "printer" port should be FAX: (Unknown Local Port). Do not designate a standard communications port, such as COM1 or COM2, for this purpose.

 You might want to create a desktop shortcut for the Microsoft Fax item that's in your Printers folder. (To do so, simply drag the Microsoft Fax icon from the Printers folder to the desktop.) Then you can send faxes by dragging documents and dropping them on the shortcut.

In addition to the property sheet shown in Figure 24-1, you need to know about a second, identically named but different, property sheet. Figure 24-2 shows the Message tab of this second property sheet. To get here, open Exchange, choose Microsoft Fax Tools from the Tools menu, and then choose Options from the submenu that appears.

On the Message tab of this property sheet, you can set defaults governing the way your faxes are sent: whether they should be transmitted immediately or at particular times, whether they should use the best-available format, and which cover page should be included—if any.

On other tabs you can supply dialing parameters (including the number of times Fax should retry sending a fax if it cannot connect at first), the name of the modem that Fax should use (in case you have access to more than one), and information about yourself that Fax will

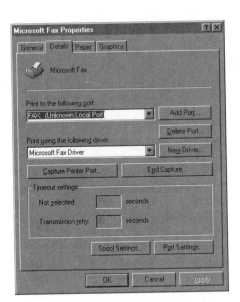

FIGURE 24-1.

Installing Fax creates a logical printer called Microsoft Fax.

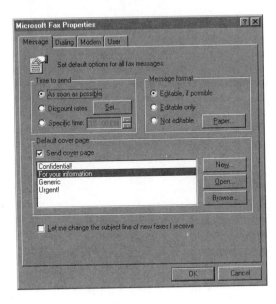

FIGURE 24-2.

In this property sheet, accessible through Microsoft Exchange's Microsoft Fax Tools command, you tell Microsoft Fax how you want your faxes sent by default.

include on its cover pages. Although you can easily override any of the property sheet's defaults for any particular message, you'll save yourself some time and trouble if you wander through all four tabs, just to make sure everything is filled out appropriately.

Adding Fax Recipients to Your Personal Address Book

Microsoft Exchange does not maintain a separate address book for fax recipients. Instead it lets you add fax recipients to your personal address book. To add a new recipient there, follow these steps:

1. In Exchange, click the Address Book tool or choose Address Book from the Tools menu.

2. With any address book displayed, click the New Entry tool (the first tool on the left side of the toolbar) or choose New Entry from the File menu.

3. In the drop-down list at the bottom of the New Entry dialog box, select Personal Address Book. In the top part of the dialog box, under the Microsoft Fax list entry, select Fax. Then click OK.

These steps bring you to the New Fax property sheet, shown in Figure 24-3.

FIGURE 24-3.

Using this property sheet, you can enter fax recipients in your personal address book.

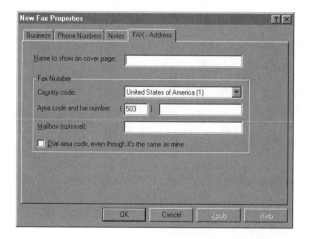

The Name line and the phone number boxes in this property sheet are mandatory fields. (Fax requires the Name information for its cover pages.) Everything else is optional. Filling out the Business tab, however, also provides Fax with information it can use on cover pages—such things as the name of your recipient, his or her voice phone number, and so on.

NOTE: You do not need to create an address-book entry for everyone you send faxes to, but if you fax to particular people repeatedly, you'll find it convenient to be able to select them from your personal address book.

Sending a Fax

Because Microsoft Exchange regards Microsoft Fax as an installed mail system, comparable to Microsoft Mail or The Microsoft Network online service, you can compose fax messages using the same procedures you would use to compose any other kind of e-mail message. That is, you can use the New Message command from Exchange's Compose menu and include one or more fax recipients as addressees for your message. For more information about composing messages in Exchange, see "Creating Mail," page 600.

But Microsoft Fax also supplies its own wizard to help you compose fax messages and select options regarding the way in which faxes are sent. You can get to this wizard in a variety of ways. If you're just faxing a note that doesn't exist anywhere in a disk file, you'll probably want to use either of the following methods:

- From the Start menu, choose Programs, then Accessories, then Fax. From the Fax menu, choose Compose New Fax.

- From Exchange's Compose menu, choose New Fax.

The Start-menu command is handy because it doesn't require that you have Exchange running. But both methods lead you to the wizard.

As we'll see in a moment, you can attach files to fax messages generated with either version of the Compose New Fax command. But if you're sending a document that already exists in a disk file, you might prefer to take one of these routes:

- Right-click the document in a folder or Windows Explorer window and choose Send To from the object menu. Choose Fax Recipient from the Send To menu.

- Drag the document and drop it on the Microsoft Fax item in your Printers folder—or on a shortcut to that item. Note that this always generates a rendered fax; you can't send an editable message by "printing" to the fax device.

- Open the document in a mail-enabled application. Then choose the Send (or equivalent) command and address the document to a fax recipient.

Meet the Compose New Fax Wizard

However you invoke the wizard, it greets you with the screen shown in Figure 24-4. If you're working from the road, make sure the dialing location shown in this initial screen is correct. If it's not, click Dialing Properties and choose your current location from the I Am Dialing From drop-down.

FIGURE 24-4.

The Compose New Fax wizard begins by asking you where you're faxing from.

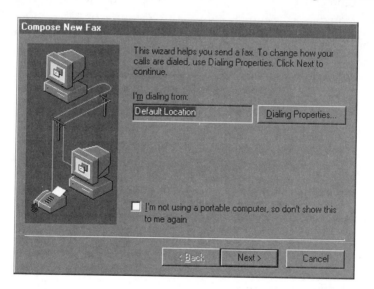

If you have not defined multiple dialing locations, the wizard's screen includes the check box shown at the bottom of Figure 24-4. If the computer you're working at never strays from its desktop, you'll probably want to select this check box. Then, the next time you compose a fax you won't have to identify your calling location. (If you change your mind and define some new calling locations, this first wizard screen will reappear.)

Clicking Next in the wizard's initial screen takes you to the screen shown in Figure 24-5. Here you specify addressees, either by clicking Address Book and selecting from lists or by simply typing names and addresses directly. If you type directly into this dialog box, click the Add To List button after supplying a recipient's name and fax number.

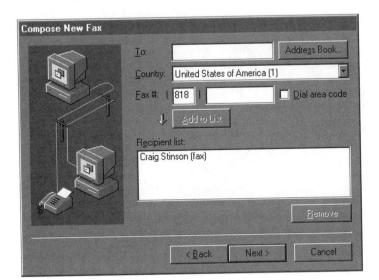

FIGURE 24-5.

In this wizard dialog box, enter the name and number for one or more recipients, or click Address Book and select recipients from lists.

 You can specify both fax recipients and non-fax recipients in the dialog box shown in Figure 24-5. Non-fax address-ees will receive your message as ordinary e-mail. To spec-ify a non-fax recipient, simply click Address Book and select from the appropriate address book. You can also specify fax and non-fax distribution lists. For information about creating and using distribution lists, see "Creating Personal Distribution Lists," page 625.

The area code portion of the dialog box initially displays the area code you're dialing from. If you're faxing to someone in your own area code, Fax will not dial the area code unless you select the Dial Area Code check box.

When you've finished identifying recipients, another click on Next takes you to the dialog box shown in Figure 24-6 on the next page. Here you can choose a cover page, if you want one. By clicking the Options button in this dialog box, you can also tell Fax when and how to deliver your message.

FIGURE 24-6.

Microsoft Fax supplies standard cover pages and a program to help you design your own. Here you tell the wizard what cover page to use.

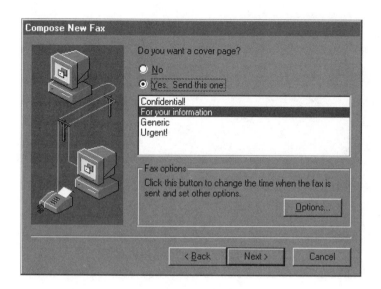

If you don't want a cover page, click the No option button. If you have created a cover page that doesn't appear on the list in this dialog box, click Options. In the Options dialog box, click the Browse button and navigate to the cover page you want. Also click Options if you want to use anything other than the defaults you've set up in your Microsoft Fax property sheet (the property sheet shown in Figure 24-2 on page 645). We'll return to the Options button in a moment.

After you click Next in the dialog box shown in Figure 24-6, the wizard displays the dialog box shown in Figure 24-7. This is your opportunity to write a subject heading and a note. If your cover page includes a Subject field, what you type on the top line of this dialog box will appear in that field.

Clicking Next again takes you to the dialog box shown in Figure 24-8, where you can specify one or more document files to be transmitted with your fax. If your recipient's system supports BFT and you have asked Microsoft Fax to send an editable message, the files you specify will arrive as embedded objects. Otherwise, Fax will render the document and transmit an image of it.

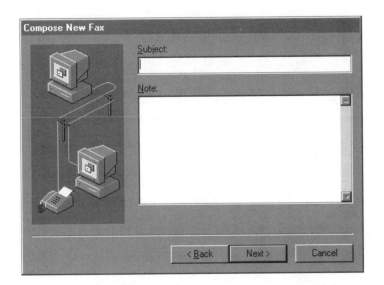

FIGURE 24-7.

In this dialog box, you can compose a message. The Subject heading can appear in your cover page.

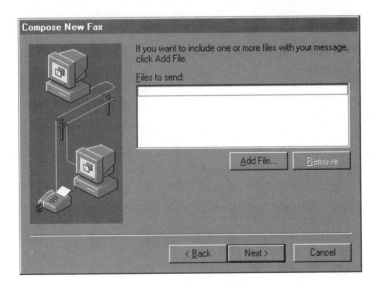

FIGURE 24-8.

Here you can specify one or more document files to be included with your fax.

After specifying any files you want to send, click Next one more time to arrive at the Finish line. Depending on options you've chosen (or the defaults set in your Microsoft Fax property sheet), when you leave the wizard your fax either is transmitted immediately or joins the queue of outbound faxes.

For information about *dialing locations,* see "Setting Up Your Modem for Multiple Calling Locations," page 370.

For information about *creating custom cover pages,* see "Using Cover Page Editor," page 660.

Options for Sending Faxes

By clicking the Options button in the dialog box shown in Figure 24-6 on page 650, you can do any of the following:

- Tell Fax whether to send your message immediately, when discount telephone rates are in effect, or at a prescribed time.

- Tell Fax not to transmit your message unless each addressee can receive it as an editable document.

- Tell Fax to send your message as a rendered (not editable) document, even if addressees can receive it in editable form.

- Tell Fax what paper size, image quality, and orientation to use in the event that it sends your message in rendered form.

- Tell Fax to use a cover page that did not appear in the dialog box shown in Figure 24-6.

- Specify the number of times Fax should retry in the event that it can't connect immediately with one or more addressees—as well as the amount of time Fax should pause between retries.

- Specify whether Fax should employ any security measures when sending this message.

If you've created your fax by choosing New Message from Exchange's Compose menu, you can set any of the options in this list by choosing Send Options from the Message window's File menu and then clicking the Fax tab in the ensuing dialog box. These steps take you to the dialog box shown in Figure 24-9.

Figure 24-9 shows the dialog box that appears when you click the Options button in the dialog box shown in Figure 24-6.

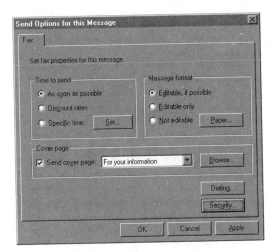

FIGURE 24-9.

In the Send Options dialog box you can specify a time for your fax to be sent, whether your fax should be rendered at a particular orientation, and other matters.

Telling Fax When to Send

Fax can transmit messages immediately, during telephone-rate discount hours, or at a specific time you prescribe. To set a specific send time, click the Set button shown in Figure 24-9 and use the spinner in the dialog box that appears.

Unless you tell it otherwise, Fax assumes that telephone rates are discounted from 5:00 P.M. to 8:00 A.M. daily. If you want to change these hours (you might want to change the discount starting time to 11:00 P.M., for example, when rates are usually discounted more), you must visit the Microsoft Fax property sheet shown in Figure 24-2 on page 645. In that dialog box, click the Set button.

Specifying Editable or Non-Editable Format

The "factory-default" format for Microsoft Fax messages is Editable If Possible (which is also sometimes described as "best available"). If you send in this mode, Fax transmits an editable message to any addressee whose system supports Binary File Transfer. (Typically, this means anyone using Microsoft Fax under Windows 95 or Windows for Workgroups 3.11, or anyone using any Microsoft At Work fax platform.) Files attached to your message appear as icons along with the text of your message. To view an attached file, your recipient simply double-clicks its icon.

When you send in Editable If Possible format to a standard Group 3 fax machine or to any other recipient who cannot accept BFT, Microsoft Fax transmits a rendered image of your document. Any files attached to your message are also transmitted as rendered images.

> **NOTE:** Microsoft Fax cannot send a file attachment to a rendered fax unless the file is associated with an application capable of printing it. To determine if your document can be sent in rendered format, right-click the document's icon in a folder or Windows Explorer window. If Print appears on the object menu, you can send the document as an attachment to a rendered fax.

If you must send an editable message, choose Editable Only in the dialog box shown in Figure 24-9. Fax will then return an error notification if one or more of your recipients cannot receive editable messages. If you want your recipients to receive a rendered message, regardless of what kind of system they're using, choose Not Editable.

Specifying Paper Size, Image Quality, and Orientation for Rendered Faxes

By default, Fax composes rendered messages at standard letter-size dimensions (8½ inches by 11 inches), in portrait mode, and at the best available image quality. You can override any of these defaults by clicking the Paper button in the dialog box shown in Figure 24-9.

Specifying an Unlisted Cover Page

The dialog box shown in Figure 24-6 on page 650 lists all cover pages (files created with Cover Page Editor) that are stored in your Windows directory. To choose a cover page stored elsewhere, click the Browse button in the dialog box shown in Figure 24-9.

See Also: For information about *custom cover pages*, see "Using Cover Page Editor," page 660.

Setting Retry Options

By default, if Fax can't connect with a recipient on the first try, it tries again three times, waiting five minutes between tries. (If you've made changes to the property sheet shown in Figure 24-2 on page 645, these defaults might be different on your system.) To specify different retry settings for the current message, click the Dialing button in the dialog box shown in Figure 24-9.

Setting Security Options

To keep unauthorized recipients from reading your fax, you can encrypt an editable fax or assign it a password. You can also attach a "digital signature" to any files enclosed in your message. Your recipient can then verify your signature to prove that the enclosures came from you and were not modified after you signed them.

 For information about *using these security features*, see "Encrypting or Password-Protecting Your Faxes," page 667.

Inspecting the Queue of Outbound Faxes

If one or more faxes are waiting to be sent, a document icon with cartoon-style motion lines appears in your notification area. You can see how many faxes are in the queue by resting your mouse on this icon, or you can double-click the icon to take a closer look at the queue. (Alternatively, you can display the queue by choosing Microsoft Fax Tools from Exchange's Tools menu, and then choosing Show Outgoing Faxes.) Figure 24-10 shows a sample of the outbound fax queue.

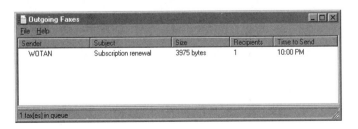

FIGURE 24-10.

The Outgoing Faxes window shows what messages are scheduled for delivery and when they'll be sent.

If you decide not to send a fax that's scheduled for transmission, select it in the Outgoing Faxes window and choose Cancel Fax from the File menu. Or, delete it from your Exchange Outbox folder.

What Happens If Microsoft Fax Cannot Send Your Message

If one or more of your recipients fail to receive your fax, your Exchange Inbox folder will receive an administrative message. The message tells you who didn't get the message and, in some cases, why they didn't get it. The administrative message appears in a special form, which includes a Send Again button. Click Send Again to try again.

Receiving Faxes

By default, Microsoft Fax automatically answers incoming calls whenever you have Exchange running. Because Fax is a "TAPI-aware" program (that is, it uses the Microsoft telephony applications programming interface), Fax can "monitor" your communications port in this manner without interfering with the operation of other TAPI-aware communications programs. You can connect with The Microsoft Network online information service, for example, while Fax "listens" for incoming messages. (If you have only a single phone line and a single modem, you won't receive any faxes while you're on line with The Microsoft Network. The feature that TAPI brings in this case, then, is the ability to use your modem to call MSN and other services without first shutting down your fax-monitoring application.)

 To use a non-TAPI-aware communications program, you don't have to quit Exchange. Instead, simply open the Fax Modem property sheet (see Figure 24-11) and switch Fax temporarily to Don't Answer.

Changing the Answer Mode and Other Modem Settings

Any time Fax is running (that is, any time you have Exchange running with Fax in the current profile), a fax-machine icon appears in your notification area. To verify that Fax is running in Auto Answer mode, rest your mouse pointer on this icon for a moment and read the message that pops up. To switch to manual answer mode, or to change other settings that affect your modem's behavior, double-click the notification-area icon. In the Status window that appears, choose Modem Properties from the Options menu. (Alternatively, choose Services from Exchange's Tools menu, select Microsoft Fax, and click Properties. Then click the Modem tab and click the Properties button.) Figure 24-11 shows the Fax Modem property sheet.

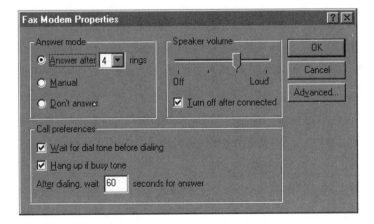

FIGURE 24-11.

Among other things, this property sheet lets you switch your modem to Manual answer mode or turn answering off altogether so that you can use a non-TAPI-aware communications program.

If you switch the answer mode to Manual, Fax continues to monitor your communications port, but it won't answer an incoming call until you tell it to. To make it answer, display the status window (double-click the notification-area icon if the window isn't visible) and click the Answer Now button.

If you switch the answer mode to Don't Answer, the icon remains in your notification area, but Fax "releases" the communications port. In this mode, you can use another, non-TAPI-aware, communication program.

Reading and Replying to Incoming Faxes

Depending on how they're sent to you, you may receive faxes either as editable messages or as rendered images. Either way, your faxes arrive in your Exchange Inbox folder, and you'll receive notification in the manner you've specified on the General tab that's displayed by Exchange's Options command.

Editable messages appear as ordinary e-mail. That is, they are indistinguishable from messages sent via your LAN-based e-mail system, CompuServe mail, or any other service you use through Exchange.

Microsoft Fax uses a Fax Viewer application to display rendered messages. Figure 24-12 shows an example of Fax Viewer. Table 24-1 describes Fax Viewer's toolbar buttons.

FIGURE 24-12.

Microsoft Fax uses a viewer program to display rendered faxes.

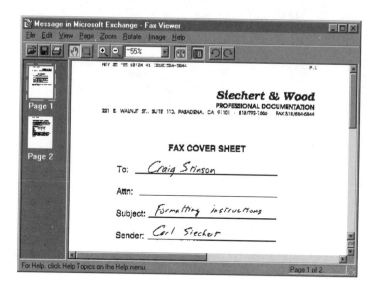

To reply to or forward an editable fax message, simply use standard Exchange tools and commands. To reply to or forward a rendered fax, first select the item in your Exchange Inbox (or other) folder. Then use standard Exchange tools and commands. You cannot reply from within the Fax Viewer application.

Table 24-1. Fax Viewer Toolbar

Toolbar Icon	Description
	Opens a fax document
	Saves a fax to a disk file
	Prints the document
	Drag mode; the mouse pointer changes to a hand and you can move the image within the window by dragging
	Select mode; the mouse pointer changes to a cross hair and you can select part of the image for copying
	Zooms in or zooms out
~55%	Zooms to a predefined level
	Changes the image size so the page width just fits in the Fax Viewer window
	Shows or hides the thumbnail images of all pages in Fax Viewer's left pane
	Rotates the image 90 degrees to the left or to the right

See Also: For information about *new-mail notification*, see "Notification Options," page 616.

For information about *replying to and forwarding messages*, see "Reading and Replying to Your Mail," page 616.

Using Fax Viewer

Here are some of the ways you can use the Fax Viewer application:

- To print your message, choose Print from Fax Viewer's File menu or click the Print button on the toolbar. (Or first choose Print Preview, and then choose Print from the Preview window.)

- To save the message as a separate file, choose Save Copy As from the File menu. Fax Viewer gives the file the extension .AWD.

   To reopen an .AWD file, click the Open button on the toolbar. Alternatively, double-click your .AWD file in a folder or Windows Explorer window.

- To enlarge or reduce the image of your document, choose commands from the Zoom menu, click the magnifying-glass tools on the toolbar, or choose from the preset zoom percentages in the toolbar's drop-down list.

- To change the position of the image in the Fax Viewer window, click the hand icon on the toolbar and then drag the image. (You can also use the scroll bars, of course.)

- To rotate or flip the image, choose commands from the Rotate menu or use the toolbar's Rotate Left and Rotate Right buttons.

- To invert the colors of your image, choose Invert from the Image menu. Inverting black on white to white on black may make low-resolution text easier to read.

- To display thumbnail sketches of each page in your message, choose Thumbnails from the View menu. Choose this command again to turn the thumbnails off.

Using Cover Page Editor

To help you design your own cover pages, Microsoft Fax includes an application called Cover Page Editor. To run this program, open your Start menu and choose Programs, Accessories, Fax, Cover Page Editor. (Alternatively, from the Microsoft Fax property sheet shown in Figure 24-2 on page 645, select a cover page from the list and click Open, or click New to create a new cover page.) Figure 24-13 shows Cover Page Editor with one of the cover pages supplied by Microsoft Fax.

Cover Page Editor is a sophisticated program. With it, you can insert fields that automatically display information about you, the recipient of your message, or the message itself (for example, the number of pages it includes). You can also insert "fixed" text (the word *FAX*, for example), graphics images from clip art or other files, and freehand decorative

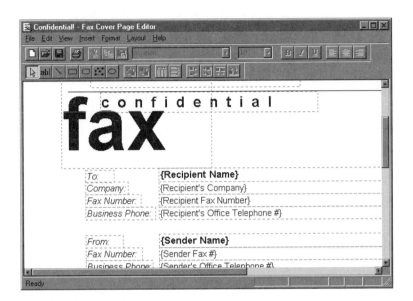

FIGURE 24-13.

With Cover Page Editor you can modify the cover pages supplied by Microsoft Fax or create your own from scratch.

 You can use any of the cover pages supplied with Microsoft Fax as a starting point for designing your own. To open an existing cover page in Cover Page Editor, double-click the page's file in a Windows Explorer or folder window. (Cover pages have the extension .CPE.) Or choose the Open command from Cover Page Editor's File menu.

objects. Using commands on Cover Page Editor's Format menu, you can adjust the appearance of your text. With commands on the Layout menu, you can modify the alignment and spacing of objects, as well as the order in which objects appear if they happen to overlap one another.

Inserting Fields

To insert a field into your cover page, open Cover Page Editor's Insert menu and choose Recipient, Sender, or Message. Each of these commands unfurls a sizable submenu of field offerings.

While you create and edit your cover page, fields are identified by text enclosed within braces. For example, the field for the subject of your message is identified as {Subject}. When you use the cover page in an actual fax, the field is replaced by the appropriate data. Whatever appears on the subject line of your message, for example, replaces {Subject} on your cover page.

Text that does not appear within braces is fixed. That is, such text is displayed as is when you use the cover page. When you choose commands on the Insert menu, Cover Page Editor inserts both a fixed text string and a replaceable field. You can work with these two objects—format them, arrange them, copy them, or delete them—independently.

Adding Text Frames

To add your own fixed text to your cover page, click the Text tool—the second tool from the left on Cover Page Editor's drawing toolbar. Your mouse pointer turns into a plus sign. Position the pointer where you want your text to begin, and then drag downward and to the right. As you do, Cover Page Editor creates a rectangle. This rectangle is a frame that will contain your text. Release the mouse button when the lower right corner of the frame is in approximately the right place. (Don't worry about exactness; you can always adjust the size and position of your frame later.) Then type your text within the frame.

NOTE: There is no menu equivalent for the Text tool.

To edit any fixed text, select it. Then type new text or delete existing text, exactly as you would in a word processor or in an Exchange message window.

NOTE: If you have trouble selecting text or any other objects on your cover page, it may be because some other shape, frame, or graphic is partially overlapping the object you want to select. See "Adjusting the Order of Overlapping Objects," page 666.

 Another way to select a particular object is to select any object, and then press Tab repeatedly until you see handles on the frame of the object you want.

Formatting Text and Frames

To format a text object, either fixed or field, start by clicking anywhere on it. Cover Page Editor confirms your selection by displaying handles on the frame containing the text. Now you can use the Format menu's Font command to change the typography of your text, the Align Text command to change its alignment, or the Line, Fill, And Color command to change its color. (The Font and Align Text commands have toolbar equivalents.) Because of the limitations of traditional fax machines, your color choices are restricted to White, Black, and three shades of gray.

To format the frame that contains a text object, select it. Then choose the Format menu's Line, Fill, And Color command. You can use this command to add lines around your text in various weights and colors, or to provide a background color for the frame. Here, as with text, "color" means black, white, or shade of gray.

 To format two or more frames at once, select all members of the group before choosing formatting commands. To select more than one object, click the Select tool (the first tool on the toolbar) and then draw a rectangle around all members of the set. Alternatively, you can hold down the Ctrl key and click each object.

Inserting Clip Art or Other Graphics

To insert a piece of clip art or some other existing graphical object, you can select it in another application, copy it to the Clipboard, and paste it into Cover Page Editor. Or you can choose the Object command from Cover Page Editor's Insert menu. In response to the latter move, Cover Page Editor displays a list of embeddable data object types. To create a new image in one of these types, choose from the list and click OK. To insert something that's already out there in a file on your disk, click the Create From File button.

See Also: For information about *embedding objects*, see "How to Embed," page 263.

Adding Freehand Drawing

Directly to the right of the Text tool, the Editor's toolbar offers five freehand drawing tools: Line, Rectangle, Rounded Rectangle, Polygon, and Ellipse. With the exception of the Polygon tool, these tools are all to be used the same way you use the Text tool: click a starting position, drag to an ending position, and release the mouse button.

 To create a square, hold down the Shift key while dragging with the Rectangle or Rounded Rectangle tool. To create a circle, hold down Shift while dragging with the Ellipse tool.

The Polygon tool lets you create closed shapes with any number of vertexes. To use this tool, click where you want your first vertex to appear. Then continue clicking where you want subsequent vertexes to be, and double-click when you're finished to close the shape.

 To create several identical shapes, create one shape and copy it. To copy a shape, first select it. Then hold down the Ctrl and Shift keys, click anywhere on or within the shape (but not on one of the black "handles" that appear in corners and midpoints of sides), and drag.

Formatting Graphical Objects

To change the border or background color of a graphical object, use the Format menu's Line, Fill, And Color command, exactly as you would use it to format a text frame.

Resizing and Repositioning Objects

To change the size of any object, first select it. Then drag one of the black handles that appear on its frame.

To change the position of an object, select it. Then drag any part of the object other than a handle.

 You can use an alignment grid to help you position objects. To turn this grid on, choose Grid Lines from the View menu. The grid is a visual aid only, however. For precise centering and alignment of objects, use commands on the Layout menu.

Controlling the Alignment of Objects

To line up two or more objects by their tops, bottoms, left edges, or right edges, first select the objects you want to align. (Click the Select tool, and then drag a rectangle around the group or hold the Ctrl key as you click each object in the group.) Choose Align Objects from the Layout menu, then Left, Right, Top, or Bottom from the submenu. You can also use commands on the Align Objects submenu to line up objects by their midpoints.

Spacing Objects Evenly

To distribute space evenly between three or more objects, first select those objects. Then choose Space Evenly from the Layout menu. From the submenu that appears, choose either Across or Down. If you choose Across, Cover Page Editor reapportions the horizontal spaces between your selected objects. If you choose Down, it evens out the spaces along the vertical dimension.

Centering Objects on the Page

To center objects between the left and right edges of your cover page, select the objects and choose Center On Page from the Layout menu. From the submenu that appears, choose Width. To center objects between the top and bottom edges, select the objects and choose Center On Page from the Layout menu. Then choose Height from the submenu.

Adjusting the Order of Overlapping Objects

If objects overlap, you can adjust their "z order"—the order in which they're stacked. To move an item forward in the stack, first select it. (If you have trouble selecting it with the mouse, press the Tab key until it's selected.) Then press the plus key to move it up one level, or choose Bring To Front from the Layout menu to move it to the top of the stack. To move an item back through the stack, select it, and then press the minus key or choose Send To Back from the Layout menu.

Note that z-order changes have no apparent effect on objects that have been formatted to be transparent.

Previewing and Printing Your Cover Page

To get a good overview of your cover page and see it as your recipients will see it (without the data that will replace field headings, of course), choose Print Preview from the File menu. From the Preview window, you can zoom in for closer inspection of particular sections of the page. You can also click the Print button to generate a hard copy of your cover page— which you may then use in a standard fax machine.

 To switch from portrait mode to landscape, or vice versa, choose Page Setup from the File menu.

Saving Your Cover Page

To save your cover page so that you can use it in your fax messages, choose Save from the File menu. The Editor assigns the extension .CPE to your saved file.

Encrypting or Password-Protecting Your Faxes

Provided your addressee can receive your faxes as binary (editable) documents, you can take the following measures to ensure the privacy of your communication:

- You can assign a password. Your recipient then has to enter the password to open your fax.

- You can use an encryption scheme developed by RSA Data Security Inc. to code your message. Your recipient then has to have a "public key" (which you supply) to read your fax.

- You can use a "digital signature" to authenticate any attachments included with your fax. Your recipient then has the option of using your public key to verify that the attachments came from you and were not altered by anyone else.

Sending a Password-Protected Fax

To send a password-protected fax, follow the steps outlined earlier in this chapter to prepare your message. If you're using the Compose New Fax wizard, click the Options button in the dialog box shown in Figure 24-6 on page 650. Then, in the Options dialog box (see Figure 24-9 on page 653), click the Security button. This takes you to the Message Security Options dialog box, shown in Figure 24-14 on the next page. Select the Password-Protected button, supply a password in the ensuing dialog box, and click OK twice to return to the Compose New Fax wizard.

If you're creating a fax by using the New Message command (instead of with the Compose New Fax wizard), choose Send Options from the message window's File menu. Then click the Security button on the Fax tab of the Options dialog box.

FIGURE 24-14.

To encrypt or password-protect a fax, choose an option button in the Security Method section of this dialog box. You can also assign digital signatures to any attachments included with your fax.

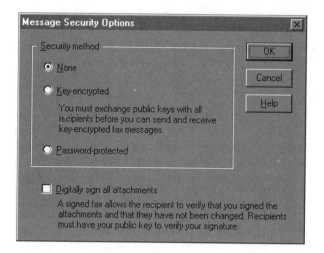

Receiving a Password-Protected Fax

If someone sends you a password-protected fax, the message will be identified in your Inbox as <Encrypted>. To read the message, double-click the message header as you normally would. Exchange then prompts you for the password. After you successfully enter the password, Exchange creates an unprotected copy of the original message, leaving the password-protected original in place. After you read the unprotected copy, you can delete it to prevent unauthorized eyes from seeing the message.

 When you delete the unprotected copy of your message, that copy moves to the Deleted Items folder. To remove the copy from your system completely, open the Deleted Items folder and delete it again.

Sending an Encrypted Fax

Before you can send an encrypted fax, you have to prepare a pair of "keys"—one private and one public. Then you need to send the public key to each person to whom you want to send encrypted faxes.

Creating the Private and Public Keys

To create a set of private and public keys, follow these steps:

1. Choose Microsoft Fax Tools from the Tools menu in Exchange, and then choose Advanced Security from the submenu that appears.

    The Advanced Security dialog box appears, as shown in Figure 24-15.

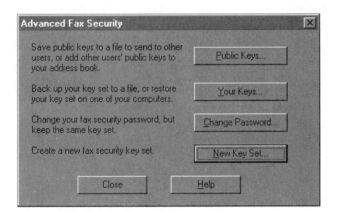

FIGURE 24-15.

Before you send encrypted faxes to someone, you must first share your public key by sending it as an attachment to an unencrypted fax.

2. Click the New Key Set button.

3. In the next dialog box that appears, type and confirm a password. This password prevents other users at your computer from doing anything with your key set.

> If your own computer is completely secure, you can save yourself the trouble of reentering your password each time you do anything with your key set—for example, each time you send your public key to a new recipient. To do this, select the check box labeled "Save the password in your password list." For more complete security, however, you should not select this check box.

4. Click OK and wait while Exchange creates your new key set.

Exchange stores your key set as part of your registry. You never actually see the keys, but you can now send your public key to your trusted fax recipients.

Sending Your Public Key to a Fax Recipient

After Exchange has created your key set, you will be at the dialog box shown in Figure 24-15. From here, you can save your public key in a file and then send that file, as an attachment to an unencrypted fax or to an e-mail message, to all parties to whom you want to be able to send encrypted faxes. When a recipient gets your message with the attached public key, he or she adds the key to your entry in his or her Personal Address Book. At that point the recipient will be prepared to decrypt any encrypted faxes you send.

The steps to send your public key are as follows:

1. If you are not already at the dialog box shown in Figure 24-15, choose Microsoft Fax Tools from the Tools menu, and then choose Advanced Security from the submenu that appears.

2. Click the Public Keys button.

3. Click the Save button to store your public key in a file.

4. In the Fax Security dialog box, select your name. Then click the To button and click OK.

5. Exchange then displays a standard Save As dialog box, proposing to save your file in your Windows folder as Yourname.awp (where Yourname is your name). Accept or alter this default, and then click Save.

6. Click Close twice to return to Exchange.

7. Compose a new fax or e-mail message, using standard procedures, and attach your newly created .AWP file. If you're faxing, you can password-protect this message for extra security.

Adding a Sender's Public Key to Your Personal Address Book

Before you can decode an encrypted message, you must add the sender's public key to the sender's entry in your Personal Address Book. Follow these steps:

1. After you receive the sender's public key as an attachment to a fax, open the message and save the attachment as a separate file. (To do this, select the attachment, choose Save As from the File menu, select the option button labeled Save These Attachments Only, and supply a filename.)

2. Choose Microsoft Fax Tools from the Tools menu, and then choose Advanced Security from the submenu that appears.

3. In the Advanced Security dialog box, click the Public Keys button.

4. In the Managing Public Keys dialog box, click the Add button.

5. Select the name of the public-key file that you want to add to your address book, and then click Open.

Receiving an Encrypted Fax

When an encrypted fax arrives, Exchange identifies it as such in your In-box. Double-click the message header to create an unencrypted copy, leaving the original intact. Read the copy, and then delete it for security. Be sure to delete it from your Deleted Items folder as well as from your Inbox!

Assigning a Digital Signature to an Attachment

Assigning a digital signature allows you to authenticate attachments included in your fax messages. Your recipients can use a Verify command to confirm that the attachments came from you and have not been altered since you attached them. To verify a signature, your recipients must have your public key. (See the preceding discussion.)

To assign a digital signature to all of a fax's attachments, first get to the Message Security Options dialog box shown in Figure 24-14. (For details, see "Sending a Password-Protected Fax," page 667.) Then select the Digitally Sign All Attachments check box.

Verifying a Digital Signature

To verify the digital signature assigned to a fax attachment, follow these steps:

1. Display the message text and select the attachment.

2. Choose Microsoft Fax Tools from the Tools menu.

3. Choose Verify Digital Signature from the submenu that appears.

You must have the sender's public key in your personal address book to verify the digital signature.

Using a Shared Faxmodem

You can use Fax with a faxmodem connected to a network server, provided the server has been set up to share the modem. If you receive messages through a shared modem, those messages will be stored in the Inbox folder on the server. A "fax receptionist" at that server will need to reroute the messages to you via your network e-mail system or some other means.

To Share a Modem

To set up a server so that its modem can be used by others, follow these steps:

1. Choose Microsoft Fax Tools from Exchange's Tools menu.

2. Choose Options.

3. Click the Modem tab.

4. Select the check box labeled "Let other people on the network use my modem to send faxes."

5. In the window that appears, accept or change the drive letter that is displayed. This is the drive that will be used to queue outgoing faxes when you share the modem. (If your computer has only one hard drive, you won't see this window.)

6. In the Share Name text box, accept or change the proposed share name.

7. Click the Properties button.

8. In the Access Type option group, choose Full. If you want to assign a password to restrict use of your shared faxmodem, enter a password in the Full Access Password text box.

9. Click OK twice to return to Exchange.

To Use a Shared Modem

To set your system up so that it uses a shared modem, follow these steps:

1. Choose Microsoft Fax Tools from Exchange's Tools menu.

2. Choose Options.

3. Click the Modem tab.

4. Click the Add button.

5. Select Network Fax Server and click OK.

6. Type the network path for the shared modem. By default, the share name is Fax. For example, if the modem is shared on the computer named Wotan, you would type *wotan**fax*.

7. Click OK.

8. Select the shared modem from the Available Fax Modems list, and then click Set As Active Fax Modem.

9. Click OK to return to Exchange.

Using a Fax-on-Demand Service

You can use Microsoft Fax to dial up a fax-on-demand service and download either all documents waiting for you there or a particular document. To do this, start by choosing Microsoft Fax Tools from Exchange's Tools menu. Then choose Request A Fax. You will be placed in the benevolent hands of the Request A Fax wizard, which looks like Figure 24-16 on the next page.

Select Retrieve Whatever Is Available or Retrieve A Specific Document. Fill out the rest of the dialog box if you're downloading a specific document. Then click Next. The rest of this wizard works exactly like the New Fax wizard detailed earlier in this chapter. Enter the name and

FIGURE 24-16.

This wizard, a close cousin of the New Fax wizard, enables you to call a fax-on-demand service and download the documents.

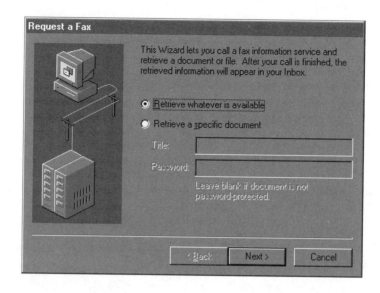

number of your fax service, follow the rest of the wizard's steps, and in a moment Fax will connect and retrieve your faxes.

25

Using The Microsoft Network

Perplexed by the information superhighway? Baffled by the Internet? Then head straight for The Microsoft Network, your friendly alternative to the wild and wooly world of the Internet.

Just like the Internet, The Microsoft Network (MSN) is a thriving community of people from all over the globe who share an interest in gathering new knowledge and meeting new people. But unlike the Internet, The Microsoft Network is an orderly and easy-to-access world, with clearly organized categories, forums for every interest, and special tools that help you get from place to place and take advantage of everything you find when you arrive. And, best of all, with The Microsoft Network, you get easy access to some favorite features of the Internet, such as the very popular Usenet newsgroups.

When you connect to The Microsoft Network by using the special software that comes with Windows 95, you can read the latest news, correspond with people on hundreds of topics, browse huge libraries of files, and even participate in lively, real-time chats about everything from the latest PC gadgetry to serious issues of home and family. Because The Microsoft Network works just like everything else in Windows 95, you navigate through MSN's forums with the same steps you use to navigate through the folders and files in your own system. Because it's as easy to find information on MSN as it is to find it in your own folders, you'll quickly grow to depend on MSN as an unlimited extension to the information that's already right on your desktop.

In this chapter, you'll learn to install the Microsoft Network software, sign on for the first time, navigate through the system, and use some of the basic features of MSN, such as the bulletin boards, chats, and e-mail. But because MSN is an ever-growing, ever-changing destination, new services appear every day, so the best way to learn about what's on the service is by diving right in and taking a look.

 See Also: For information about *accessing other Internet services*, see Chapter 26, "Roaming the Internet with Internet Explorer," page 701.

For more information about *The Microsoft Network*, see *Traveling The Microsoft Network* (Microsoft Press, 1995).

Installing the MSN Software

When you install Windows, the software for The Microsoft Network is installed only if you select the check box for The Microsoft Network during the setup process. When the setup process is complete and the Windows desktop appears, you'll be ready to sign up for The Microsoft Network.

If Windows is already installed and you'd like to add the software for The Microsoft Network, double-click the Add/Remove Programs icon in Control Panel, and then, on the Windows Setup tab, click the check box next to The Microsoft Network. When you click OK, the Setup program installs the software, prompting you for the diskettes or CD-ROM it needs.

Of course, you'll also need to make sure a modem is properly installed in Windows 95. To use MSN, you should have a modem with a speed of at least 9600 bps. MSN will be slow and difficult to use at lesser speeds.

 See Also: For information about *setting up a modem*, see "Installing a Legacy Peripheral," page 349.

Signing Up

Before you can connect to The Microsoft Network for the first time, you must sign up for the service. Follow these steps:

1. Double-click the icon for The Microsoft Network on your desktop.

    NOTE: If this icon does not appear on your desktop (and you have installed the MSN software as described in the previous section), use the Start menu's Find command to locate a file called Signup. When its icon appears in the Find window, double-click the icon to launch the Signup application.

2. In The Microsoft Network introduction window, click OK.

    From here on, you'll be guided through the process of signing up for MSN. MSN needs to know your area or city code, your name and address, a method of payment such as a credit card number, and a member ID and password. The member ID can be any combination of characters that you choose, as long as it is not already in use by another MSN member. If the member ID you enter is already taken, you'll be asked to enter a different ID. Keep in mind that this member ID will be your online identity when contributing to conversations in BBS's and chats, and when you receive mail from other systems (your Internet address will be *your memberid*@msn.com) so be sure to choose an ID that you can live with over the long run.

Signing In

After you've entered all the information that the signup program needs, the MSN software uses your modem to dial into MSN, connect to the service, and obtain an updated listing of nearby access telephone numbers from which you can choose. After you've chosen a local access number and member name, you're all set to sign in for the first time. Simply double-click the MSN icon, enter your member ID and password into the Sign In dialog box, shown in Figure 25-1, and click Connect. (The next time you sign in, your member ID will be entered automatically. Your password will be entered automatically if you select the Remember My Password check box.) The MSN software dials the service, verifies your identity, and then displays MSN Central (the main MSN screen), shown in Figure 25-2.

FIGURE 25-1.

The Sign In dialog box appears each time you want to connect to MSN.

When you first sign in, a magazine-style feature, called MSN Today, may open in a window. You can click icons to browse through MSN Today and learn about new MSN services, special scheduled events, or

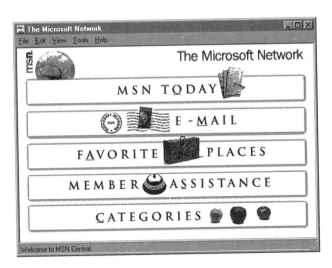

FIGURE 25-2.

MSN Central is the "main menu" for The Microsoft Network.

other news of interest to MSN users. To put away MSN Today, simply close its window. To prevent MSN Today from appearing each time you sign in, choose Options from the View menu of the MSN Central window, and then, on the General tab, clear the check box labeled "Show MSN Today title on startup."

Getting Around the System

Moving from place to place within The Microsoft Network is a simple point-and-click operation. Opening forums on MSN is just like opening the folders on your hard disk or network drive. In fact, after you've opened a folder or forum on MSN, you have a similar choice of views for browsing its contents.

The starting point for all your excursions is MSN Central, the main window that opens when you sign in. The large buttons within the MSN Central window lead to services and areas provided by The Microsoft Network.

- The MSN Today button takes you to news about world events and local developments right on The Microsoft Network. MSN Today is updated daily with information about the latest additions to The Microsoft Network.

- Clicking the E-Mail button ushers you directly to Microsoft Exchange, where you can read incoming correspondence and compose outgoing e-mail messages.

- Favorite Places takes you back to sites that you enjoyed enough to add to the Favorite Places folder.

- Member Assistance leads to a comprehensive customer service area where you can get help about using MSN, your bill, or other service-related issues.

- The Categories button leads to a display of icons, one for each of the major areas of interest within MSN. Here's where you'll begin your exploration of the forums, products, and services on The Microsoft Network. It's the top level of the MSN content tree.

The current View setting determines how the MSN categories are represented on the screen. The initial setting is probably Large Icons view, which displays the categories as large folder icons. The forums, chats, BBS's, file libraries, kiosks, and other services within the folders will be displayed as large icons, too. Other choices are Small Icons, which allows you to see a greater number of icons in each window; List, which provides a display of services as a sortable list; and Details, which also offers a sorted list but includes additional information such as the last date and time a bulletin board was modified. These four views are identical to the views you can choose while browsing the folders and files on your system with Windows Explorer.

You can also determine whether you want each new area you enter within MSN to appear in its own window, or whether to use a single window whose contents change each time you open a new service so you won't be buried under a pile of windows as you move about the system. To make your selection, choose Options from the View menu, and then choose one of the settings on the Folder tab of the Options dialog box.

See Also: For more information about *views and switching among them*, see "Folder Viewing Options," page 128.

Leaving MSN Central

To begin your travels through one of the broad areas on MSN, such as Arts and Entertainment, choose Categories from MSN Central, and then double-click one of the broad areas of interest within MSN that are represented by icons. Figure 25-3 shows the Categories display.

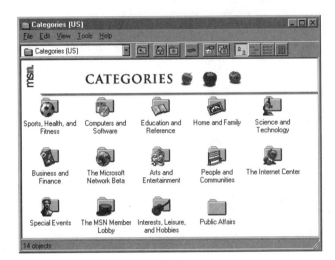

FIGURE 25-3.

The Categories display in large icon view.

When you double-click any category icon, you'll see new icons, which represent the folders and forums that reside under the category. Double-click any of these icons to move inside a folder or forum in which you'll find still more specialized icons or the services within a forum. After you've selected Arts And Entertainment, for example, you can double-click the Comedy And Humor icon to move into the Comedy Connection forum. Then you can double-click one of the icons within the forum, such as the Political Humor BBS, to move into one of the services within the forum. To leave a BBS or other service and return to the previous level, click the Up One Level button on the toolbar or press the Backspace key. If the toolbar is not visible, choose Toolbar from the View menu.

A useful alternative to moving up or down in the folder hierarchy one step at a time is to use the drop-down list at the left end of the toolbar to see your current position in the tree structure of folders on MSN. Your current location is highlighted, and all the folders above your position are displayed, as shown in Figure 25-4 on the next page. Click any folder to jump up one or more levels. You can even click The Microsoft Network, at the top of the hierarchy, to return to MSN Central. Two shortcuts for returning to MSN Central are to click the MSN Central button on the toolbar or to right-click the MSN icon in the taskbar's notification area and choose Go To MSN Central from the object menu.

FIGURE 25-4.

You can quickly navigate with the folder drop-down list.

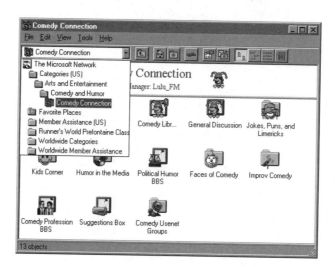

MSN provides another useful method for jumping from point to point. "Go words" let you jump immediately to any service without having to travel through the MSN hierarchy of folders. The Go word for a service is part of its properties, so you can find the Go word for a service by right-clicking its icon and choosing Properties from the object menu. To jump to a forum by entering a Go word, right-click the MSN icon in the taskbar's notification area and choose Go To from the object menu. Then enter the Go word in the Go To Service dialog box. You can also choose Go To from the Edit menu; choose Other Location from the Go To submenu to get to the Go To Service dialog box.

Exploring MSN with Windows Explorer

Anyone who has had experience using Windows Explorer to navigate through a local hard disk or network drive might prefer to transit through The Microsoft Network using the exact same tool. In one window with two panes, Windows Explorer shows both the content tree of MSN and the folders and icons in the currently selected branch of the tree. Windows Explorer also lets you jump quickly from place to place within MSN by simply clicking any folder you can see in Windows Explorer's left pane. Figure 25-5 shows MSN as viewed in Windows Explorer.

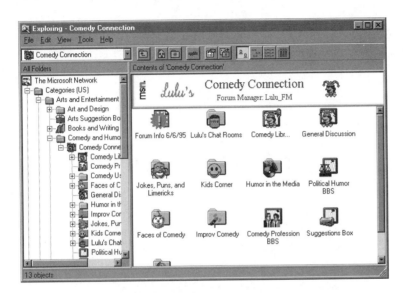

FIGURE 25-5.

You can use Windows Explorer to navigate MSN.

To sign on to The Microsoft Network in Windows Explorer view, press and hold Shift when you double-click the MSN icon or right-click the MSN icon and choose Explore.

If you're already connected to The Microsoft Network, you can open a Windows Explorer view of MSN by displaying the Categories window, right-clicking its Control-menu icon, and choosing Explore.

For more information about *using Windows Explorer to navigate through folders*, see Chapter 5, "Managing Folders and Files with Windows Explorer," page 163.

Using the Find Command

Perhaps the most powerful way to navigate through The Microsoft Network is by using Find to locate and jump directly to a site of particular interest. To use Find, click the Start button, point to Find, and then choose On The Microsoft Network from the Find submenu. (You can also get to the Find command via the Tools menu in any MSN folder window.) In the Find dialog box, enter a keyword that describes your interest. To find forums devoted to automobiles, for example, you might enter "car" as a keyword. After a moment, you'll see a list of areas in a search-results window that shows services that pertain to automobiles, as shown in Figure 25-6. Double-click any item in the search-results list to jump directly to that site on MSN.

FIGURE 25-6.

You can use wildcards and the "or" keyword to broaden your search. For details, select the Containing text box and press F1.

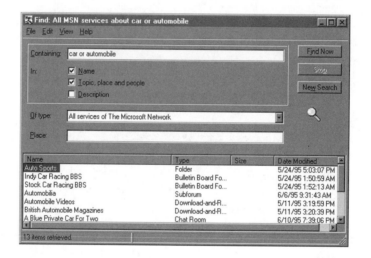

Visiting a Forum

A forum is like a club where people meet, swap stories, and share files. As you explore MSN, you'll find dozens of forums in each of the main category folders. One example of a forum is Gardening, which you'll find in the Home Interests folder under the Interests, Leisure, And Hobbies category.

To find a forum, you can wander through the folders of MSN until you stumble upon something that intrigues you, or you can use Find to quickly seek out the forums that match your interests. While visiting a forum you like, you can always add it to your Favorite Places folder. Then you'll have one-click access to the forum or any of its services. While visiting the forum or one of its services, just click the Add To Favorite Places button on the toolbar.

You'll know you've entered a forum when you open a folder and find icons inside for a variety of services. Nearly every forum has at least these three services: a Chat, a BBS, and a Kiosk.

- A Chat is a live conversation among members.

- A BBS is a bulletin board where members can post messages.

- A Kiosk is a WordPad document that contains information about the forum and the forum managers.

Participating in a Chat

Nearly every forum has a chat room, a place where members can type messages to everyone else in the chat room. To step into a chat room, simply double-click any icon that's labeled "chat." Although your arrival will be announced to everyone in the chat, you don't need to begin chatting right away. You might want to take a few minutes to follow the flow of the conversation before adding your own ".02" (two cents' worth). Figure 25-7 shows a chat in a chat window.

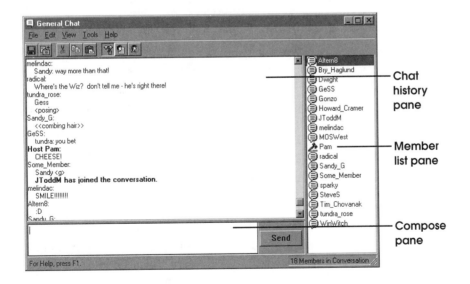

FIGURE 25-7.

A Chat is a live conversation among members.

Within a chat window, you'll see three panes. The largest pane, at the upper left, is the *chat history pane*. It displays comments as they're entered by chat participants. The vertical *member list pane* at the right contains a list of the members who have joined the chat. The small *compose pane* at the bottom, next to the Send button, is where you compose comments before sending them into the conversation for everyone to read. There, a typing cursor patiently awaits.

If this is your first visit to a chat, you may be bewildered by the jumble of comments that are flowing into the chat history pane. Most chats are unorganized free-for-alls, so don't be alarmed by the chaos that seems to be occurring. It may take you a few moments to pick out the threads of the multiple conversations.

When you're ready to speak up and contribute your own comments, simply begin typing into the compose pane. Don't worry, nothing you type will be sent out until you press Enter or click the Send button. This gives you the chance to carefully compose your thoughts by editing the text in the compose pane. (As you'll see, few people really edit their comments before freely tossing them into the mix.)

To learn more about someone who is present in a chat, double-click that member's name on the member list or click a name and then click the Member Properties button on the toolbar. A Member Properties window opens to reveal all the biographical data the member has chosen to provide in the MSN address book. (To edit your own personal information, you must modify your properties in The Microsoft Network address book. You gain access to the address book via Exchange.)

When a chat has been particularly interesting, you can save a transcript by saving the chat history. Everything from the moment you entered the chat is recorded in a file on disk. To save the chat history, choose Save History from the File menu.

When you're ready to leave a chat, say your goodbyes and then simply close the chat window. Everyone in the group sees a message that you've left.

The Language of Chat

To save chat members both time and typing, a special, cryptic chat shorthand has evolved that everyone will seem to understand at first, except you. To save you the embarrassment of asking for a translation, Table 25-1 provides a brief guide to some of chat's most popular vernacular.

Table 25-1. Chat Shorthand

Shorthand	Meaning
BRB	Be right back
<g>	Grin
<G>	Big grin
IMO	In my opinion
IMHO	In my humble opinion
LOL	Lots of laughs
ROFL	Rolling on the floor laughing
Rehi	Greeting to a member who returns to chat

Chats have begotten another contribution to contemporary discourse, called a "smiley." A smiley provides the nuances of communication that are normally conveyed by vocal inflections in a phone chat or facial expressions in a F2F (face-to-face conversation). A smiley can communicate your bantering intent in a statement that might otherwise come across as sarcastic. Smileys (also called emoticons) are easy to tack on to the end of a comment, so don't be afraid to use them freely to enhance your communication. Smileys make sense if you tilt your head to the left as you look at them. Here are some of the most popular smileys:

:-)	Smile
:-(	Frown
:->	Big grin
;-)	Wink
%-|	Dazed
:-o	Surprised
:-O	Shocked

Customizing a Chat

MSN chats offer a few customization options that can enhance your use of chat. First, you can easily ignore someone who's making less-than-valuable or even inappropriate contributions to unmoderated conversations. To ignore members, select their names on the member list, and then click the Ignore button on the toolbar or choose Ignore Members from the View menu. Their comments will no longer be visible until you select them again and turn off ignore.

You can also choose whether to be notified when members arrive or when they depart from a chat. Choose Options from the Tools menu and then click the check boxes next to the Notify Me When Members . . . options. In the same dialog box, you can choose whether MSN adds a blank line between each message. Blank lines make the chat easier to follow but allow fewer comments to fit on the screen.

Using a BBS

Another service you'll find in just about every MSN forum is a BBS, short for bulletin board system. Unlike a chat, a BBS contains an orderly and usually civil discussion among members on topics that are covered by that forum. A discussion takes the form of a series of messages interleaved with responses. Someone initiates a conversation about a topic by entering a new message and others contribute responses. Still others may respond to the responses. Before you know it, the thread of a discussion can contain dozens of messages. Any one BBS can contain hundreds of these threads, all available for your reading pleasure.

Reading a BBS

To open any BBS, simply double-click its icon. The BBS window opens and displays the messages it contains in one of three views: Conversation, List, or Attached Files.

- Conversation view displays message and response subjects, called *headers*, in an outline structure that makes it easy to follow the thread of a conversation.

- List view displays a simple list of headers in the order in which they were posted to the BBS. To sort the list another way, such as by Author, Subject, or Date, click the Author, Subject, or Date buttons at the top of the list.

- Attached Files view displays only the message headers of messages that contain files that are available for downloading.

In Conversation view, each new discussion is represented by a new message header at the top level of the outline. Responses to the initial message are indented below. Indented below these responses are further responses, and so on.

The header of each message that you have not yet read in a BBS is bold and accompanied by an arrow. The unread message symbol also appears next to the headers of messages that have unread responses.

To see only new messages that have been added to the BBS since your last visit, deactivate the Show All Messages option on the Tools menu.

When you first open a BBS, you will see only the top-level message headers, which start off each discussion, as shown in Figure 25-8. If there are any responses, they are hidden in the outline structure underneath. To reveal the responses, click the plus icon to the left of the message header. The headers of the responses will appear as a second level in the outline.

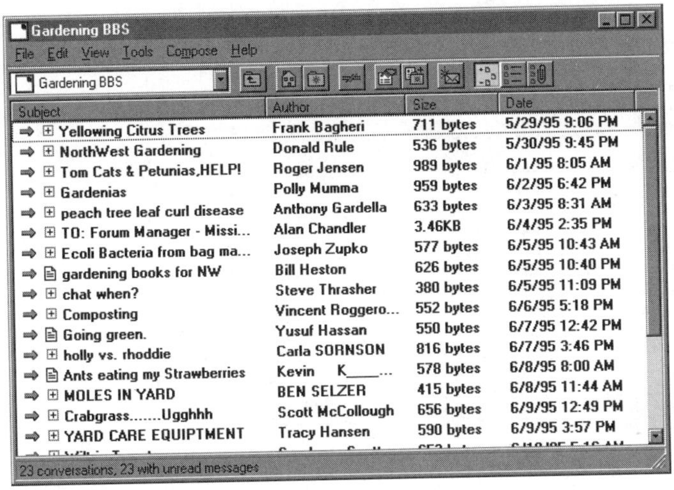

FIGURE 25-8.

Bold type indicates unread messages; an arrow in the left column indicates the presence of at least one unread message in the conversation "thread."

Figure 25-9 on the next page shows a message header that has been opened to reveal its responses. If any response has a plus icon, you can click it to reveal the responses to the response. When you reach a message that is accompanied by a message-without-responses icon, you've reached the last message in that branch of the conversation. You can either add a response of your own or click the icon next to any message header again to close the outline structure under that message. Then you can browse another branch of the current conversation, or return to the top level and browse another conversation entirely.

The following icons can appear in Conversation view:

⊞   Message with hidden responses

⊟   Message with visible responses

📄   Message without responses

 To expand a conversation outline to show all the responses without opening them one at a time, hold the Shift key when you click the plus icon in a message header.

FIGURE 25-9.

Conversation view uses outline-style indenting to show the sequence of responses.

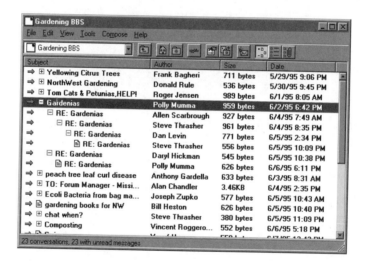

If you'd like, you can use the keyboard to navigate through the outline structure of a discussion. To open the outline structure under any message, move the highlight to the message header with the arrow keys and then press the Plus key. To close the outline under a message header, highlight the message header and press the Minus key.

To read a message in a conversation, double-click the message header or highlight the header and press Enter. While the message window is still open, you can use the navigation buttons on the toolbar to move to the next or previous message, next unread message, or next or previous conversation. You can also close the message and return to Conversation view by pressing the Esc key. Table 25-2 describes the navigation and other buttons on the BBS message toolbar.

Table 25-2. BBS Message Toolbar

Toolbar Icon	Description
	Creates a new BBS message
	Saves this message to disk
	Prints this message
	Standard Clipboard operations: cut, copy, and paste
	Creates a reply to this message
	Displays the previous or next message
	Displays the next unread message
	Displays the first message in the previous or next conversation
	Displays the first message in the next unread conversation
	Displays the File Transfer Status window

Contributing to a BBS

To post a message about a new topic, click the New Message button on the toolbar or choose New Message from the Compose menu. A window opens in which you can enter the text of your comment or query. This window offers the text formatting capabilities of WordPad so you can change fonts, font sizes, and even the font color within a message.

To reply to any message in a BBS, open the message and then click the Reply To BBS button on the toolbar. When you finish composing a message or a response, click the Send button at the left end of the toolbar or press Ctrl-Enter. Your message will show up in the BBS when you either choose Refresh from the View menu or reopen the BBS at a later time. Other users who enter the BBS after you send a message will see the message immediately. Your message stays in the BBS for a preset interval, after which old messages are deleted.

 Rather than post a public reply on the BBS, you can send a private reply by e-mail simply by choosing Reply By E-mail from the Compose menu or pressing Ctrl-R.

 For more information about *formatting text in a message,* see "Changing Fonts," page 458.

Downloading Files from a BBS

When a BBS message contains a file that you can download from MSN to your own computer, you'll see a paper-clip icon next to the message header in List view. To learn more about the downloadable file, open the message. The message will contain both a description of the file and a file icon. For detailed information about the file, such as its size, the time it will take to download, and whether a fee will be charged to your account to retrieve the file, right-click the file icon, choose File Object from the object menu, and then choose Properties. To go ahead and download the file, choose Download rather than Properties from the File Object menu. More simply, you can double-click the file icon. The file will be added to the download queue so it will begin downloading as soon as any other files you may be downloading are finished. A File Transfer Status window will open to reveal the files that you've already placed in the download queue. The File Transfer Status window is shown in Figure 25-10.

If a file is compressed, you can have MSN automatically uncompress the file after it is transferred, and even delete the original compressed version. In the File Transfer Status window, choose Options from the Tools menu to activate this feature. In the same dialog box, you can also choose to "Pause files as they are queued," so you can add files to the download queue at different times during an MSN session and only start their downloading when you are finished with your other work on the service. If you choose this option, you may also want to click the Transfer And Disconnect

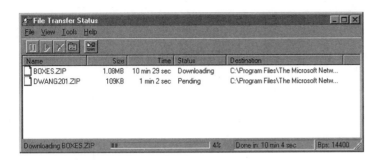

FIGURE 25-10.

The File Transfer
Status window
tracks the progress
of files you are
downloading from
MSN.

button on the File Transfer Status toolbar so MSN will hang up automatically after you receive the last file from the queue.

Because MSN takes advantage of the multitasking capabilities of Windows, your other option is to continue with your exploration of MSN even while files are downloading in the background. Be aware that MSN may operate more slowly because the MSN software at your end is also busy working to transfer files.

Downloading Files from a File Library

In some forums, you'll find a special service called a *file library*, which contains files that you can download from MSN to your own computer. Hardware and software manufacturers use file libraries to make software updates and hardware drivers available to users of their products. Other forums use file libraries to provide news and information in downloadable text files, or to offer shareware software programs that anyone can download. Still other forums may offer files that you can purchase and download immediately. The charge for these files will be added to your MSN bill. Figure 25-11 on the next page shows a file library.

A file library is very much like a BBS except that its postings are messages that contain files rather than contributions to a conversation. Each message header describes the file that is contained within the message. Figure 25-11 shows the contents of a typical file library when it is first opened. In many file libraries, messages are grouped into folders that represent categories of files. Double-click any folder to view the messages it contains. Figure 25-12 on the next page shows the contents of the Demos folder depicted in Figure 25-11.

FIGURE 25-11.

A file library contains files that you can download, or folders that contain files.

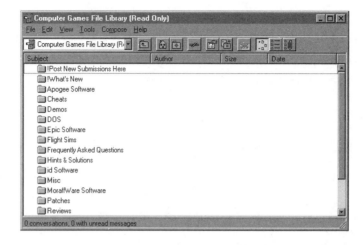

FIGURE 25-12.

A file library looks much like a BBS.

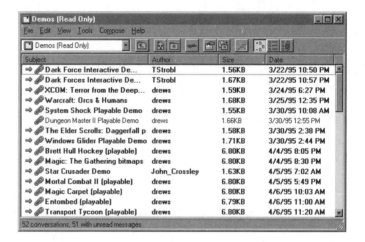

When you open one of these messages, you'll see a description of the file or files represented by file icons that are also in the message. Just as you would in a BBS message that contains a file, you can learn more about the file by right-clicking its icon and checking its properties. You can also add any file to the download queue by double-clicking its icon.

If you'd like to contribute a file to a public file library, you must compose a new message, enter information about the file, and then insert the file into the message by clicking the paper-clip icon, by choosing File from the Insert menu and specifying the filename in the Insert File dialog box, or by dragging the file to your message from a folder window. When you click the Send button, your message and the file it contains will be sent to the manager of the forum. Your file will not appear until the forum manager has checked to ensure that it works, infringes no copyright, and contains no viruses, so it may be a short interval before your file becomes available for everyone to download.

Sending and Receiving E-Mail

For some people, the best thing about The Microsoft Network will be its extraordinary electronic mail (e-mail) capabilities. MSN e-mail makes it easy to send private messages to someone else on The Microsoft Network or anyone who has a mailbox that is reachable through the Internet. That means you can send e-mail to the electronic mailboxes of millions of people, organizations, and companies all around the world.

When you send a message to another MSN member, you gain a special advantage. In your message, you can change the font, size, and styling for any of the text, and even change the text color to anything other than basic black. Figure 25-13 shows an example of some of the text formatting that's possible in an e-mail message between MSN members.

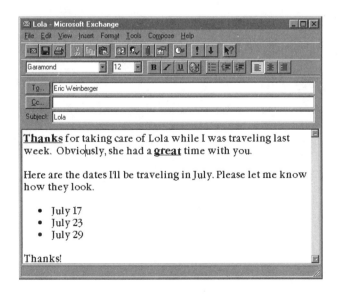

FIGURE 25-13.

Messages between MSN members can have text formatting.

As if that's not enough improvement over other e-mail systems, you can also embed in your messages objects that you've created in Windows-based applications, such as Microsoft Word or Microsoft Excel. An object appears as an icon in an e-mail message; the recipient can double-click the icon to open the object. While creating a message, you can insert a Microsoft Word file as an icon, for example. When the recipient, who also has Word, opens the message and then double-clicks the icon of the Word file, Word starts and then opens the document automatically.

Microsoft Exchange, the universal inbox of Windows 95, is the power behind MSN e-mail. Exchange is the same program that handles incoming and outgoing mail from other electronic mail sources to which you are connected, such as the Microsoft Mail server on your office network.

After you sign in to MSN, you can open Exchange by clicking the E-Mail button in the MSN Central window. Exchange retrieves any incoming messages and sends any outgoing mail that you've written. If you are notified that you have new mail when you sign in to MSN, you can simply click Yes when the message asks whether to retrieve your new mail. Exchange opens automatically, gets your e-mail, and places it in your Inbox folder.

Once MSN e-mail arrives in your Inbox, it looks and acts just like e-mail from any other source with which you communicate using Microsoft Exchange, such as a Microsoft Mail server on your office network. Within the Microsoft Exchange window, the folders you use to store incoming and outgoing messages are at the left. When you click any folder, you see its contents listed within the right side of the Exchange window. Message headers that are bold represent new, unread messages.

See Also: For more information about *sending and receiving messages with Exchange*, see Chapter 23, "Using Microsoft Exchange," page 587.

Previewing Your Incoming E-Mail

If you receive tons of e-mail each day or if you get messages with large embedded files, Exchange offers a special option you can use to get a list of waiting e-mail messages without actually taking the time to download them all. When you review the list, you can mark certain messages for retrieval, leave other messages on MSN for later, and even delete messages without reading them. Take *that,* e-mail advertisers!

To use this feature, called remote preview, open Exchange before you connect to MSN and then choose Remote Mail from the Tools menu. On the Remote Mail submenu, choose The Microsoft Network and then click the Update Headers button on the toolbar in the Remote Mail window. Exchange connects with MSN, opens your mailbox on MSN, retrieves the list of waiting messages, and then disconnects. Now you can work through the list of message headers in the Remote Mail window, marking messages to be retrieved, left alone, or deleted. To accomplish this, select a message to be retrieved and then click the Mark To Retrieve or Mark To Retrieve A Copy button (to leave the original on the system), and then select the messages to be deleted and click the Mark To Delete button. Messages that you do not mark remain in your mailbox on MSN and are not transferred to your Inbox in Exchange. After you mark the list, click the Transfer Mail button to have Exchange sign back on, handle the messages according to your bidding, and then sign off again. In the Exchange Inbox, you can now review and reply to the messages you've chosen to receive. Figure 25-14 shows the Remote Mail window.

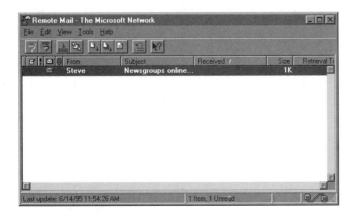

FIGURE 25-14.

The Remote Mail window lets you review message headers before you download messages to your Inbox.

To create a new message before you connect to MSN, open Microsoft Exchange and click the New Message button on the Exchange toolbar or choose New Message from the Compose menu. If you are connected to MSN already, open Exchange by either clicking E-Mail in the MSN Central window, or right-clicking the MSN icon in the taskbar's notification area and choosing Send Mail from the object menu.

 For more information about *remote preview*, see "Using Remote Mail with Local and Dial-Up Connections," page 637.

Keeping Up with the Internet Newsgroups

Internet newsgroups, available under The Internet Center in the Categories window, are much like the bulletin boards in the forums of MSN. They offer similar strands of messages on hundreds and hundreds of subjects, but they are accessible to everyone who has access to the Internet, not just the members of MSN. Because most everyone with access to the Internet can read and contribute to these newsgroups, you'll find an incredible array of topics from which to choose and an amazing depth of discussion in any one topic. There's a newsgroup on the Internet for every conceivable profession, hobby, political interest, and sexual persuasion. The big difference between the Internet newsgroups and the BBS's on MSN is that the newsgroups arrive from somewhere out on the Internet. Therefore, they can be an interesting supplement to the BBS's, which contain local conversations that occur within MSN forums.

To visit an Internet newsgroup, choose Categories from MSN Central and double-click The Internet Center icon. Then double-click the Newsgroups icon. The Internet newsgroups are organized into categories represented by folders. Double-click any folder to see more detailed sub-folders inside. Continue double-clicking subfolders until you get to the actual newsgroups, in which you'll find messages that appear just as the messages in BBS's, except that the senders have Internet addresses rather than MSN member names.

You can browse through the newsgroup discussions using all the same techniques you use to browse through MSN BBS's. You can even contribute a posting to a newsgroup by following the same procedure you'd use to add a comment in a BBS.

> **NOTE:** Because the Internet newsgroups emanate from sources outside MSN, they're not subject to the examination that forum managers give to the MSN BBS's for profane, indecent, or even illegal topics and comments. So be forewarned that the newsgroups are uncontrolled and uncontrollable. Should you find their content objectionable, you can stay away and restrict your children's access.

 To navigate through the complex categories and subcategories of the Internet newsgroups, you may want to open Internet Newsgroups with Windows Explorer, or take advantage of the drop-down folder hierarchy display at the left end of the toolbar.

Customizing MSN

As you travel MSN, you're bound to find certain services that interest you especially. To make it simple to frequent them, you may want to add them to your Favorite Places folder. To make it even easier to jump to a specific MSN area, you can place a shortcut icon for a service right on your Windows desktop. Then you can jump to a service on MSN even if you're not connected to MSN at the time. If necessary, you'll be signed in to MSN automatically and transferred immediately to the service you want.

Adding MSN Services to Favorite Places

While visiting a forum, BBS, chat, or newsgroup, you can always click the Add To Favorite Places button or choose Add To Favorite Places from the File menu. This personalizes MSN by adding icons for your favorite services to the Favorite Places folder. You open this folder by clicking Favorite Places in the MSN Central window, clicking the Favorite Places button on the toolbar of any MSN window, or right-clicking the MSN icon in the taskbar's notification area and then choosing View Favorite Places from the object menu. To delete a service from Favorite Places, simply select the icon and choose Delete from the File menu.

Creating Shortcuts

An option for personalizing MSN even further is to create a shortcut for any MSN service right on your Windows desktop. Simply select the folder or icon of the service you want and then choose Create Shortcut from the File menu. You'll see a new shortcut icon appear on your Windows desktop. Double-clicking this icon jumps directly to the service it represents, even if it means connecting with MSN first.

Shortcuts are enormously powerful because they allow you to create an environment on your desktop in which the information stored in folders on MSN is just as accessible as the information stored in folders on your own disk. You can even mail a shortcut to a friend that will lead to a service by simply dragging the shortcut from your desktop to a mail message you're composing.

26

Roaming the Internet with Internet Explorer

nternet Explorer is an application that allows you to explore the part of the Internet known as the World Wide Web. Internet Explorer includes many features that make accessing information on the Internet as simple as pointing and clicking on items that interest you.

Internet Explorer is included with Microsoft Plus! for Windows 95. You can also obtain Internet Explorer on The Microsoft Network. If you have an MSN account, you will be automatically provided with Internet Explorer once it becomes available on The Microsoft Network.

This chapter assumes that you already have access to the Internet. This means that you have one of the following:

- A modem and a PPP account with an Internet service provider

- A local-area network (LAN) connection to the Internet

- A modem and an account with The Microsoft Network

If you have one of the above setups, you can run the Internet Setup wizard that comes with Internet Explorer. This wizard walks you through the process of setting up your computer to connect to the Internet. To start the Internet Setup wizard, go to the Start menu and choose Programs, Accessories, Internet Tools, Internet Setup Wizard.

Most of the features and commands in Internet Explorer allow you to work directly with material on the World Wide Web. Before you start using these features, it is important to know a few things about the Web itself. If you are already familiar with the Internet and with the World Wide Web, you should probably skip ahead to "Getting Started with Internet Explorer," page 704.

See Also: For more information about *Microsoft Plus! for Windows 95,* see Appendix A, "Using the Power of Your 486 or Pentium with Microsoft Plus!," page 727.

For information about *The Microsoft Network,* see Chapter 25, "Using The Microsoft Network," page 675.

Introducing the World Wide Web

The World Wide Web is a system of information that can be accessed on the Internet. Each section of information on the Web is called a *page*. Any individual page may have links, or pointers, to other World Wide Web pages. To move around the World Wide Web, you simply start at one page, and then use links on that page to jump to other pages that interest you.

Because you will be moving around from page to page quite frequently, it can be hard to remember what pages you have already seen. Internet Explorer has several features to help you keep track of where you've been and what pages you like to look at.

Important Things to Know About the World Wide Web

Internet Explorer makes using the World Wide Web fairly simple. However, it's helpful to know some terms and concepts. You can refer to this short list of terms when they are used elsewhere in this chapter.

Internet. The Internet is a worldwide network of computers. If you have access to the Internet, you can view information from any public computer on the Internet.

World Wide Web. The World Wide Web, or WWW, is a system of interconnected documents that are placed on the Internet. Each individual document is usually called a *page*.

World Wide Web browser. A browser is any application that allows you to view pages on the World Wide Web. Internet Explorer is an example of such an application.

Home page. The first screen that you see at any WWW site is usually called the *home page* for that site. Home page can also refer to the first WWW page you see when you start your browser, although Internet Explorer uses the term *start page* to describe that page.

URL. URL stands for Uniform Resource Locator. This is an address that identifies a World Wide Web page or other resource on the Internet. For example, the URL for Microsoft Corporation's Web site is *http://www.microsoft.com.*

Link. A link is any highlighted information in a World Wide Web page that takes you to another page when you click it. You can tell if an item is a link by putting the mouse pointer over it. If the pointer icon changes to a "hand" pointer, then the item under it is a link.

HTML. HTML, which stands for Hypertext Markup Language, is the document language that all World Wide Web documents are created with.

HTTP. The protocol that is used to send HTML documents across the Internet is called HTTP, which stands for Hypertext Transfer Protocol.

FTP. FTP, which stands for File Transfer Protocol, is a simple way to send any kind of file across the Internet.

Gopher. Gopher is another system for sending information across the Internet. Unlike FTP, gopher provides simple text menus to help you find your way.

Getting Started with Internet Explorer

To start Internet Explorer, simply double-click the icon labeled "The Internet" on your desktop. If this icon was not created when you installed Internet Explorer, you should be able to start Internet Explorer by opening the Start menu, and then choosing Programs, Accessories, Internet Tools, Internet Explorer.

The Internet Explorer Window

Before you start exploring the World Wide Web, it is important to understand the components of the Internet Explorer window. Once you know what the different items do, using Internet Explorer is pretty simple. Figure 26-1 points out the various components of the window.

■ The *toolbar* allows quick access to commands that you use most often. (For details, see "Using the Toolbar," page 706.) All of the commands on the toolbar can also be accessed with the menus on the menu bar.

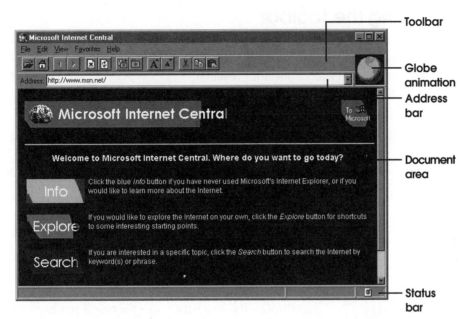

Toolbar

Globe animation

Address bar

Document area

Status bar

FIGURE 26-1.

The Internet Explorer main window has a small set of tools and controls surrounding the document viewing area

- The *address bar* displays the Internet address of the World Wide Web page you're currently viewing. If the page is located on your own computer, the full path to the page is displayed. You can also use the address bar for navigation: type the address of a page you want to go to in the address bar.

- The *globe animation* indicates when Internet Explorer is waiting to receive information from a remote computer on the Internet; the globe rotates while Internet Explorer waits.

- The *status bar* gives you information about what Internet Explorer is currently doing. The icon at the far right of the bar shows detailed information when the pointer is placed over it; while Internet Explorer retrieves data from the Internet, the detailed information also appears at the status bar's left end.

- The *document area* displays the World Wide Web page you're currently viewing. Any items that are highlighted are links, and clicking them takes you to the page they point to.

Using the Toolbar

The most often used Internet Explorer commands can be accessed by using the appropriate button on the toolbar. Table 26-1 provides a description of the command each button represents.

Table 26-1. Internet Explorer Toolbar

Toolbar Icon	Description
	Brings up a dialog box in which you can specify the Internet address (URL) of a World Wide Web page or the path to a file stored on your computer—allowing you to view the page or file
	Displays the Internet Explorer start page
	Displays the previous page that you looked at (available only if you have viewed any page other than the current page)
	Displays the next page (available only if you have used the Back button to display a previous page)
	Stops loading the current page; use this if the page is very long and is taking a lot of time to be received, or if you accidentally start downloading an image you do not want
	Refreshes (i.e., rereads from the server) the current page
	Adds an entry for the current page to the Favorites folder
	Opens the Favorites folder, which provides quick access to your favorite Web pages
	Increases the size of the screen font
	Decreases the size of the screen font
	Standard Clipboard operations: cut, copy, and paste

Viewing the Document Area

The document area of Internet Explorer is where World Wide Web pages are displayed. When Internet Explorer is started, it automatically loads a document called the *start page* into the document area of the window. The start page contains sample material that will help you to learn about and use Internet Explorer. (See the document area of Figure 26-1.)

Use the scroll bars to view parts of the page not currently displayed in the window. Within the window, you can click a link to jump to another page or right-click any area to display an object menu. A different object menu appears depending on whether you right-click a link, a graphic, or the document's background area.

Understanding the Status Bar

When you access pages on the World Wide Web, getting information from a site on the Internet to your computer can sometimes take a fair amount of time. In situations like this, it can be helpful to have more information about what Internet Explorer is actually doing.

The status bar provides several pieces of additional information, including the Internet address that a link points to, progress information about downloading the current page, and detailed information about what action Internet Explorer is trying to complete.

At the far right of the status bar is an icon that represents the current page. If you place the mouse pointer over this icon for a few moments, information about the current page appears. This feature can be extremely useful if you're not sure what Internet Explorer is currently doing.

Navigating on the World Wide Web

Internet Explorer offers several routes for navigating the World Wide Web. You can:

- Click a link to go to a page

- Enter an Internet address (URL) to go to a specific page

- Use the Forward and Back commands to revisit previously viewed pages

- Go further back in your Web-browsing history with commands on the File menu

- Return to your favorite pages by saving pointers to them

When you visit a World Wide Web site, Internet Explorer records the information in a *cache*, a set of files on your disk. When you click a link or shortcut, Internet Explorer looks in the cache to see if it has the page you are looking for. If it does, it loads the page from the cache instead of connecting to the Internet.

If Internet Explorer cannot find the page in the cache, it starts the procedure for connecting to the Internet—either by dialing your Internet service provider or by accessing the Internet through your LAN. This is called *AutoDial;* Internet Explorer automatically dials the Internet when you try to access information that is on the Internet.

If you connect to the Internet via The Microsoft Network or a dial-up service provider, Internet Explorer displays a connection dialog box when it needs to connect to the Internet. Simply click Connect to establish the connection. When you no longer need the connection, activate the Dial-Up Networking connection window (see Figure 26-2) by clicking its task-bar button (its title begins with the name of the connection); then click the Disconnect button.

FIGURE 26-2.

To end an online Internet session, open the Dial-Up Networking connection window and click Disconnect.

 If you use a modem to connect to the Internet, be sure to enable Auto Disconnect. Doing so allows Internet Explorer to disconnect from the Internet after a specified time without any activity by you. To enable Auto Disconnect, right-click the desktop Internet icon and choose Properties. Select the Auto Disconnect check box and specify a timeout value.

Using Links to Get to Other Pages

The World Wide Web works in a fashion similar to the Help feature in most Windows-based software products. In Help, any word that is underlined or highlighted is an item that you can click in order to get more information. On the World Wide Web, these items are called *links*.

Each page on the World Wide Web can have an unlimited number of links to other pages. You can identify a link by moving the pointer over a text or graphic item on a page. If the pointer icon changes to a hand when you pass over that item, as shown in Figure 26-3, then the item is a link. Notice also that the status bar displays information about the link.

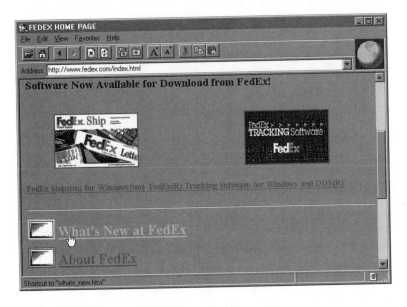

FIGURE 26-3.

The mouse pointer changes to a hand when pointing to a link. Links initially appear in blue; they turn green after you visit the page that the link points to.

To use a link, all you have to do is click it. When you do this, Internet Explorer takes you to the World Wide Web page that the link is pointing to.

Once you have clicked a link and gone to a particular page, Internet Explorer remembers that you have used that link. To let you know that you've already used a link, Internet Explorer changes the color of the text for that link from blue to green.

Viewing Multiple Documents Simultaneously

Internet Explorer allows you to specify whether you want to open a particular World Wide Web page in a new window or in the current window. This feature allows you to view one page while you are waiting to connect to another. You might find this capability useful for viewing graphics-laden pages, which can take a long time to display. To use this feature, choose Open from the File menu, type the Internet address for the item you want to view, and then select the Open In New Window check box. Click the OK button, and this new page will be loaded in a new Internet Explorer window.

If you want to display a linked page in a new window, Internet Explorer offers two shortcuts for using this feature, allowing you to bypass the Open Internet Address dialog box. You can right-click a link and choose Open In New Window from the object menu or, more simply, hold down the Shift key when you click the link.

Getting to a Specific World Wide Web Page

If you happen to know the address of a specific Web page, Internet Explorer provides two easy ways to get there. You can use the address bar or the File Open command.

The address bar is the strip of information right below the toolbar. The text field in the address bar always displays the URL of the current WWW page. However, you can also type any URL into the text field. Once you type it in and press Enter, Internet Explorer will take you there. Follow these steps to enter an address into the address bar:

1. Press Tab or click the Address text entry box. This highlights whatever text is currently in the box.

2. Type the URL or World Wide Web address for the page you want to go to. The address should look something like this:

   `http://www.microsoft.com`

3. Press Enter. This tells Internet Explorer to find the page that you want. It may take a few seconds for the World Wide Web page to respond to Internet Explorer's request for information.

You can use the Open command either by clicking the leftmost toolbar button or by choosing the command from the File menu. To use the Open command to get to a specific World Wide Web page, follow these steps:

1. Click the Open toolbar button or choose Open from the File menu. This displays the Open Internet Address dialog box, shown in Figure 26-3.

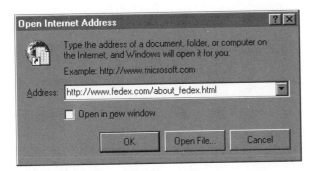

FIGURE 26-4.

You can type the URL of a document to go directly to that page. If you want to display the page in a separate Internet Explorer window, select Open In New Window.

2. Type the URL or World Wide Web address for the page you want to go to. The address should look something like this:

```
http://www.microsoft.com
```

3. Click OK. This tells Internet Explorer to find the page that you want. It may take a few seconds for the World Wide Web page to respond to Internet Explorer's request for information.

 For most Internet addresses, Internet Explorer can identify what protocol—HTTP, FTP, and so on—it should use. This means that most of the time you can leave off the first part of the address. So for the example address listed in step 2 above, you need to type only *www.microsoft.com*.

Using the Forward and Back Commands

The Forward and Back commands provide a simple way to move between pages that you have already viewed. Internet Explorer keeps a list of these pages; the Forward and Back commands simply move you through that list so that you can easily get to places you have already seen. Try out the commands with a simple example:

1. From the start page, click any link on this page. (To identify a link, move the pointer over a text or graphic item, and if the pointer icon changes to a hand, it's a link.)

2. Now use the Back command by clicking the Back button on the toolbar or by choosing the command from the View menu. (After you do this, notice that the Forward command and toolbar button become active.)

3. Now use the Forward command, which returns you to the original page.

 The Forward and Back commands come in handy when you have gotten lost on the World Wide Web. By using the Back command, you can retrace your steps until you find a familiar page.

Working with History

The Forward and Back commands are pretty simple to use. However, the more places that you go to, the harder it is to keep track of exactly how many steps back a specific page is. Internet Explorer provides an additional feature called *history*, which gives you an easier way to move several steps back at a time.

Internet Explorer treats World Wide Web pages like files. Like Microsoft Word and many other applications, Internet Explorer shows a list of the most recently visited World Wide Web pages at the bottom of the File menu. To go to one of these pages, simply choose it from the list.

Figure 26-4 shows where to find the listing of recently viewed World Wide Web pages.

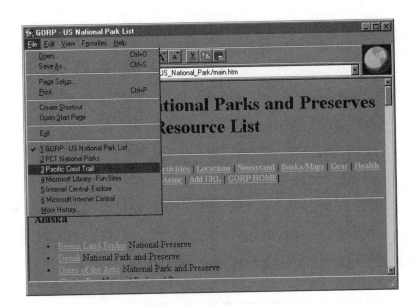

FIGURE 26-5.

The File menu lists
your recently visited
sites.

Going Further Back in History

The history list in the File menu shows the last several pages that you have viewed during the current session. Internet Explorer also has a way to view a much larger history list.

Whenever you visit a page, Internet Explorer creates a shortcut for that page in a folder called History. You can access the entire contents of the History folder by choosing the More History command from the File menu.

The More History command simply opens up the History folder, similar to the one shown in Figure 26-6 on the next page, which contains shortcuts for the last 300 pages you have been to. To go to any of these pages, double-click the shortcut for the page that you want.

Because the items in the History folder are shortcuts to World Wide Web pages, they merely tell Internet Explorer where to find the content of a particular page. When you double-click an item, Internet Explorer first tries to find the page in the cache it maintains. If the page is not in the cache, Internet Explorer connects you to the Internet and retrieves the page that you want.

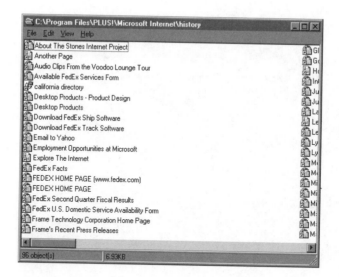

For more information about *shortcuts*, see "Using Shortcuts to Run Programs and Open Documents," page 71.

Keeping Track of Your Favorite Places

As you use Internet Explorer and discover pages on the World Wide Web that you like, you will probably want to get back to those places easily. Internet Explorer provides a feature, called *favorites*, that allows you to create a list of your favorite pages and to organize them into groupings or folders.

Using the Add To Favorites Command

The Add To Favorites command allows you to create a favorite-place listing for the page you are currently viewing. You can have as many favorite pages as you like. When you are at a page that you want to add to this list, follow these steps:

1. Click the Add To Favorites toolbar button or choose Add To Favorites from the Favorites menu. This opens the Add To Favorites dialog box, shown in Figure 26-7.

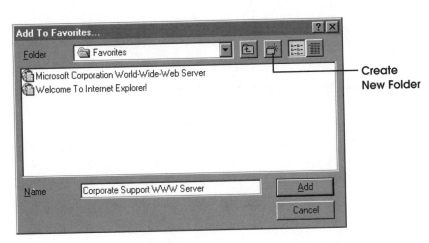

The Add To Favorites dialog box is similar to the common File Save dialog box seen in many applications for Windows.

2. In the Add To Favorites dialog box, change the page's name if you want to. Then click the Add button. This creates a favorite-place listing for the current page.

To go to a favorite place, simply go to the Favorites menu and select the page you want to go to from the list.

Organizing Your Favorite Places with Folders

After you have created five or six favorite places, you might have difficulty finding the particular favorite page that you are looking for. To help you organize your favorite places, Internet Explorer allows you to create folders of favorite places.

To create folders for your favorite places with the Add To Favorites command, follow these steps:

1. Choose the Add To Favorites command by clicking the toolbar button or by selecting it from the Favorites menu. This brings up the Add To Favorites dialog box.

2. Click the Create New Folder button, the third button from the right. (See Figure 26-7.) A new folder appears in the listing of favorites.

3. Type a name for your new folder and press Enter.

4. Click Cancel to close the dialog box.

The Favorites menu now includes a cascading item with a folder icon that has the name of the folder you created. Creating such a menu structure lets you group your favorite places logically.

After you have created a new folder, you can add favorites to it by double-clicking the folder you want in the Add To Favorites dialog box and then clicking the Add button.

Using the Open Favorites Command

The Open Favorites command allows you to view, organize, and return to your favorite places. When you click the Open Favorites toolbar button or choose the Open Favorites command from the Favorites menu, you will be presented with a window displaying the contents of the Favorites folder. This window functions exactly the same as any other Windows 95 folder. You can create new folders, rename items, and organize things as you see fit. Double-click an item in the folder to display that page.

For more information about *working with folders*, see Chapter 4, "Working with Folders," page 115.

Working with Displayed Pages

Navigating around the globe is fine, but what can you *do* with the information displayed by Internet Explorer? This section describes how to do the following:

- Print a page
- Save an entire page as a document on your computer
- Download files, such as graphics or programs, to your computer
- Create a shortcut to a page that you can reuse or share with others
- Use drag and drop to move images and text from Internet Explorer to your desktop or to a document
- Use a displayed image as your desktop wallpaper
- Search for text within a page
- Use the currently displayed page as your start page
- Set options that control the appearance of pages in Internet Explorer

Printing a Page

Internet Explorer allows you to print any World Wide Web page; simply go to the File menu and choose Print. This brings up the common Print dialog box. This capability can be very useful when viewing long pages, or if you want to read some information while you are away from the computer.

 See Also: For more information about *the common Print dialog box,* see "Printing from an Application," page 227.

Saving a Page to Disk

With Internet Explorer you can save any World Wide Web page to a disk file on your computer. However, because all World Wide Web documents are created using HTML, you will have to consider what format to save them in. When you choose the Save As command from the File Menu, you can save a World Wide Web page in either of two different formats: HTML and Text.

If you save the page in HTML format, all of the special HTML formatting codes will remain intact, but you need a World Wide Web browser, such as Internet Explorer, to view it properly. If you save the page in Text format, you will lose all of the HTML formatting commands, but you can load the text in almost any application.

 You can also view and edit HTML-formatted documents with the Internet Assistant add-on for Microsoft Word, which is available from Microsoft Corporation's World Wide Web site at *www.microsoft.com.*

Downloading Files from the Internet

On some World Wide Web sites, files are available for you to download to your computer via the Internet. These files are usually displayed by Internet Explorer as links. To download a file, simply click the link that represents the file. Internet Explorer then brings up the Save As dialog box, which asks you where to save the file on your computer.

 If you accidentally start downloading a file that you don't want, simply click the Stop button on the toolbar to stop the download.

 You can download a file in one window while you continue browsing in another. To do so, hold down the Shift key while you click the link that downloads a file.

Creating Shortcuts to World Wide Web Pages

Internet Explorer provides the capability to use shortcuts to pages on the World Wide Web. These shortcuts can point to information that is anywhere on the Internet. Once you have created an Internet shortcut, you can keep it on the desktop, send it in an e-mail message to your friends, or embed it into a document in another application.

To create a shortcut for the current World Wide Web page in Internet Explorer, simply go to the File menu and choose the Create Shortcut command. (The shortcut you create, in fact, is identical to those stored in the History folder and in the Favorites folder. The Create Shortcut command simply provides an easy way to create a shortcut on your desktop.)

Once the shortcut has been created, you can move it, copy it, or rename it as you see fit. To use the shortcut, simply double-click its icon, and Internet Explorer will take you to that World Wide Web page. You can use the shortcut even if Internet Explorer is not running; like other document shortcuts, shortcuts to Internet destinations launch their associated application if it's not already running.

For more information about *shortcuts in Windows 95*, see "Using Shortcuts to Run Programs and Open Documents," page 71.

Using Drag and Drop of Images and Text

With Internet Explorer, you can drag and drop images and text from the Internet Explorer document area to other applications or to the desktop. For example, suppose you are at the Microsoft World Wide Web home page, and you like one of the graphic images on the page. You decide you would like to make a copy of that image and place it in a file on the desktop. You can do this by following these steps:

1. Make sure that Internet Explorer is not maximized, and that a portion of the desktop is visible.

2. Click the image that you want to make a copy of. Keep the mouse button pressed down.

3. Drag the mouse pointer to the desktop. You should see the pointer icon change once you start moving the mouse.

4. Release the mouse button when the pointer is on the desktop. You should see an icon appear representing the image you just copied.

You can drag and drop images to areas other than the desktop. Basically any application that can understand what an image file is can receive an image by drag and drop.

You can drag and drop text by selecting the text that you want, and then using the same procedure described above. Of course, you can also move information via the Clipboard—standard Cut, Copy, and Paste commands are available on Internet Explorer's Edit menu and on the toolbar.

 You can quickly select an entire page by right-clicking in the document's background and choosing Select All from the object menu.

Turning an Image into Windows Wallpaper

If you happen to see an image that you like on a World Wide Web page, Internet Explorer can save that image and install it as your Windows desktop wallpaper. To do this, all you have to do is right-click any image in Internet Explorer. This brings up an object menu with three options: Save As, Copy Picture, and Set As Desktop Wallpaper. Select the last option to turn that image into your Windows wallpaper.

 See Also: For more information about *wallpaper*, see "Using Patterns, Wallpaper, and Screen Savers," page 106.

Finding Text on a World Wide Web Page

Many pages on the Internet have large amounts of text for you to read. To find a specific phrase or word in a long document, you can use Internet Explorer's Find command. Follow these steps to use this command:

1. Display the page on which you want to find a specific word or phrase. The Find command works only on a single page at a time.

2. Choose the Find command from the Edit menu.

3. Type the text that you are looking for. You can type part of a word or the entire word.

4. Click the Find Next button, and Internet Explorer takes you to the next occurrence of your search text in the document.

Changing the Start Page

After using Internet Explorer for awhile, you might find that you don't want to see the standard start page, and would rather see the home page of one of your favorite World Wide Web sites when you start Internet Explorer. To do this you would follow these steps:

1. Display the page you want to use as your start page by typing its address, by selecting it from favorites, or by double-clicking its shortcut.

2. Choose Options from the View menu.

3. Click the Start Page tab.

4. Click Use Current.

To reset the start page to the way it was the first time you used Internet Explorer, click Use Default in the Options dialog box.

Setting Options

Internet Explorer allows you to customize some of its features to suit your preferences and needs. To see what options are available, choose Options from the View menu. This brings up the Options dialog box, shown in Figure 26-8. From here you can select any of the four tabs:

■ The Appearance tab allows you to set colors for foreground, background, and links (shortcuts). You can also control the way information appears in the status bar.

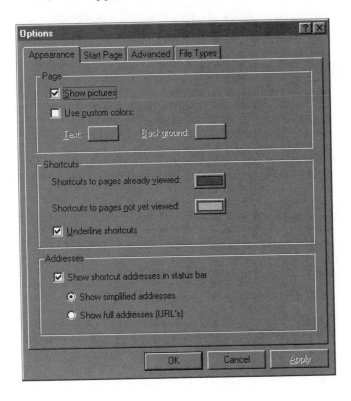

FIGURE 26-8.

From the Options dialog box you can customize many of Internet Explorer's features.

- The Start Page tab lets you specify what World Wide Web page you want to see when you start Internet Explorer. For details, see "Changing the Start Page," page 720.

- The Advanced tab lets you specify how many items will be kept in the History folder and how large the cache for Internet content should be.

- The File Types tab lets you associate a program with a particular file type. For example, if you encounter a .ZIP or other compressed file, you can specify what application Internet Explorer should use to uncompress it. (For details, see "Working with the File Types List," page 155.)

Connecting to FTP and Gopher Sites

Some parts of the Internet are set up differently than the World Wide Web. Two common types are FTP (file transfer protocol) and gopher sites. Internet Explorer provides the same interface for these systems as it does for the World Wide Web, so you don't need to learn anything new to use information from these types of sites.

 The easiest way to distinguish what type of site you are viewing is by the address: each Internet address usually has the name of the service at the beginning. For example, the URL for Microsoft's FTP server is *ftp.microsoft.com*.

To connect to an FTP or gopher site, simply enter the URL for the site you want to connect to in the same way you would for a World Wide Web page. Just as with World Wide Web addresses, you can do this with the address bar or with the File Open command.

For example, an anonymous connection (one that doesn't require a password) to the Microsoft Corporation FTP site looks like this:

```
ftp://ftp.microsoft.com
```

To connect to an FTP server that requires you to provide your user-name and password, use this format:

```
ftp://name:password@ftp.microsoft.com
```

(Replace *name* and *password* with the logon information assigned by the server administrator.)

Appendix

Using the Power of Your 486 or Pentium with Microsoft Plus!

Microsoft Plus! is a set of "add-on" goodies for Windows 95. If your system uses an 80486 or later microprocessor, includes at least 8 megabytes of memory, and has a display adapter capable of displaying at least 256 colors, you can take advantage of the features in Plus!:

- Desktop Themes, to give your Windows system a topical "look and spiel"

- Assorted other visual enhancements

- A System Agent to run maintenance chores and other programs at prearranged times

- An improved version of DriveSpace (called DriveSpace 3) that can give you a higher degree of file compression and larger compressed volume files

- A Compression Agent that works together with DriveSpace 3 to achieve even higher compression ratios for particular files

- Internet tools, including Internet Explorer, a program for browsing the World Wide Web

- Software that lets your system host a Dial-Up Networking session

- The 3-D Pinball game

Using Desktop Themes

Desktop themes add thematically consistent sounds and sights to your system, using wallpaper, specially designed icons, sound schemes, color schemes, fonts, animated mouse pointers, and screen savers. If you choose the Travel theme, for example, you get a train station for wallpaper, assorted propellers and clocks for mouse pointers, an airplane for a screen saver, and various toots, honks, beeps, and a-oogas to enliven your day. You can install any of these thematic elements separately (just the horns, without the propellers, for example), or accept the whole package.

Eleven themes are offered (some of which require 24-bit color): Dangerous Creatures, Inside Your Computer, Leonardo da Vinci, Mystery, Nature, Science, Sports, The 60's USA, The Golden Era, Travel, and Windows 95. You can also save your own collection of settings as a theme.

After you install Plus!, you apply desktop themes via the Desktop Themes item in Control Panel.

Other Visual Enhancements

With Plus!, you can also dress up the appearance of your desktop in the following ways:

- You can substitute alternative icons for My Computer, Network Neighborhood, and Recycle Bin.

- You can use full-window drag. With this feature on, as you drag a window, you see the entire window move, not just a frame.

- You can turn on font smoothing. Font smoothing eliminates jagged edges on large screen fonts.

- You can have Windows automatically scale wallpaper images to fill your screen.

Click the Display property sheet's Plus! tab to access these features.

Scheduling Programs with System Agent

System Agent is a utility that runs in the background and carries out preassigned tasks at scheduled times. You can use it, for example, to check, defragment, and back up your hard disks at regular intervals. When you schedule a task with System Agent, you can stipulate that the task run only if the computer has been idle for a certain period of time, and that the Agent try again at regular intervals if the computer is not idle at the appointed hour.

To run System Agent, double-click its icon in the taskbar's notification area. (If its icon doesn't appear in the notification area, open the Start menu and choose Programs, Accessories, System Tools, System Agent.)

Putting on the Squeeze with DriveSpace 3

DriveSpace 3 is an enhanced version of the file-compression technology that comes with Windows 95. The standard compression system (Drive-Space) cannot create compressed volume files (CVFs) larger than 512 MB. DriveSpace 3, however, can create CVFs as large as 2 gigabytes (2048 MB).

With DriveSpace 3, you also have a choice of two compression methods. The standard method, comparable to that used by DriveSpace, creates compression ratios on the order of 2:1. The HiPack method achieves significantly higher compression ratios, but files may take slightly longer to read and write.

To run DriveSpace 3, open the Start menu and choose Programs, Accessories, System Tools, DriveSpace.

See Also: For information about *DriveSpace*, see "Doubling Your Disk with DriveSpace," page 390.

Optimizing Compression with Compression Agent

With Compression Agent you can balance speed with performance in an optimal way by applying high-compression techniques to particular files. Compression Agent can squeeze your files using either the HiPack method or an ultra-high-compression algorithm called UltraPack. (You can also use Compression Agent to remove compression from particular files.) You can tell Compression Agent to use its UltraPack method only on files meeting a particular description, such as files that you haven't worked with during the most recent 30 days. Like System Agent, Compression Agent is designed to operate in the background at scheduled intervals. If you leave your computer on 24 hours a day, for example, you can have Compression Agent run every night so that your system remains in optimal condition at all times.

To run Compression Agent, open the Start menu and choose Programs, Accessories, System Tools, Compression Agent.

Exploring the Internet

Microsoft Plus! includes the following tools to facilitate your use of resources on the Internet:

- An Internet setup wizard
- Internet Explorer, a program that lets you browse the World Wide Web
- The ability to create desktop shortcuts for favorite web sites
- An Internet mail driver, allowing you to send and receive Internet mail from your Exchange inbox
- One month of free Internet use from The Microsoft Network
- The Microsoft Network version 1.05 (an enhancement to the version shipped with Windows 95)

 See Also: For information about *Internet Explorer,* see Chapter 26, "Roaming the Internet with Internet Explorer," page 701.

Using Your Computer as a Remote-Access Server

The Dial-Up Networking component of Windows 95 allows your computer to act as a client to a remote-access server. With Plus!, a remote user can log on to your computer.

To enable this feature, open the Dial-Up Networking folder and choose Dial-Up Server from the Connections menu.

See Also: For information about *Dial-Up Networking*, see "Using Dial-Up Networking," page 372.

Pinball Madness

Finally, if you long for the good old days of noisy pinball games, Plus! has something special for you: a three-dimensional re-creation of a traditional game, complete with flippers, tilt keys, sound effects, music, and high-score recording. Up to four players can compete.

To play 3-D Pinball, open the Start menu and choose Programs, Accessories, Games, 3-D Pinball.

Index

Index

Index

documents, *continued*
   linking files, 267–68
   margins, 458, 463–64
   opening from applications, 126–27, *447*, 483
   opening from Find window, 67
   opening from folders, 62–63, 121
   opening from Start menu, 61–62
   opening with Run command, 70–71
   opening with Send To command, 147
   opening with shortcuts, 72
   pausing printing, 237
   printing from applications, 227–30
   printing from Paint, 512–13
   printing from WordPad, *447*, 474–75
   printing to disk, 243
   printing with drag and drop, 230–31
   printing with Send To command, 147, 232
   saving, 126–27, *447*, 449, 472, 481
   selecting, 136–37
   updating links, 270–72, 471
   using fonts in, 216
   viewing, xxxvi, 28, 67–69
Documents submenu (Start menu), 61–62
document windows, 21, *22*
dog-earred–page icon, 135
domains, network, 7, 190
DOS Protected-Mode Interface (DPMI) memory, 325–26
DOS. *See* MS-DOS
double-clicking, 18, 27, 62, 436
double-click speed, adjusting, 112
DoubleSpace, 392. *See also* DriveSpace
Down arrow key, 42
downloading files, 528–32, 692–95, 717–18
DPMI (DOS Protected Mode Interface) memory, 325–26
drag and drop
   creating scrap files, 273
   installing fonts, 215
   from Internet Explorer, 719
   Microsoft Backup, 419
   moving or copying data, 257, 259
   moving or copying folders, files, or shortcuts, 142–46
   and OLE object technology, 257
   printer installation, 234
   printing, 75, 230–31

drag and drop, *continued*
   Recycle Bin, 149
   sending faxes, 644, 647
   shortcuts to desktop, 74
   shortcuts to Start button, 83
   Windows Explorer, 165, 175
Drag And Drop command (Microsoft Backup), 419
dragging, 18, 436
drawing. *See also* Paint
   curved lines, 495
   free-form shapes, 493–94
   irregular shapes, 496–97, 664
   ovals and circles, 496, 664
   rectangles and squares, 495–96, 664
   straight lines, 493, 494, 664
drawing area (Paint), *479*, 480
Draw Opaque command (Paint), 506
drive letters, mapping network folders, *124*, 187–89
drive letters for compressed drives, 393
DriveSpace
   compressing disks, 392–95
   compressing free space only, 394
   drive letters, 393
   vs. DriveSpace 3, 731
   formatting floppy disks, 395–96
   host drives, 393
   installing, 393
   introduction, 390–91
   and Microsoft Backup, 417
   performance, 390–91
   and ScanDisk, 382, 387
   starting, 392
   and swap files, 381
   uncompressing disks, 396
DriveSpace 3, 392, 731
drop-down list boxes, 32–33
drop-down menus, 25–26
duplex printing, 248
Dvorak keyboard layout, 297, 438
dynamic data exchange (DDE), 255
dynamic-link library (.DLL) files, 132, 344
Dynamic Memory Allocation option (MS-DOS–based applications), 329
dynamic swap files, 380

E

Index

G

game ports, 566
games
    3-D Pinball, 733
    "boss key", 568
    FreeCell, 581–83
    Hearts, 572–76
    installing, 568
    introduction, 565–66
    Minesweeper, 569–72
    MS-DOS based, 566–67
    setting up, 568
    Solitaire, 576–81
General tab (Accessibility property sheet), *437*
General tab (device property sheet), *399*
General tab (file property sheet), *139*, 140, 319
General tab (folder property sheet), *138*, 319
General tab (modem property sheet), *289*
General tab (Modems property sheet), *288*
General tab (printer property sheet), *245*
Get Colors command (Paint), 510
globe (Internet Explorer), 705
glossary of terms
    dialog boxes, 30
    fonts, 207–10
    Internet, 703–4
    Microsoft Backup, 408
    mouse, 18
    OLE object technology, 254, 256–57
    windows, 15–17
    Windows 95, 8
gopher, 704, 722
Go To command (Windows Explorer), 174–75
Go words, 682
graphics
    adding to fax cover pages, 663–64
    copying from Internet Explorer, 719
    editing (*see* Paint)
    printing, 230, 248–50
Graphics tab (printer property sheet), *249*
gray commands, 27
grayed-out commands, 27
green text in help, 48
grid, displaying in Paint, 509
Grid Lines command (Cover Page Editor), 665

groups of items
    moving or copying, 145
    property sheets for, 140–41
    selecting, 137, 140
guest computer, 361

H

handheld computers. *See* portable computers
handicaps, features for people with. *See*
    accessibility features
hanging indents, 462
hard disks
    checking available space, 170
    compressing, 390–96, 731–32
    defragmenting, 388–89
    repairing with ScanDisk, 381–87
    uncompressing, 396
    upgrading, 403
hardware
    device conflicts, 398–400
    installing, 349–52, 540
    requirements, 542–44
    uninstalling, 353–54
hearing-impaired users, features for, 431–33
Hearts
    customization options, 575
    playing over network, 572
    rules and scoring, 573–74
    shooting the moon, 575
    starting, 568
    starting a game, 572–73
    strategy, 575–76
help
    annotations, 50
    Back button, 49
    buttons, 48, *49*
    Contents tab, 45–46
    copying topics, 49–50
    for dialog boxes, 50–51
    Find tab, 45, 46–47, *48*
    for MS-DOS commands, 334
    glossary terms, 48
    green text, 48
    Index tab, 45, 46, *46*
    printing topics, 50

Index

Index

Index

U

Index

Craig Stinson   An industry journalist since 1981, Craig Stinson is a contributing editor of *PC Magazine* and was formerly editor of *Softalk for the IBM Personal Computer*. Stinson is a coauthor of *Running Excel 5 for Windows* and *Running Windows NT*, both published by Microsoft Press. In addition to his numerous computer publications, Stinson has written music reviews for *Billboard*, the *Boston Globe*, the *Christian Science Monitor, Musical America*, and other publications. He lives with his wife and children in Eugene, Oregon.

The manuscript for this book was prepared and submitted to Microsoft Press in electronic form. Text files were prepared using Microsoft Word 6.0 for Windows. Pages were composed by Siechert & Wood using FrameMaker for Windows, with text in Garamond and display text in Avant Garde Demi. Composed pages were delivered to the printer as electronic prepress files.

Cover Designer
Rebecca Geisler

Cover Color Separator
Color Service Inc.

Interior Graphic Designer
Kim Eggleston

Principal Editorial Compositor
Paula J. Kausch

WELCOME TO THE WORLD OF WINDOWS® 95 ·

The MICROSOFT® WINDOWS® 95 RESOURCE KIT provides you with all of the information necessary to plan for and implement Windows 95 in your organization.

ISBN 1-55615-678-2
1376 pages, $49.95 ($67.95 Canada)
Three 3.5" disks

Details on how to install, configure, and support Windows 95 will save you hours of time and help ensure that you get the most from your computing investment. This exclusive Microsoft publication, written in cooperation with the Windows 95 development team, is the perfect technical companion for network administrators, support professionals, systems integrators, and computer professionals.

The MICROSOFT WINDOWS 95 RESOURCE KIT contains important information that will help you get the most out of Windows 95. Whether you support Windows 95 in your company or just want to know more about it, the MICROSOFT WINDOWS 95 RESOURCE KIT is a valuable addition to your reference library.

Microsoft®_Press_

YOU CAN GET THERE from here!

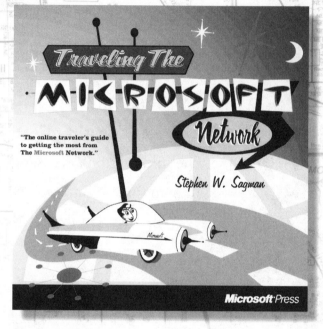

ISBN 1-55615-817-3, 352 pages, $19.95 ($26.95 Canada)

This entertaining and in-depth book about The Microsoft® Network is the online traveler's guide to getting the most from Microsoft's new online service. The best books about online services read like the best travel guides; they show you where to go, what to do, who to meet. TRAVELING THE MICROSOFT NETWORK does all this, plus tells interesting stories about the online world that will encourage you to explore, enhancing your experience along the way.

Available August 1995!

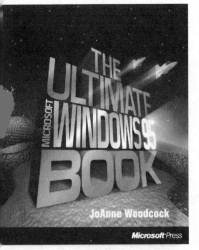

A colorful, fact-filled, and entertaining guide to getting the most from Microsoft® Windows® 95.

Written in a humorous style that makes learning enjoyable, THE ULTIMATE MICROSOFT WINDOWS 95 BOOK is the perfect introduction to Microsoft Windows 95. THE ULTIMATE MICROSOFT WINDOWS 95 BOOK takes you on a guided tour of the user interface basics and then gives you an up-close-and-personal look at individual Windows 95 features. This colorful and engaging book delivers hundreds of the best hints, tips, and tricks for using Windows 95—and it's fun to read.

ISBN 1-55615-670-7, 352 pages, $24.95 ($33.95 Canada)

THE ULTIMATE MICROSOFT WINDOWS 95 BOOK shows you how to manage your computer, your applications, your documents, and your printer. You'll learn how to:

- Accomplish the most common computing tasks with ease, such as starting applications, copying files, and arranging things nicely on screen.

- Customize Windows 95 behavior to make your computer work more like you do.

- Manage files, folders, and disks.

- Find your way around the network neighborhood and work with other printers and computers.

- Merge painlessly onto the much-touted information superhighway.

Hands-On sections are step-by-step examples that let you try out what you've been reading about in the text.

Definitions provide on-the-spot explanations of terms and acronyms.

Tabs let you turn instantly to the section you need.

Tips give you practical advice.

What's more, the book includes dozens of the most-asked questions about Windows 95, gleaned from Microsoft Corporation's Product Support Group. These are real questions followed by answers in plain English.

Entertaining and packed with easy-to-find information, THE ULTIMATE MICROSOFT WINDOWS 95 BOOK is the one book you'll want close to your PC. Don't just take our word for it—open it up and see.

Microsoft Press® books are available wherever quality books are sold and through CompuServe's Electronic Mall—**GO MSP**.
Call **1-800-MSPRESS** for more information or to place a credit card order.* Please refer to **BBK** when placing your order. Prices subject to change.
*In Canada, contact Macmillan Canada, Attn: Microsoft Press Dept., 164 Commander Blvd., Agincourt, Ontario, Canada M1S 3C7, or call 1-800-667-1115.
Outside the U.S. and Canada, write to International Coordinator, Microsoft Press, One Microsoft Way, Redmond, WA 98052-6399, or fax +1-206-936-7329.

MICROSOFT LICENSE AGREEMENT

(Book Companion Disks)

097-000-680

Windows Explorer

You can use Windows Explorer to navigate through the folders and files on your computer. Change the view to see a list of items or to see each item as an icon.

Windows Explorer's toolbar helps you access network drives as well as cut, copy, and paste objects. Rest the mouse pointer on a tool for a few seconds to see the tool tip that tells you what that tool does.

The drop-down list shows all the drives available to you.

The left pane shows the hierarchical "tree" of objects available from your computer. Click + to expand the tree.

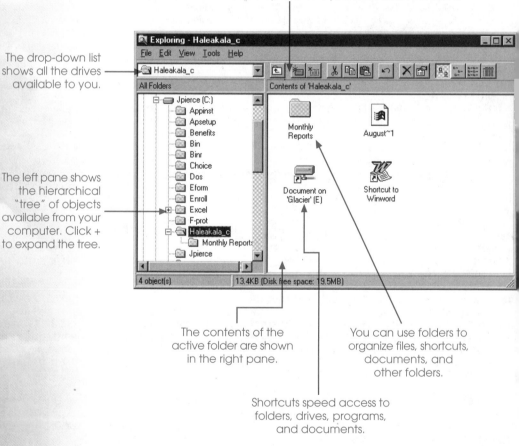

The contents of the active folder are shown in the right pane.

You can use folders to organize files, shortcuts, documents, and other folders.

Shortcuts speed access to folders, drives, programs, and documents.